QUESTIONS* EVERY PATIENT SHOULD ASK ABOUT PRESCRIPTION MEDICINES

1. What is the name of the drug and what is it supposed to do?

2. How and when do I take it—and for how long?

3. What foods, drinks, other medications, or activities should I avoid while taking this drug?

4. Are there any side effects, and what do I do if they occur?

5. Is there any written information available about the drug?

*Questions prepared by the National Council on Patient Information and Education (NCPIE)

D1570499

PRESCRIPTION DRUGS

AN INDISPENSABLE GUIDE FOR PEOPLE OVER 50

BRIAN S. KATCHER, PHARM.D.

AVON BOOKS ◆ NEW YORK

Although great care was taken in the preparation of this book, medical information changes constantly and is often subject to interpretation. Furthermore, this book does not claim to present every possible adverse effect or interaction for the drugs presented. Finally, the reader is reminded that the circumstances of drug therapy vary, and no book can be considered a substitute for the professional judgment of a physician or pharmacist.

AVON BOOKS
A division of
The Hearst Corporation
1350 Avenue of the Americas
New York, New York 10019

Copyright © 1988 by Brian S. Katcher, Pharm. D.
Published by arrangement with Atheneum/Macmillan Publishing Company
Library of Congress Catalog Card Number: 87-19587
ISBN: 0-380-70670-9

First Avon Books Printing: July 1989

AVON TRADEMARK REG. U.S. PAT. OFF. AND IN OTHER COUNTRIES, MARCA REGISTRADA, HECHO EN CANADA.

Printed in Canada.

UNV 10 9 8 7 6 5 4 3 2

To my mother and father

CONTENTS

INTRODUCTION

This book grew out of my long-standing interest in how age affects drug response. I hope it will be a useful resource for people over the age of fifty who need practical information about prescription drugs.

I am a pharmacist. I have worked in hospital and community pharmacies, taught at a school of pharmacy, and edited pharmacy textbooks. I wrote this book because I believe that many of the older people who take prescription drugs are interested in how those drugs affect them. I knew that no such book existed; that people over the age of fifty constitute a little more than a quarter of a general population but consume more than half of the prescription drugs; that many drugs exert their effects differently in older bodies than in younger bodies; and that most adverse drug reactions and interactions take place in older people.

This book is divided into two parts. The first part describes how aging affects your response to drugs. It also offers some strategies for minimizing the risk of adverse drug reactions. The second part, which is the bulk of the book, is intended as a practical resource for information on the drugs most commonly prescribed for those over the age of fifty.

When I began the research for this book, I was struck by the way that age determines which drugs people take. For example, antibiotics, which are among the drugs most commonly dispensed in pharmacies, do not rank among the fifteen most commonly prescribed drug groups for older people. The most important prescription drugs for those over the age of fifty are drugs for arthritis, for high blood pressure, for heart problems, for diabetes—drugs for problems that increase in frequency with advancing age and remain for life. These are the drugs that are emphasized in this book.

Most of these drugs are not new. Some, like digoxin

or quinidine, were used in their crude plant forms more than a hundred years ago. Most of the others became widely used during the last ten to twenty-five years. There is, however, a wealth of new information about these drugs.

There is new information about how drugs work and how they interact with other drugs. In some instances, new techniques for monitoring drug therapy have made dosing more precise. And, most recently, the effect of age on drug response has become a major area of study. This new information is woven throughout the pages that follow.

Although you may know your drugs by their brand names, you will find that I refer to them by their generic (common) names. I do this because there are often many brand names for a single drug. For example, the diuretic hydrochlorothiazide (which, I'll admit, doesn't quite roll off the tongue like some of its brand names) is sold by many drug manufacturers under different brand names. Esidrix, HydroDIURIL, Oretic, and Thiuretic are just a few of the brand or trade names for hydrochlorothiazide tablets. To find information about your drugs, use the index at the back of the book. If the drug name you are looking up is a brand or trade name, and if the drug is in this book, you will be referred to the appropriate generic name. If you are taking a tablet or capsule that contains more than one ingredient, the index will refer you to each of the ingredient names.

The subject of drugs is extremely complex, and the amount of published information is vast. Although I made good use of the drug literature in distilling the information for this book, I have tried to retain a conversational tone and to focus on what is likely to be important. In doing so, I had to leave out some information. I might have made a wrong decision in anticipating information that might have been helpful to you. If you are unable to find all the answers you need in this book, I apologize and hope you will understand that I couldn't include everything and still maintain a clear and readable book of reasonable size. Also, medical information changes daily, so something between these covers may be outdated, despite my best efforts. Finally, no book can be a substitute for the personal attention of health professionals who know you as an individual.

PART ONE

The Pharmacology
of Aging

YOUR BODY

Age brings important changes in our bodies. Subtle signs of aging begin after the third decade of life. By the time we are forty, every one of our organ systems is on a lifelong course of steady decline. No matter how much or how little grace we can muster to face this decline, normal aging affects all of our physiological processes. Therefore, it affects our responses to drugs.

Drugs work by causing subtle changes in the body's chemistry. When they are present in the right concentration in the blood, they exert their desired effect on the heart, the joints, the brain—whatever organ or tissue is being treated. Pharmacologists call this the *target organ* or *target tissue*. The effects of drugs are not always localized, of course, and this is one of the reasons that drugs have side effects. Maintaining the right concentration of drug in your blood is very important. If there is too little drug, it will not have any effect. If there is too much, you will be more likely to experience side effects. Let's look at what your body does with the medicines that you take.

After you swallow a drug, it passes through the stomach and into the small intestine, where it is usually *absorbed* into the bloodstream. Once in the blood, the drug is *distributed* throughout the body—to muscle, to fat, to all the major organs. Some of the drug dose will reach the target organ or tissue, where it will have its effect. As long as the drug is circulating in the blood (that is, as long as there is some of the drug left in the body), some of the drug dose will go to the liver and the kidneys. In the liver, many drugs are *metabolized*—that is, their chemical structure is changed. Sometimes the metabolized (changed) drug is pharmacologically active; sometimes it is not. In either case, the metabolized drug keeps circulating with the blood and is distributed throughout the body. All the blood circulating

3

in the body goes through the kidneys, which filter out waste products. The drug, its pharmacologically active metabolites, and its inactive metabolites are all filtered out of the blood by the kidneys and *excreted* into the urine. Eventually, the concentration of drug in the blood falls so low that it has no effect on the target organ. Usually, you take another dose of drug before this happens.

Why do we need to concern ourselves with all this? Because many of these processes are affected by aging, although the effect that age has on these processes varies from drug to drug.

DRUG ABSORPTION AND DISTRIBUTION Age does not usually have much effect on drug *absorption*, but the *distribution* of drugs within the body can be markedly altered with age. Your body's composition changes as you get older. Muscle mass tends to decrease. Body fat tends to increase. The results of these changes on drug distribution vary from drug to drug. With some drugs, these changes result in a greater concentration of drug in the blood immediately after it is taken. Alcohol is such a drug. As you get older, you may find that the effects of alcohol hit you sooner than they used to. With other drugs, such as diazepam (Valium) or flurazepam (Dalmane), it takes longer for the full effects of repeated doses to become apparent. Excess sedation or confusion from too much diazepam or too much flurazepam may, therefore, occur several weeks after taking daily doses that were well tolerated at first.

DRUG METABOLISM AND EXCRETION Many drugs are inactivated by metabolism in the liver. With increasing age, there is less blood flow to the liver. (The amount of blood your heart can pump in a minute's time decreases by about 1 percent per year.) In addition, the liver gets smaller with age. As a result, your liver becomes less efficient in metabolizing some drugs. Drugs that rely on your liver for inactivation will remain in the blood longer before they are metabolized. Your doctor will therefore give you smaller doses of these drugs, to prevent the drug from accumulating to a higher concentration than you need. Of course, your liver may not decline in its metabolizing ability at the same rate as someone else's, and routine laboratory tests are not very good at measuring the liver's metabolizing ability. Also, some drugs are easier for the liver to metabolize than others. Therefore, with some drugs, your doctor will be especially careful to observe whether you are experiencing too much or too little effect from what would seem to be an appropriate daily dose.

The kidneys also become less efficient with age. They become slower at removing drugs and drug metabolites from the blood and excreting them into the urine. Drugs that are not inactivated by the liver usually depend on the kidneys for termination of their effect. There is considerable variation among individuals, but, on the average, an older person's kidneys are about half as efficient as they were when they were in their prime. Unlike the liver, the kidney's drug-filtering ability can be predicted with standard laboratory tests. For some drugs, your doctor will use this information in determining the correct daily dose for you. For many drugs, your doctor will prescribe a smaller dose than he or she would for a younger person because of this slower removal of drugs by the kidneys.

SENSITIVITY TO DRUGS Finally, with age, many organs or organ systems become more sensitive to drug effects. The brain becomes more sensitive to the sedative effect of drugs, and oversedation is a common problem among older people. With aging, the stabilizing mechanisms that maintain constant blood pressure with changing body position becomes less efficient, so dizziness from standing up too quickly becomes a common problem. Many drugs will make this problem worse. The changes in drug distribution, elimination, and organ sensitivity that occur with aging are often cumulative and result in a greater sensitivity to drugs.

INCREASED USE OF DRUGS Increased sensitivity to drugs isn't the only consequence of aging. The bodily changes that occur with aging bring with them a greater need for drugs. Wear and tear on joints brings osteoarthritis, the most common form of arthritis. Not surprisingly, drugs for arthritis are among those most commonly prescribed for older people. The incidence of many other chronic diseases also increases with advancing age. Four out of five older persons have at least one chronic disease. The majority of older people have several chronic medical problems. The older you are, the more likely you will be to require drug treatment for diabetes, high blood pressure, angina, heart failure, or some other medical problem. Individuals over the age of fifty comprise only a quarter of the population, but they consume more than half of the prescription drugs. Persons over the age of sixty-five consume three times more prescription drugs than persons below this age. Whatever your age, it is likely that your need for drugs will increase as you get older.

PROBLEMS WITH DRUGS   Since advancing age is accompanied by both a greater sensitivity to drugs and an increased use of drugs, you might expect to find more problems with drugs in older people than in younger people. There is good evidence to support this supposition. In a three-year study of admissions to a large university teaching hospital, it was found that drug-induced disease was responsible for 3 percent of all the admissions. Forty percent of these patients with drug-induced disease were older than sixty years; the admissions rate due to drug-induced illness in this age group was fifteen times higher than it was among younger patients. In another large study of hospital admissions, which looked at hospital admissions for any cause among older people, it was found that drug-induced problems accounted for 10 percent of the admissions. Other studies, of both ambulatory and hospitalized patients, have shown that adverse drug reactions occur more frequently in older people than they do in younger people.

What can be done about this problem? Most adverse drug reactions are preventable. Doctors are more aware of the problem than they were a decade ago. In addition, you can and should take an active role in supervising your drug therapy. The best insurance against adverse drug effects is understanding on your part.

Several years ago, the National Council on Patient Information and Education (NCPIE), a nonprofit organization committed to improving the dialogue between health professionals and patients, began promoting a list of questions that every patient should ask about prescription medicines. This list of questions, which is the basis of their "Get the Answers" campaign, is as follows:

1. What is the name of the drug and what is it supposed to do?
2. How and when do I take it—and for how long?
3. What foods, drinks, other medications, or activities should I avoid while taking this drug?
4. Are there any side effects, and what do I do if they occur?
5. Is there any written information available about the drug?

THE TROUBLE WITH DRUGS

The trouble with drugs is that they can make you sick. As you get older, the likelihood that you might run into a problem with drugs increases.

But let me say from the start, I don't think that drugs are bad. When used as directed, their benefits almost always outweigh their negative effects, which include cost, inconvenience, minor discomforts, and the risk of more serious adverse effects. We can adjust ourselves to the minor discomforts. We can even feel comfortable with them, if we can appreciate the trade-off between their existence and some measure of protection against symptoms or possibly life-threatening events. Serious adverse effects, on the other hand, are cause for real concern. Although they are infrequent, if not rare occurrences, they may take unexpected forms. The list of possible adverse effects attributed to each drug is almost always long, even though most patients do not experience any of them. These adverse effects are more like accidents than predictable occurrences. Like accidents, they are associated with risk factors that can be identified, and the majority of serious adverse drug effects can be prevented.

PREVENTION Prevention of drug-induced disease is a major objective of this book, and much of what you find here is about side effects, drug interactions, and problems you might experience because of your age. I hope you won't get the wrong impression. Think of what it would be like if you were teaching someone to drive an automobile. You would warn about looking in the rearview mirror, waiting and signaling when moving about in traffic, not driving too fast or too slow, wearing a seat belt, not driving while intoxicated, watching out for other cars, watching out for pedestrians, and so on. To impress your student with the seriousness of it all, you might show some movies or photographs of traffic accidents, possibly including injured people. It could easily become overwhelming, and one might temporarily lose sight of the marvelous benefits associated with being able to get around in one's own automobile. So it is with drugs. Although they can also cause diseases of their own, they are a powerful means for controlling the chronic illnesses that occur with aging.

The main risk factors for drug-induced diseases are described in the following pages. All of them are related to advancing age, which explains why a person who is sixty to seventy years old is nearly twice as likely to experience a problem with drug therapy as is a person thirty to forty years of age.

AGE Our bodies change as we age. As pointed out in the previous chapter, advancing age is usually accompanied by increasing sensitivity to drugs. Therefore, side effects that usually occur only with large doses in young adults sometimes occur with normal doses in older adults. Before taking a drug, find out what side effects are likely to occur. Watch for signs of too much drug effect.

DRUG INTERACTIONS Many adverse drug reactions are the result of drug *interactions*. The more drugs you take, the more likely they will be to interact in some way. It is not uncommon for an older person to take several prescription medications in addition to one or more nonprescription medications. The most important drug interactions for the most commonly prescribed drugs are described throughout this book. Make use of a pharmacist who keeps a separate, preferably computerized, record of all the drugs you take, and ask how he or she goes about checking for drug interactions. Keep your own list of drugs as well. Make it your business to be sure that none of your medications interact in a dangerous way.

OTHER DISEASES Diseases can modify your response to drugs. If you are being treated for a single disease, it's easy to keep things straight. But the number of chronic medical problems increases with advancing age, and it's not uncommon for older people to take a variety of drugs for several medical problems. Your high-blood-pressure medicine might cause a problem with your diabetes. A kidney problem might make you overly sensitive to the drug you are taking for your heart. Your arthritis medicine might worsen your heart failure. And so on. Be sure that each of your physicians knows all the drugs you are taking, including nonprescription drugs. Don't be afraid to ask questions about your drugs.

DRUG MISUSE Are all your medicines in the bottles they came in? If not, you might confuse one tablet with another and get an unexpected response.

If you have trouble opening your prescription bottles or reading their labels, ask your pharmacist to correct the problem. Federal law requires that prescriptions be dispensed in child-proof containers, unless conventional containers are requested by the patient, because poisoning from overdoses of prescription drugs is a serious problem among children. Unfortunately, child-proof containers are often adult-proof for older individuals with arthritis in their hands. Ask that your drug be dispensed in a container you can open easily. Be sure to store your drugs out of the reach of any visiting children. (A recent study found that more than a third of the accidental overdoses of prescription drugs in children came from grandparents' medication containers.)

Do you take so many different drugs at different times of day that the whole thing becomes confusing? If so, see if your physician or pharmacist can't devise a more simplified schedule.

Finally, don't share your medicines with anyone else, and don't take any prescription drugs that weren't prescribed for you. Discard old bottles of drugs you are no longer taking.

UNPREVENTABLE PROBLEMS Sometimes drug problems occur despite every effort to prevent them.

An allergy may occur; an unexpected toxicity may manifest itself. Going back to the analogy of driving an automobile, being a safe driver doesn't guarantee that you won't have an accident. This raises the issue of risk versus benefit. For most drugs, risks are quite small in comparison with the benefits. You should, however, know what benefits are to be expected. Find out what your drugs are supposed to do and how long you're supposed to take them. If you should develop any unexpected symptoms, check with your doctor as soon as possible.

PART TWO

Commonly Prescribed Drugs

PART TWO

Commonly Prescribed
Drugs

ACETAMINOPHEN

OTHER NAMES   Acetaminophen (pronounced *a-seat-a-MEE-noe-fen*) is the common or generic name of this drug. In Great Britain, acetaminophen is called paracetamol, which is also a generic name. Some frequently used brand names for acetaminophen as a nonprescription drug are Aceta, Datril, Tempra, and Tylenol. Acetaminophen is sometimes included as an ingredient in brand-name nonprescription products that also contain aspirin or other ingredients. Acetaminophen is also an active ingredient in many brand-name prescription medications that contain other pain relievers, such as Darvocet-N (propoxyphene and acetaminophen), Tylenol with Codeine (codeine and acetaminophen), and others.

WHAT IS IT SUPPOSED TO DO?   Acetaminophen relieves mild to moderate pain, and it lowers fever. It is roughly equivalent to aspirin in accomplishing these tasks. Unlike aspirin, it does not relieve inflammation when taken in higher doses, but it can relieve mild arthritic pain.

SIDE EFFECTS   Unlike aspirin, acetaminophen does not cause stomach upset. However, you should be careful not to exceed the dosage recommended on the bottle. Overdosage with acetaminophen can cause severe liver damage.

Side effects from acetaminophen taken in recommended doses are too rare to list here. Contact your doctor if you experience any unexpected symptoms.

DRUG INTERACTIONS   Acetaminophen can be taken safely with most drugs. These are the only drug interactions that merit special concern:

Cholestyramine Resin (Questran), which is used for the itching that sometimes accompanies jaundice and is also used to lower the concentration of cholesterol in the blood, inhibits the absorption of acetaminophen.

If cholestyramine therapy is necessary, you should take your acetaminophen doses at least an hour before your cholestyramine doses.

Phenobarbital, when taken regularly for seizure prevention or other reasons, stimulates the metabolism of acetaminophen and thereby reduces its effects. More importantly, regular use of phenobarbital will make you more sensitive to the effects of acetaminophen overdose. Be sure to observe the dosage recommendations on your acetaminophen bottle.

ALCOHOLIC BEVERAGES   Acetaminophen can be taken with alcohol without problems. However, chronic alcoholism causes changes in the liver that increase its sensitivity to the toxic effects of acetaminophen overdose.

FOOD   Food slows the absorption of acetaminophen and makes its effects less intense. For the fastest and most complete pain relief, you should take acetaminophen on an empty stomach, an hour before a meal. However, the effect of food is not so great as to overcome the effects of acetaminophen, and if you are taking regular doses (for example, every four hours), this interaction with food is less important, because food also prolongs the effects of each dose.

HOW DOES AGE AFFECT THE RESPONSE TO THIS DRUG?   The rate at which acetaminophen is inactivated by the liver does not change with advancing age.

ACETAZOLAMIDE

OTHER NAMES   Acetazolamide (pronounced *a-set-a-ZOLE-a-mide)* is the common or generic name of this drug. A frequently used brand name for acetazolamide is Diamox. Acetazolamide belongs to a group of drugs called carbonic-anhydrase inhibitors.

WHAT IS IT SUPPOSED TO DO?   Acetazolamide is most often used in the treatment of glaucoma. It reduces intraocular pressure, the pressure inside the eye, by slowing the rate of formation of aqueous humor, the fluid within the front part of the eye. If untreated, excess intraocular pressure can lead to loss of vision. Acetazolamide is also a diuretic, but its use for this purpose has been replaced by more potent drugs. Occasionally, it is used in the prevention of seizures.

SIDE EFFECTS Acetazolamide can cause loss of appetite, nausea, or vomiting. To minimize any gastrointestinal discomfort, avoid taking acetazolamide on an empty stomach.

Some people experience drowsiness, dizziness, or a decrease in alertness while taking acetazolamide. Tingling, numbness, or burning sensations in the feet, hands, lips, or tongue occur in some individuals. If these problems are severe, you should check with your doctor; the dosage may be too high for you. Before driving an automobile, observe for yourself whether or not this drug causes any decrease in your alertness.

Other side effects are too rare to list here. Contact your doctor if you experience any unusual symptoms.

DRUG INTERACTIONS Several drugs can interact with acetazolamide. These are the most important interactions:

Aspirin. Acetazolamide often causes the blood to become mildly acidic, particularly in older individuals. This can pose a problem when aspirin is taken in large doses, such as twelve or more tablets per day. When the blood becomes even mildly acidic, aspirin enters the brain more readily, and aspirin toxicity is more likely to occur. A number of patients who were previously accustomed to taking large doses of aspirin or other salicylates have developed aspirin toxicity after starting to take acetazolamide. Check with your doctor if you are taking large doses of aspirin; it may be necessary to decrease the dosage somewhat. Occasional doses of aspirin do not interact with acetazolamide.

Digoxin (Lanoxin), which is used in the treatment of congestive heart failure and certain kinds of irregular heartbeats, is more likely to cause toxicity in individuals who have low concentrations of potassium in their blood. Since acetazolamide causes an increase in the excretion of potassium in the urine, the concentration of potassium in your blood may become low. Normally, dietary potassium provides adequate replacement. However, if you are taking digoxin, your doctor will measure the concentration of potassium in your blood at regular intervals and may prescribe additional medication.

Ephedrine, which is contained in many nonprescription cold and hay fever remedies, is eliminated from the body more slowly while you are taking acetazolamide. You will, therefore, be more likely to experience the adverse effects of ephedrine (nervousness, insomnia, palpitations) if the dosage is not reduced.

Methenamine (Mandelamine), which is used in the treatment of urinary tract infections, requires an acidic urine in order to be effective. Since acetazolamide causes the urine to become alkaline, it renders methenamine ineffective. Other drugs must be used for urinary tract infections while you are taking acetazolamide.

Phenytoin (Dilantin), which is used to prevent seizures and to treat certain kinds of irregular heartbeats, can cause softening of the bones in rare instances. The risk for this phenytoin side effect is increased during treatment with acetazolamide. If you are taking both drugs, your doctor should watch for this side effect during regular checkups.

Quinidine (Cardioquin, Quinidex, Quinaglute, others), which is used to treat certain kinds of irregular heartbeats, is eliminated from the body more slowly while you are taking acetazolamide. It may be necessary for your doctor to decrease the dosage of your quinidine while you are taking acetazolamide.

ALCOHOLIC BEVERAGES   There is no reason to refrain from drinking alcoholic beverages while taking acetazolamide. However, if acetazolamide makes you drowsy or decreases your alertness, you should be extremely careful in your use of alcohol.

FOOD Take your acetazolamide with food to avoid upset stomach.

HOW DOES AGE AFFECT THE RESPONSE TO THIS DRUG? There is some evidence that advancing age is accompanied by increased sensitivity to the effects of acetazolamide. Your doctor will take your age into consideration in determining the dosage that is likely to be appropriate for you.

ACETOHEXAMIDE

OTHER NAMES Acetohexamide (pronounced *a-set-oh-HEX-a-mide)* is the common or generic name of this drug. A frequently used brand name for acetohexamide is Dymelor. Acetohexamide belongs to a group of chemically related drugs called sulfonylureas.

WHAT IS IT SUPPOSED TO DO? Acetohexamide decreases the concentration of glucose (a form of sugar) in the blood. Therefore, it is used in the treatment of certain types of diabetes. Acetohexamide works by making the body more sensitive to its own insulin. It was originally thought to increase insulin production by the pancreas, but this effect does not persist with normal continued use.

Diabetes that begins in middle or late life is usually best controlled by diet and exercise, but if these measures fail to decrease the concentration of glucose in the blood, either insulin or a sulfonylurea drug such as acetohexamide may be required in addition. The symptoms of too high a concentration of glucose in the blood (*hyper*glycemia) are excessive thirst, excessive urination, fatigue (which can lead to loss of consciousness and coma), and low resistance to infection. But even if you don't have any symptoms, your doctor will want you to control your blood glucose. Control of blood glucose is essential in preventing or reducing the complications of diabetes, which include damage to vision, loss of feeling in the extremities, kidney damage, heart attack, and stroke.

SIDE EFFECTS   *Hypo*glycemia (too low a concentration of glucose in the blood) can occur from any drug that lowers the blood sugar. Acetohexamide is no exception, although this problem is not likely to occur unless you stop eating, are severely ill, or follow an extremely irregular diet. The symptoms of hypoglycemia, which include lethargy, nausea, cold sweats, pounding or racing heartbeat, shakiness, headache, confusion, and dizziness, are quickly reversed with a glass of fruit juice or with food. If untreated, hypoglycemia can lead to loss of consciousness and coma. If you think you are experiencing hypoglycemia, have something to eat and contact your doctor.

Other side effects from acetohexamide are infrequent. Stomach upset occurs in one or two persons per hundred; take it with food if this problem bothers you. Rash occurs in about one person per hundred; contact your doctor if rash occurs.

Other side effects are too rare to list here. Contact your doctor if you experience any unusual symptoms.

DRUG INTERACTIONS   A number of drugs can interact with acetohexamide or affect your diabetes. These are the most likely to cause problems:

Aspirin. Large doses of aspirin (for example, twelve or more tablets a day) have a mild antidiabetic effect. This effect is too mild to be considered a treatment for diabetes, but it adds to the effect of acetohexamide. If you are taking large doses of aspirin, you should be aware of this effect. If you start or stop using large doses of aspirin, ask your doctor to determine whether it is necessary to alter the dosage of your acetohexamide. Occasional use of aspirin will not affect your response to acetohexamide.

Some *beta-blocking drugs,* such as *propranolol (Inderal), pindolol (Visken), nadolol (Corgard), or timolol (Blocadren).* Diabetic patients should not take these drugs unless there is no other alternative. They can block some of the warning signs of hypoglycemia (especially rapid heartbeat or palpitations), delay the recovery from hypoglycemia, cause high blood pressure episodes during hypoglycemia, and impair circulation to the extremities in diabetics. Other beta-blocking drugs, like metoprolol (Lopressor) and atenolol (Tenormin), are less likely to cause these problems, but there is some risk. If a beta-blocker is required, keep in mind that sweating, but not rapid heartbeat, is a sign of hypoglycemia.

Clofibrate (Atromid-S), which is sometimes used to lower the concentration of triglycerides in blood, may increase the response to acetohexamide in some patients. If you start or stop taking clofibrate, ask your doctor to reevaluate your response to acetohexamide.

Corticosteroids, such as *dexamethasone, hydrocortisone, or prednisone*, can make diabetes more difficult to control. This effect is well known. If you require a corticosteroid, your doctor will check your blood glucose concentration and may increase the dosage of your acetohexamide.

Diuretics, such as *furosemide (Lasix)* or *hydrochlorothiazide (Hydro-DIURIL)*, can reduce the effects of acetohexamide. If your diuretic causes your blood glucose concentration to increase, your doctor may increase the dosage of your acetohexamide.

Guanethidine (Ismelin), which is sometimes used to treat high blood pressure, increases the effects of acetohexamide. Do not start or stop taking guanethidine without asking your doctor to reevaluate your response to acetohexamide.

Nifedipine (Procardia), which is used in the treatment of angina, may decrease your response to acetohexamide. If you start or stop taking nifedipine, ask your doctor to reevaluate your response to acetohexamide.

Phenylbutazone (Butazolidin) and *oxyphenbutazone*, which are sometimes used for brief periods to control gout attacks or severe arthritic pain, can markedly increase the effects of acetohexamide. Since hypoglycemia could result, your doctor may temporarily decrease the dosage of your acetohexamide. Check with your doctor.

Smoking antagonizes the effects of insulin and may impair your response to acetohexamide as well.

Sulfonamides, which are used in treating infections, may increase your response to acetohexamide. If you start or stop taking a sulfonamide, ask your doctor to reevaluate your response to acetohexamide.

Thyroid hormones can affect your response to acetohexamide. If you are starting to take thyroid, or if the dosage of your thyroid hormone is being changed, ask your doctor to reevaluate your response to acetohexamide.

ALCOHOLIC BEVERAGES A number of potential problems can arise from your use of alcoholic beverages. Some doctors tell their patients to avoid alcohol. Others advise their patients to limit their alcohol intake to a glass of wine or two with dinner. The American Diabetes Association allows the inclusion of small amounts of alcoholic beverages in the diet of diabetics. You should avoid sweetened alcoholic beverages. Here is a summary of the potential problems that alcohol can cause:

First, alcohol temporarily lowers the concentration of glucose in the blood. If you drink alcohol on an empty stomach, it can cause hypoglycemia. The risk of hypoglycemia is increased while you are taking acetohexamide. Therefore, you should avoid large amounts of alcohol and avoid drinking on an empty stomach. If you drink small amounts of alcohol with meals, hypoglycemia is not likely to occur.

Second, some people who take acetohexamide develop a flushing reaction when they drink alcohol. This reaction occurs in fewer than 5 percent of those who take acetohexamide. It is known as the disulfiram or Antabuse reaction, because disulfiram (Antabuse), which is more reliable in causing this reaction, is given to alcoholics for precisely this reason. The reaction is usually harmless, but may be unpleasant and may be accompanied by headache. If you are bothered by this reaction and your doctor says it is all right for you to drink small amounts of alcohol with meals, you might try taking an aspirin tablet about an hour before any meal that will include a glass of wine.

FOOD Acetohexamide does not replace diet as the primary means for controlling blood glucose. In addition to avoiding simple sugars, you should increase the amount of roughage (such as fruits, vegetables, and whole grains) in your diet. These foods slow the absorption of complex carbohydrates. Furthermore, you should restrict your consumption of saturated fats (butter, animal fat), because they increase the risk of cardiovascular disease, and cardiovascular disease is more common among diabetics. Finally, most diabetics who take acetohexamide are overweight. Obesity causes resistance to the body's natural insulin and increases the concentration of glucose in the blood. Weight loss, even if you remain a little heavy, will help control your diabetes. Follow the diabetic diet prescribed by your doctor.

A regular diet is important. If you skip meals because of illness or some other reason, you may experience hypoglycemia (see Side Effects). If you cannot eat because of illness, check with your doctor.

Acetohexamide is best taken at the start of a meal to prevent stomach upset and to help you remember to take it. Food does not affect the absorption of acetohexamide tablets. Hypoglycemia can occur if you fail to eat within an hour or two after taking it on an empty stomach.

HOW DOES AGE AFFECT THE RESPONSE TO THIS DRUG? Hypoglycemia from drugs like acetohexamide is more common among older people than it is among younger people. Be sure to take your acetohexamide as directed, follow a careful but regular diet, and be sure that you and those around you are familiar with the signs and symptoms of hypoglycemia.

Acetohexamide is metabolized by the liver to another, more potent drug. This metabolite is removed from the body by the kidneys, and the kidneys become less efficient with advancing age. Therefore, the metabolite may accumulate to somewhat higher concentrations in the bodies of older people. As a result, some older people will experience greater effects from this metabolite of acetohexamide than younger people who are given the same dose. Your doctor will take your age and kidney function into account (see appendix) in determining which dose of acetohexamide is likely to be appropriate for you. Nevertheless, you should always be alert for signs of hypoglycemia from acetohexamide (see Side Effects).

Another effect of age on the kidneys is the way they respond to high concentrations of glucose in the blood. In younger people, when the concentration of glucose in the blood gets much higher than normal, glucose appears in the urine. The threshold for glucose spilling into the urine increases with age, and older people can have much higher concentrations of glucose in their blood without having any in their urine. This effect varies from individual to individual, of course, but urine tests for glucose may be less reliable as indicators of blood glucose in older people. So don't be misled by negative urine tests for glucose. Your doctor can compare your blood glucose with your urine glucose to give you some idea of how reliable urine tests might be for you.

ALLOPURINOL

OTHER NAMES Allopurinol (pronounced *al-oh-PURE-i-nole)* is the common or generic name of this drug. Some frequently used brand names for allopurinol are Lopurin and Zyloprim.

WHAT IS IT SUPPOSED TO DO? Allopurinol prevents gout attacks and gouty arthritis by decreasing the formation of uric acid. Too high a concentration of uric acid in the blood is the cause of gout attacks. (The drug has no effect on gout attacks that are already in progress.) Allopurinol also prevents the rapid increase of uric acid concentration in the blood that occurs because of the rapid breakdown of cells during some forms of cancer therapy. In this situation, its ability to prevent the formation of uric acid decreases the risk of kidney damage that might otherwise occur if the kidneys were presented with a lot more uric acid than is normal. It is also used to prevent the formation of some types of kidney stones.

SIDE EFFECTS The most commonly encountered problem is allergy, which occurs in less than 1 percent of the patients who take allopurinol. Allergy usually manifests itself as a rash. Allergic reactions can also become apparent in the form of fever, chills, joint pain, nausea and vomiting, sore throat with fever, yellowing of the eyes or skin, unusual bleeding or bruising, or other symptoms. Stop taking your allopurinol and promptly report these or any other possible symptoms of allergy to your doctor. Allergy can occur after you have taken allopurinol for some time without problem.

Infrequently, allopurinol causes diarrhea, nausea, stomach pain, or drowsiness. If any of these are severe or persistent, contact your doctor. Do not drive an automobile until you are certain that allopurinol does not affect your alertness.

Infrequently, gout attacks occur at the beginning of allopurinol therapy. Your doctor will treat these with other drugs.

Rarely, kidney stones occur as a result of allopurinol therapy. Contact your doctor if you experience painful or bloody urination, difficult urination, or lower back pain.

Other side effects are too rare to list here. Contact your doctor if you experience any unexpected symptoms.

DRUG INTERACTIONS Several drugs can interact with allopurinol. These are the ones that are most likely to cause problems:

Anticoagulants, such as *dicumarol* and possibly *warfarin (Coumadin).* The metabolism of these drugs may be slowed by allopurinol, which would increase their effects. Your doctor will monitor your anticoagulant therapy with special care while you are taking allopurinol. It may be necessary to decrease the dosage of your anticoagulant.

Anticancer drugs. The metabolism of both *azathioprine (Imuran)* and *mercaptopurine (6-MP, Purinethol)* are slowed by allopurinol, and their effects are thereby increased. Your doctor will reduce the dosage of these drugs when they are to be taken with allopurinol. In addition, allopurinol may increase the effect of *cyclophosphamide (Cytoxan);* the mechanism for this reaction is unknown.

Ampicillin and amoxicillin, which are antibiotics, are much more likely to cause rashes when taken with allopurinol. Any rash that occurs while taking allopurinol should be promptly reported to your doctor.

Thiazide diuretics, such as *hydrochlorothiazide (HydroDIURIL),* apparently increase the concentration of oxypurinol, the active metabolite of allopurinol, in the blood. In those with decreased kidney function, this increase in oxypurinol concentration is considerable and can lead to a serious allergic reaction to allopurinol (and oxypurinol). If you are taking a thiazide diuretic, ask your doctor to evaluate your kidney function by determining your creatinine clearance (see appendix) and, if necessary, adjust the dosage of your allopurinol. Allopurinol is not recommended for the asymptomatic hyperuricemia (elevated concentration of uric acid in the blood without symptoms of gout) that is sometimes caused by thiazide diuretics.

ALCOHOLIC BEVERAGES Heavy consumption of alcohol provokes gout attacks in susceptible individuals. If allopurinol affects your alertness, be careful in your use of alcohol.

FOOD It's probably best to take your allopurinol with food or after a meal to avoid gastrointestinal irritation. It is especially important to drink plenty of fluid while taking allopurinol. This will help prevent kidney stones.

HOW DOES AGE AFFECT THE RESPONSE TO THIS DRUG? Advancing age is likely to be associated with the need for smaller doses of allopurinol.

Allopurinol is metabolized by the liver to another drug, oxypurinol, which shares allopurinol's pharmacological effects. Oxypurinol is slowly eliminated from the body by the kidneys, and it accumulates to high concentrations in the blood of people with poor kidney function. There is good evidence that this accumulation leads to dangerous allergic reactions unless allopurinol dosage is reduced in accordance with kidney function. Although there is currently no direct evidence that normal decline in kidney function is sufficient to cause problems, many doctors routinely assess their older patients' kidney functions and use those assessments in determining allopurinol dosages that are likely to be safe and effective. The assessment of kidney function in older individuals is described in the appendix.

ALPRAZOLAM

OTHER NAMES Alprazolam (pronounced *al-PRAY-zo-lam)* is the common or generic name of this drug. A frequently used brand name for alprazolam is Xanax. Alprazolam belongs to a large group of similar drugs called benzodiazepines.

WHAT IS IT SUPPOSED TO DO? Alprazolam relieves the symptoms of anxiety and tension.

SIDE EFFECTS Drowsiness is the principal side effect from alprazolam. You may find yourself unsteady on your feet as well. Evaluate these effects for yourself and regulate your activities accordingly. You should be especially cautious about driving an automobile. If drowsiness or unsteadiness is persistent, stop taking the drug and contact your doctor.

Infrequently, alprazolam causes dizziness, fainting, weakness, confusion, impaired memory, or loss of coordination. If you experience any of these effects, which suggest you are extremely sensitive to alprazolam, stop taking it and contact your doctor.

If you have been taking alprazolam regularly for a long time and in large doses, you may experience mild withdrawal symptoms several days after stopping this drug. Typical symptoms include difficulty in sleeping, unusual irritability, and unusual nervousness. If these occur, contact your doctor.

Other side effects from alprazolam are too rare to list here. Contact your doctor if you experience any unusual symptoms.

DRUG INTERACTIONS Sedation is a common side effect of antidepressant drugs, antihistamines, tranquilizers, narcotic analgesics, and other drugs. Be careful of additive effects if you are taking alprazolam with any of these drugs.

In addition, several drugs can interact with alprazolam by other mechanisms. These are the interactions most likely to cause problems:

Cimetidine (Tagamet), which is used for the treatment of ulcers, may slow the metabolism of alprazolam and thereby enhance its effects. It may be necessary to decrease the dosage of your alprazolam while taking both drugs; ask your doctor.

Disulfiram (Antabuse), which is used in the treatment of alcoholism, may slow the metabolism of alprazolam and thereby enhance its effects. It may be necessary to decrease the dosage of your alprazolam while taking both drugs; ask your doctor.

Levodopa (Dopar, Larodopa, L-dopa) is used in the treatment of Parkinson's disease, and alprazolam may block its effect. If you are taking both drugs and notice a worsening of your parkinsonism, stop taking your alprazolam and contact your doctor.

ALCOHOLIC BEVERAGES Alprazolam adds to alcohol's depressant effects on the nervous system. You should limit your alcohol consumption to small amounts while taking alprazolam. Needless to say, the effects of this combination on driving can be dangerous.

FOOD Alprazolam can be taken with food or on an empty stomach.

HOW DOES AGE AFFECT THE RESPONSE TO THIS DRUG? The older you are, the more sensitive you will be to alprazolam. There are at least two mechanisms involved:

First, older people are inherently more sensitive to the effects of alprazolam. This may have something to do with the effects of aging on the brain. Second, the metabolism of alprazolam slows with aging. Therefore, older people accumulate higher concentrations of alprazolam in their blood after repeated doses, and they therefore experience more effect than younger people taking the same doses.

In any case, side effects increase with age. Confusion, weakness, fainting, dizziness, impaired memory, and loss of coordination, which are infrequent side effects from alprazolam, occur more often in older people than they do in younger people.

Your doctor will take your age into consideration in selecting a dose and dosage schedule that are appropriate for you.

AMILORIDE

OTHER NAMES Amiloride (pronounced *a-MILL-oh-ride*) is the common or generic name of this drug. A frequently used brand name for amiloride is Midamor. Amiloride is often prescribed in tablets that also contain hydrochlorothiazide, another diuretic but one with different properties. A frequently used brand name for this hydrochlorothiazide plus amiloride combination is Moduretic. Pharmacologists refer to amiloride as a potassium-sparing diuretic.

WHAT IS IT SUPPOSED TO DO? Amiloride is a diuretic—it acts on the kidneys, causing them to eliminate extra water and salt from the body and into the urine. It is used in treating high blood pressure and in relieving the symptoms of edema, the abnormal swelling in tissues or congestion in the lungs that results from heart failure or other medical problems. Because amiloride is a mild diuretic, it is usually taken with another diuretic, such as hydrochlorothiazide or furosemide. Unlike hydrochlorothiazide or furosemide, amiloride conserves potassium in the body rather than promoting its loss. Therefore, when used in combination with these more potent diuretics, amiloride counteracts their principal side effect—potassium loss.

SIDE EFFECTS At first you will notice a need to urinate frequently. This effect will decrease with continued use. You should avoid taking amiloride too close to bedtime. Otherwise, you may find yourself being frequently awakened by a need to urinate.

Infrequently, amiloride causes headache, nausea, vomiting, or diarrhea. If they occur, these side effects may go away with continued use. Contact your doctor if they are persistent. (You should contact your doctor whenever you experience continued vomiting or diarrhea, because these can cause dehydration and electrolyte imbalance.)

The most serious side effect from amiloride is hyperkalemia (too high a concentration of potassium in the blood), but this occurs infrequently. To prevent this side effect, which can cause dangerously irregular heartbeats, you should not take any form of potassium supplement while you are taking amiloride. Your doctor will periodically measure the concentration of potassium in your blood while you are taking this drug. Numbness or tingling in the hands, feet, or lips; weakness; or confusion may be signs of hyperkalemia—contact your doctor if any of these occur.

Rarely, amiloride causes dizziness, confusion, dry mouth, weakness, or skin rashes. These may be signs that you are extremely sensitive or allergic to the drug; contact your doctor.

Other side effects are too rare to list here. Contact your doctor if you experience any unexpected problems.

DRUG INTERACTIONS Several drugs can interact with amiloride, and some of these interactions have potentially serious consequences:

Angiotensin-converting-enzyme (ACE) inhibitors, such as *captopril (Capoten, Capozide)* or *enalapril (Vaseretic, Vasotec),* which are used in the treatment of congestive heart failure and high blood pressure, cause potassium to be conserved by the body. To minimize the risk of too high a concentration of potassium in the blood (hyperkalemia), amiloride should be used with these drugs only when the concentration of potassium in the blood has been demonstrated to be too low. If you are taking this combination, be sure your doctor is monitoring the concentration of potassium in your blood.

Indomethacin (Indocin), an anti-inflammatory drug, can impair kidney function when taken with amiloride. Amiloride causes a slight reduction of blood flow in the kidney, which the kidney compensates for by producing prostaglandins. Indomethacin prevents the formation of prostaglandins—it is among the most potent inhibitors of prostaglandin synthesis. These two drugs should not be used together.

Potassium supplements (KCl, potassium chloride). Amiloride causes potassium to be conserved by the body. When supplemental potassium is taken with amiloride, too high a concentration of potassium in the blood (hyperkalemia) can occur.

Other *potassium-sparing diuretics*, such as *spironolactone (Aldactone, Aldactazide) or triamterene (Dyazide, Dyrenium, Maxzide)*, should not be taken with amiloride. There is no reason for taking more than one potassium-sparing diuretic at a time. Such a combination would substantially increase the risk of developing too high a concentration of potassium in the blood (hyperkalemia).

Salt substitutes and *low-salt milk* contain potassium chloride. Therefore, they can interact with amiloride in the same way as potassium supplements (see above) if used in sufficient amounts. Check with your doctor before using these products.

ALCOHOLIC BEVERAGES Unless you have other medical reasons for restricting their use, you can continue drinking them. There is no interaction.

FOOD Unless your doctor has advised otherwise, take your amiloride with meals to decrease any gastrointestinal upset that it might cause and to help you set up a routine for taking it regularly.

If you are on a restricted-salt diet, be sure to follow it, and avoid using salt substitutes (see Drug Interactions). Since foods vary in their potassium content, you should not make a radical change in your regular diet without first checking with your doctor.

HOW DOES AGE AFFECT THE RESPONSE TO THIS DRUG?   The risk of hyperkalemia (see Side Effects) from amiloride increases because of the steady decline in kidney function that occurs with advancing age. Both potassium and amiloride are eliminated from the body by the kidneys, and both can accumulate to high concentrations in the blood if kidney function is sufficiently reduced. Evidence of this risk was recently illustrated by a study of hospitalized patients with hyperkalemia of various causes, in which age over sixty was associated with a threefold greater incidence of this problem. Two-thirds of the cases of hyperkalemia in this study were caused by drugs. Your doctor will evaluate your kidney function (see appendix) before prescribing amiloride and periodically thereafter.

Older age is more often accompanied by medical problems that add to the risk of hyperkalemia. For example, in some instances, diabetics may be more prone to develop hyperkalemia than nondiabetics. Likewise, individuals with malignancies are more likely to develop hyperkalemia.

Lastly, older individuals are more likely to experience adverse effects from drug interactions that don't ordinarily cause problems. For example, amiloride and nonsteroidal anti-inflammatory drugs (NSAIDs), such as ibuprofen, fenoprofen, and naproxen, are commonly taken together without problem, despite the fact that these drugs have the potential for interacting with amiloride in a manner similar to indomethacin (see Drug Interactions). This interaction is probably too rare to warrant routine precautionary warnings, but in someone whose kidneys are already stressed by uncorrected congestive heart failure or by dehydration, it could cause kidney failure (usually reversible), depending on the dosage level and the condition of the individual.

Furthermore, the potassium-retaining properties of the NSAIDs, which are ordinarily not clinically apparent, may be additive to those of amiloride in people with poor kidney function.

Regular checkups should prevent these problems. Despite this list of potentially serious consequences, amiloride is one of the most commonly used drugs among older people and it seldom causes serious side effects.

AMITRIPTYLINE

OTHER NAMES Amitriptyline (pronounced *a-mee-TRIP-ti-leen)* is the common or generic name of this drug. Some frequently used brand names for amitriptyline are Amitril, Elavil, Emitrip, Endep, and Enovil. Sometimes amitriptyline is prescribed as tablets that also contain a second drug. Examples of these combinations are amitriptyline with the benzodiazepine sedative chlordiazepoxide (Limbitrol) and amitriptyline with the tranquilizer perphenazine (Etrafon, Triavil). Amitriptyline belongs to a group of drugs called tricyclic antidepressants. (*Tricyclic* describes their chemical structure; *antidepressant* refers to their principal pharmacological effect.)

WHAT IS IT SUPPOSED TO DO? Amitriptyline relieves mental depression. The precise means by which it works has not been established, but its mechanism of action involves an increase in the concentration of certain naturally occurring substances (serotonin and norepinephrine) within the brain. Elevation of mood and reversal of the various symptoms that can accompany depression (such as sleep problems, decreased energy, or loss of appetite) require a minimum of several weeks of regular use. Your doctor may prescribe less than several weeks' supply of medication initially, so it is important that you return to your pharmacy to have your prescription refilled. Your doctor may want you to continue taking amitriptyline for several months after your mood returns to normal.

SIDE EFFECTS Nearly everyone experiences dry mouth while taking amitriptyline. It doesn't seem to be related to dosage, and it tends to diminish with time. Sugar-free candy or gum is often helpful in alleviating this problem.

Drowsiness is another common side effect. Avoid driving until you are sure that your alertness and coordination are not impaired.

The most common, potentially serious side effect involves the temporary decrease in blood pressure that occurs when you stand up quickly. This decrease in blood pressure is exaggerated by amitriptyline and is likely to make you dizzy, lightheaded, or faint if you stand up too quickly. If this side effect is severe (especially if it causes you to fall or your heart to pound or race), contact your doctor. Be very careful to stand up slowly.

The dry mouth caused by amitriptyline is an example of what pharmacologists call an anticholinergic effect. It can be caused by any drug that blocks the receptors for acetylcholine, a substance the body produces to regulate certain functions that are beyond conscious control. When amitriptyline is taken with other drugs that have anticholinergic side effects, these side effects are more likely to cause problems (see Drug Interactions). Another common anticholinegric side effect is constipation. Ask your pharmacist for appropriate treatment; a stool softener is often helpful. Contact your doctor if constipation becomes severe. A third anticholingeric side effect is the sudden onset of confusion or disorientation, sometimes with visual hallucinations. If this occurs, contact your doctor; it is a sign that the dosage is too high for you. Other anticholinergic side effects that require your doctor's attention (and these are infrequent or rare) include blurred vision, difficulty in urinating (more common in older men with prostate difficulties), and eye pain (a possible indication that narrow-angle glaucoma, not the usual type of glaucoma, has been aggravated).

Effects on the heart—excessively fast, slow, or irregular heartbeat—are infrequent. Contact your doctor if any of these occur.

Other side effects include nausea, unpleasant taste, diarrhea (infrequent), and excessive sweating (infrequent). These side effects may diminish or go away as your body adjusts to the effects of this drug. Contact your doctor if they are severe or bothersome. A fine tremor is not an uncommon side effect in older people; tell your doctor if this occurs.

Other side effects are too infrequent to list here. Contact your doctor if you experience any unexpected symptoms.

DRUG INTERACTIONS Amitriptyline interacts with a number of drugs. Here are the most common sources of potential problems:

Anticholinergic drugs, such as *belladonna (Donnatal) or propantheline (Pro-Banthine),* which are used for peptic-ulcer disease; *benztropine (Cogentin),* which is used in the treatment of Parkinson's disease and to treat the side effects sometimes caused by tranquilizers; and *scopolamine (Transderm Scōp),* which is used to prevent motion sickness, all work by blocking acetylcholine (see Side Effects). These drugs are more likely to cause anticholinergic side effects when taken with amitriptyline. In many cases, the anticholinergic effects of amitriptyline obviate the need for these other drugs. Check with your doctor before taking them.

Antihistamines, which are included in many nonprescription cold and allergy medicines, have sedative and anticholinergic (see above) side effects. Avoid these products while taking amitriptyline.

Antihypertensive drugs can interact with amitriptyline by several mechanisms. First, some of them (beta-blockers, clonidine, methyldopa, and reserpine) can cause depression as a side effect. Second, the action of a few antihypertensive drugs is blocked by amitriptyline. If you are taking clonidine (Catapres, Combipres), guanethidine (Ismelin), or guanadrel (Hylorel), your doctor will need to prescribe another drug to control your blood pressure. Third, if your antihypertensive drug causes dizziness, amitriptyline will make this side effect worse. Your doctor may need to decrease the dose of your antihypertensive drug before you start taking amitriptyline.

Cimetidine (Tagamet), which is used in the treatment of peptic-ulcer disease, slows the metabolism of amitriptyline and thereby increases its effects. Contact your doctor if you experience an increase in amitriptyline side effects while taking cimetidine; your doctor may have to temporarily lower the dosage of your amitriptyline.

Monoamine-oxidase inhibitors, such as *isocarboxazid (Marplan), phenelzine (Nardil), or tranylcypromine (Parnate)*, which are also used in the treatment of depression, sometimes cause dangerous toxic reactions when taken with amitriptyline. This combination of drugs should be used only in hospitalized patients who are under careful observation. Normally, one or two weeks are allowed to elapse between the use of amitriptyline and one of these drugs.

Phenobarbital, which is used to prevent seizures and is also sometimes included as an ingredient in certain medications for its sedative effects, stimulates the metabolism of amitriptyline and thereby decreases its effects. If you require treatment with phenobarbital, your doctor will take this into consideration in adjusting your amitriptyline dosage. Otherwise, your doctor may replace your phenobarbital-containing medication with another drug product.

Phenothiazine tranquilizers, such as *perphenazine (Trilafon), thioridazine (Mellaril), and trifluoperazine (Stelazine)*, are more likely to cause anticholinergic side effects (see Side Effects) when taken with amitriptyline. In addition, these drugs may slow the metabolism of amitriptyline and thereby increase its effects. There are instances when these drugs need to be given with amitriptyline, but you should be sure that your doctor intends that you take this combination.

ALCOHOLIC BEVERAGES   Alcohol will increase the dizziness or faintness that you may feel upon standing up too quickly. It will also add to any drowsiness that amitriptyline might cause. Therefore, you should avoid alcohol or use it sparingly while taking amitriptyline.

FOOD   Take your amitriptyline with meals to help you maintain a regular schedule and to prevent any nausea that it might cause.

HOW DOES AGE AFFECT THE RESPONSE TO THIS DRUG?   There is considerable variation among individuals in the rate at which amitriptyline is removed from the blood by metabolism in the liver. However, several studies have shown that advancing age is accompanied by a slower metabolism of amitriptyline, and that older people tend to develop higher concentrations of amitriptyline in their blood. Therefore, older people usually require smaller doses than younger people.

In addition, older people are more sensitive to side effects from amitriptyline. Your doctor will try to prescribe a dose that is likely to be effective without causing serious side effects, but you should contact your doctor promptly if you experience extreme dizziness or faintness (which could cause you to fall), confusion or disorientation (which is alarming but goes away when the dose is reduced or the drug is stopped), or any other serious side effect. Your doctor may make use of a laboratory test that measures the concentration of amitriptyline in your blood in order to evaluate your amitriptyline dosage.

ASPIRIN

OTHER NAMES   Aspirin (pronounced *AS-pir-in)* is the common or generic name of this drug. It is sometimes referred to by its chemical name, acetylsalicylic acid, which is abbreviated ASA.

Aspirin is sold without prescription in a variety of forms and under a variety of brand names. There are many brands of plain aspirin tables. Buffered aspirin tablets (Ascriptin, Bufferin, others) contain a small amount of antacid and, it is claimed, work faster and cause less stomach irritation than plain aspirin tablets, because presumably they go into solution faster. These claims, however, are based on studies of tablets that contained much more antacid than is present in commercially available tablets. Enteric-coated aspirin (A.S.A. Enseals, Ecotrin, others) release aspirin after it leaves the stomach, which protects against irritation to the stomach (but not the rest of the gastrointestinal tract). Alka-Seltzer is a brand of aspirin that is taken in solution, making it the fastest-acting aspirin product, but each dose contains a large amount of sodium. Therefore, it should be used with appropriate caution and never on a regular basis. Many nonprescription aspirin products contain caffeine (Anacin, others), which does not contribute in any helpful way to aspirin's effects. Most pharmacologists agree that none of these various forms of aspirin has substantial advantages over plain aspirin tablets. However, the marketplace for aspirin is busy—more than ten thousand tons of aspirin are consumed annually in the United States alone, and every form and brand of aspirin has its adherents. If a particular form of aspirin works well for you, or if your doctor has recommended a particular form for you, you should use it.

Aspirin is an active ingredient in many brand-name prescription medications. Among these are Darvon Compound (aspirin, caffeine, and propoxyphene), Empirin with Codeine (aspirin and codeine), Equagesic (aspirin and meprobamate), Fiorinal (aspirin, a barbiturate, and caffeine), and Percodan (aspirin and a derivative of codeine).

Aspirin belongs to a group of chemically related drugs called salicylates. It is also sometimes referred to as a nonsteroidal anti-inflammatory drug, abbreviated in medical journals and textbooks as NSAID.

WHAT IS IT SUPPOSED TO DO?   Aspirin relieves mild to moderate pain, such as joint or muscle pain, or headache. It also lowers fever. In higher doses, it relieves inflammation. Sometimes doctors ask certain of their patients to take small amounts of aspirin, such as a tablet a day or every other day, to prevent harmful blood clots.

Contrary to popular belief, aspirin is at least as effective in relieving pain as codeine, and it causes fewer side effects. However, the combination of these two drugs is more effective than either codeine or aspirin by itself.

SIDE EFFECTS The most common side effect from aspirin is gastrointestinal upset, which usually takes the form of mild discomfort in the area of the stomach but can also manifest itself as heartburn, indigestion, cramps, nausea, or vomiting. In addition, aspirin can cause painless gastric bleeding. In most cases, the amount of blood lost is insignificant, but it can cause anemia in regular users of aspirin. You can decrease these gastrointestinal effects by taking each dose with a full glass of water. The amount of antacid in buffered aspirin tablets is probably inadequate to be of much help. A more important consideration in choosing an aspirin tablet that will be easiest on your stomach is freshness of the tablets. Aspirin breaks down, especially in the presence of moisture, to salicylic acid, which is extremely irritating. The other product of decomposed aspirin is acetic acid, or vinegar. That is why aspirin always smells a little sour. Never take aspirin that has a strong vinegarlike odor. Keep your aspirin bottle tightly closed, and don't store it anywhere near your shower or other source of dampness.

Stomach upset from aspirin is not the same as allergy to aspirin. If you have ever had a rash, hives, or itching from aspirin, you are probably allergic to aspirin and other salicylates. If you have ever had an asthma attack because of aspirin, you are probably allergic to aspirin, all other nonsteroidal anti-inflammatory drugs, a yellow dye called tartrazine (FD&C yellow No. 5) that is used in some foods and drugs, and sodium benzoate (a widely used preservative).

On rare occasions, aspirin causes significant bleeding in the gastrointestinal tract. The symptoms include bloody or black tarry stools, severe stomach pain, or vomiting of blood or material that looks like coffee grounds. Contact your doctor at once if any of these symptoms occur.

If you take large daily doses of aspirin for arthritis (for example, twelve or more tablets per day), you should watch for signs of overdose. Most commonly, the first sign is a ringing or buzzing in the ears, followed by some loss of hearing. If you already have a hearing impairment, which is common with increasing age, you may not notice any of these signs. Other signs of overdose are dizziness, confusion, drowsiness, dim vision, sweating, fever, rapid breathing, nausea, vomiting, and diarrhea. Contact your doctor promptly if any of these signs occur.

Other side effects from aspirin are too rare to list here. Contact your doctor if any unexpected symptoms occur.

DRUG INTERACTIONS These are the most important drug interactions with aspirin. Most of them require large amounts of aspirin before they become significant.

Acetazolamide (Diamox), which is sometimes used in the treatment of glaucoma, may make you more sensitive to large doses of aspirin. It may be necessary to decrease your daily dosage of aspirin.

Antacids, in large amounts, can increase the urinary excretion of salicylate and thereby decrease the effect of aspirin. This interaction occurs only with large daily doses of aspirin. It doesn't occur with occasional doses. If you take both drugs regularly in large amounts, you should be alert for the possibility of too much aspirin effect if you suddenly stop taking your antacid.

Antidiabetic drugs, such as *insulin* or the *sulfonylureas,* interact with aspirin by several mechanisms that may increase their effects. First, large doses of aspirin (twelve or more tablets per day) tend to decrease the blood sugar. This effect is usually not significant by itself, but it can add to the effect of an antidiabetic drug. Second, aspirin can displace some sulfonylurea antidiabetic drugs from storage areas in the blood (on circulating proteins) and thereby increase their effects. This doesn't usually cause problems, but it should be watched for. Third, aspirin may interfere with the excretion of chlorpropamide (Diabinese) by the kidneys and thereby increase its effects. Small doses of aspirin are not likely to cause problems with antidiabetic drugs, with the exception of chlorpropamide (Diabinese). If you are taking a drug for diabetes, don't start or stop taking large doses of aspirin without first checking with your doctor.

Corticosteroids, such as *dexamethasone, hydrocortisone, or prednisone*, may increase the urinary excretion of aspirin and its active metabolites and thereby decrease its effects. Because both aspirin and corticosteroids reduce inflammation, this combination is often used to good therapeutic advantage. However, when large amounts of aspirin are taken with a corticosteroid and the corticosteroid dosage is cut back, the aspirin dosage may have to be reduced as well.

Methotrexate, which is used in treating some forms of cancer, severe psoriasis, and severe rheumatoid arthritis, is removed from the body by the kidneys. Aspirin impairs this process and also displaces methotrexate from its storage sites in the blood. Both of these effects increase the toxicity of methotrexate. Therefore, aspirin should be avoided while taking methotrexate.

Uricosuric drugs, such as *probenecid (Benemid) and sulfinpyrazone (Anturane)*, prevent gout attacks by increasing the urinary excretion of uric acid. Aspirin in anything more than an occasional small dose blocks their effect.

Warfarin (Coumadin), an anticoagulant, interacts with aspirin by several mechanisms, all of which increase the risk of bleeding. You should avoid aspirin while taking warfarin.

ALCOHOLIC BEVERAGES Both alcohol and aspirin are irritating to the stomach, so you should avoid taking them at the same time. Alcohol substantially increases the amount of minor gastric bleeding from aspirin.

FOOD It's a good idea to take aspirin after meals or with a snack, because food acts as a buffer to decrease the gastric effects of aspirin.

HOW DOES AGE AFFECT THE RESPONSE TO THIS DRUG? Several studies have found no correlation between age and the response to aspirin. There is considerable variation among individuals in the dosages required to achieve equal concentrations of aspirin and its active metabolites in the blood, but age does not appear to play a major role in this variation.

ATENOLOL

OTHER NAMES Atenolol (pronounced *a-TEN-oh-lole)* is the common or generic name of this drug. A frequently used brand name for atenolol is Tenormin. Tablets that contain a combination of atenolol and chlorthalidone, a thiazide diuretic, are marketed under the brand name Tenoretic. Atenolol belongs to a group of drugs known as beta-blockers. Health professionals sometimes refer to atenolol as a cardioselective beta-blocker or a $beta_1$-blocker, names that are precise pharmacological descriptions of how atenolol works.

WHAT IS IT SUPPOSED TO DO? Atenolol lowers blood pressure, prevents angina attacks, and reduces the risk of recurrent heart attack. It accomplishes these beneficial effects by acting on the autonomic nervous system, the part of the nervous system that is beyond our conscious control—the part that regulates the heart, blood vessels, and various internal organs. Needless to say, the autonomic nervous system is complex. It has parasympathetic and sympathetic parts that generally work in opposition to one another. The sympathetic part responds to two types of stimulation, alpha and beta.

Atenolol molecules temporarily bind with highly specialized nervous tissues called beta-receptors, thereby preventing them from recognizing the chemical messengers that normally set them off. (That is why pharmacologists refer to atenolol as a beta-blocker.) The beta-receptors are one of several means by which the cardiovascular system gets the messages that tell it what to do. An increase in heart rate and an increase in blood pressure are examples of beta responses that are blocked by atenolol.

There are beta-receptors throughout the body, but they are not all the same. The beta-receptors in the heart and kidneys, which are more sensitive to the effects of atenolol, are called $beta_1$-receptors. The beta-receptors in the lungs and pancreas, which are called $beta_2$-receptors, are less sensitive to the effects of atenolol. This relative lack of effect on $beta_2$-receptors is particularly desirable in people who have lung problems or diabetes, because beta-blockers that are not as selective in their action as atenolol can complicate these conditions. Because atenolol has a greater affinity for $beta_1$-receptors, and therefore greater selectivity for cardiovascular beta-blocking effects, pharmacologists call it a cardioselective beta-blocker.

SIDE EFFECTS   Despite the wide distribution of beta-receptors throughout the body, side effects from atenolol are infrequent and generally mild. Most people experience no side effects at all.

The most important side effect you should know about is the possibility of withdrawal symptoms if you suddenly stop taking atenolol after taking it regularly. This side effect can be understood by considering how atenolol works (see above). While the beta-receptors are blocked by atenolol, they can become overly sensitive to the chemical messengers that normally set them off. If atenolol is withdrawn abruptly, these receptors will overrespond. The most common symptom is headache, but there is also the danger of angina attacks, a sudden rise in blood pressure, irregular heart-beats, or even a heart attack, depending on what condition was being treated initially. If your doctor wants you to stop taking atenolol, he will gradually reduce the dose or he may substitute another drug that has similar effects.

Your doctor will carefully check your heart before prescribing atenolol. When atenolol is taken by individuals with untreated congestive heart failure, a condition in which the heart is unable to do the job of pumping blood through the circulatory system adequately, this heart failure is likely to be worsened. Infrequently, it causes congestive heart failure in individuals with no previous symptoms. Most patients whose congestive heart failure is corrected by other drugs are able to take atenolol without problem. You should contact your doctor at once if you experience swelling of the feet or ankles, sudden weight gain, or difficulty in breathing. Atenolol's ability to slow the heart and lower the blood pressure is usually beneficial, but occasional individuals experience an excess of these effects. An unusually slow pulse rate (less than fifty beats per minute) or dizziness (possibly from abnormally low blood pressure) are other reasons to get in touch with your doctor.

Stomach upset, constipation, or diarrhea occur infrequently from atenolol. When any of these side effects do occur, they often go away with continued use of the drug. If they continue to be bothersome, contact your doctor.

Although atenolol enters the brain, its effects there are usually imperceptible, except for occasional drowsiness. However, it sometimes causes adverse mental effects, including dizziness, fatigue, confusion, nightmares, insomnia, and depression. There is some evidence that atenolol is less likely than other beta-blockers to cause these side effects, but if you experience any unusual and persistent mental symptoms, contact your doctor.

Other side effects are too rare to mention here. Contact your doctor if you experience any unusual symptoms.

DRUG INTERACTIONS Several drugs can interact with atenolol. Your doctor will monitor your therapy with special care if you are taking any of these drugs.

Antacids can impair the absorption of atenolol. Therefore, antacid and atenolol doses should be taken at least one hour apart.

Antidiabetic drugs, such as *insulin* or the *sulfonylureas.* Atenolol can block the rapid heartbeat or palpitations that occur as warning signs of hypoglycemia (too low a concentration of glucose in the blood), although sweating and dizziness remain as signs of hypoglycemia. Overdosage of atenolol can delay the recovery from hypoglycemia.

Breathing medications, such as *isoproterenol (Isuprel) inhalation, terbutaline (Brethine, Bricanyl), or theophylline (Elixophyllin, Slo-Phyllin, Theobid, Theo-Dur, and others),* which are used for the treatment of asthma, emphysema, or other lung problems, stimulate $beta_2$-receptors whereas atenolol blocks $beta_1$-receptors. Theoretically, there should be no interaction, but large doses of atenolol will also block $beta_2$-receptors and will therefore block the ability of breathing medications to open up the air passages in the lungs. These drugs can be used together safely, but you should be alert for the possibility of poor response from your respiratory medication. If this occurs, contact your doctor.

Clonidine (Catapres), which is used to control high blood pressure, can cause a rebound hypertensive reaction if it is stopped abruptly. This reaction is worse in patients who are also taking atenolol. If you are taking both of these drugs and must stop taking clonidine, your doctor may slowly discontinue your atenolol first. In any case, don't stop taking this drug combination without careful supervision.

ALCOHOLIC BEVERAGES Usually there is no interaction between atenolol and alcohol. However, you should establish for yourself that atenolol does not make you drowsy or dizzy before you drink anything with alcohol in it.

FOOD It's a good idea to take atenolol with meals to help develop a regular routine. Food does not affect its absorption. If your doctor has prescribed a restricted-salt or restricted-calorie diet, be sure to follow it.

HOW DOES AGE AFFECT THE RESPONSE TO THIS DRUG? Aging slows the rate at which atenolol is removed from the body by the kidneys, thereby allowing it to accumulate to higher concentrations in the blood. However, advancing age also brings changes in the beta-receptors that make them less sensitive to drug effects. These two effects tend to offset each other. Therefore, older people usually respond similarly to the doses required by younger people. There is, however, wide variation in the doses required by different individuals, regardless of age.

The risk for side effects, particularly those related to the heart (see Side Effects), increases with advancing age. Be sure to return to your doctor for regular checkups. Most older people, including those who have achieved considerable age, are able to take atenolol without problems.

BENDROFLUMETHIAZIDE

OTHER NAMES Bendroflumethiazide (pronounced *ben-dro-flu-meh-THIGH-a-zide)* is the common or generic name of this drug. In Great Britain, its generic name is bendrofluazide. A frequently used brand name for bendroflumethiazide is Naturetin. Bendroflumethiazide is sometimes prescribed in tablets that contain other drugs. Corzide is the brand name of tablets that contain bendroflumethiazide and the antihypertensive drug nadolol. Naturetin with K tablets contain potassium in addition to bendroflumethiazide. Rauzide is the brand name of tablets that contain bendroflumethiazide and the antihypertensive drug reserpine. Rautrax-N is the brand name of tablets that contain bendroflu-

methiazide, reserpine, and potassium. Bendroflumethiazide belongs to a group of closely related drugs
called thiazide diuretics.

WHAT IS IT SUPPOSED TO DO?   Bendroflumethiazide is a diuretic, meaning that it increases the amount
of urine that is excreted from the body. Bendroflumethiazide acts on the kidneys, causing them to eliminate
extra water and salt from the body and into the urine.
It is used to treat congestive heart failure, high blood
pressure, and other medical problems.

Use in Congestive Heart Failure. Extra salt and water
may accumulate in the body for a variety of reasons,
but congestive heart failure is a common cause in older
persons. In congestive heart failure, which is the result
of some types of heart disease, the heart's pumping
action weakens and the circulation slows. When the
kidneys do not get enough circulation, they become
less efficient in removing extra salt and water from the
body. As a result, veins become swollen, and fluid leaks
out of them and into surrounding tissue. Usually, the
first symptom of this problem is swelling of the ankles
and lower legs. (The medical term for this swelling,
which can also be caused by less potentially serious
circulatory problems, is edema.) Later, fluid accumulates in the lungs, causing shortness of breath. Bendroflumethiazide's ability to promote salt and water
removal by the kidneys is the basis for its use in congestive heart failure.

Use in Hypertension. The diuretic effects of bendroflumethiazide are important here because too much salt
in the body may be part of the cause of hypertension
(high blood pressure). In addition, and perhaps more
important in hypertension, bendroflumethiazide causes
small blood vessels to dilate. This dilation of blood vessels eases the resistance to blood flow, and blood pressure is thereby lowered. Whether your hypertension is
mild or severe, bendroflumethiazide may be the first
drug your doctor prescribes to control it.

SIDE EFFECTS Serious side effects from bendroflumethiazide are rare. The most annoying side effect you will notice when you begin taking this drug is a need to urinate frequently. You should avoid taking bendroflumethiazide too late in the day. Otherwise, you may find yourself being frequently awakened from sleep by a need to urinate.

Bendroflumethiazide causes potassium to be removed from the body along with salt and water. In most cases, this causes no problem. Dietary sources of potassium usually prevent potassium deficiency from occurring. However, your doctor may prescribe either a potassium supplement or a second diuretic that conserves potassium to prevent this effect, especially if you are also taking digoxin (see Drug Interactions). In any case, your doctor will periodically order a laboratory test that measures the concentration of potassium in your blood. The symptoms of too low a concentration of potassium in the blood include profound muscle weakness, muscle cramps or pain, and irregular heartbeat. If you experience any of these symptoms, contact your doctor.

Bendroflumethiazide sometimes causes an increase in the amount of glucose in the blood, which could unmask latent diabetes or require an increase in your insulin or other drug requirement if you already have diabetes. Prevention of excess potassium loss decreases the risk for this problem. Bendroflumethiazide can also increase the amount of uric acid in your blood, but it rarely causes gout, the clinical manifestation of this condition. Your doctor will order periodic laboratory tests to monitor for these and other, rarer possible problems before they cause symptoms.

All diuretics have the potential for causing dehydration when fluid loss is accelerated by hot weather or flulike illness. Whenever you experience fever, vomiting, or diarrhea, whatever the cause, be sure to increase your fluid intake to prevent dehydration. If the symptoms are severe, you should contact your doctor.

Other side effects are too rare to list here. If you should develop a rash or any other unusual symptom while taking this drug, contact your doctor.

DRUG INTERACTIONS Several drugs interact with bendroflumethiazide, and your doctor will take special precautions to ensure that no problems occur if you must take any of these drugs with bendroflumethiazide:

Antidiabetic drugs, such as *insulin* or the *sulfonylureas.* Bendroflumethiazide can increase the concentration of glucose in the blood. If this occurs, despite the protective effect of correcting for potassium loss, your doctor may increase the dosage of your diabetic medication. If you are taking chlorpropamide (Diabinese) or tolbutamide (Orinase), your doctor will monitor for a second, less frequent, possible interaction. These drugs sometimes decrease the concentration of sodium in the blood. (Other sulfonylureas do not share this property.) In some older individuals, this combination of drugs can lead to too low a concentration of sodium in the blood (hyponatremia)—if you experience weakness, confusion, or muscle cramps, contact your doctor.

Bile-acid sequestrants, such as *cholestyramine resin (Questran) and colestipol (Colestid),* are used to lower the concentration of cholesterol in the blood. They are also used to treat the itching that sometimes occurs with jaundice. These drugs may bind to bendroflumethiazide in the gastrointestinal tract and thereby prevent its full absorption. If therapy with one of these drugs is necessary, the bendroflumethiazide dose should be taken two hours before the cholestyramine or colestipol dose to minimize any interaction.

Corticosteroids, such as *dexamethasone, hydrocortisone, or prednisone,* cause potassium to be lost from the body, and this side effect is additive with that of bendroflumethiazide. To prevent problems, your doctor will periodically order a laboratory test that measures the concentration of potassium in your blood and, if necessary, will prescribe either a potassium supplement or a second diuretic that conserves potassium.

Digoxin (Lanoxin). Although bendroflumethiazide is often prescribed together with digoxin, an interaction can occur because of bendroflumethiazide's promotion of potassium loss from the body. If the amount of potassium in the blood becomes too low, then digoxin toxicity may develop. To prevent this problem, your doctor will periodically order a laboratory test that measures the concentration of potassium in the blood and, if necessary, will prescribe either a potassium supplement or a second diuretic that conserves potassium.

Lithium (Eskalith, Lithane, and others), a drug that is prescribed by psychiatrists for mood problems, is removed from the body by the kidneys. Bendroflumethiazide significantly slows this removal, and the concentration of lithium in the blood increases, sometimes to toxic levels. When these drugs must be used together, your doctor will probably decrease your lithium dose, using a laboratory test for monitoring the concentration of lithium in your blood as a guide.

Nonsteroidal anti-inflammatory drugs (NSAIDs), such as *diflunisal, ibuprofen, indomethacin, fenoprofen, meclofenamate, naproxen, piroxicam, sulindac, tolmetin, or large amounts of aspirin.* These drugs can cause fluid retention and edema in older people who are sensitive to this effect. If you are taking bendroflumethiazide for fluid retention and edema (such as that caused by congestive heart failure or liver disease) and you experience a worsening of your symptoms while taking one of these NSAIDs, stop taking the NSAID and contact your doctor.

ALCOHOLIC BEVERAGES Alcoholic beverages have a more pronounced effect on some people than on others; if you become dizzy when drinking, bendroflumethiazide might make things worse. You can carefully evaluate this effect for yourself. Most people do not notice any effect at all.

FOOD Many pharmacists recommend taking bendroflumethiazide with meals. Food does not impair its absorption, and some people (probably fewer than one in a hundred) experience an upset stomach when they take bendroflumethiazide on an empty stomach. Taking it with a meal will also help you set up a routine and thereby prevent you from missing too many doses. Take your morning dose with breakfast and, if you take a second daily dose, take it with a late-afternoon snack or dinner.

Be sure to follow any dietary advice, such as restricting salt intake or increasing potassium-containing foods (such as bananas, orange juice, raisins), you may have been given with your prescription.

HOW DOES AGE AFFECT THE RESPONSE TO THIS DRUG?   Older people are more sensitive to the effects of diuretics. The effects of too much diuretic, which are rare in younger people, are more likely to occur with advancing age. The most common problem is dizziness or faintness from abnormally low blood pressure. If you experience such a symptom, contact your doctor. Another problem, which is infrequent, is too low a concentration of sodium in the blood. If you experience weakness, confusion, or muscle cramps, contact your doctor.

Your doctor will take your age into consideration in selecting a dosage that is likely to be appropriate for you.

BUMETANIDE

OTHER NAMES   Bumetanide (pronounced *byoo-MET-a-nide)* is the common or generic name of this drug. A frequently used brand name for bumetanide is Bumex. Bumetanide belongs to a group of drugs called high-ceiling diuretics (*high-ceiling* denoting great potency) or loop diuretics (*loop* referring to the loop of Henle, the anatomical part of the kidney where these drugs work).

WHAT IS IT SUPPOSED TO DO?   Bumetanide is a diuretic, meaning that it increases the amount of urine which is excreted from the body. It acts on the kidneys, causing them to eliminate extra water and salt from the body and into the urine. Bumetanide is one of the most potent diuretics available. It is used to remove the excess salt and water that has accumulated as a result of congestive heart failure, kidney failure, or liver disease. It is also used to treat high blood pressure that is accompanied by heart or kidney failure.

Use in Congestive Heart Failure. Extra salt and water may accumulate in the body for a variety of reasons, but congestive heart failure is a common cause in older persons. In congestive heart failure, which is the result of some types of heart disease, the heart's pumping action weakens and the circulation slows. When the kidneys don't get enough circulation, they become less efficient in removing extra salt and water from the body. As a result, veins become swollen, and fluid leaks out of them and into surrounding tissues. This leads to swelling, first of the ankles and lower legs, later of the arms. There is general weight gain from excess fluid accumulation. Fluid also accumulates in the lungs, causing shortness of breath. Bumetanide promotes rapid and substantial salt and water removal by the kidneys, and it increases blood flow to the kidneys. Therefore, it is effective in relieving the symptoms of congestive heart failure.

SIDE EFFECTS You will find yourself needing to urinate frequently, especially at first. You should anticipate this need so that it won't become an inconvenience to you. The effects of a dose of bumetanide usually become apparent within thirty minutes to an hour, and you will probably notice increased urination for several hours. As with other diuretics, you should try to avoid taking bumetanide too close to bedtime so that you won't be frequently awakened by a need to urinate.

Because it is such a potent diuretic, the side effects of profound diuresis are more prominent with bumetanide than with other diuretics. You may experience dizziness or faintness, particularly when standing up too fast. If dizziness or faintness is persistent or severe, contact your doctor.

Bumetanide causes potassium to be removed from the body along with salt and water. Dietary sources of potassium often prevent potassium deficiency from occurring. However, your doctor may prescribe either a potassium supplement or a second diuretic that conserves potassium to prevent this effect, especially if you are also taking digoxin (see Drug Interactions). In any case, your doctor will periodically order a laboratory test that measures the concentration of potassium in the blood. The symptoms of too low a concentration of potassium in the blood include profound muscle weakness, muscle cramps or pain, and irregular heartbeats. If you experience any of these symptoms, contact your doctor.

Bumetanide sometimes causes an increase in the amount of glucose in the blood, which could unmask latent diabetes or require an increase in your insulin or other drug requirement if you already have diabetes. Prevention of excess potassium loss decreases the risk of this problem. Bumetanide can also increase the concentration of uric acid in your blood, but it rarely causes gout, the clinical manifestation of this condition. Your doctor will order periodic laboratory tests to monitor for these and other, rarer possible problems before they cause symptoms.

All diuretics have the potential for causing dehydration when fluid loss is accelerated by hot weather or flulike illness. Whenever you experience fever, vomiting, or diarrhea, whatever the case, be sure to increase your fluid intake to prevent dehydration. If the symptoms are severe, you should contact your doctor.

Other side effects are too rare to list here. If you experience any unusual symptoms, contact your doctor.

DRUG INTERACTIONS Several drugs can interact with bumetanide. Your doctor will take special precautions to ensure that no problems occur if you are taking any of these drugs with bumetanide:

Antidiabetic drugs, such as *insulin* or the *sulfonylureas.* Bumetanide can increase the concentration of glucose in the blood. If this occurs, despite the protective effect of correcting for potassium loss, your doctor may increase the dosage of your diabetic medication to compensate for this interaction. If you are taking chlorpropamide (Diabinese) or tolbutamide (Orinase), your doctor will monitor for a second, less frequent, possible interaction. These drugs sometimes decrease the concentration of sodium in the blood. (Other sulfonylureas do not share this property.) In some older individuals, this combination of drugs can lead to too low a concentration of sodium in the blood (hyponatremia)—if you experience weakness, confusion, or muscle cramps, contact your doctor.

Corticosteroids, such as *dexamethasone, hydrocortisone, and prednisone,* cause potassium to be lost from the body, and this side effect is additive with that of bumetanide. To prevent problems, your doctor will monitor the concentration of potassium in your blood and may prescribe a potassium supplement or a potassium-conserving diuretic in addition to bumetanide.

Digoxin (Lanoxin) and bumetanide are often prescribed together because they work by different and complementary mechanisms to relieve the symptoms of congestive heart failure. However, an interaction can occur because of bumetanide's promotion of potassium loss from the body. If the amount of potassium in the blood becomes too low, digoxin toxicity may develop. To prevent this problem, your doctor will monitor the concentration of potassium in your blood and may prescribe a potassium supplement or a potassium-conserving diuretic in addition to bumetanide.

Indomethacin (Indocin) and perhaps other *nonsteroidal anti-inflammatory drugs,* which are used for the treatment of arthritis, may decrease the effects of bumetanide. If such an interaction occurs, your doctor may have to increase the dose of bumetanide or prescribe another anti-inflammatory drug.

ALCOHOLIC BEVERAGES Bumetanide will make you more sensitive to the blood-pressure-lowering effects of alcohol. Limit your consumption of alcoholic beverages, and watch for excessive dizziness.

FOOD If bumetanide upsets your stomach, a rare problem, take it with food.

Be sure to follow any dietary advice, such as decreased salt intake or increased potassium-containing foods (such as bananas, orange juice, raisins), you may have been given with your prescription.

HOW DOES AGE AFFECT THE RESPONSE TO THIS DRUG? Advancing age is accompanied by greater sensitivity to dehydration, excessive potassium loss, and excessive sodium loss from potent diuretics like bumetanide. Therefore, the older you are, the more carefully your doctor will monitor your response to this drug.

BUSPIRONE

OTHER NAMES Buspirone (pronounced *byue-SPEAR-ohn)* is the common or generic name of this drug. A frequently used brand name for buspirone is BuSpar. Buspirone is the first representative of a new group of drugs, the azaspirodecanediones. It is often called a nonbenzodiazepine, to underscore the fact that it is completely different from the benzodiazepines, widely used drugs with which it is often compared.

WHAT IS IT SUPPOSED TO DO? Buspirone relieves the symptoms of anxiety caused by stress or trauma. It acts on several naturally occurring substances within the brain in a way that decreases anxiety without affecting alertness. It is as effective in relieving anxiety as diazepam (Valium) and other benzodiazepines.

SIDE EFFECTS The most common side effects are stomach upset, headache, and dizziness. Less common are light-headedness, nausea, and nervousness. If any of these are unacceptably bothersome, contact your doctor.

Unlike the widely used benzodiazepine drugs, buspirone does *not* cause drowsiness, fatigue, or impaired coordination.

Other side effects are too rare to list here. If you

experience any unexpected symptoms, contact your doctor.

DRUG INTERACTIONS Preliminary studies with several drugs have found no drug interactions with buspirone. However, this is a new drug, and interactions may become apparent with more widespread use. If you notice a change in any drug side effect, or the appearance of a new symptom while taking buspirone, contact your doctor.

ALCOHOLIC BEVERAGES When taken in usual dosages, buspirone does not add to the impairment caused by alcohol.

FOOD Buspirone should be taken with meals or with a snack. Food increases its effectiveness by slowing its metabolism.

HOW DOES AGE AFFECT THE RESPONSE TO THIS DRUG? In a preliminary study that compared the concentration of buspirone and its metabolites in the blood in a dozen younger (aged twenty-one to thirty-nine) and a dozen older (over sixty-five years of age) volunteers given the same amount of the drug, there were no significant differences between the two groups. Older and younger individuals seem to require the same doses of buspirone.

In a larger study that compared the effects of buspirone on more than six hundred patients over the age of sixty with more than two thousand younger patients, the response in younger and older patients was similar. However, stomach complaints and dizziness were more frequent among the older patients.

CALCIUM CARBONATE

OTHER NAMES Calcium carbonate (pronounced *KAL-see-um KAR-boe-nate*) is the common or generic name of this drug, which occurs in nature as chalk, limestone, sea shells, and other forms. Frequently used brand names for calcium carbonate are Amitone, Biocal, Calcilac, Cal-Sup, Caltrate, Chooz, Dicarbosil, Os-Cal 500, Titralac, and Tums.

WHAT IS IT SUPPOSED TO DO?   Calcium carbonate is prescribed as an antacid, as a source of calcium for those with hypocalcemia (too low a concentration of calcium in the blood), and as a supplement to dietary calcium for the prevention of osteoporosis.

Use as an Antacid. Calcium carbonate neutralizes excess stomach acid and is therefore effective in relieving the symptoms of heartburn or acid stomach. It is also used in the treatment of gastric and duodenal ulcers.

Use in Preventing Osteoporosis. Calcium, which is an essential element in the body's skeletal structure, is supplied from dietary sources (especially milk products) and can be supplemented by a variety of calcium salts. Osteoporosis, which is loss of enough bone mass with aging to increase the risk of fractures markedly, is a common health problem, and it might be prevented by increasing the daily intake of calcium. Although many people take calcium supplements, there is some controversy over their benefit in preventing osteoporosis (see How Does Age ...). Of the various calcium salts, calcium carbonate contains the most calcium per unit of weight. Calcium carbonate is 40 percent calcium; a 500 mg tablet (Tums, for example) contains 200 mg of calcium.

The current Recommended Daily Allowance for calcium is 800 mg per day. However, many investigators feel that 1,000 to 1,500 mg per day is more appropriate for older people, because calcium absorption becomes less efficient with aging. In addition, the average daily intake of calcium is often low in older people (500 mg per day in one large study), so some doctors recommend supplemental calcium in the form of calcium carbonate.

If you are taking an estrogen, which is the most effective means of preventing osteoporosis in middle-aged women, the addition of calcium will provide more protection than either drug alone.

There is some evidence than calcium supplementation will help prevent the osteoporosis caused by the long-term use of corticosteroids, such as prednisone or dexamethasone.

SIDE EFFECTS   Belching and chalky taste are the most common side effects from calcium carbonate. Occasionally, it causes mild constipation. If any of these side effects become bothersome, check with your doctor.

Increased calcium intake can cause kidney stones in susceptible individuals. However, if you have never had kidney stones and don't have kidney disease or any of several conditions (such as hyperparathyroidism) that would turn up with routine medical exams, this problem is not likely to occur. Contact your doctor if difficult or painful urination should occur.

There is a rare disorder, called the milk-alkali syndrome, that has occurred in people taking extremely large doses of calcium carbonate as an antacid (for example, 2,000 mg every hour). The name of this disorder is derived from a now obsolete form of ulcer therapy that utilized high doses of easily absorbed alkali, such as sodium bicarbonate (baking soda), together with calcium carbonate and milk. The symptoms include nausea, vomiting, diarrhea, headache, and lethargy. It is unlikely to occur from the smaller doses of calcium carbonate that are used for calcium supplementation or as an antacid, and it is less likely to occur with advancing age because of decreased calcium absorption. But it is a serious condition that requires prompt medical attention. Certain diseases and vitamin D intoxication can lead to this problem. If you are taking calcium carbonate regularly, don't take vitamin D capsules without your doctor's supervision; the amounts of vitamin D in milk and in most multiple vitamins are not likely to cause problems.

Other side effects are too rare to list here. Contact

your doctor if you experience any unexpected symptoms.

DRUG INTERACTIONS Calcium carbonate can interact with several drugs:

The effects of *calcium channel blockers,* such as *diltiazem (Cardizem), nifedipine (Procardia), or verapamil (Calan, Isoptin),* which are used for various heart problems and in the treatment of high blood pressure, can be antagonized if the concentration of calcium in the blood is significantly increased. This interaction is not likely to occur with ordinary use of calcium carbonate, but it has been reported in one patient who was taking a calcium supplement with vitamin D, and intravenous calcium (which causes high concentrations of calcium in the blood) has been used to treat overdoses of calcium channel blockers. If you are responding poorly to your calcium channel blocker, calcium carbonate might be suspected as a possible cause, but your doctor will consider other possible causes as well.

Iron supplements should not be taken at the same time of day as calcium carbonate, which may decrease the absorption of iron. Space the doses at least two hours apart.

Tetracycline antibiotics should not be taken at the same time of day as calcium carbonate, because calcium decreases their absorption. Space the doses at least two hours apart.

ALCOHOLIC BEVERAGES There is no interaction between alcohol and calcium carbonate. However, excessive alcohol use will increase your risk of osteoporosis.

FOOD If you are taking calcium carbonate as a supplement to your dietary calcium, you should take it with meals; this increases its absorption. Milk products are the best source of calcium (300 mg per cup of milk) and an excellent source of protein; they are often supplemented with vitamin D to aid calcium absorption and need not contain an excess of fat (nonfat milk often contains more calcium than regular milk).

HOW DOES AGE AFFECT THE RESPONSE TO THIS DRUG?   Age should not affect your response to the antacid effects of calcium carbonate. However, the production of stomach acid decreases with advancing age, so your need for antacids may decline as you get older.

Although calcium absorption becomes less efficient with aging, more calcium is absorbed if the daily calcium intake is increased. In 1984, the National Institutes of Health held a consensus conference on osteoporosis, and the researchers at this meeting unanimously agreed that the current Recommended Daily Allowance of calcium should be increased from 800 mg per day to 1,000 mg per day in men and 1,500 mg per day in postmenopausal women. This consensus, which was based on the research then available, led to a calcium boom, and now millions of Americans consume calcium supplements.

Meanwhile, however, some researchers were expressing doubts about the efficacy of calcium in preventing osteoporosis, particularly in postmenopausal women. Some studies showed calcium to be beneficial, while others showed it to have little or no effect. During 1986, studies demonstrated that menopause brings about an impairment in calcium absorption that is more severe than was previously appreciated. For some postmenopausal women who don't take estrogens, even 1,500 mg per day will not be enough calcium to prevent bone loss. Larger doses cannot be recommended for the prevention of osteoporosis, because safety and efficacy have not been established. Studies finding no correlation between calcium intake and osteoporosis after menopause continue to be reported.

The effect of aging, particularly the effect of menopause, on the response to calcium for the prevention of osteoporosis remains controversial. It now appears that older people should try to get at least 1,000 mg of calcium per day in their diet (with or without supplementation), and women in their fifties should discuss the potential benefits and risks of estrogen therapy with their doctors.

:e:e:e:e:e:e:e

CAPTOPRIL

OTHER NAMES Captopril (pronounced *CAP-toe-pril*) is the common or generic name of this drug. The most frequently used brand name for captopril is Capoten. Captopril is sometimes prescribed as tablets that also contain the diuretic hydrochlorothiazide. A frequently used brand name for this drug combination is Capozide. Captopril belongs to a new class of drugs called angiotensin-converting-enzyme (ACE) inhibitors.

WHAT IS IT SUPPOSED TO DO? Captopril lowers high blood pressure and relieves the symptoms of congestive heart failure by preventing the body from making a hormone called angiotensin II, which is instrumental in both of these diseases. Angiotensin II is the most potent elevator of blood pressure currently known. Angiotensin II also stimulates the adrenal glands to produce another hormone, aldosterone, which acts on the kidneys to retain salt and water and excrete potassium. Captopril inhibits an enzyme (angiotensin-converting enzyme) required for the formation of angiotensin II and thereby prevents its undesirable effects.

Use in Hypertension. Captopril is very effective in lowering high blood pressure. People who respond poorly to other antihypertensive drugs usually respond well to captopril. In addition, it causes fewer unpleasant side effects than most other antihypertensives. It is sometimes prescribed with a thiazide diuretic, which increases its effects.

Use in Congestive Heart Failure. Captopril reverses several of the complex events that contribute to congestive heart failure. By lowering blood pressure, it decreases the heart's workload. Improved blood flow to the kidneys and decreased secretion of aldosterone (see above) cause excess fluid to be removed from the body. Captopril is often prescribed in addition to diuretics and digoxin, which work by other mechanisms to relieve congestive heart failure.

SIDE EFFECTS   Side effects from captopril are infrequent.

The most common side effect is a rash that appears during the first month of therapy. Contact your doctor if this happens. Your doctor may tell you to continue the captopril, perhaps at a smaller dosage, and wait for the rash to disappear, or he may prescribe an alternate drug. Any rash should be promptly reported.

Other side effects, which occur infrequently or rarely, include dizziness, light-headedness, or fainting; swelling of the face, mouth, hands, or feet; and chest pain. If these or any other symptoms occur, you should contact your doctor promptly.

Diarrhea or vomiting can cause substantial loss of sodium and water from the body, and this can make you more than usually sensitive to captopril's effects on blood pressure. Therefore, you should check with your doctor whenever you are sick with continuing vomiting or diarrhea.

If you are taking captopril for congestive heart failure, you will probably notice that your capacity for exercise or exertion is improved. It is important to avoid overdoing it. Ask your doctor how much activity is safe for you.

Rarely, captopril causes changes in the sense of taste. When this happens, flavor sensation is usually lost, but some people report a bitter or metallic taste. This side effect may go away with continued use, but if it is bothersome, contact your doctor.

A rare but very serious side effect is suppression of the formation of white blood cells, which are essential in fighting off infection. Your doctor will check your blood periodically, but you should contact your doctor promptly whenever you experience fever, chills, or sore throat. The risk for this side effect is greater in people with collagen disease such as lupus and in people with kidney problems.

Other side effects are too rare to list here. Contact your doctor if you experience any unexpected symptoms.

DRUG INTERACTIONS   Several drugs can interact adversely with captopril:

Diuretics, such as *hydrochlorothiazide (HydroDIURIL) or furosemide (Lasix)*, can interact adversely with the initial dose of captopril. People who have been taking diuretics sometimes have low concentrations of sodium in their blood. In this situation, captopril can cause an unusually profound drop in blood pressure after the first dose. The risk of this side effect, which can cause you to faint, is greatest in those with congestive heart failure and in those who have been taking large doses of a diuretic and restricting the amount of salt in their diets. If you have been taking a diuretic and are about to start taking captopril, your doctor may measure the concentration of sodium in your blood (to be sure it is not too low) and then begin your captopril therapy with small doses. Your doctor may tell you to temporarily stop taking your diuretic or temporarily increase your salt intake before starting to take captopril. The diuretic is usually resumed once your body becomes accustomed to the effects of captopril. Diuretics are often used in combination with captopril, because the two drugs work by mechanisms that are complementary. Diuretics enhance the effects of captopril, and captopril prevents diuretic-induced potassium loss.

Indomethacin (Indocin), which is used for arthritic pain and related problems, can block the antihypertensive effect of captopril. Your doctor will check for this interaction and may need to prescribe another antiinflammatory drug. Other nonsteroidal anti-inflammatory drugs have not been studied for their effect on captopril response, but it is likely that they interact in a similar way, although to a lesser degree.

Potassium supplements and *potassium-conserving diuretics*, such as *triamterene (Dyazide, Dyrenium, Maxzide), amiloride (Midamor, Moduretic), or spironolactone (Aldactazide, Aldactone)*, can cause too high a concentration of potassium in the blood (hyperkalemia) if taken with captopril. As explained above, captopril prevents aldosterone secretion, thereby causing potassium to be retained by the body. These drugs should be taken with captopril only when the concentration of potassium in the blood has been demonstrated to be too low. If you are taking this combination, be sure your doctor is monitoring the concentration of potassium in your blood.

ALCOHOLIC BEVERAGES   Captopril should not affect your response to alcohol.

FOOD   Captopril is best absorbed when taken on an empty stomach, an hour before a meal. However, there is preliminary evidence that food does not significantly impair the response to captopril.

If your doctor has prescribed a low-salt diet, be sure to follow it. Do not use salt substitutes without first checking with your doctor; salt substitutes contain potassium chloride, which may interact with captopril if used in sufficient amounts (see Drug Interactions, Potassium Supplements).

HOW DOES AGE AFFECT THE RESPONSE TO THIS DRUG?   Older people tend to be more sensitive to the effects of captopril. Significantly reduced kidney function, which is more likely to occur in older people, increases the risk of adverse reactions from captopril, unless the dosage is reduced accordingly. Your doctor will assess your kidney function (see appendix) in determining a dosage of captopril that is likely to be appropriate for you.

CHLORDIAZEPOXIDE

OTHER NAMES   Chlordiazepoxide (pronounced *klor-dye-az-e-POX-ide*) is the common or generic name of this drug. Frequently used brand names for chlordiazepoxide are Libritabs and Librium. Chlordiazepoxide is sometimes prescribed as tablets or capsules that contain a second drug. Examples of such brand-name combinations are Menrium (chlordiazepoxide with estrogens), Limbitrol (chlordiazepoxide with the antidepressant amitriptyline), and Librax (chlordiazepoxide with the atropinelike drug clidinium). Chlordiazepoxide belongs to a large group of similar drugs called benzodiazepines.

WHAT IS IT SUPPOSED TO DO? Chlordiazepoxide relieves the symptoms of anxiety and tension.

SIDE EFFECTS Drowsiness is the principal side effect from chlordiazepoxide. You may find yourself unsteady on your feet as well. Evaluate these effects for yourself and regulate your activities accordingly. You should be especially cautious about driving an automobile. If drowsiness or unsteadiness persists, stop taking the drug and contact your doctor.

Infrequently, chlordiazepoxide causes dizziness, weakness, confusion, impaired memory, or loss of coordination. If you experience any of these effects, which suggest you are extremely sensitive to chlordiazepoxide, stop taking it and contact your doctor.

If you have been taking chlordiazepoxide regularly for a long time and in large doses, you may experience mild withdrawal symptoms several days after stopping this drug. Typical symptoms include difficulty in sleeping, unusual irritability, and unusual nervousness. If these occur, contact your doctor.

Other side effects are too rare to list here. Contact your doctor if you experience any unusual symptoms.

DRUG INTERACTIONS Sedation is a common side effect of antidepressant drugs, antihistamines, tranquilizers, narcotic analgesics, and other drugs. Be careful of the additive effects of chlordiazepoxide taken in combination with any of these drugs.

In addition, several drugs can interact with chlordiazepoxide by other mechanisms. These are the interactions most likely to cause problems:

Cimetidine (Tagamet), which is used for the treatment of ulcers, slows the metabolism of chlordiazepoxide and thereby enhances its effects. It may be necessary to decrease the dosage of your chlordiazepoxide while taking both drugs; ask your doctor.

Disulfiram (Antabuse), which is used in the treatment of alcoholism, slows the metabolism of chlordiazepoxide and thereby enhances its effects. It may be necessary to decrease the dosage of your chlordiazepoxide while taking both drugs; ask your doctor.

Levodopa (Dopar, Larodopa, L-dopa) is used in the treatment of Parkinson's disease, and chlordiazepoxide may block its effects. If you are taking both drugs and notice a worsening of your parkinsonism, stop taking your chlordiazepoxide and contact your doctor.

ALCOHOLIC BEVERAGES   Chlordiazepoxide adds to alcohol's depressive effects on the nervous system. If you are taking chlordiazepoxide regularly, the combined effects of alcohol and chlordiazepoxide might occur even if you haven't taken chlordiazepoxide for twenty-four hours, or even several days. Chlordiazepoxide and its active metabolites remain in the body for many days. Therefore, you should limit your alcohol consumption while taking chlordiazepoxide. Needless to say, the effects of this combination on driving can be dangerous.

FOOD   Chlordiazepoxide can be taken either with meals or on an empty stomach.

HOW DOES AGE AFFECT THE RESPONSE TO THIS DRUG?   The older you are, the more sensitive you will be to chlordiazepoxide. There are several mechanisms involved:

First, older people are inherently more sensitive to the effects of chlordiazepoxide and its active metabolites. This may have something to do with the effects of aging on the brain.

Second, aging changes the distribution of chlordiazepoxide and its active metabolites within the body. As a result, it takes much longer for the maximum effect of repeated doses to become apparent. An older person who takes the same amount of chlordiazepoxide every day will experience slightly more effect each day for several weeks, and *then* repeated doses will maintain the same level of effect. If the dosage is too high for you, you may not notice it as soon as you might expect.

Third, the metabolism of chlordiazepoxide slows with aging. Therefore, some older people develop higher concentrations of the drug in their blood than would be expected and they are more likely to develop side effects.

In any case, side effects increase with age. Confusion, weakness, fainting, dizziness, impaired memory, and loss of coordination, which are infrequent side effects from chlordiazepoxide, occur far more often in older people than they do in younger people. All of these side effects are reversible, but because their onset can be so slow, they are sometimes not associated with the offending drug. Furthermore, just as these side effects are often slow to appear, they are equally slow in disappearing after chlordiazepoxide is stopped. If you are aware of this possibility, it probably won't become a problem for you.

Your doctor will take your age into consideration in selecting a dose and dosage schedule that are likely to be appropriate for you.

CHLOROTHIAZIDE

OTHER NAMES   Chlorothiazide (pronounced *klor-oh-THYE-a-zide)* is the common or generic name of this drug. Frequently used brand names for chlorothiazide are Diuril and SK-Chlorothiazide. Chlorothiazide is sometimes prescribed as tablets that contain a second drug. Aldoclor is the brand name of tablets that contain chlorothiazide and methyldopa. Diupres is the brand name of tablets that contain chlorothiazide and reserpine. Chlorothiazide is the oldest member of a group of closely related drugs called the thiazides.

WHAT IS IT SUPPOSED TO DO?   Chlorothiazide is a diuretic, meaning that it increases the amount of urine that is excreted from the body. Chlorothiazide acts on the kidneys, causing them to eliminate extra water and salt from the body and into the urine. It is used to treat congestive heart failure, high blood pressure, and other medical problems.

Use in Congestive Heart Failure. Extra salt and water may accumulate in the body for a variety of reasons, but congestive heart failure is a common cause in older persons. In congestive heart failure, which is a result of some types of heart disease, the heart's pumping action weakens and the circulation slows. When the kidneys do not get enough circulation, they become less efficient in removing extra salt and water from the body. As a result, veins become swollen, and fluid leaks out of them and into surrounding tissues. Usually, the first symptom of this problem is swelling of the ankles and lower legs. (The medical term for this swelling, which can also be caused by less potentially serious circulatory problems, is edema.) Later, fluid accumulates in the lungs, causing shortness of breath. Chlorothiazide's ability to promote salt and water removal by the kidneys is the basis for its use in congestive heart failure.

Use in Hypertension. The diuretic effects of chlorothiazide are important here because too much salt in the body may be part of the cause of hypertension (high blood pressure). In addition, and perhaps more important in hypertension, chlorothiazide causes small blood vessels to dilate. This dilation of blood vessels eases the resistance to blood flow, and blood pressure is thereby lowered. Whether your hypertension is mild or severe, chlorothiazide may be the first drug that your doctor prescribes to control it.

SIDE EFFECTS Serious side effects from chlorothiazide are rare. The most annoying side effect you will notice when you begin taking this drug is a need to urinate frequently. You should avoid taking chlorothiazide too close to bedtime. Otherwise, you may find yourself being frequently awakened from sleep by the need to urinate.

Chlorothiazide causes potassium to be removed from the body along with salt and water. In most cases, this causes no problem. Dietary sources of potassium usually prevent potassium deficiency from occurring. However, your doctor may prescribe either a potassium supplement or a second diuretic that conserves potassium to prevent this effect, especially if you are also taking digoxin (see Drug Interactions). In any case, your doctor will periodically order a laboratory test that measures the concentration of potassium in the blood. The symptoms of too low a concentration of potassium in the blood include profound muscle weakness, muscle cramps or pain, and irregular heartbeat. If you experience any of these symptoms, contact your doctor.

Chlorothiazide sometimes causes an increase in the amount of glucose in the blood, which could unmask latent diabetes or require an increase in your insulin or other drug requirement if you already have diabetes. Prevention of excess potassium loss reduces the risk for this problem. Chlorothiazide can also increase the amount of uric acid in your blood, but it rarely causes gout, the clinical manifestation of this condition. Your doctor will order periodic laboratory tests to monitor for these and other, rarer possible problems before they cause symptoms.

Other side effects are too rare to list here. If you should develop a rash or any other unusual symptom while taking this drug, contact your doctor.

DRUG INTERACTIONS   Several drugs interact with chlorothiazide, and your doctor will take special precautions to ensure that no problems occur if you are taking any of these drugs with chlorothiazide:

Antidiabetic drugs, such as *insulin* or the *sulfonylureas.* Chlorothiazide can increase the concentration of glucose in the blood. If this occurs, despite the protective effect of correcting for potassium loss, your doctor may increase the dosage of your diabetic medication to compensate for this interaction. If you are taking chlorpropamide (Diabinese) or tolbutamide (Orinase), your doctor will monitor for a second, less frequent, possible interaction. These drugs sometimes decrease the concentration of sodium in the blood. (Other sulfonylureas do not share this property.) In some older individuals, this combination of drugs can lead to too low a concentration of sodium in the blood (hyponatremia). If you experience weakness, confusion, or muscle cramps, contact your doctor.

Bile-acid sequestrants, such as *cholestyramine resin (Questran) and colestipol (Colestid),* are used to lower the concentration of cholesterol in the blood. They are also used to treat the itching that sometimes occurs with jaundice. These drugs may bind to chlorothiazide in the gastrointestinal tract and thereby prevent its full absorption. If therapy with one of these drugs is necessary, the chlorothiazide dose should be taken two hours before the cholestyramine or colestipol dose to minimize any interaction.

Corticosteroids, such as *dexamethasone, hydrocortisone, or prednisone,* cause potassium loss, and this side effect is additive with that of chlorothiazide. To prevent problems, your doctor will periodically order a laboratory test that measures the concentration of potassium in the blood and, if necessary, will prescribe either a potassium supplement or a second diuretic that conserves potassium.

Digoxin (Lanoxin). Although chlorothiazide is often prescribed together with digoxin, an interaction can occur because of chlorothiazide's promotion of potassium loss from the body. If the amount of potassium in the blood becomes too low, then digoxin toxicity may develop. To prevent this problem, your doctor will periodically order a laboratory test that measures the concentration of potassium in the blood and, if necessary, will prescribe either a potassium supplement or a second diuretic that conserves potassium.

Lithium (Eskalith, Lithane, and others), a drug that is prescribed by psychiatrists for mood problems, is removed from the body by the kidneys. Chlorothiazide significantly slows this removal, and the concentration of lithium in the blood increases, sometimes to toxic levels. When these drugs must be used together, your doctor will probably decrease the dose of your lithium, using a laboratory test for monitoring the concentration of lithium in your blood as a guide.

Nonsteroidal anti-inflammatory drugs (NSAIDs), such as *diflunisal, ibuprofen, indomethacin, fenoprofen, meclofenamate, naproxen, piroxicam, sulindac, tolmetin, or large amounts of aspirin.* These drugs can cause fluid retention and edema in older people who are sensitive to this effect. If you are taking chlorothiazide for fluid retention and edema (such as that caused by congestive heart failure or liver disease) and you experience a worsening of your symptoms while taking one of these NSAIDs, stop taking the NSAID and contact your doctor.

ALCOHOLIC BEVERAGES Alcoholic beverages have a more profound effect on some people than on others; if you become dizzy when drinking, chlorothiazide might make things worse. You can carefully evaluate this effect for yourself. Most people do not notice any effect at all.

FOOD Many pharmacists recommend taking chlorothiazide with meals. Food may improve its absorption, and some people (probably fewer than one in a hundred) experience an upset stomach when they take chlorothiazide on an empty stomach. Taking it with a meal will also help you set up a routine and thereby prevent you from missing too many doses. Take your morning dose with breakfast and, if you take a second daily dose, take it with a late-afternoon snack or dinner.

Be sure to follow any dietary advice, such as limiting salt intake or increasing potassium-containing foods (such as bananas, orange juice, raisins), you may have been given with your prescription.

HOW DOES AGE AFFECT THE RESPONSE TO THIS DRUG? Older people are more sensitive to the effects of diuretics. The effects of too much diuretic, which are rare in younger people, are more likely to occur with advancing age. The most common problem is dizziness or faintness from abnormally low blood pressure. If you experience such a symptom, contact your doctor. Another problem, which is infrequent, is too low a concentration of sodium in the blood. If you experience weakness, confusion, or muscle cramps, contact your doctor.

Your doctor will take your age into consideration in selecting a dosage that is likely to be appropriate for you.

CHLORPROPAMIDE

OTHER NAMES   Chlorpropamide (pronounced *klor-PRO-pa-mide)* is the generic or common name of this drug. A frequently used brand name for chlorprop-amide is Diabinese. Chlorpropamide belongs to a group of chemically related drugs called sulfonylureas.

WHAT IS IT SUPPOSED TO DO?   Chlorpropamide decreases the concentration of glucose (a form of sugar) in the blood. Therefore, it is used in the treatment of certain types of diabetes. Chlorpropamide works by making the body more sensitive to its own insulin. It was originally thought to increase insulin production by the pancreas, but this effect does not persist with normal continued use.

Diabetes that begins in middle and late life is usually best controlled by diet and exercise. But if these mea-sures fail to decrease the concentration of glucose in the blood, either insulin or a sulfonylurea drug such as chlorpropamide may be required in addition. The symptoms of too high a concentration of glucose in the blood (*hyper*glycemia) are excessive thirst, excessive ur-ination, fatigue (which can lead to loss of consciousness and coma), and low resistance to infection. Even if you don't have any symptoms, your doctor will want you to control your blood glucose. Control of blood glucose is essential in preventing or reducing the complications of diabetes, which include damage to vision, loss of feeling in the extremities, kidney damage, heart attack, and stroke.

SIDE EFFECTS   *Hypo*glycemia (too low a concentration of glucose in the blood) can occur from any drug that lowers the blood sugar. Chlorpropamide is no exception, although this problem is not likely to occur unless you stop eating, are severely ill, or follow an extremely irregular diet. The symptoms of hypoglycemia, which include lethargy, nausea, cold sweats, pounding or racing heartbeat, shakiness, headache, confusion, and dizziness, are quickly reversed with a glass of fruit juice or with food. If untreated, hypoglycemia can lead to loss of consciousness and coma. If you think you are experiencing hypoglycemia, have something to eat and contact your doctor.

Other side effects from chlorpropamide are infrequent. Stomach upset occurs in about two persons per hundred; take it with food if this problem bothers you. Rash occurs in two or three per hundred; contact your doctor if you experience a rash.

Other side effects are too rare to list here. Contact your doctor if you experience any unusual symptoms.

DRUG INTERACTIONS   A number of drugs can interact with chlorpropamide or affect your diabetes. These are the most likely to cause problems:

Aspirin. Large doses of aspirin (for example, 12 or more tablets a day) have a mild antidiabetic effect. This effect is too mild to be used as a treatment for diabetes, but it adds to the effect of chlorpropamide. If you are taking large doses of aspirin, you should be aware of this effect. If you start or stop using large doses of aspirin, ask your doctor to determine if it is necessary to alter the dosage of your chlorpropamide. Occasional use of aspirin will not affect your response to chlorpropamide.

Some *beta-blocking drugs,* such as *propranolol (Inderal), pindolol (Visken), nadolol (Corgard), or timolol (Blocadren).* Diabetic patients should not take these drugs unless there is no alternative. They can block some of the warning signs of hypoglycemia (especially rapid heartbeat or palpitations), delay the recovery from hypoglycemia, cause high-blood-pressure episodes during hypoglycemia, and impair circulation to the extremities in diabetics. Other beta-blocking drugs, like metoprolol (Lopressor) and atenolol (Tenormin), are less likely to cause these problems, but there is some risk. If a beta-blocker is required, keep in mind that sweating, but not rapid heartbeat, is a sign of hypoglycemia.

Clofibrate (Atromid-S), which is sometimes used to lower the concentration of triglycerides in the blood, may increase the response to chlorpropamide in some patients. If you start or stop taking clofibrate, ask your doctor to reevaluate your response to chlorpropamide.

Corticosteroids, such as *dexamethasone or prednisone*, can make diabetes more difficult to control. This effect is well known. If you require a corticosteroid, your doctor will check your blood glucose concentration and may increase the dosage of your chlorpropamide.

Diuretics, such as *hydrochlorothiazide (HydroDIURIL) or furosemide (Lasix)*, can reduce the effects of chlorpropamide. If your diuretic causes your blood glucose concentration to increase, your doctor may increase the dosage of your chlorpropamide. There is a second possible interaction between chlorpropamide and diuretics. Diuretics and chlorpropamide both tend to lower the concentration of sodium in the blood, but they do this by separate mechanisms. In some older individuals, this combination of drugs may lead to too low a concentration of sodium in the blood (hyponatremia). Your doctor will periodically order a laboratory test that measures the concentration of sodium in the blood. Contact your doctor if you experience weakness, confusion, or muscle cramps, which may be symptoms of this problem.

Guanethidine (Ismelin), which is sometimes used to treat high blood pressure, increases the effects of chlorpropamide. If you start or stop taking guanethidine, ask your doctor to reevaluate your response to chlorpropamide.

Nifedipine (Procardia), which is used in the treatment of angina, may decrease your response to chlorpropamide. If you start or stop taking nifedipine, ask your doctor to reevaluate your response to chlorpropamide.

Phenylbutazone (Butazolidin) and *oxyphenbutazone*, which are sometimes used for brief periods to control gout attacks or severe arthritic pain, can markedly increase the effects of chlorpropamide. Since hypoglycemia could result, your doctor may want to decrease the dosage of your chlorpropamide temporarily. Check with your doctor.

Smoking antagonizes the effect of insulin and may impair your response to chlorpropamide as well.

Sulfonamides, which are used in treating infections, may increase your response to chlorpropamide. If you start or stop taking a sulfonamide, ask your doctor to reevaluate your response to chlorpropamide.

Thyroid hormones can affect your response to chlorpropamide. If you are starting to take thyroid, or if the dosage of your thyroid hormone is being changed, ask your doctor to reevaluate your response to chlorpropamide.

ALCOHOLIC BEVERAGES A number of potential problems can arise from your use of alcoholic beverages. Some doctors tell their patients to avoid alcohol. Others advise their patients to limit their alcohol use to a glass of wine or two with dinner. The American Diabetes Association allows the inclusion of small amounts of alcoholic beverages in the diet of diabetics. You should avoid sweetened alcoholic beverages. Here is a summary of the potential problems that alcohol can cause:

First, alcohol temporarily lowers the concentration of glucose in the blood. If you drink alcohol on an empty stomach, it can cause hypoglycemia. The risk of hypoglycemia is increased while you are taking chlorpropamide. Therefore, you should avoid large amounts of alcohol and avoid drinking on an empty stomach. If you drink small amounts of alcohol with meals, hypoglycemia is not likely to occur.

Second, some people who take chlorpropamide develop a flushing reaction when they drink alcohol. This reaction may occur in as many as half of those who take chlorpropamide. It is known as the disulfiram or Antabuse reaction, because disulfiram (Antabuse), which is more reliable in causing this reaction, is given to alcoholics for precisely this reason. The reaction is usually harmless, but may be unpleasant and may be accompanied by headache. If you are bothered by this reaction, and your doctor says it is all right for you to drink small amounts of alcohol with meals, you might try taking an aspirin tablet about an hour before any meal that will include a glass of wine.

Third, regular *heavy* use of alcohol stimulates the enzymes that metabolize chlorpropamide, thereby causing it to be eliminated from the body more rapidly. As a result, the effects of chlorpropamide are decreased. Alcohol consumption should be limited to small amounts for this reason, and because of the danger of hypoglycemia during acute alcohol intoxication.

FOOD   Chlorpropamide does not replace diet as the primary means for controlling blood glucose. In addition to avoiding simple sugars, you should increase the amount of roughage (such as fruits, vegetables, and whole grains) in your diet. These foods slow the absorption of complex carbohydrates. Furthermore, you should restrict your consumption of saturated fats (butter, animal fat), because they increase the risk of cardiovascular disease, and cardiovascular disease is more common among diabetics. Finally, most diabetics who take chlorpropamide are overweight. Obesity causes resistance to the body's natural insulin and increases the concentration of glucose in the blood. Weight loss, even if you remain a little heavy, will help control your diabetes. Follow the diabetic diet prescribed by your doctor.

A regular diet is important. If you skip meals because of illness or some other reason, you may experience hypoglycemia (see Side Effects). If you cannot eat because of illness, check with your doctor.

Chlorpropamide is best taken at the start of a meal to prevent stomach upset and to help you remember to take it. Food does not affect the absorption of chlorpropamide tablets. Hypoglycemia can occur if you fail to eat within an hour or two after taking it on an empty stomach.

HOW DOES AGE AFFECT THE RESPONSE TO THIS DRUG?

Hypoglycemia from drugs like chlorpropamide is more common among older people than it is among younger people. Be sure to take your chlorpropamide as directed, follow a careful but regular diet, and be sure that you and those around you are familiar with the signs and symptoms of hypoglycemia.

Chlorpropamide is removed from the body by the kidneys, and the kidneys become less efficient with advancing age. Therefore, some older people will experience greater effects from chlorpropamide than younger people given the same dose. Your doctor will take your age and kidney function into account (see appendix) in determining which dose of chlorpropamide is likely to be appropriate for you. Nevertheless, you should always be alert for signs of hypoglycemia from chlorpropamide (see Side Effects).

Another consequence of age on the kidneys is the way they respond to high concentrations of glucose in the blood. In younger people, when the concentration of glucose in the blood gets much higher than normal, glucose appears in the urine. The threshold for glucose spilling into the urine increases with age, and older people can have much higher concentrations of glucose in their blood without having any in their urine. This effect varies from individual to individual, of course, but urine tests for glucose may be less reliable as indicators of blood glucose in older people. So don't be misled by negative urine tests for glucose. Your doctor can compare your blood glucose with your urine glucose and give you some idea of how reliable urine tests might be for you.

CHLORTHALIDONE

OTHER NAMES   Chlorthalidone (pronounced *klor-THAL-i-doan*) is the common or generic name of this drug. Frequently used brand names for chlorthalidone are Hygroton and Thalitone. Chlorthalidone is sometimes prescribed in tablets that contain other drugs. Combipres is the brand name of tablets that contain chlorthalidone and the antihypertensive drug clonidine. Demi-Regroton and Regroton are the brand names of tablets that contain chlorthalidone and the antihypertensive drug reserpine. Chlorthalidone belongs to a group of closely related drugs called thiazide diuretics.

WHAT IS IT SUPPOSED TO DO?   Chlorthalidone is a diuretic, meaning that it increases the amount of urine that is excreted from the body. Chlorthalidone acts on the kidneys, causing them to eliminate extra water and salt from the body and into the urine. It is used to treat congestive heart failure, high blood pressure, and other medical problems.

Use in Congestive Heart Failure. Extra salt and water may accumulate in the body for a variety of reasons, but congestive heart failure is a common cause in older persons. In congestive heart failure, which is the result of some types of heart disease, the heart's pumping action weakens and the circulation slows down. When the kidneys do not get enough circulation, they become less efficient in removing extra salt and water from the body. As a result, veins become swollen, and fluid leaks out of them and into surrounding tissue. Usually, the first symptom of this problem is swelling of the ankles and lower legs. (The medical term for this swelling, which can also be caused by less potentially serious circulatory problems, is edema.) Later, fluid accumulates in the lungs, causing shortness of breath. Chlorthalidone's ability to promote salt and water removal by the kidneys is the basis for its use in congestive heart failure.

Use in Hypertension. The diuretic effects of chlorthalidone are important here because too much salt in the body may be part of the cause of hypertension (high blood pressure). In addition, and perhaps more important in hypertension, chlorthalidone causes small blood vessels to dilate. This dilation of blood vessels eases the resistance to blood flow, and blood pressure is thereby lowered. Whether your hypertension is mild or severe, chlorthalidone may be the first drug that your doctor prescribes to control it.

SIDE EFFECTS Serious side effects from chlorthalidone are rare. The most annoying side effect you will notice when you begin taking this drug is a need to urinate frequently. You should avoid taking chlorthalidone too late in the day. Otherwise, you may find yourself being frequently awakened from sleep by the need to urinate.

Chlorthalidone causes potassium to be removed from the body along with salt and water. In most cases, this causes no problem. Dietary sources of potassium usually prevent potassium deficiency from occurring. However, your doctor may prescribe either a potassium supplement or a second diuretic that conserves potassium to prevent this effect, especially if you are also taking digoxin (see Drug Interactions). In any case, your doctor will periodically order a laboratory test that measures the concentration of potassium in the blood. The symptoms of too low a concentration of potassium in the blood include profound muscle weakness, muscle cramps or pain, and irregular heartbeat. If you experience any of these symptoms, contact your doctor.

Chlorthalidone sometimes causes an increase in the amount of glucose in the blood, which could unmask latent diabetes or require an increase in your insulin or other drug requirement if you already have diabetes. Prevention of excess potassium loss reduces the risk of this problem. Chlorthalidone can also increase the amount of uric acid in your blood, but it rarely causes gout, the clinical manifestation of this condition. Your doctor will order periodic laboratory tests to monitor for these and other, rarer possible problems before they cause symptoms.

All diuretics have the potential for causing dehydration when fluid loss is accelerated by hot weather or flulike illness. Whenever you experience fever, vomiting, or diarrhea, whatever the cause, be sure to increase your fluid intake to prevent dehydration. If the symptoms are severe, you should contact your doctor.

Other side effects are too rare to list here. If you should develop a rash or any other unusual symptom while taking this drug, contact your doctor.

DRUG INTERACTIONS Several drugs interact with chlorthalidone, and your doctor will take special precautions to ensure that no problems occur if you are taking them:

Antidiabetic drugs, such as *insulin* or the *sulfonylureas.* Chlorthalidone can increase the concentration of glucose in the blood. If this occurs, despite the protective effect of correcting for potassium loss, your doctor may increase the dosage of your diabetic medication to compensate for this interaction. If you are taking chlorpropamide (Diabinese) or tolbutamide (Orinase), your doctor will monitor for a second, less frequent, possible interaction. These drugs sometimes decrease the concentration of sodium in the blood. (Other sulfonylureas do not share this property.) In some older individuals, this combination of drugs can lead to too low a concentration of sodium in the blood (hyponatremia). If you experience weakness, confusion, or muscle cramps, contact your doctor.

Bile-acid sequestrants, such as *cholestyramine resin (Questran) and colestipol (Colestid),* are used to lower the concentration of cholesterol in the blood. They are also used to treat the itching that sometimes occurs with jaundice. These drugs may bind to chlorthalidone in the gastrointestinal tract and thereby prevent its full absorption. If therapy with one of these drugs is nec-

essary, the chlorthalidone dose should be taken two
hours before the cholestyramine or colestipol dose to
minimize any interaction.

Corticosteroids, such as *dexamethasone, hydrocortisone, or prednisone*, cause potassium to be lost from
the body, and this side effect is additive with that of
chlorthalidone. To prevent problems, your doctor will
periodically order a laboratory test that measures the
concentration of potassium in the blood and, if necessary, will prescribe either a potassium supplement or a
second diuretic that conserves potassium.

Digoxin (Lanoxin). Although chlorthalidone is often
prescribed together with digoxin, an interaction can occur because of chlorthalidone's promotion of potassium
loss from the body. If the amount of potassium in the
blood becomes too low, then digoxin toxicity may develop. To prevent this problem, your doctor will periodically order a laboratory test that measures the
concentration of potassium in the blood and, if necessary, will prescribe either a potassium supplement or a
second diuretic that conserves potassium.

Lithium (Eskalith, Lithane, and others), a drug that is
prescribed by psychiatrists for mood problems, is removed from the body by the kidneys. Chlorthalidone
significantly slows this removal, and the concentration
of lithium in the blood increases, sometimes to toxic
levels. When these drugs must be used together, your
doctor will probably decrease the dose of your lithium,
using a laboratory test for monitoring the concentration of lithium in your blood as a guide.

Nonsteroidal anti-inflammatory drugs (NSAIDs), such
as *diflunisal, ibuprofen, indomethacin, fenoprofen, meclofenamate, naproxen, piroxicam, sulindac, tolmetin,
or large amounts of aspirin*. These drugs can cause fluid
retention and edema in older people who are sensitive
to this effect. If you are taking chlorthalidone for fluid
retention and edema (such as that caused by congestive
heart failure or liver disease) and you experience a
worsening of your symptoms while taking one of these
NSAIDs, stop taking the NSAID and contact your doctor.

ALCOHOLIC BEVERAGES Alcoholic beverages have a more pronounced effect on some people than on others; if you become dizzy when drinking, chlorthalidone might make things worse. You can carefully evaluate this effect for yourself. Most people do not notice any effect at all.

FOOD Many pharmacists recommend taking chlorthalidone with meals. Food does not impair its absorption, and some people (probably fewer than one in a hundred) experience an upset stomach when they take chlorthalidone on an empty stomach. Taking it with a meal will also help you set up a routine and thereby prevent you from missing too many doses. Take your morning dose with breakfast and, if you take a second daily dose, take it with a late-afternoon snack or dinner.

Be sure to follow any dietary advice, such as limiting salt intake or increasing potassium-containing foods (such as bananas, orange juice, raisins), you may have been given with your prescription.

HOW DOES AGE AFFECT THE RESPONSE TO THIS DRUG? Older people are more sensitive to the effects of diuretics. The effects of too much diuretic, which are rare in younger people, are more likely to occur with advancing age. The most common problem is dizziness or faintness from abnormally low blood pressure. If you experience such a symptom, contact your doctor. Another problem, which is infrequent, is too low a concentration of sodium in the blood. If you experience weakness, confusion, or muscle cramps, contact your doctor.

Your doctor will take your age into consideration in selecting a dosage that is likely to be appropriate for you.

CIMETIDINE

OTHER NAMES Cimetidine (pronounced *sye-MET-i-deen)* is the common or generic name of this drug. Its principal brand name is Tagamet. Pharmacologists refer to cimetidine as a histamine H_2-receptor blocker. Cimetidine became available in 1977 as the first member of this new class of drugs and has since become one of the most widely prescribed drugs.

WHAT IS IT SUPPOSED TO DO? Cimetidine decreases the secretion of stomach acid. Therefore, it is used to treat peptic ulcers and related problems.

Cimetidine works by decreasing the effect that histamine has on the stomach. Histamine, a substance the body produces to regulate a number of its functions, reacts with specialized receptors in the stomach to stimulate the flow of gastric juices. Too great a flow of gastric juices (too much stomach acid, too much pepsin), along with too little tissue resistance to their effects, is the cause of peptic-ulcer disease and related problems. Decreasing gastric-juice production is a key component in the medical treatment of these problems. For years, pharmacologists tried to use antihistamines (like the ones you can buy without prescription) to block the effect of histamine on stomach-acid secretion, but without good results. The histamine receptors in the stomach are H_2-receptors, which are different from the histamine receptors in the rest of the body. Antihistamines are histamine H_1-receptor blockers; they block the effect of histamine on allergic reactions, but not on gastric-acid secretion. Cimetidine, on the other hand, blocks the effect of histamine on the histamine H_2-receptors in the stomach. The primary location of histamine H_2-receptors in the body is in the stomach.

SIDE EFFECTS Side effects from cimetidine are infrequent.

Cimetidine does not usually cause any perceptible mental effects, but it can cause confusional states (with symptoms of psychosis, anxiety, disorientation, depression, or dementia) as an infrequent side effect. Tiredness, weakness, slurred speech, dizziness, and headache have also been reported. Contact your doctor if you experience any adverse mental effects.

Muscle or joint pain also occur infrequently and may

disappear with continued use; contact your doctor if this side effect is bothersome or persistent. The same may be said of diarrhea, which also occurs infrequently.

On rare occasions, cimetidine causes temporary impotence. It can also cause breast swelling and tenderness in both men and women. Contact your doctor if you develop either of these rare side effects.

Other side effects are too rare to list here. Contact your doctor if you develop any other unexpected symptoms.

DRUG INTERACTIONS Cimetidine interacts with a number of drugs:

Antacids can decrease the absorption of cimetidine, so don't take both at the same time of day. If you take your cimetidine with a meal and then take the antacid an hour or more afterward, this interaction is not likely to cause any problems.

Antidepressants, such as *amitriptyline (Elavil), desipramine (Pertofrane, Norpramin), imipramine (Tofranil), and nortiptyline (Aventyl).* Cimetidine slows the metabolism of these drugs and thereby increases their effects. Your doctor may have to give you smaller doses of these antidepressants while you are taking cimetidine. If you experience a worsening of antidepressant side effects, contact your doctor.

Some *benzodiazepines,* such as *alprazolam (Xanax), chlordiazepoxide (Librium), clorazepate (Tranxene), diazepam (Valium), flurazepam (Dalmane), halazepam (Paxipam), prazepam (Centrax), and triazolam (Halcion).* The metabolism of these drugs, which are used for the treatment of anxiety and insomnia, is slowed considerably by cimetidine. If the dosages of these drugs are not decreased while you are taking cimetidine, you may experience confusion or excess drowsiness from too much benzodiazepine effect. The benzodiazepines lorazepam (Ativan), oxazepam (Serax), and temazepam (Restoril) do not seem to be affected by cimetidine.

Metoprolol (Lopressor), which is used in the treatment of high blood pressure, is metabolized fairly rapidly by the liver. Cimetidine slows metoprolol's metabolism, thereby enhancing its effects. Your doctor may need to lower your metoprolol dosage temporarily while you are taking cimetidine. Contact your doctor if you experience metoprolol side effects while taking cimetidine.

Phenytoin (Dilantin), which is used to prevent seizures and to treat certain kinds of irregular heartbeats, is metabolized in the liver by a process that is slowed by cimetidine. The result could be too much phenytoin effect when both drugs are taken together. Your doctor may have to decrease the dosage of your phenytoin temporarily while you are taking cimetidine. Contact your doctor if you experience phenytoin side effects.

Procainamide (Pronestyl), which is used to treat certain kinds of irregular heartbeats, and its active metabolite (the formation of which is not affected by cimetidine) are removed from the body by the kidneys. There is preliminary evidence that cimetidine slows their elimination by the kidneys. Your doctor will carefully monitor your procainamide therapy while you are taking cimetidine and may temporarily lower the dosage of your procainamide. Contact your doctor if you experience any procainamide side effects.

Propranolol (Inderal), which is used in the treatment of high blood pressure, angina, and a number of other medical problems, is metabolized fairly rapidly by the liver. Cimetidine slows propranolol's metabolism, thereby enhancing its effects. Your doctor may need to lower your propranolol dosage temporarily while you are taking cimetidine. Contact your doctor if you experience propranolol side effects while taking cimetidine.

Quinidine (Quinora, Quinaglute, Cardioquin, and others), which is used to treat certain kinds of irregular heartbeats, is metabolized in the liver by a process that may be slowed by cimetidine. This could lead to too much quinidine effect. Your doctor will monitor your response to quinidine while you are taking cimetidine and may temporarily decrease the dose of your quinidine.

Smoking increases the production of stomach acid and may therefore decrease the beneficial effects of cimetidine.

Theophylline (Elixophyllin, Slo-Phyllin, Theobid, Theo-Dur, and others). Theophylline, which is used to treat asthma, emphysema, and other breathing problems, is metabolized by a process that is slowed by cimetidine. Your doctor may need to decrease the dose of your theophylline temporarily while you are taking cimetidine.

Warfarin (Coumadin). Cimetidine slows the metabolism of this anticoagulant, although it takes more than a week for the effect to become apparent clinically. Since a possible consequence of this interaction is increased risk of bleeding, many physicians, when faced with this interaction, prescribe another H_2-blocker, ranitidine (Zantac), which does not appear to interact with warfarin.

ALCOHOLIC BEVERAGES You can drink alcoholic beverages while you are taking cimetidine, but alcohol's effects are usually intensified by this drug. Cimetidine slows the metabolism of alcohol, thereby increasing the concentration of alcohol in the blood. The result isn't always dramatic, but alcohol intoxication occurs more quickly and lasts longer. A second effect, which occurs only when there is a lot of alcohol in the blood (enough to make you feel drunk), is a slowing of the metabolism of cimetidine by alcohol, which results in greater cimetidine effect. Since cimetidine itself can cause mental effects, and is more likely to do so in older people, this combination could be unpleasant. Finally, alcoholic beverages can be irritating to the stomach.

FOOD It's a good idea to take cimetidine with meals. Food slows its absorption and makes its effects last longer. When you take cimetidine this way, it will still be exerting its effect long after your stomach has emptied. This is what you want from the drug: reduced stomach acid while the stomach is empty.

Avoid foods that are irritating to your stomach. Special diets are no longer commonly used in the treatment of peptic-ulcer disease, but you should heed the messages sent by your stomach.

HOW DOES AGE AFFECT THE RESPONSE TO THIS DRUG? Advancing age is associated with slowed elimination of cimetidine by the liver and the kidneys. Therefore, smaller doses are required. There is a clear correlation between the progressive age-related decline in kidney function and the rate at which cimetidine is eliminated from the body. Your doctor will evaluate your kidney function (see appendix) in determining the correct dosage of cimetidine for you.

Although confusion is an infrequent side effect from cimetidine, it is most likely to occur in people over the age of fifty. Furthermore, many of the drugs whose metabolism is slowed by cimetidine (for example, benzodiazepines, antidepressants, phenytoin) can cause confusion when they accumulate to too high a concentration in the blood. Since the metabolism of these drugs is already slowed by aging, further slowing by cimetidine increases the risk that these drugs will accumulate to concentrations that cause confusion. (Assuming, of course, that the dosages of these drugs are not adjusted for age and interaction with cimetidine.) The degree to which cimetidine slows drug metabolism is the same in adults of all ages.

CLONIDINE

OTHER NAMES Clonidine (pronounced *KLOE-ni-deen)* is the common or generic name of this drug. Its most frequently used brand name is Catapres. It is prescribed both as conventional tablets and as a specially formulated patch from which the drug is slowly absorbed through the skin. Clonidine is sometimes prescribed as tablets that also contain the thiazide diuretic chlorthalidone; the brand name of this combination is Combipres.

WHAT IS IT SUPPOSED TO DO?   Clonidine works inside the brain (by stimulating alpha$_2$-adrenergic receptors) to lower blood pressure. It is often used in combination with a thiazide diuretic, which lowers the blood pressure by additional mechanisms.

Hypertension (high blood pressure) causes no symptoms, but untreated hypertension substantially increases the risk for the subsequent development of congestive heart failure, angina, heart attack, stroke, kidney problems, or visual problems. Antihypertensive drugs such as clonidine decrease these risks.

SIDE EFFECTS   The most common side effects from clonidine are drowsiness, dry mouth, and dizziness (especially when standing or sitting up quickly). Less frequently, the dry mouth may be accompanied by painful salivary glands (located just below and in front of each ear), dry eyes, and dry nasal mucosa as well. Other less common side effects are constipation, nausea, loss of appetite, difficulty in sleeping, and decreased sexual ability. All of these side effects are frequent during the first weeks of therapy, but they tend to go away. If any of these side effects is persistent or bothersome, contact your doctor.

Your doctor will begin clonidine therapy with small doses in order to minimize any drowsiness or dizziness that may occur. However, you should be especially careful when performing tasks that require alertness, such as driving, especially during the first week after starting to take clonidine. Be careful not to stand up too quickly.

Clonidine can cause salt and water retention, but this is usually prevented by the diuretic that is often prescribed along with it. If you experience swelling of your feet or lower legs, contact your doctor.

Rarely, clonidine causes adverse mental effects. If you experience vivid dreams or nightmares, or if you feel depressed, contact your doctor.

One of the most serious side effects from clonidine is

a withdrawal syndrome that can occur from stopping the drug suddenly. This syndrome, called rebound hypertension, can be life threatening. It includes a sharp rise in blood pressure, sweating, nervousness, palpitations, headache, tremor, and increased salivation. If you have been taking clonidine for more than a few weeks, this reaction is likely to be severe. It can be avoided entirely by slowly decreasing the dose if therapy must be stopped. Be sure you always have an adequate supply of clonidine.

Other side effects are too rare to list here. If you experience any unusual symptoms, contact your doctor.

DRUG INTERACTIONS   Special caution is warranted when clonidine is prescribed with these drugs:

Antidepressants, such as *amitriptyline (Elavil), desipramine (Norpramin, Pertofrane), imipramine (Tofranil), and others,* can cause a dangerous increase in blood pressure if taken with clonidine. This combination should be avoided.

Beta-blocking drugs, such as *atenolol (Tenormin), propranolol (Inderal), and others,* which are used in the treatment of hypertension and other medical problems, increase the danger of rebound hypertension from sudden withdrawal of clonidine (see Side Effects).

ALCOHOLIC BEVERAGES   Alcohol will add to any drowsiness or dizziness that clonidine might cause. Cautiously observe for yourself how this combination affects you.

FOOD   Clonidine can be taken with food or on an empty stomach. Some people take it with a meal to help them remember to take it.

If your doctor has prescribed a salt-restricted diet, be sure to follow it.

HOW DOES AGE AFFECT THE RESPONSE TO THIS DRUG?   Drowsiness, which is the most common side effect from clonidine, is more often a persistent problem in older people.

CLORAZEPATE

OTHER NAMES   Clorazepate (pronounced *klor-AZ-e-pate)* is the common or generic name of this drug. A frequently used brand name for clorazepate is Tranxene. Clorazepate belongs to a large group of similar drugs called benzodiazepines.

WHAT IS IT SUPPOSED TO DO?   Clorazepate relieves the symptoms of anxiety and tension.

SIDE EFFECTS   Drowsiness is the principal side effect from clorazepate. You may find yourself unsteady on your feet as well. Evaluate these effects for yourself and regulate your activities accordingly. You should be especially cautious about driving an automobile. If drowsiness or unsteadiness persists, stop taking the drug and contact your doctor.

Infrequently, clorazepate causes dizziness, weakness, confusion, impaired memory, or loss of coordination. If you experience any of these effects, which suggest you are extremely sensitive to clorazepate, stop taking it and contact your physician.

If you have been taking clorazepate regularly for a long time and in large doses, you may experience mild withdrawal symptoms several days after stopping this drug. Typical symptoms include difficulty in sleeping, unusual irritability, and unusual nervousness. If these occur, contact your doctor.

Other side effects are too rare to list here. Contact your doctor if you experience any unusual symptoms.

DRUG INTERACTIONS   Sedation is a common side effect of antidepressant drugs, antihistamines, tranquilizers, narcotic analgesics, and other drugs. Be careful of additive effects when clorazepate is taken with any of these drugs.

In addition, several drugs can interact with clorazepate by other mechanisms. These are the interactions most likely to cause problems:

Cimetidine (Tagamet), which is used for the treatment of ulcers, slows the metabolism of clorazepate and thereby enhances its effects. It may be necessary to decrease the dosage of your clorazepate while taking both drugs; ask your doctor.

Disulfiram (Antabuse), which is used in the treatment of alcoholism, slows the metabolism of clorazepate and thereby enhances its effects. It may be necessary to decrease the dosage of your clorazepate while taking both drugs; ask your doctor.

Isoniazid (INH), which is used in the treatment of tuberculosis, may slow the metabolism of clorazepate and thereby enhance its effect. It may be necessary to decrease the dosage of your clorazepate while taking both drugs; ask your doctor. Rifampin, another drug used in the treatment of tuberculosis, has the opposite effect (see below). When rifampin and isoniazid are used together, the effects of rifampin predominate in the interaction with clorazepate.

Levodopa (Dopar, Larodopa, L-dopa) is used in the treatment of Parkinson's disease, and clorazepate may block its effect. If you are taking both drugs and notice a worsening of your parkinsonism, stop taking your clorazepate and contact your doctor.

Rifampin (Rifadin, Rimactane), which is used in the treatment of tuberculosis, increases the metabolism of clorazepate and thereby decreases its effect. If your doctor increases the dosage of your clorazepate to compensate for this interaction, remind him to readjust your clorazepate dosage when you stop taking rifampin.

ALCOHOLIC BEVERAGES Clorazepate adds to alcohol's depressive effects on the nervous system. If you are taking clorazepate regularly, the combined effects of alcohol and clorazepate can occur even if you haven't taken the clorazepate for twenty-four hours, or even several days. The active metabolites of clorazepate remain in the body for many days. Therefore, you should limit your alcohol consumption to small amounts while taking clorazepate. Needless to say, the effects of this combination on driving can be dangerous.

FOOD Clorazepate can be taken with food or on an empty stomach.

HOW DOES AGE AFFECT THE RESPONSE TO THIS DRUG? The older you are, the more sensitive you will be to clorazepate. There are several mechanisms involved:

First, older people are inherently more sensitive to the effects of clorazepate. This may have something to do with the effects of aging on the brain. There is good evidence that older people experience much more sedation than younger people with the same concentration of the drug in their blood.

Second, aging changes the distribution of desmethyldiazepam, the principal active metabolite of clorazepate, within the body. As a result, it takes much longer for the maximum effect of repeated doses to become apparent. An older person who takes clorazepate every day will experience slightly more effect each day for several weeks, and *then* repeated doses will maintain the same level of effect. If the dosage is too high for you, you may not notice it as soon as you might expect.

Third, and for some unknown reason this applies more to men than to women, the metabolism of desmethyldiazepam, the active metabolite of clorazepate, becomes slower with advanced age. Therefore, some older people develop higher concentrations of drug in their blood than would be expected, and they are more likely to develop side effects. In these individuals, it may take longer than a month before the full effects of repeated doses become apparent.

In any case, side effects increase with age. Confusion, weakness, fainting, dizziness, impaired memory, and loss of coordination, which are infrequent side effects from clorazepate, occur far more often in older people than they do in younger people. All of these side effects are reversible, but because their onset can be so slow, they are sometimes not associated with the offending drug. Furthermore, just as these side effects are often slow to appear, they are equally slow to disappear after clorazepate is stopped. If you are aware of this possibility, it probably won't become a problem for you.

Your doctor will take your age into consideration in selecting a dose and dosage schedule that are likely to be appropriate for you.

CODEINE

OTHER NAMES   Codeine (pronounced *KOE-deen)* is so well known by its common or generic name that it does not have a brand name. However, many brand-name prescription drug products contain codeine as an ingredient in combination with one or more other drugs. Some are combinations of acetaminophen and codeine (Aceta with Codeine, Codap, Empracet with Codeine, Phenaphen with Codeine, Tylenol with Codeine). Others are combinations of aspirin and codeine (Empirin with Codeine) or buffered aspirin and codeine (Ascriptin with Codeine, Bufferin with Codeine). Still others contain caffeine with aspirin and codeine (A.S.A. and Codeine Compound) or phenacetin and caffeine with aspirin and codeine (A.P.C. with Codeine). Codeine is also an ingredient in many cough syrups.

Codeine is one of the drugs that occur naturally in the opium poppy. Therefore, it is sometimes referred to as an opiate or opioid. Because opium causes sedation and sleep if taken in large enough amounts, opiates became known as narcotics, a derivative of the Greek word for stupor.

WHAT IS IT SUPPOSED TO DO?   Codeine works within the brain to alter the sensation of pain. When taken orally, 30 mg of codeine (a usual dose) is about equal to one aspirin tablet in pain-relieving potency. When taken in combination with aspirin or acetaminophen, which relieve pain by other mechanisms, codeine is a very effective pain reliever. Codeine also suppresses cough, and it is sometimes taken for this purpose.

SIDE EFFECTS   Codeine sometimes causes nausea or vomiting, especially after the first few doses. Nausea often goes away if you lie down for a while. If vomiting is persistent, contact your doctor.

Other side effects include dizziness, mental cloudiness, drowsiness, stomach pain, and itching. If any of these is persistent or severe, contact your doctor.

Avoid driving while taking codeine.

Codeine is constipating when taken in repeated doses.

Codeine is addicting if enough of it is taken regularly for a long enough time. Follow your doctor's instructions—the risk is small if taken as directed when needed for pain.

Other side effects are too rare to be listed here. Contact your doctor if you experience any unexpected symptoms.

DRUG INTERACTIONS   Any drug that shares codeine's ability to depress the central nervous system (alcohol, antihistamines, barbiturates, benzodiazepine sedatives, MAO inhibitors, tricyclic antidepressants) can intensify codeine's adverse effects in susceptible individuals. Check with your doctor or pharmacist.

ALCOHOLIC BEVERAGES   Limit your use of alcohol to small amounts. Alcohol may intensify any dizziness or light-headedness you feel from codeine, and the codeine will intensify the intoxicating effects of alcohol. Excessive amounts of both drugs can depress breathing.

FOOD   Codeine can be taken with food or on an empty stomach. If your codeine medication contains aspirin, take it with a full glass of water and with something to eat.

HOW DOES AGE AFFECT THE RESPONSE TO THIS DRUG?   Advancing age is accompanied by greater sensitivity to codeine. Your doctor will take your age into consideration in prescribing a dose that is likely to be effective without causing too many side effects.

DESIPRAMINE

OTHER NAMES   Desipramine (pronounced *dess-IP-ra-meen)* is the common or generic name of this drug. Frequently used brand names for desipramine are Nor-pramin and Pertofrane. Desipramine belongs to a group of drugs called tricyclic antidepressants. *(Tricyclic* describes their chemical structure; *antidepressant* refers to their pharmacological effect.)

WHAT IS IT SUPPOSED TO DO?   Desipramine relieves mental depression. The precise means by which it works has not been established, but its mechanism of action involves an increase in the concentration of certain naturally occurring substances within the brain (particularly norepinephrine). Elevation of mood and reversal of the various symptoms that can accompany depression (such as sleep problems, decreased energy, or loss of appetite) require a minimum of several weeks of regular use. Your doctor may prescribe less than several weeks' supply of medication initially, so it is important that you return to your pharmacy to have your prescription refilled. Your doctor may want you to continue taking desipramine for several months after your mood returns to normal.

SIDE EFFECTS   Although desipramine causes fewer side effects than most other tricyclic antidepressants, side effects are not uncommon. Nearly everyone experiences dry mouth while taking desipramine. It doesn't seem to be related to dosage, and it tends to diminish with time. Sugar-free candy or gum is often helpful in alleviating this problem.

The most common potentially serious side effect involves the temporary decrease in blood pressure that occurs when you stand up. This decrease in blood pressure is exaggerated by desipramine and is likely to make you dizzy, light-headed, or faint if you stand up too quickly. If this side effect is severe (especially if it causes you to fall or causes your heart to pound or race), contact your doctor. Be very careful to stand up slowly.

The dry mouth caused by desipramine is an example of what pharmacologists call an anticholinergic effect. It can be caused by any drug that blocks the receptors for acetylcholine, a substance produced by the body to regulate certain functions that are beyond conscious control. When desipramine is taken with other drugs that have anticholinergic side effects, these side effects are more likely to cause problems (see Drug Interactions). Although desipramine causes fewer anticholinergic effects than most other antidepressants, it occasionally causes constipation. Ask your pharmacist for appropriate treatment; a stool softener is often helpful. Contact your doctor if constipation becomes severe. Another anticholinergic side effect is the sudden onset of confusion or disorientation, sometimes with visual hallucinations. If this occurs, contact your doctor; it is a sign that the dosage is too high for you. Other anticholinergic side effects that require your doctor's attention (and these are infrequent or rare) include blurred vision, difficulty in urinating (more common in older men with prostate difficulties), and eye pain (a possible indication that narrow-angle glaucoma, not the usual type of glaucoma, has been aggravated).

Other side effects include drowsiness, nausea, unpleasant taste, diarrhea (infrequent), and excessive sweating (infrequent). These side effects may diminish or go away as your body adjusts to the effects of this drug. Contact your doctor if they are severe or bothersome. A fine tremor is not an uncommon side effect in older people; tell your doctor if this occurs.

Effects on the heart—excessively fast, slow, or irregular heartbeats—are infrequent. Contact your doctor if any of these occur.

Other side effects are too infrequent to list here. Contact your doctor if you experience any unexpected symptoms.

DRUG INTERACTIONS Desipramine interacts with a number of drugs. Here are the most common sources of potential problems:

Anticholinergic drugs, such as *belladonna (Donnatal)* or *propantheline (Pro-Banthine),* which are used for peptic-ulcer disease, *benztropine (Cogentin),* which is used in the treatment of Parkinson's disease and to treat the side effects sometimes caused by tranquilizers, and *scopolamine (Transderm Scōp),* which is used to prevent sickness, all work by blocking acetylcholine (see Side Effects). These drugs are more likely to cause anticholinergic side effects when taken with desipramine. In some cases, the anticholinergic side effects of desipramine obviate the need for these other drugs. Check with your doctor before taking them with desipramine.

Antihistamines, which are included in many nonprescription cold and allergy medicines, have sedative and anticholinergic (see above) side effects. Avoid these products while taking desipramine.

Antihypertensive drugs can interact with desipramine by several mechanisms. First, some of them (beta-blockers, clonidine, methyldopa, and reserpine) can cause depression as a side effect. Second, the action of a few antihypertensive drugs is blocked by desipramine. If you are taking clonidine (Catapres, Combipres), guanethidine (Ismelin), or guanadrel (Hylorel), your doctor will need to prescribe another drug to control your blood pressure. Third, if your antihypertensive drug causes dizziness, desipramine will make this side effect worse. Your doctor may need to decrease the dose of your antihypertensive drug before you start taking desipramine.

Cimetidine (Tagamet), which is used in the treatment of peptic-ulcer disease, slows the metabolism of desipramine and thereby increases its effects. Contact your doctor if you experience an increase in desipramine side effects while taking cimetidine; your doctor may have to lower the dosage of your desipramine temporarily.

Monoamine oxidase inhibitors, such as *isocarboxazid (Marplan), phenelzine (Nardil), and tranylcypromine (Parnate),* which are also used in the treatment of depression, sometimes cause dangerous toxic reactions when taken with desipramine. This combination of drugs should only be used in hospitalized patients who are under careful observation. Normally, one or two weeks are allowed to elapse between the use of desipramine and one of these drugs.

Phenobarbital, which is used to prevent seizures and is also sometimes included as an ingredient in certain medications for its sedative effects, stimulates the metabolism of desipramine and thereby decreases its effects. If you require treatment with phenobarbital, your doctor will take this into consideration in adjusting your desipramine dosage. Otherwise, your doctor may replace your phenobarbital-containing medication with another drug product.

Phenothiazine tranquilizers, such as *perphenazine (Trilafon), thioridazine (Mellaril), and trifluoperazine (Stelazine),* are more likely to cause anticholinergic side effects (see Side Effects) when taken with desipramine. In addition, these drugs may slow the metabolism of desipramine and thereby increase its effects. There are instances when these drugs need to be given with desipramine, but you should be sure that your doctor intends that you take this combination.

ALCOHOLIC BEVERAGES   Alcohol will increase the dizziness or faintness that you may feel upon standing up too quickly. It will also add to any drowsiness that desipramine might cause. Therefore, you should avoid alcohol or use it sparingly while taking desipramine.

FOOD   Take your desipramine with meals to help you maintain a regular schedule for taking it and to prevent any nausea it might cause.

HOW DOES AGE AFFECT THE RESPONSE TO THIS DRUG?   There is considerable variation among individuals in the rate at which desipramine is metabolized and removed from the body, but advancing age does not appear to influence these processes. The currently available evidence suggests that the beneficial effects of desipramine require several weeks of treatment with similar doses (and similar concentrations of the drug in the blood) for both older and younger people.

However, advancing age is clearly associated with a higher incidence of adverse reactions from desipramine. In a study of serious side effects from desipramine in hospitalized patients, these side effects occurred in four out of fifty-six (7 percent) of those who were younger than sixty and eleven out of twenty-eight (39 percent) of those who were older than sixty. Other studies have also found a greater incidence of side effects in older people. Therefore, your doctor may begin your treatment with smaller doses that are gradually increased. Contact your doctor promptly if you experience extreme dizziness or faintness (which could cause you to fall). Your doctor may prescribe a laboratory test that measures the concentration of desipramine in your blood in order to evaluate your desipramine dosage.

DIAZEPAM

OTHER NAMES   Diazepam (pronounced *dye-AZ-eh-pam)* is the common or generic name of this drug. A frequently used brand name for diazepam is Valium. Diazepam belongs to a large group of similar drugs called benzodiazepines.

WHAT IS IT SUPPOSED TO DO?   Diazepam relieves the symptoms of anxiety and tension.

SIDE EFFECTS   Drowsiness is the principal side effect from diazepam. You may find yourself unsteady on your feet as well. Evaluate these effects for yourself and regulate your activities accordingly. You should be especially cautious about driving an automobile. If drowsiness or unsteadiness persists, stop taking the drug and contact your doctor.

Infrequently, diazepam causes dizziness, weakness, impaired memory, confusion, or loss of coordination. If you experience any of these effects, which suggest you are extremely sensitive to diazepam, stop taking it and contact your doctor.

If you have been taking diazepam regularly for a long time and in large doses, you may experience mild withdrawal symptoms several days after stopping this drug. Typical symptoms include difficulty in sleeping, unusual irritability, and unusual nervousness. If these occur, contact your doctor.

Other side effects are too rare to list here. Contact your doctor if you experience any unusual symptoms.

DRUG INTERACTIONS Sedation is a common side effect of antidepressant drugs, antihistamines, tranquilizers, narcotic analgesics, and other drugs. Be careful of additive effects between diazepam and any of these drugs.

In addition, several drugs can interact with diazepam by other mechanisms. These are the interactions most likely to cause problems:

Cimetidine (Tagamet), which is used for the treatment of ulcers, slows the metabolism of diazepam and thereby enhances its effects. It may be necessary to decrease the dosage of your diazepam while taking both drugs; ask your doctor.

Disulfiram (Antabuse), which is used in the treatment of alcoholism, slows the metabolism of diazepam and thereby enhances its effects. It may be necessary to decrease the dosage of your diazepam while taking both drugs; ask your doctor.

Isoniazid (INH), which is used in the treatment of tuberculosis, may slow the metabolism of diazepam and thereby enhance its effect. It may be necessary to decrease the dosage of your diazepam while taking both drugs; ask your doctor. Rifampin, another drug that is used for tuberculosis, has the opposite effect (see below). When isoniazid and rifampin are used together for the treatment of tuberculosis, the effects of rifampin predominate in the interaction with diazepam.

Levodopa (Dopar, Larodopa, L-dopa) is used in the treatment of Parkinson's disease, and diazepam may block its effect. If you are taking both drugs and notice a worsening of your parkinsonism, stop taking your diazepam and contact your doctor.

Rifampin (Rifadin, Rimactane), which is used in the treatment of tuberculosis, increases the metabolism of diazepam and thereby decreases its effect. If your doctor increases the dosage of your diazepam to compensate for this interaction, remind him or her to readjust your diazepam dosage when you stop taking rifampin.

ALCOHOLIC BEVERAGES Diazepam adds to alcohol's depressive effects on the nervous system. If you are taking diazepam regularly, the combined effects of diazepam and alcohol can occur even if the last time you took diazepam was on the previous day, or even several days previously. Diazepam and its active metabolites remain in the body for many days. Therefore, you should limit your alcohol consumption to small amounts while taking diazepam.

In addition, alcohol increases the absorption of diazepam from the gastrointestinal tract and slows its metabolism. Both of these effects of alcohol increase the effects of diazepam. To avoid increased diazepam absorption, you should not take diazepam within two hours of drinking alcohol.

Needless to say, the effects of this combination on driving can be dangerous.

FOOD Food slows the absorption of diazepam from the gastrointestinal tract. You may wish to take your diazepam with food if you find that its effects are too intense after taking it on an empty stomach.

HOW DOES AGE AFFECT THE RESPONSE TO THIS DRUG? The older you are, the more sensitive you will be to diazepam. There are several mechanisms involved:

First, older people are inherently more sensitive to the effects of diazepam. This may have something to do with the effects of aging on the brain. It may also have something to do with changes in the blood that sometimes occur with aging—diazepam is highly bound to certain proteins that circulate in the blood. With aging, the concentration of these proteins tends to decrease, and the percentage of diazepam that is *not* bound to these proteins increases substantially. It's the unbound diazepam that gets into the brain. There is good evidence that older people experience much more sedation than younger people with the same concentration of diazepam in their blood.

Second, aging changes the distribution of diazepam within the body. As a result, it takes much longer for the maximum effect of repeated doses to become apparent. An older person who takes the same amount of diazepam every day will experience slightly more effect each successive day for several weeks, and *then* repeated doses will maintain the same level of effect. If the dosage is too high for you, you may not notice it as soon as you might expect. Younger people experience their maximum response to repeated doses more quickly.

Third, and for some unknown reason this applies more to men than to women, the metabolism of diazepam and its principal active metabolite, desmethyldiazepam, become slower with advanced age. Therefore, some older people develop higher concentrations of drug in their blood than would be expected, and they are more likely to develop side effects. In these individuals, it may take longer than a month before the full effects of repeated doses become apparent.

In any case, side effects increase with age. Confusion, weakness, fainting, dizziness, impaired memory, and loss of coordination, which are infrequent side effects from diazepam, occur far more often in older people than they do in younger people. All of these side effects are reversible. However, because their onset can be so slow, they are sometimes not associated with the offending drug. Furthermore, just as these side effects are often slow to appear, they are equally slow in disappearing after diazepam is stopped. If you are aware of this possibility, it probably won't become a problem for you.

Your doctor will take your age into consideration in

selecting a dose and dosage schedule that are likely to be appropriate for you.

DIFLUNISAL

OTHER NAMES   Diflunisal (pronounced *dye-FLOO-ni-sal)* is the common or generic name of this drug. A frequently used brand name for diflunisal is Dolobid. Diflunisal belongs to a large group of drugs called non-steroidal anti-inflammatory drugs (NSAIDs). It is chemically related to aspirin and other salicylate drugs.

WHAT IS IT SUPPOSED TO DO?   Diflunisal relieves the pain, inflammation, swelling, and stiffness associated with arthritis. It also relieves the pain caused by injuries, surgery, or cancer.

Although some relief of arthritic symptoms should be apparent shortly after the first dose, maximum relief occurs after a week or more of regular use.

SIDE EFFECTS   Indigestion, heartburn, nausea, stomach discomfort, excessive gas, diarrhea, and other problems related to the digestive tract are the most common side effects. These can sometimes be prevented by taking diflunisal with a full glass of water. (Always swallow diflunisal tablets whole; never break or crush them.) If gastrointestinal side effects persist, or if they are severe, stop taking the drug and contact your doctor.

Rarely, diflunisal causes more severe problems in the digestive tract. These include ulcer with bleeding into the gastrointestinal tract (evidenced by bloody stools or stools that are discolored dark red or black) and small amounts of painless blood loss (which can cause anemia). The risk of these problems is lower than it is with aspirin.

Diflunisal can also cause mental effects such as drowsiness, headache, or dizziness. Because diflunisal can cause decreased alertness in some individuals, you should evaluate how this drug affects you before you drive an automobile or operate any potentially dangerous machinery. If you should develop any sort of visual difficulty (such as blurred or dim vision) or hearing problem (such as buzzing or ringing in your ears), stop taking the drug and contact your doctor.

Kidney problems caused by diflunisal and similar drugs are relatively rare, but most of the cases that have been reported in the medical literature involved older individuals. Some of the medical problems that are more prevalent among older people place them at greater risk for this side effect. When kidneys are stressed by congestive heart failure, dehydration, or any kind of kidney impairment (even modest impairment), the body responds by producing substances called prostaglandins. Prostaglandins increase the flow of blood to the kidneys and increase their efficiency. Diflunisal and related drugs can block this compensatory response, and kidney failure (usually reversible) can occur as a result. (All nonsteroidal anti-inflammatory drugs work by preventing the body from manufacturing prostaglandins, which are also mediators of pain and inflammation.) Considering the widespread use of diflunisal among older people and the extremely small number of kidney problems that have been reported, the risk appears to be quite small. However, you should return to your doctor for regular medical checkups while taking this drug. Contact your doctor promptly if you experience sudden weight gain, swelling of your feet or ankles, or markedly decreased urine production.

Skin problems such as rashes or unusual reactions to the sun are rarely associated with diflunisal. Contact your doctor if you experience anything unusual.

When taken regularly, diflunisal prevents fever from occurring. This effect, combined with its pain-relieving and anti-inflammatory actions, could be considered a side effect if the signs of an infection were masked, and the infection went undetected (and untreated) too long.

If you have ever developed asthma as an allergic reaction to aspirin, you should not take diflunisal, because a similar allergic reaction could occur.

Other side effects from diflunisal are too rare to list

here. Contact your doctor if you experience any unusual symptoms.

DRUG INTERACTIONS   Several drugs have the potential to interact with diflunisal:

Antacids decrease the absorption of diflunisal when
both are taken on an empty stomach. This interaction
does not appear to be significant when diflunisal is
taken with food.

Aspirin is potentially irritating to the digestive tract,
and its irritant effects could become troublesome when
added to those of diflunisal. Check with your doctor
before taking this drug combination.

Diuretics, such as *hydrochlorothiazide (HydroDIURIL
and other brands) or furosemide (Lasix).* Infrequently,
diflunisal causes fluid retention and edema. If you are
taking a diuretic for fluid retention and edema (such as
that caused by congestive heart failure or liver disease)
and you experience a worsening of your symptoms
while taking diflunisal, stop taking your diflunisal and
contact your doctor.

Warfarin (Coumadin). Diflunisal may increase the effects of warfarin by displacing it from the proteins in
the blood where it is stored. In addition, diflunisal can
cause some gastrointestinal bleeding, which could be
worsened by the anticoagulant effects of warfarin.
Other NSAIDs are probably safer with warfarin.

ALCOHOLIC BEVERAGES   Alcohol adds to the
gastric-irritant effects of diflunisal. Avoid taking them
at the same time.

FOOD   Food slows the absorption of diflunisal somewhat, but it doesn't impair its absorption. It's a good
idea to take your diflunisal with food to minimize any
gastric irritation that might occur.

**HOW DOES AGE AFFECT THE RESPONSE TO THIS
DRUG?**   Older individuals are more sensitive to side
effects from diflunisal.

DIGOXIN

OTHER NAMES Digoxin (pronounced *di-JOX-in)* is the common or generic name of this drug. Its principal brand names are Lanoxin and Lanoxicaps. These brands provide the most reliable dosage forms of this drug, which has a narrow margin for safe use. Digoxin is a purified derivative of one of the species of digitalis plants, *Digitalis lanata,* a close relative of the common foxglove plant. The dried leaves of digitalis plants, which have been used medicinally for more than two centuries, contain several drugs that have similar effects on the heart. Although these drugs differ markedly from one another in their onset and duration of action, they are all referred to as digitalis. Digoxin is the most widely used form of digitalis.

WHAT IS IT SUPPOSED TO DO? Digoxin makes the heart beat more forcefully. It also slows the heart and makes it beat more regularly.

Use in Congestive Heart Failure. Congestive heart failure, a frequent complaint with advancing age, has many causes, but the results are always the same. When the heart's pumping action is inadequate, the circulation becomes congested, and salt and water leak out of veins, causing abnormal fluid accumulation in tissues. Eventually, fluid accumulation occurs in the lungs, and breathing becomes labored. (There are, of course, many other causes of respiratory difficulty.) The treatment of congestive heart failure includes limitation of activity (at least temporarily), removal of its causes (if possible), restriction of salt intake, treatment with diuretics, and, for many individuals, digoxin. Unlike diuretics, which relieve congestive heart failure by virtue of their effects on the kidneys, digoxin acts directly on the heart, causing it to contract more forcefully and efficiently. Circulation is improved, and the symptoms are reversed. Of course, your physician will determine the cause and severity of your congestive heart failure before deciding that digoxin is an appropriate treatment.

Use in Irregular Heart Rhythms. In addition to its principal effect of increasing the forcefulness of the heart's contractions, digoxin slows the heart and makes it beat more regularly. These properties are beneficial in certain types of cardiac arrhythmia, or irregular heartbeat. It is most often used in the treatment of atrial fibrillation, a condition in which the normal rhythmical contractions of the smaller chambers of the heart are replaced by rapid, irregular twitchings, which in turn cause the larger chambers of the heart to beat too rapidly. In this situation, digoxin slows the heart and makes it work more efficiently.

SIDE EFFECTS Under normal circumstances, you will not experience any side effects. However, the therapeutic (effective) dose and the toxic dose of digoxin are closer together than they are for most drugs. The amount of digoxin that is required for its tonic effects on the heart is only slightly less than the amount that can cause dangerous abnormal heartbeats. For this reason, it is essential that you take your digoxin exactly as prescribed and that you promptly contact your physician should you develop any signs that might be indicative of digoxin toxicity.

The most common signs of digoxin toxicity are marked loss of appetite, nausea, and vomiting. Unfortunately, these are rather nonspecific signs; they often occur in people who aren't even taking digoxin. To be safe, however, you should take them as an indication to contact your doctor. Other common signs of digoxin toxicity are confusion; abnormally colored vision, blurred vision, or any visual disturbance; diarrhea; extremely slow pulse rate or irregular pulse; and sudden and severe mood change. By examining you, possibly with the aid of an electrocardiogram and a blood test that measures the concentration of digoxin in your blood, your doctor can determine whether or not your symptoms are due to digoxin toxicity.

DRUG INTERACTIONS   Several drugs can interact with digoxin. Special precautions should be taken if any of the following drugs need to be taken with digoxin:

Antacids can impair the absorption of digoxin. Don't take antacids at the same time that you take your daily dose of digoxin. If you require an antacid, take it two hours before or one hour after your digoxin dose.

Bile-acid sequestrants, such as *cholestyramine resin (Questran) and colestipol (Colestid),* are used to lower the concentration of cholesterol in the blood. They are also used to treat the itching that sometimes occurs with jaundice. These drugs may bind to digoxin in the gastrointestinal tract and thereby prevent its full absorption. If therapy with one of these drugs is necessary, the digoxin dose should be taken at least two hours before the cholestyramine or colestipol dose to minimize any interaction.

Diuretics, such as *hydrochlorothiazide (Esidrex, HydroDIURIL, and others), furosemide (Lasix), and others,* interact with digoxin in a way that is so well known among physicians and pharmacists that it seldom becomes a problem. Diuretics act on the kidneys to cause the removal of excess salt and water from the body. They are often used with digoxin for the treatment of congestive heart failure, both drugs working by different mechanisms to help the heart do its job more efficiently. However, one of the side effects of potent diuretics is the promotion of potassium loss from the body. If the amount of potassium in the blood becomes too low, then digoxin toxicity might occur. To prevent this problem, physicians monitor the concentration of potassium in the blood and sometimes prescribe either a potassium supplement or second diuretic that conserves potassium.

Kaolin-pectin (Kaopectate and others), which is used to treat diarrhea, can impair the absorption of digoxin. Don't take kaolin-pectin at the same time that you take your daily dose of digoxin. The digoxin can be taken two hours after or one hour before the kaolin-pectin.

Quinidine (Cardioquin, Quinidex, Quinora, and others), which is used to make the heart beat more regularly, can cause a substantial increase in the concentration of digoxin in your body. If both drugs are required (a common occurrence), your doctor will give you a smaller dose of digoxin than would otherwise be required.

Spironolactone (Aldactone) is a mild diuretic that causes potassium to be retained by the body rather than being lost (see Diuretics, above). Spironolactone interferes with certain of the assays used to measure the concentration of digoxin in the blood, causing false reports of elevated digoxin concentrations. In addition, there is limited evidence that spironolactone may also decrease the elimination of digoxin from the body, causing true elevations of the concentration of digoxin in the blood and thereby increasing the risk of digoxin toxicity. If you are taking spironolactone with digoxin, be sure your doctor is aware that you are taking both drugs.

Sympathomimetics, which are contained in some nonprescription remedies for nasal congestion, can cause the heart to beat irregularly in some individuals. The risk is probably greater when you are taking digoxin. Check with your pharmacist before taking any medication for nasal congestion.

Verapamil (Calan, Isoptin), which is used to prevent irregular heart rhythms and to prevent angina attacks, increases the concentration of digoxin in the blood. Ask your doctor to reevaluate your digoxin dosage if you start or stop taking verapamil.

ALCOHOLIC BEVERAGES Digoxin does not interact with alcoholic beverages.

FOOD Food does not impair the absorption of digoxin in any significant way. You may want to take your digoxin with breakfast, along with any other drugs you are taking (unless there is some interaction—see Drug Interactions), if this will help you remember to take it.

Be sure to follow any dietary advice, such as low-salt diet, that you may have received with your prescription.

HOW DOES AGE AFFECT THE RESPONSE TO THIS DRUG?   Generally speaking, advancing age is accompanied by greater sensitivity to digoxin. Because digoxin is removed from the body by the kidneys, and kidney function steadily decreases with age, older people require smaller doses of digoxin. Your doctor will take your age, weight, kidney function, and type of heart problem into consideration in determining the correct dose of digoxin for you.

In order to calculate the correct dose of digoxin for you, your doctor will need to evaluate how efficiently your kidneys are carrying out their work. This assessment is most commonly based on a blood test that measures the concentration of creatinine in the blood. Creatinine is a normal metabolic waste product that is filtered out of the blood by the kidneys and excreted in the urine. A decrease in kidney function is usually accompanied by an elevated concentration of creatinine in the blood. However, your age will be considered in interpreting this test. Because muscle tissue is the source of creatinine in the blood and muscle mass decreases with age, creatinine production decreases with age. Therefore, a seventy-year-old person, whose kidney function has steadily decreased during the past thirty years, may have the same concentration of creatinine in his blood as someone who is thirty years old. To get around this problem, your doctor will apply a formula to the measured concentration of creatinine and modify it with respect to your age, sex, and weight (see appendix).

During the past fifteen years, a great deal of research has been directed toward developing assays for measuring the concentration of digoxin in the blood and correlating these concentrations with therapeutic and toxic effects. Although these assays are not perfect in their assessment of drug effect, they are widely used, and they have reduced the incidence of digoxin toxicity.

The assessment of kidney function and, to some extent, the measurement of digoxin concentration in the blood allow digoxin doses to be tailored for each pa-

tient so that the response will be the same regardless of age.

DILTIAZEM

OTHER NAMES   Diltiazem (pronounced *dill-TIE-a-zem*) is the common or generic name of this drug. Its most frequently used brand name is Cardizem. Pharmacologists refer to diltiazem as a calcium channel blocker.

WHAT IS IT SUPPOSED TO DO?   Diltiazem deceases the occurrence of angina pectoris, the chest pain that is caused by a deficiency in oxygen supply to the heart muscle. It works by inhibiting the movement of calcium into the cells of the specialized muscle tissue in the walls of certain blood vessels (arterioles), thereby causing a relaxation of this muscle and dilation of the blood vessel. This widening in the diameter of the vessels that carry blood to the heart muscle improves its circulation and supplies it with more oxygen. Diltiazem also causes a widening in the diameter of the blood vessels that the heart pumps into (the ones that create a resistance to the heart's pumping action). The heart's workload is thereby decreased because it is pumping against less resistance—pharmacologists call this a decrease in afterload. This decrease in workload causes the heart to use less oxygen.

Although the current primary use of diltiazem is for angina, its effects on blood vessels are of value in the treatment of high blood pressure. Diltiazem also has some effect on the heart muscle itself, which may prove to be of value in preventing certain types of irregular heartbeats.

Like other calcium channel blockers, diltiazem's effects on calcium are limited to specialized muscle tissues. It has no effect on the concentration of calcium in the blood, and, under normal circumstances, it is unaffected by calcium in the diet or by calcium supplements.

SIDE EFFECTS Side effects from diltiazem are infrequent. In a study of nearly four thousand patients, the incidence of side effects was less than 2 percent, and none of these were serious. Possible side effects include nausea and loss of appetite (there is one report of altered sense of smell and taste), headache, dizziness, and tiredness. If any of these become persistent or bothersome, contact your doctor.

Because diltiazem also has a direct effect on the heart muscle, you should learn to take your pulse and contact your doctor if it should become slower than fifty beats per minute. Likewise, you should contact your doctor if you develop shortness of breath or swollen feet or ankles (possible signs of congestive heart failure). These side effects are infrequent. Rash, another infrequent side effect, should also be brought to your doctor's attention.

Other side effects are too rare to list here. Contact your doctor if you experience any unexpected symptoms.

DRUG INTERACTIONS Several drugs can interact with diltiazem:

Antidiabetic drugs, such as *insulin* or the *sulfonylureas.* Other calcium channel blockers have caused an increase in the concentration of sugar in the blood of some individuals, and there is one report of diltiazem causing this effect. Therefore, your diabetes therapy should be reevaluated after you begin taking diltiazem.

Beta-blocking drugs, such as *atenolol (Tenormin), metoprolol (Lopressor), nadolol (Corgard), propranolol (Inderal), pindolol (Visken), or timolol (Blocadren).* A beta-blocking drug is sometimes prescribed together with diltiazem because the two drugs work by different mechanisms that complement each other in the treatment of angina or hypertension. For most patients, it's a beneficial combination. However, in rare instances this drug combination can cause either abnormally low blood pressure (dizziness, fainting), too slow a pulse rate (less than fifty beats per minute), or congestive heart failure (swelling of feet or ankles, difficulty in breathing). Contact your doctor if you experience these or other unexpected symptoms.

Calcium, if taken in large enough amounts, can block the effects of diltiazem. This is true of intravenous infusions of calcium and calcium taken in combination with large doses of vitamin D. It is unlikely that a diet rich in calcium or one that is modestly supplemented with calcium would cause this effect. However, you should be alert for the possibility of loss of diltiazem effect if you are taking calcium supplements.

Digoxin (Lanoxin), which is used in the treatment of congestive heart failure and to prevent certain types of irregular heartbeats, slows the heart rate. Diltiazem can cause further slowing of the heart rate. Contact your doctor if your pulse becomes slower than fifty beats per minute or if you think you are experiencing a worsening of your congestive heart failure. There is limited evidence that diltiazem can cause slight increases in the concentration of digoxin in the blood, so your digoxin therapy should be reevaluated after you start taking diltiazem. (There is also some evidence that diltiazem has no effect on the concentration of digoxin in the blood.) A large number of patients have taken digoxin and diltiazem together without adverse effect.

ALCOHOLIC BEVERAGES   Alcohol is more likely to cause dizziness or unsteadiness while you are taking diltiazem. Be careful until you determine the effects of this combination.

FOOD   Take your diltiazem with meals to help you maintain a regular schedule for taking it.

HOW DOES AGE AFFECT THE RESPONSE TO THIS DRUG?   There is preliminary evidence that aging slows the removal of diltiazem from the body (it is metabolized by the liver), which suggests that smaller doses are appropriate for older people. Your doctor will prescribe a dosage that is likely to be appropriate for you.

DIPHENHYDRAMINE

OTHER NAMES Diphenhydramine (pronounced *dye-fen-HYE-dra-meen)* is the common or generic name of this drug. The most frequently used brand name for diphenhydramine in capsule form is Benadryl. Some frequently used brand names for liquid diphenhydramine are Benadryl and Benylin. There are many nonprescription sleeping tablets that contain diphenhydramine as their active ingredient. Among these are Compoz, Nytol with DPH, Sleep-Eze 3, and Sominex Formula 2. A prescription cough remedy called Ambenyl Cough Syrup contains diphenhydramine and codeine. Diphenhydramine belongs to a large and chemically diverse group of drugs called antihistamines.

WHAT IS IT SUPPOSED TO DO? Like other antihistamines, diphenhydramine blocks the effect of histamine, a chemical the body produces in large amounts during allergic reactions. Even in the absence of allergy, histamine is present in many tissues throughout the body.

Diphenhydramine is used for the relief of allergic symptoms such as runny nose, watery eyes, and itching. Because it causes drowsiness in most people, it is often used to induce sleep. It also suppresses cough, prevents motion sickness, decreases the stiffness and tremor of Parkinson's disease, and alleviates nausea.

SIDE EFFECTS The most common side effect from diphenhydramine is drowsiness, an effect that is beneficial in some instances. Avoid driving while under the influence of this drug. Less frequently, it causes dizziness, weakness, or clumsiness.

In addition to blocking some of the receptors for histamine, diphenhydramine blocks the receptors for acetylcholine, another substance produced by the body. This accounts for the dry mouth you may experience from diphenhydramine. If the dose is too high for you or if you are taking other drugs that also block the effects of acetylcholine—anticholinergic drugs (see Drug Interactions), you may experience other anticholinergic effects, including blurred vision, difficult urination (more common in older men), nervousness or restlessness, confusion or disorientation, and racing or pounding heartbeat. Contact your doctor if you experience any of these infrequent symptoms.

Other side effects are too rare to list here. If you experience any unusual symptoms, contact your doctor.

DRUG INTERACTIONS   Several drugs interact with diphenhydramine. These are most likely to cause problems:

Anticholinergic drugs, such as *belladonna (Donnatal) or propantheline (Pro-Banthine),* sometimes used in the treatment of peptic-ulcer disease, *benztropine (Cogentin) or trihexyphenidyl (Artane),* used to treat Parkinson's disease and the side effects of some tranquilizers, and *scopolamine (Transderm Scōp),* used to prevent motion sickness, all work by blocking the effects of acetylcholine, which is what *anticholinergic* means. In addition to these primarily anticholinergic drugs, many drugs have anticholinergic side effects. The most important are *tranquilizers,* such as *thioridazine (Mellaril) and trifluoperazine (Stelazine);* the *tricyclic antidepressants,* such as *amitriptyline (Elavil), desipramine (Norpramin, Pertofrane), doxepin (Sinequan), imipramine (Tofranil), or nortriptyline (Aventyl);* and the antiarrhythmic drug *disopyramide (Norpace).* Because diphenhydramine also blocks acetylcholine, it is more likely to cause anticholinergic side effects when taken with these drugs (see Side Effects).

The *sedative effects* of drugs like the *anticholinergic drugs* listed above, *benzodiazepines, narcotics, and barbiturates* will be increased by diphenhydramine.

ALCOHOLIC BEVERAGES   Alcohol will increase the drowsiness from diphenhydramine. Avoid alcohol or limit your use to small amounts; the combined effects could lead to falls or accidents.

FOOD Diphenhydramine works most rapidly when taken on an empty stomach. If you are among the few people who experience upset stomach from diphenhydramine, take it with food.

HOW DOES AGE AFFECT THE RESPONSE TO THIS DRUG? Age does not affect the rate at which diphenhydramine is metabolized and removed from the blood. However, changes in the brain that occur with aging make anticholinergic side effects more likely to occur.

DIPYRIDAMOLE

OTHER NAMES Dipyridamole (pronounced *dye-peer-ID-a-mole)* is the common or generic name of this drug. Some frequently used brand names for dipyridamole are Persantine, Pyridamole, and SK-Dipyridamole.

WHAT IS IT SUPPOSED TO DO? Dipyridamole is sometimes prescribed in combination with small doses of aspirin or aspirin plus a beta-blocking drug to prevent the recurrence of heart attacks. It is also sometimes used in combination with warfarin to prevent blood clots after heart surgery.

Dipyridamole may prevent angina attacks in some individuals, but it will not relieve angina pain once an attack has occurred.

SIDE EFFECTS In the doses that are usually used, side effects from dipyridamole are not common. Infrequent side effects are dizziness, flushing, headache, nausea, and stomach discomfort. If any of these is persistent or bothersome, contact your doctor.

Rarely, it causes chest pain in patients with angina, usually at the beginning of therapy. Contact your doctor if this occurs.

Other side effects are too rare to list here. Contact your doctor if you experience any unexpected symptoms.

DRUG INTERACTIONS It is unlikely that this drug will interact in an adverse way with your other medications, but if you are taking other drugs that share dipyridamole's infrequent side effects, then the risk of these side effects will be increased.

ALCOHOLIC BEVERAGES   Be careful until you have determined whether this drug affects your response to alcohol. Dizziness or light-headedness from alcohol are more likely to occur.

FOOD   Dipyridamole works best when taken on an empty stomach, with a full glass of water or other non-irritating liquid, at least an hour before meals. If it upsets your stomach, however, take it with meals or with a snack.

HOW DOES AGE AFFECT THE RESPONSE TO THIS DRUG?   Dizziness, an infrequent side effect that may occur from large doses, or smaller doses in sensitive individuals, is more likely to occur with advancing age. Be careful not to stand up too quickly. If this side effect is bothersome, contact your doctor.

DISOPYRAMIDE

OTHER NAMES   Disopyramide (pronounced *dye-so-PEER-a-mide*) is the common or generic name of this drug. A frequently used brand name for disopyramide is Norpace.

WHAT IS IT SUPPOSED TO DO?   Disopyramide acts directly on the heart muscle to slow it and make it beat more regularly. It prevents certain irregular heartbeats.

SIDE EFFECTS   The most common side effect from disopyramide is dry mouth. This side effect may decrease in intensity as you become accustomed to the drug, but if it is unacceptably bothersome, contact your doctor. Sugarless candy or gum may provide some relief.

The dry mouth caused by disopyramide is an example of what pharmacologists call an anticholinergic effect. It can be caused by any drug that blocks the receptors for acetylcholine, a substance that the body produces to regulate certain functions that are beyond conscious control. When disopyramide is taken with other drugs that have anticholinergic side effects, these side effects are more likely to cause problems (see Drug Interactions). Other, less frequent anticholinergic effects that may be bothersome include constipation, blurred vision, and dry eyes or nose.

Disopyramide's propensity to cause anticholinergic side effects can lead to problems that require medical attention. The most frequent is difficult urination, which is more likely to occur in older men. (An unusually frequent urge to urinate is an infrequent side effect that does not require medical attention unless it is unacceptably bothersome.) An infrequent anticholinergic side effect is confusion or disorientation, sometimes with visual hallucinations. Eye pain is a possible sign that glaucoma has been aggravated by the anticholinergic effects of the drug.

Other adverse effects can be caused by disopyramide's effect on the heart. Contact your doctor if you experience chest pain; dizziness, light-headedness, fainting (from abnormally low blood pressure); unusually slow or fast heartbeat; or rapid weight gain, swelling of the feet or lower legs, or unexplained shortness of breath (possible signs of congestive heart failure); or weakness.

Rarely, disopyramide decreases the concentration of glucose (the body's form of sugar) in the blood. Most of the individuals who experienced this side effect also had congestive heart failure, poor nutrition, liver disease, or poor kidney function. The signs of too low a concentration of glucose in the blood (hypoglycemia) are rapid onset of weakness, hunger or nausea, cold sweats, pounding or racing heartbeat, shakiness, headache, nervousness, tingling lips or mouth, drowsiness, confusion, light-headedness, or dizziness. If any of these signs occur, contact your doctor.

Other side effects are too rare to list here. If you experience any unusual symptoms, contact your doctor.

DRUG INTERACTIONS   These drugs can cause problems when taken with disopyramide:

Other *antiarrhythmic drugs* (drugs for irregular heartbeat) will increase the likelihood of disopyramide side effects related to the heart (see Side Effects). Do not take any other antiarrhythmic drugs while taking disopyramide without checking with your doctor.

Anticholinergic drugs (so named because they block the effects of acetylcholine), such as *belladonna (Donnatal) or propantheline (Pro-Banthine)*, which are sometimes used in the treatment of peptic-ulcer disease, *benztropine (Cogentin) or trihexyphenidyl (Artane)*, which are used in the treatment of Parkinson's disease and to treat the side effects sometimes caused by tranquilizers, and *scopolamine (Transderm Scōp)*, which is used to prevent motion sickness, compound the anticholinergic side effects of disopyramide (see Side Effects). In addition, many drugs have anticholinergic side effects. The most important are *tranquilizers*, such as *thioridazine (Mellaril) and trifluoperazine (Stelazine); tricyclic antidepressants*, such as *amitriptyline (Elavil), desipramine (Norpramin, Pertofrane), doxepin (Sinequan), imipramine (Tofranil), and nortriptyline (Aventyl);* and *antihistamines*. These drugs are more likely to cause anticholinergic side effects when taken with disopyramide. Check with your doctor before taking them together.

Smoking is not advisable in the presence of serious heart-rhythm problems. In addition, there is some evidence that disopyramide is more rapidly removed from the bodies of heavy smokers than nonsmokers. This interaction is significant in older but not younger individuals. Heavy smokers may require relatively larger doses than they would if they were nonsmokers.

ALCOHOLIC BEVERAGES   Use alcohol in moderation or avoid it entirely. Alcohol may cause dizziness when taken with disopyramide. Drinking on an empty stomach may predispose you to hypoglycemia.

FOOD   Disopyramide can be taken with food or on an empty stomach. You should avoid fasting, which increases the risk of hypoglycemia from disopyramide.

HOW DOES AGE AFFECT THE RESPONSE TO THIS DRUG?   Disopyramide is removed from the body more slowly with advancing age. Older people require smaller doses than younger people of the same body weight. Part of the greater sensitivity of older people to disopyramide can be explained by the normal decline in kidney function that occurs with aging; more than half of each dose of disopyramide is eliminated unchanged by the kidneys. Your doctor will evaluate your kidney function (see appendix) in determining an appropriate dosage for you.

DOXEPIN

OTHER NAMES   Doxepin (pronounced *DOX-e-pin)* is the common or generic name of this drug. Some frequently used brand names for doxepin are Adapin and Sinequan. Doxepin belongs to a group of drugs called tricyclic antidepressants. *Tricyclic* describes their structure; *antidepressant* refers to their principal pharmacological effect.

WHAT IS IT SUPPOSED TO DO?   Doxepin relieves mental depression. The precise means by which it works has not been established, but its mechanism of action involves an increase in the concentration of certain naturally occurring substances (serotonin and norepinephrine) within the brain. Elevation of mood and reversal of the various symptoms that can accompany depression (such as sleep problems, decreased energy, or loss of appetite) require a minimum of several weeks of regular use. Your doctor may prescribe less than several weeks' supply of medication initially, so it is important that you return to your pharmacy to have your prescription refilled. Your doctor may want you to continue taking doxepin for several months after your mood returns to normal.

SIDE EFFECTS Nearly everyone experiences dry mouth while taking doxepin. It doesn't seem to be related to dosage, and it tends to diminish with time. Sugar-free candy or gum is often helpful in alleviating this problem.

Drowsiness is another common side effect. Avoid driving until you are sure that your alertness and coordination are not impaired.

The most common potentially serious side effect involves the temporary decrease in blood pressure that occurs when you stand up quickly. This decrease in blood pressure is exaggerated by doxepin and is likely to make you dizzy, light-headed, or faint if you stand up too quickly. If this side effect is severe (especially if it causes you to fall or causes your heart to pound or race), contact your doctor. Be very careful to stand up slowly.

The dry mouth caused by doxepin is an example of what pharmacologists call an anticholinergic effect. It can be caused by any drug that blocks the receptors for acetylcholine, a substance the body produces to regulate certain functions that are beyond conscious control. When doxepin is taken with other drugs that have anticholinergic side effects, these side effects are more likely to cause problems (see Drug Interactions). A common anticholinergic side effect is constipation. Ask your pharmacist for appropriate treatment; a stool softener is often helpful. Contact your doctor if constipation becomes severe. Another anticholinergic side effect is the sudden onset of confusion or disorientation, sometimes with visual hallucinations. If this occurs, contact your doctor; it is a sign that the dosage is too high for you. Other anticholinergic side effects that require your doctor's attention (and these are infrequent or rare) include blurred vision, difficulty in urinating (more common in older men with prostate difficulties), and eye pain (a possible indication that narrow-angle glaucoma, not the usual type of glaucoma, has been aggravated)

Effects on the heart—excessively fast, slow, or irregular heartbeat—are infrequent. Contact your doctor if any of these occur.

Other side effects include nausea, unpleasant taste, diarrhea (infrequent), and excessive sweating (infrequent). These side effects may diminish or go away as your body adjusts to the effects of this drug. Contact your doctor if they are severe or bothersome. A fine tremor is not an uncommon side effect in older people; tell your doctor if this occurs.

Other side effects are too infrequent to list here. Contact your doctor if you experience any unexpected symptoms.

DRUG INTERACTIONS Doxepin interacts with a number of drugs. Here are the most common sources of potential problems:

Anticholinergic drugs, such as *belladonna (Donnatal) or propantheline (Pro-Banthine),* which are used for peptic-ulcer disease, *benztropine (Cogentin),* which is used in the treatment of Parkinson's disease and to treat the side effects sometimes caused by tranquilizers, and *scopolamine (Transderm Scōp),* which is used to prevent motion sickness, all work by blocking acetylcholine (see Side Effects). These drugs are more likely to cause anticholinergic side effects when taken with doxepin. In many cases, the anticholinergic side effects of doxepin obviate the need for these other drugs. Check with your doctor before taking them.

Antihistamines, which are included in many nonprescription cold and allergy medicines, have sedative and anticholinergic (see above) side effects. Avoid these products while taking doxepin.

Antihypertensive drugs can interact with doxepin by several mechanisms. First, some of them (beta-blockers, clonidine, methyldopa, and reserpine) can cause depression as a side effect. Second, the action of a few antihypertensive drugs is blocked by doxepin. If you are taking clonidine (Catapres, Combipres), guanethidine (Ismelin), or guanadrel (Hylorel), your doctor will need to prescribe another drug to control your blood pressure. Third, if your antihypertensive drug causes dizziness, doxepin will make this side effect worse. Your doctor may need to decrease the dose of your antihypertensive drug before you start taking doxepin.

Cimetidine (Tagamet), which is used in the treatment of peptic-ulcer disease, slows the metabolism of doxepin and thereby increases its effects. Contact your doctor if you experience an increase in doxepin side effects while taking cimetidine; your doctor may have to lower the dosage of your doxepin temporarily.

Monoamine oxidase inhibitors, such as *isocarboxazid (Marplan), phenelzine (Nardil),* or *tranylcypromine (Parnate),* which are also used in the treatment of depression, sometimes cause dangerous toxic reactions when taken with doxepin. This combination of drugs should only be used in hospitalized patients who are under careful observation. Normally, one or two weeks are allowed to elapse between the use of doxepin and one of these drugs.

Phenobarbital, which is used to prevent seizures and is also sometimes included as an ingredient in certain medications for its sedative effects, stimulates the metabolism of doxepin and thereby decreases its effects. If you require treatment with phenobarbital, your doctor will take this into consideration in adjusting your doxepin dosage. Otherwise, your doctor may replace your phenobarbital-containing medication with another drug product.

Phenothiazine tranquilizers, such as *perphenazine (Trilafon), thioridazine (Mellaril),* or *trifluoperazine (Stelazine),* are more likely to cause anticholinergic side effects (see Side Effects) when taken with doxepin. In addition, these drugs may slow the metabolism of doxepin and thereby increase its effects. There are instances when these drugs need to be given with doxepin, but you should be sure that your doctor intends for you take this combination.

Propoxyphene (Darvocet-N, Darvon), which is taken for the relief of pain, slows the metabolism of doxepin and increases the concentration of doxepin in the blood. Because this combination may cause doxepin toxicity, another pain reliever should be used.

ALCOHOLIC BEVERAGES Alcohol will increase the dizziness or faintness you may feel upon standing up too quickly. It will also add to the drowsiness that doxepin often causes. Therefore, you should avoid alcohol or use it sparingly while taking doxepin.

FOOD Take your doxepin with meals to help you maintain a regular schedule for taking it and to prevent any nausea it might cause.

HOW DOES AGE AFFECT THE RESPONSE TO THIS DRUG? Doxepin is metabolized in the liver by a process that slows with aging, and, although there is considerable variation among individuals, older people tend to develop higher concentrations of doxepin in their blood. Therefore, older people usually require smaller doses than younger people.

In addition, older people are more sensitive to side effects from doxepin. Your doctor will try to prescribe a dose that is likely to be effective without causing serious side effects.

ENALAPRIL

OTHER NAMES Enalapril (pronounced *en-AL-a-pril*) is the common or generic name of this drug. The most frequently used brand name for enalapril is Vasotec. A combination of enalapril and the diuretic hydrochlorothiazide is frequently prescribed under the brand name Vaseretic. Enalapril belongs to a new class of drugs called angiotensin-converting-enzyme (ACE) inhibitors.

WHAT IS IT SUPPOSED TO DO? Enalapril lowers high blood pressure. It also relieves the symptoms of congestive heart failure. Enalapril prevents the body from making a hormone called angiotensin II, which is instrumental in both of these diseases. Angiotensin II is the most potent elevator of blood pressure currently known. Angiotensin II also stimulates the adrenal glands to produce another hormone, aldosterone, which acts on the kidneys to retain salt and water and excrete potassium. Enalapril inhibits an enzyme (angiotensin-converting enzyme) required for the formation of angiotensin II and thereby prevents its undesirable effects.

Use in Hypertension. Enalapril is very effective in lowering high blood pressure. People who respond poorly to other antihypertensive drugs usually respond well to enalapril. In addition, it causes fewer unpleasant side effects than most other antihypertensives. It is sometimes prescribed with a thiazide diuretic, which increases its effects.

Use in Congestive Heart Failure. Enalapril reverses several of the complex events that contribute to congestive heart failure. By lowering blood pressure, it decreases the heart's workload. Improved blood flow to the kidneys and decreased secretion of aldosterone (see above) cause excess fluid to be removed from the body. Enalapril is often prescribed in addition to diuretics and digoxin, which work by other mechanisms to relieve congestive heart failure.

SIDE EFFECTS Side effects from enalapril are infrequent.

Infrequent or rare side effects include dizziness, lightheadedness, or fainting; swelling of the face, mouth, hands, or feet; rash; and chest pain. If these or any other symptoms occur, you should contact your doctor promptly.

Diarrhea or vomiting can cause substantial loss of sodium and water from the body, and this can make you overly sensitive to enalapril's effects on blood pressure. Therefore, you should check with your doctor whenever you are sick with continued vomiting or diarrhea.

If you are taking enalapril for congestive heart failure, you will probably notice that your capacity for exercise or exertion is improved. It is important to avoid overdoing it—ask your doctor how much activity is safe for you.

Rarely, enalapril causes changes in the sense of taste. This side effect usually goes away with continued use, but if it is bothersome, contact your doctor.

Other side effects are too rare to list here. Contact your doctor if you experience any unexpected symptoms.

DRUG INTERACTIONS Several drugs can interact adversely with enalapril:

Diuretics, such as *hydrochlorothiazide (HydroDIURIL) or furosemide (Lasix),* can interact adversely with the initial dose of enalapril. People who have been taking diuretics sometimes have low concentrations of sodium in their blood. In this situation, enalapril can cause an unusually profound drop in blood pressure after the first dose. The risk of this side effect, which can cause you to faint, is greatest in those with congestive heart failure and in those who have been taking large doses of a diuretic and restricting the amount of salt in their diets. If you have been taking a diuretic and are about to start taking enalapril, your doctor may measure the concentration of sodium in your blood (to be sure it is not too low) and then begin your enalapril therapy with small doses. Your doctor may tell you to temporarily stop taking your diuretic or temporarily increase your salt intake before starting to take enalapril. The diuretic is usually resumed once your body becomes accustomed to the effects of enalapril. Diuretics are often used in combination with enalapril because they work by mechanisms that are complementary to those of enalapril. Diuretics enhance the effects of enalapril, and enalapril prevents diuretic-induced potassium loss.

Indomethacin (Indocin), which is used for arthritic pain and related problems, may block the antihypertensive effect of enalapril. Your doctor will check for this interaction and may need to prescribe another anti-inflammatory drug. Other nonsteroidal anti-inflammatory drugs have not been studied for their effect on enalapril response, but it is likely that they interact in a similar way but to a lesser degree.

Potassium supplements and *potassium-conserving di-*

uretics, such as triamterene (Dyazide, Dyrenium, Maxzide), amiloride (Midamor, Moduretic), or spironolactone (Aldactazide, Aldactone), can cause too high a concentration of potassium in the blood (hyperkalemia) if taken with enalaparil. As explained above, enalapril prevents aldosterone secretion, thereby causing potassium to be retained by the body. These drugs should be taken with enalapril only when the concentration of potassium in the blood has been demonstrated to be too low. If you are taking this combination, be sure your doctor is monitoring the concentration of potassium in your blood.

ALCOHOLIC BEVERAGES Enalapril should not affect your response to alcohol.

FOOD Enalapril can either be taken with food or on a empty stomach; food does not affect its absorption.

If your doctor has prescribed a low-salt diet, be sure to follow it. Do not use salt substitutes without first checking with your doctor; salt substitutes contain potassium chloride, which may interact with enalapril if used in sufficient amounts (see Drug Interactions, Potassium Supplements).

HOW DOES AGE AFFECT THE RESPONSE TO THIS DRUG? Older people tend to be more sensitive to the effects of enalapril. Significantly reduced kidney function, which is more likely to occur in older people, increases the risk of adverse reactions from enalapril, unless the dosage is reduced accordingly. Therefore, your doctor will assess your kidney function (see appendix) in determining a dosage of enalapril that is likely to be appropriate for you.

ERYTHRITYL TETRANITRATE

OTHER NAMES Erythrityl tetranitrate (pronounced *e-RI-thri-til tet-ra-NYE-trate)* is the common or generic name of this drug. Another, similar generic name for this drug is erythritol tetranitrate. A frequently used brand name for erythrityl tetranitrate is Cardilate. It is available as two types of tablets—regular tablets, which can be either swallowed or dissolved under the tongue, and chewable tablets, which are flavored to prevent unpleasant taste when they are chewed and held in the mouth as long as possible. Be sure you know how to take your erythrityl tetranitrate; the way you take it will determine the rate at which the drug is released into your blood. Erythrityl tetranitrate belongs to a large group of drugs called organic nitrates, which have been used in the treatment of angina for more than a hundred years.

WHAT IS IT SUPPOSED TO DO? Angina pectoris, the chest pain that may be precipitated by exercise, stress, or meals, is caused by a deficiency of oxygen in the heart muscle. Erythrityl tetranitrate relaxes the smooth muscle within the walls of veins and arteries, causing them to dilate (their diameter gets wider). This dilation is beneficial in angina for two reasons. First, blood flow (and therefore oxygen supply) within the heart muscle is increased. Second, circulatory changes throughout the body decrease the heart's workload and therefore its demand for oxygen.

Erythrityl tetranitrate is taken to prevent angina attacks. It works too slowly, even when dissolved under the tongue, to relieve an angina attack that has already started. Chewed or sublingual (dissolved under the tongue) administration results in an effect that begins within about five minutes, is maximal at thirty to forty-five minutes, and persists up to two hours (as long as four hours when chewed). The effects of swallowed tablets begin in about thirty minutes and reach their peak after sixty to ninety minutes.

Although the prevention of angina is the most common use of erythrityl tetranitrate, it is sometimes used in the treatment of congestive heart failure (because of its ability to decrease the heart's workload).

SIDE EFFECTS Although the circulatory changes brought about by erythrityl tetranitrate are beneficial to the heart, they can cause unpleasant effects elsewhere in the body. Headache is the most common side effect. Headache often decreases with continued use. Acetaminophen or aspirin may provide some relief. If your headaches are particularly severe, ask your doctor if the dose can be decreased. You may experience dizziness and weakness, especially when you are standing up. Sit or lie down if you feel dizzy or light-headed (if you don't, you might faint); this will restore circulation to your brain. Exercise, hot weather, standing in one position for a long time, and alcohol can provoke this drug-induced dizziness or light-headedness. Flushing of the face and neck, rapid pulse (unless you are taking a beta-blocker), and nausea can also occur as a result of the circulatory changes brought about by this drug. Contact your doctor if any of these side effects is persistent or severe; the dosage may be too high for you.

After taking erythrityl tetranitrate on a regular basis for a while, you may develop some tolerance to it, and stopping it suddenly could cause a withdrawal reaction. The likelihood of such tolerance is unknown at this time; it may be only a theoretical risk. To be safe, don't stop taking erythrityl tetranitrate without first checking with your doctor, who may wish that you slowly decrease the dosage when stopping it.

Blurred vision, dry mouth, and rash are rare side effects. Contact your doctor if you experience these or any other unexpected symptoms.

DRUG INTERACTIONS Any drug that lowers the blood pressure (as a therapeutic effect or side effect) will make you more sensitive to the dizziness or light-headedness that erythrityl tetranitrate may cause. Nasal decongestants often contain drugs that can provoke an angina attack; check with your pharmacist before using such drugs.

ALCOHOLIC BEVERAGES Alcohol can add significantly to the dilation of blood vessels caused by erythrityl tetranitrate, making dizziness, light-headedness, or fainting much more likely to occur. Be very careful to limit the amount of alcohol you drink.

FOOD   Remember that overeating can cause angina attacks. Exercise immediately after meals is another situation you should avoid. Also, obesity places a strain on your heart and increases the likelihood that you will have angina attacks.

HOW DOES AGE AFFECT THE RESPONSE TO THIS DRUG?   Advancing age increases the susceptibility to dizziness or light-headedness from erythrityl tetranitrate. Therefore, your doctor will begin treatment with small doses. However, there is considerable variation among individuals in the dosages they require.

ESTROGENS

OTHER NAMES   Estrogens (pronounced *ESS-troe-jenz*) are female hormones that the body produces in fluctuating amounts, depending on the time of month and whether pregnancy occurs, from puberty until menopause. After menopause, estrogen production decreases markedly. Men produce only small amounts of estrogens. Estrogens from a variety of synthetic and animal sources are used as drugs. When taken in equivalent doses, all estrogens have similar effects. In the United States, the most commonly prescribed form of estrogen for women over the age of fifty is conjugated estrogens. The most frequently used brand name for conjugated estrogens is Premarin. Other commonly prescribed forms of estrogen for women over fifty (with most frequently used brand names in parentheses) are estradiol (Estrace), ethinyl estradiol (Estinyl), estropipate (Ogen), esterified estrogens (Estratab, Menest), diethylstibestrol, and chlortrianisene (TACE).

WHAT IS IT SUPPOSED TO DO?   In women over the age of fifty, estrogens are most often prescribed to replace the naturally occurring estrogens that the ovaries stop making after menopause. Although the ovaries are the major source of estrogens before menopause, estrogens are also manufactured elsewhere in the body, both before and after menopause.

Nevertheless, about 80 percent of women experience symptoms of estrogen withdrawal at menopause, and this decrease in estrogen can lead to other problems, which are described below.

There are other medical uses for estrogens, such as in the treatment of certain cancers in both men and women and a variety of uses in younger women, most commonly as a constituent of birth control pills, but I am assuming that you are taking the smaller doses that are most commonly prescribed after menopause. These doses are typically the equivalent of 0.625 mg of conjugated estrogens (Premarin) taken daily for the first twenty-five days of each month, followed by no tablets for the remainder of the month to mimic the body's normal production cycle for estrogens. A progestin (a drug that works like the natural hormone, progesterone) is often taken with the estrogen during the sixteenth to twentieth-fifth days of the month to further mimic the body's natural hormone cycle.

Estrogens are the major cause of the changes that take place in girls at puberty. After puberty, estrogens bring about the cyclical buildup of the endometrium (lining of the uterus) and they also control ovulation. When the ovaries temporarily stop making estrogens (and progesterone) at the end of each monthly cycle (if pregnancy has not occurred), the endometrium is shed and menstruation occurs. After menopause, which most often occurs around the age of fifty, there is a marked and permanent decrease in estrogen production, and menstruation no longer occurs. Since menopause and the marked decrease in estrogen production that accompanies it are normal events, why does anyone need to take estrogens after menopause? All women do not need to take estrogens after menopause, but there are several benefits to estrogen use, including the control of the following:

Hot Flashes. The onset of menopause is often accompanied by symptoms of "hot flashes" or "hot flushes"— sudden and intense episodes of sweating or heat throughout the body. Warmth in the face, neck, and chest are related symptoms. Hot flashes during the night cause abrupt awakening from sleep. All of these symptoms are caused by a deficiency of estrogen. Under normal circumstances, the body adjusts to this estrogen deficiency over a period of months to years. However, these symptoms are reversed by small doses of estrogens. Until recently, the treatment of hot flashes was the most common reason for estrogen prescriptions, but the prevention of osteoporosis, which is a more serious threat to health, is now emerging as a more common use.

Osteoporosis. Osteoporosis, or loss of enough bone mass to markedly increase the risk of fractures, is an important health problem among older women. Osteoporosis is responsible for more than 1.2 million fractures per year in the United States alone; these are fractures from simple falls or even less traumatic events. Both men and women achieve their greatest bone mass at age thirty; thereafter, bone density gradually decreases with age. In women, however, the rate of bone loss is markedly accelerated by the estrogen deficiency that occurs with menopause. After age fifty, the average age of menopause, women are many times more likely than men to break bones.

Although women lose the most bone mass during the first seven years after the onset of menopause, most problems occur later. One-third of women over sixty-five have vertebral fractures. These fractures can be either painless or cause temporary back pain. Vertebral fractures cause loss of height, and in some women they can cause back deformities that may lead to a "dowager's hump" posture with chronic back pain.

An even greater problem is hip fracture. Seventy-five to 80 percent of all hip fractures occur in women, and they are most likely to occur after the age of eighty. A woman who lives to be eighty has a remaining life expectancy of nine more years, but a broken hip will significantly decrease her chance of living for more than another year. For those who do survive broken hips, it is often the event that precipitates long-term nursing care. Since about one-third of all women who reach age fifty can expect to live to age eighty-one, these statistics are pertinent to women who are experiencing the first symptoms of menopause.

The greatest likelihood of osteoporosis is in white women and in Asian women. Black women, both in the United States and in Africa, have more bone mass and are far less likely than white women to suffer from osteoporosis. The risk for Hispanic women is not yet known. Thin women are at greater risk than heavy women. Heavy alcohol consumption, cigarette smoking, and deficiency in dietary calcium all increase the risk of osteoporosis. Exercise decreases the risk of osteoporosis. Thiazide diuretics, because they cause the kidneys to conserve calcium, have a mild protective effect against bone loss; it is still too early to know whether this effect is consistent enough or of enough magnitude to be of therapeutic value. The currently available techniques for measuring bone mass are of limited usefulness in predicting the risk of osteoporosis, but more reliable techniques will no doubt become available in the future.

Estrogen-replacement therapy is the most effective means of preventing the bone loss that occurs after menopause. Since the benefits of estrogens in this regard are lost within a few years after therapy is stopped, estrogen replacement to prevent bone loss is a long-term proposition. Therefore, the decision to embark on such a course should be made only after discussing the risks and benefits with your doctor.

Vaginal and Urinary Problems. Symptoms of vaginal dryness, painful sexual intercourse, burning, itching, and discharge can occur because of the estrogen deficiency that occurs with menopause. These symptoms are prevented or can be treated with estrogens that are taken as tablets or applied as a vaginal cream. The estrogen from estrogen creams is absorbed in sufficient quantities to cause systemic effects. Painful urination, increased frequency of urination, and urinary problems can be caused by estrogen deficiency. These problems can be prevented or treated with estrogens.

Other Uses. Although medical controversy remains, there is a growing consensus that estrogens, in the lower doses that are used after menopause, may protect against cardiovascular disease. The evidence that they are beneficial in this regard is not sufficient for them to be used solely for this purpose, and it is unknown whether the progestins that are commonly prescribed with estrogens to prevent uterine cancer will cancel this beneficial effect. Because of the prevalence of cardiovascular disease among older women, this benefit, if established, will have widespread public-health implications.

There is no substantial evidence that estrogens have any beneficial effects on aging skin or in preventing emotional changes that may occur with menopause.

SIDE EFFECTS Estrogen side effects are dose related. I am assuming that you are taking a small dose for the purposes described above. Estrogens should not be taken by anyone with breast or uterine cancer, a history of blood clots, migraine headaches, or severe liver disease.

Nausea, fluid retention, swelling of the ankles or feet, and breast tenderness are occasional side effects that often disappear with continuous use. If these side effects are persistent or troublesome, contact your doctor.

As pointed out above, a primary role of estrogens during the menstrual cycles that occur before menopause is to promote the buildup of the endometrium, or lining of the uterus. The end of the menstrual cycle is marked by decreased production of estrogen and progesterone, and the endometrium sloughs off, causing menstruation. There is now good evidence for the supposition that when estrogens are taken after menopause, the endometrium builds up without sloughing off and the risk for endometrial cancer (cancer of the lining of the uterus) is increased. There is some evidence that this risk is lessened with smaller doses of estrogens and by cyclic administration (for example, three weeks of taking pills, followed by one week without pills). More important, however, is the recent evidence that the risk of endometrial cancer is further reduced when a progestin (to replace progesterone, another hormone that the ovaries stop making after menopause) is given with the estrogen during the last ten days of the estrogen-taking cycle. In fact, women who take a progestin with their estrogen in this way have a lesser risk of getting endometrial cancer than women who take no hormones at all.

If you are among the many women who has had a hysterectomy (surgical removal of the uterus), and you don't have any health problems that preclude estrogen use, your response to estrogens will not be affected by your hysterectomy.

There is some evidence that estrogens, even in smaller doses, increase the risk of gallbladder disease.

There is some evidence that estrogens can increase the blood pressure. However, this effect is not likely to be of any significance at lower doses that are used for estrogen replacement after menopause.

It is essential that you return to your doctor for regular checkups while taking estrogens. Any abnormal bleeding, breast changes, or any unexpected symptoms should be promptly reported to your doctor.

The ability of estrogens to cause cancer, heart attacks, and strokes has been widely publicized. However, it should be understood that the effects of estrogens in birth control pills are not the same as the effects of the smaller doses that are now used for postmenopausal estrogen-replacement therapy. Although there is still some medical controversy, there is now enough information to place the following risks in some perspective:

Breast Cancer. The risk of breast cancer increases with advancing age, so the question of whether or not the use of estrogens after menopause might further increase this risk has received much attention. Most studies show that this use of estrogens does not increase the risk of breast cancer. There is some evidence that combined estrogen-progestin therapy *decreases* the risk of breast cancer.

Heart Disease. Unlike young men, young women rarely have heart attacks. Heart disease increases rapidly after menopause. Because estrogens have a favorable effect on lipids in the blood, it has long been thought that they might be beneficial in preventing heart disease. The bulk of medical evidence suggests that estrogen use after menopause protects against heart disease, although some controversy remains. It is possible that progestins may negate these beneficial effects.

Blood Clots. Estrogens have been shown to increase the concentration of clotting factors in the blood. In low doses, this effect is not likely to be significant. However, you are at greater risk for blood clots if you are immobile, have had a recent traumatic injury or surgery, or if you have congestive heart failure. Several studies have found no correlation between postmenopausal estrogen use and stroke.

In summary, despite the considerable amount of publicity that estrogen side effects have received, the only serious side effect that should cause real concern is the increased risk of endometrial cancer, and this increased risk is avoided if a progestin is taken with the estrogen. For many women, the benefits of estrogens outweigh their risks.

DRUG INTERACTIONS These are the most important interactions with estrogens:

Prednisone. Estrogens slow the metabolism of prednisone and thereby increase both its effects and its side effects. Although this effect is less than that obtained with the estrogens in birth control pills, it is still significant. Your doctor may be able to treat you with smaller doses of prednisone while you are taking estrogens.

Smoking. Smoking increases the risk of heart disease, stroke, cancer, and osteoporosis. Smoking increases the metabolism of estrogens and thereby decreases their concentration in the blood; this interaction probably decreases their beneficial effects.

ALCOHOLIC BEVERAGES Estrogens will not affect your response to alcohol. However, excessive alcohol use promotes osteoporosis.

FOOD Estrogens can be taken either with meals or on an empty stomach.

If you are bothered by fluid retention, which estrogens can worsen, your doctor may advise you to restrict your salt intake.

You should try to increase the amount of calcium in your diet because calcium increases the effectiveness of estrogens in preventing osteoporosis. Dairy products are the best source of calcium; one cup of nonfat milk contains 300 mg of elemental calcium. The Recommended Daily Allowance for calcium is 800 mg per day, but some doctors feel that postmenopausal women should get 1,000 to 1,500 mg per day.

HOW DOES AGE AFFECT THE RESPONSE TO THIS DRUG Estrogens are most effective in preventing osteoporosis if they are started as soon as possible after menopause and continued for many years. More than half of all the bone that will be lost because of estrogen deficiency after menopause is lost during the first seven years. However, estrogens will prevent bone loss when given at any age.

FAMOTIDINE

OTHER NAMES Famotidine (pronounced *fa-MOT-te-deen*) is the common or generic name of this drug. Its most frequently used brand name is Pepcid. Pharmacologists refer to famotidine as a histamine H_2-receptor blocker.

WHAT IS IT SUPPOSED TO DO? Famotidine decreases the secretion of stomach acid. Therefore, it is used to treat peptic ulcers and related problems.

Famotidine works by decreasing the effect that histamine has on the stomach. Histamine, a substance the body produces to regulate a number of its functions, reacts with specialized receptors in the stomach to stimulate the flow of gastric juices. Too great a flow of gastric juices (too much stomach acid, too much pepsin), along with too little tissue resistance to their effects, is the cause of peptic-ulcer disease and related problems. Decreasing gastric-juice production is a key component in the medical treatment of these problems. For years, pharmacologists tried to use antihistamines (like the ones you can buy without prescription) to block the effect of histamine on stomach-acid secretion, but without good results. The histamine receptors in the stomach are H_2-receptors, which are different from the histamine receptors in the rest of the body. Antihistamines are histamine H_1-receptor blockers; they block the effect of histamine on allergic reactions, but not on gastric-acid secretion. Famotidine, on the other hand, blocks the effect of histamine on the histamine H_2-receptors in the stomach. The primary location of histamine H_2-receptors in the body is in the stomach.

SIDE EFFECTS Headache, diarrhea, and muscle cramps are infrequent side effects. Contact your doctor if any of these side effects is persistent or bothersome.

Famotidine does not usually cause any perceptible mental effects, but it can cause confusional states (with symptoms of psychosis, anxiety, disorientation, depression, or dementia) as a rare side effect. Contact your doctor promptly if you experience any of these rare side effects.

Other side effects are too rare to list here. Contact your doctor if you develop any other unexpected symptoms.

DRUG INTERACTIONS These are the most important interactions with famotidine:

Antacids can decrease the absorption of famotidine, so don't take both at the same time of day. If you take your famotidine with a meal and then take the antacid an hour or more afterward, this interaction is not likely to cause any problems.

Smoking increases the production of stomach acid and may therefore decrease the beneficial effects of famotidine.

ALCOHOLIC BEVERAGES   You can drink alcoholic beverages while you are taking famotidine, but you should remember that they can be irritating to the stomach.

FOOD   Take your famotidine with food. Avoid foods that are irritating to your stomach. Special diets are no longer commonly used in the treatment of peptic-ulcer disease.

HOW DOES AGE AFFECT THE RESPONSE TO THIS DRUG?   The elimination of famotidine from the blood, which occurs by metabolism in the liver and excretion by the kidneys, may be slower in older people than it is in younger people, so older people may require smaller doses. Your doctor will take your age and kidney function into consideration in determining a dosage of famotidine that is likely to be appropriate for you.

FENOPROFEN

OTHER NAMES   Fenoprofen (pronounced *fen-oh-PRO-fen)* is the common or generic name of this drug. A frequently used brand name for fenoprofen is Nalfon. Fenoprofen belongs to a large group of drugs called nonsteroidal anti-inflammatory drugs (NSAIDs).

WHAT IS IT SUPPOSED TO DO?   Fenoprofen relieves the pain, inflammation, swelling, and stiffness associated with arthritis. It is also relieves the pain caused by injuries, surgery, or cancer.

Although some relief from arthritic pain should become apparent shortly after you begin taking fenoprofen, maximum benefit occurs after one or two weeks of regular use.

SIDE EFFECTS   Indigestion. heartburn, nausea, stomach discomfort, excessive gas, diarrhea, and other problems related to the digestive tract are the most common side effects from fenoprofen. These side effects can sometimes be prevented by taking your fenoprofen with a full glass of water, perhaps with the addition of food or an antacid. If they persist, or if they are severe, stop taking the drug and contact your doctor.

Rarely, fenoprofen causes more severe problems in the digestive tract. These include ulcer with bleeding into the gastrointestinal tract (evidenced by bloody stools or stools that are discolored dark red or black) and small amounts of painless blood loss (which can cause anemia). The risk of these problems is lower than it is with aspirin.

Fenoprofen can also cause mental effects, such as drowsiness, headache, or dizziness. Because fenoprofen can cause decreased alertness in some individuals, you should evaluate how this drug affects you before you drive an automobile or operate any potentially dangerous machinery. If you should develop any sort of visual difficulty (such as blurred or dim vision) or hearing problem (such as buzzing or ringing in your ears), stop taking the drug and contact your doctor.

Kidney problems caused by fenoprofen and similar drugs are relatively rare, but most of the cases that have been reported in the medical literature involved older individuals. Some of the medical problems that are more prevalent among older people place them at greater risk for this side effect. When the kidneys are stressed by congestive heart failure, dehydration, or any kind of kidney impairment (even modest impairment), the body responds by producing substances called prostaglandins. Prostaglandins increase the flow of blood to the kidneys and increase their efficiency. Fenoprofen and related drugs can block this compensatory response, and kidney failure (usually reversible) can occur as a result. (All nonsteroidal anti-inflammatory drugs work by preventing the body from manufacturing prostaglandins, which are also mediators of pain and inflammation.) Considering the widespread use of fenoprofen among older people and the relatively small number of kidney problems that have been reported, the risk is probably small. However, you should be sure to return to your doctor for regular medical checkups while taking this drug. Contact your doctor promptly if you experience sudden weight gain, swelling of your feet or ankles, or markedly decreased urine production.

Skin problems such as rashes or unusual reactions to the sun are rare side effects from fenoprofen. Contact your doctor if you experience anything unusual.

Fenoprofen is very effective in lowering fever. This effect, combined with its pain-relieving and anti-inflammatory actions, could be considered a side effect if the signs of an infection were masked and the infection went undetected (and untreated) too long.

If you have ever developed asthma as an allergic reaction to aspirin, you should not take fenoprofen, because a similar allergic reaction could occur.

Other side effects are too rare to list here. Contact your doctor if you experience any unusual symptoms.

DRUG INTERACTIONS Several drugs have the potential to interact with fenoprofen:

Aspirin is potentially irritating to the digestive tract, and its irritant effects could become troublesome when added to those of fenoprofen. Check with your doctor before taking this drug combination.

Diuretics, such as *hydrochlorothiazide (HydroDIURIL and other brands) or furosemide (Lasix).* Infrequently, fenoprofen causes fluid retention and edema. If you are taking a diuretic for fluid retention and edema (such as that caused by congestive heart failure or liver disease) and you experience a worsening of your symptoms while taking fenoprofen, stop taking your fenoprofen and contact your doctor.

Warfarin (Coumadin). Fenoprofen can cause some gastrointestinal bleeding, which could be worsened by the anticoagulant effects of warfarin. In addition, fenoprofen decreases the effectiveness of blood platelets in forming blood clots, so the risk of side effects from warfarin is increased somewhat while you are taking fenoprofen.

ALCOHOLIC BEVERAGES Alcohol will add to the gastric-irritant effects of fenoprofen. Avoid taking them at the same time.

FOOD Food slows the absorption of fenoprofen somewhat, but it doesn't impair its absorption. It's a good idea to take your fenoprofen with food to minimize any gastric irritation that might occur.

HOW DOES AGE AFFECT THE RESPONSE TO THIS DRUG? Advancing age increases the risk of side effects from fenoprofen.

FERROUS SULFATE

OTHER NAMES Ferrous sulfate (pronounced *FER-us SUL-fate)* is the common or generic name of this drug. Frequently used brand names for ferrous sulfate are Feosol, Fer-In-Sol, Fero-Gradumet, and Mol-Iron. Ferrous sulfate is a form of iron.

WHAT IS IT SUPPOSED TO DO? Ferrous sulfate is prescribed to correct or prevent iron deficiency. Iron is essential to the body because it is a necessary part of hemoglobin, the specialized protein that carries oxygen in red blood cells. Red blood cells, which are filled with hemoglobin, transport oxygen from the lungs to tissues throughout the body. Iron deficiency depletes the supply of hemoglobin, impairing this process. It is the most common cause of anemia (a word whose Greek roots mean "without blood").

Iron deficiency is most often diagnosed before it causes any symptoms of anemia. Your doctor will rely on laboratory tests to determine whether iron deficiency is the cause of your anemia. (Other common causes of anemia are vitamin B_{12} deficiency and folate deficiency.) If your anemia is due to iron deficiency, your doctor will try to find its cause. Common causes of iron deficiency are not enough iron in the diet, poor absorption of iron, recent blood-bank donation, and chronic blood loss caused by some medical problems or by drugs such as aspirin or nonsteroidal anti-inflammatory drugs.

SIDE EFFECTS   Ferrous sulfate sometimes causes stomach upset in the form of heartburn, nausea, cramps, constipation, or diarrhea. These side effects do not usually require medical attention. However, if they are unacceptably severe, contact your doctor.

Ferrous sulfate will cause your stools to become black. This black color is unabsorbed ferrous sulfate and is harmless. However, in rare cases, black stools of a sticky consistency occur along with other symptoms such as prolonged stomach pain and red streaks in the stool; this requires prompt medical attention.

Be careful to store your ferrous sulfate out of the reach of children. Overdose from sugar-coated ferrous sulfate tablets has caused many deaths in toddlers.

If you are taking a liquid form of ferrous sulfate, you can avoid temporarily staining your teeth by mixing each dose with water or fruit juice and drinking it through a straw. If stains do occur, they can usually be removed from the teeth by brushing with baking soda.

If you experience prolonged stomach pain, prolonged cramping, or pain on swallowing (all rare), contact your doctor.

Other side effects are too rare to list here. Contact your doctor if you experience any unexpected symptoms.

DRUG INTERACTIONS   Ferrous sulfate interacts with several drugs. These are the interactions most likely to cause problems:

Antacids can decrease the absorption of ferrous sulfate. Calcium carbonate (Titralac) is more likely to cause problems than aluminum and magnesium hydroxides (Maalox, Mylanta, Riopan). Check with your doctor before taking any antacid with your ferrous sulfate.

Penicillamine (Cuprimine), a drug that is sometimes prescribed for severe rheumatoid arthritis, is poorly absorbed when taken with ferrous sulfate. Space the doses of the two drugs as far apart as possible.

Tetracycline antibiotics are poorly absorbed when taken with ferrous sulfate. The doses of the two drugs should be spaced as far apart as possible.

Vitamin C (ascorbic acid) increases the absorption of ferrous sulfate, but it also increases the likelihood of stomach upset from ferrous sulfate.

ALCOHOLIC BEVERAGES   Ferrous sulfate will not affect your response to alcohol. However, you should not drink alcoholic beverages with ferrous sulfate, because both are potentially irritating to the stomach.

FOOD   Ferrous sulfate is best absorbed when taken with a full glass of water or juice on an empty stomach, one hour before meals or two hours after meals. Food decreases the absorption of ferrous sulfate by about 50 percent.

If your doctor says it is all right for you to take your ferrous sulfate with food to decrease its upsetting effects on your stomach (be sure to ask—many doctors, when faced with complaints of upset stomach, tell their patients to take a smaller dose on an empty stomach), there are certain foods you should avoid. Cheese, milk, ice cream, eggs, spinach, tea, coffee, whole-grain breads, and cereals are most likely to impair the absorption of ferrous sulfate.

You should also strive to increase the iron in your diet. Meat, fish, and fowl are excellent dietary sources of iron, and the iron in these foods (which is already in the heme form) is better absorbed by older people than the iron in other foods. Other foods that contain iron are brewer's yeast, wheat germ, egg yolks, oysters, most green vegetables, most cereals, and certain dried beans and fruits. Milk products contain almost no iron. Cooking in an iron skillet will increase the iron in your diet.

HOW DOES AGE AFFECT THE RESPONSE TO THIS DRUG?   The absorption of ferrous sulfate tends to decrease with advancing age, probably because of decreased stomach-acid secretion.

FLURAZEPAM

OTHER NAMES Flurazepam (pronounced *flur-AZ-eh-pam*) is the common or generic name of this drug. A frequently used brand name for flurazepam is Dalmane. Flurazepam belongs to a large group of similar drugs called benzodiazepines.

WHAT IS IT SUPPOSED TO DO? Flurazepam induces and maintains sleep. It is therefore used for the treatment of insomnia.

There is some controversy over the use of drugs for insomnia. It is generally agreed that they are useful for brief episodes of insomnia caused by grief or stress. In such a situation, the drug helps to provide restful sleep. However, most physicians feel that sleeping pills should not be taken every night on a regular basis.

There are several arguments against regular use of sleeping pills. First, individuals vary in their requirement for sleep, and many people seem to function quite well with less sleep than they might think they require. Second, most effective sleeping pills cause some residual effect on the following day (see Side Effects). Third, all sleeping pills are potentially habit forming, although they can be slowly discontinued after prolonged use. Fourth, some medical problems can be complicated by their use.

Furthermore, it is quite normal for your sleep pattern to change as you get older. You are likely to awaken more often during the night and to sleep fewer hours.

SIDE EFFECTS Ideally, a drug for sleep would cause you to fall asleep and its effects would last all night, disappearing in the morning, when you would wake up refreshed. If the drug is too short-acting, you might wake up after a few hours. If it is too long-acting, you will feel its effects the following day.

Although flurazepam is rather long-acting and it has

several active metabolites that are even longer-acting, the effects of these drugs wane early in the morning as they are redistributed from the brain to the body's fatty tissue and muscle. However, if the dose is too large, you may find yourself somewhat drowsy the next day.

Infrequently, flurazepam causes light-headedness, dizziness, headache, weakness, confusion, blurred vision, or lack of coordination on the following day.

If you have been taking flurazepam regularly for a long time and in large doses, you may experience mild withdrawal symptoms several days after stopping this drug. Typical symptoms include difficulty in sleeping, unusual irritability, and unusual nervousness. If these occur, contact your doctor.

Other side effects are too rare to list here. Contact your doctor if you experience any unusual symptoms.

DRUG INTERACTIONS Sedation is a common side effect of antidepressant drugs, antihistamines, tranquilizers, narcotic analgesics, and other drugs. These drugs will add to any residual daytime sedation you might experience from flurazepam.

In addition, several drugs can interact with flurazepam by other mechanisms. These are the interactions most likely to cause problems:

Cimetidine (Tagamet), which is used for the treatment of ulcers, slows the metabolism of flurazepam and thereby prolongs its effects. You will be more susceptible to side effects from flurazepam while taking cimetidine.

Disulfiram (Antabuse), which is used in the treatment of alcoholism, slows the metabolism of flurazepam and thereby prolongs its effects. You will be more susceptible to side effects from flurazepam while taking both drugs.

Isoniazid (INH), which is used in the treatment of tuberculosis, may slow the metabolism of flurazepam and thereby prolong its effect. You will be more susceptible to side effects from flurazepam while taking both drugs. Rifampin, another drug which is used for tuberculosis, has the opposite effect (see below). When isoniazid and rifampin are used together for the treatment of tuber-culosis, the effects of rifampin predominate in the in-teraction with flurazepam.

Levodopa (Dopar, Larodopa, L-dopa) is used in the treatment of Parkinson's disease, and flurazepam may block its effect. If you are taking both drugs and you notice a worsening of your parkinsonism, stop taking flurazepam and contact your doctor.

Rifampin (Rifadin, Rimactane), which is used in the treatment of tuberculosis, increases the metabolism of flurazepam and thereby decreases its effects. If your doctor increases the dosage of your flurazepam to com-pensate for this interaction and you stop taking rifam-pin while continuing to take the same dosage of flurazepam, you may experience side effects from flur-azepam.

ALCOHOLIC BEVERAGES   Flurazepam adds to al-cohol's depressant effects on the nervous system. Do not take flurazepam if you have been drinking during the evening.

If you are taking flurazepam regularly, the combined effects of alcohol and flurazepam can occur even if the last time you took your flurazepam was on the previous day, or even several days previously. Flurazepam and its active metabolites remain in the body for many days. This will make you more sensitive to the effects of al-cohol.

FOOD   Food will delay the effects of flurazepam.

HOW DOES AGE AFFECT THE RESPONSE TO THIS DRUG?   Older people are more sensitive to the ef-fects of flurazepam. In addition, aging changes the way flurazepam is distributed within the body; its effects are prolonged with advancing age. The 30 mg dose, which is well tolerated by most younger people, often causes residual effects (side effects on the following day) in older people. The 15 mg dose is less likely to cause residual effects in older people.

Although lowering the dose to 15 mg usually pre-vents problems on the following day, the active metabolites accumulate very slowly in older people who take repeated nightly doses. It is possible that nightly use could lead eventually (for example, after several weeks) to confusion, weakness, or other side effects. Such a slow appearance of the problem might not be associated with the drug. Furthermore, just as the problem was slow to appear, it would be slow to disappear.

Men, for some unknown reason, metabolize this drug more slowly as they get older. This is apparently not true of women. At any rate, regular use for more than a few nights is most likely to cause residual effects in older men.

FUROSEMIDE

OTHER NAMES Furosemide (pronounced *fur-OH-se-mide)* is the common or generic name of this drug. In Great Britain, its generic name is frusemide. A frequently used brand name for furosemide is Lasix. Furosemide belongs to a group of drugs called high-ceiling diuretics *(high-ceiling* denoting great potency) or loop diuretics *(loop* referring to the loop of Henle, the anatomical part of the kidney where these drugs work).

WHAT IS IT SUPPOSED TO DO? Furosemide is a diuretic, meaning that it increases the amount of urine that is excreted from the body. It acts on the kidneys, causing them to eliminate extra water and salt from the body and into the urine. Furosemide is one of the most potent diuretics available. It is used to remove excess salt and water that have accumulated as a result of congestive heart failure, kidney failure, or liver disease. It is also used to treat high blood pressure that is accompanied by heart or kidney failure.

Use in Congestive Heart Failure. Extra salt and water may accumulate in the body for a variety of reasons, but congestive heart failure is a common cause in older persons. In congestive heart failure, which is the result of some types of heart disease, the heart's pumping action weakens and the circulation slows. When the kidneys don't get enough circulation, they become less efficient in removing extra salt and water from the body. As a result, veins become swollen, and fluid leaks out of them and into surrounding tissues. This leads to swelling, first of the ankles and lower legs, later of the arms. There is general weight gain from excess fluid accumulation. Fluid also accumulates in the lungs, causing shortness of breath. Furosemide promotes rapid and substantial salt and water removal by the kidneys, and it increases circulation to the kidneys. Therefore, it is effective in relieving the symptoms of congestive heart failure.

SIDE EFFECTS   You will find yourself needing to urinate frequently, especially at first. You should anticipate this need so that it won't become an inconvenience to you. The effects of a dose of furosemide usually become apparent within thirty minutes to an hour, and you will probably notice increased urination for several hours. Avoid taking it too close to bedtime so you won't be frequently awakened by a need to urinate.

Because it is such a potent diuretic, the side effects of profound diuresis are more prominent with furosemide than with other diuretics. You may experience dizziness or faintness, particularly when standing up too fast. If dizziness or faintness is persistent or severe, contact your doctor.

Furosemide causes potassium to be removed from the body along with salt and water. Dietary sources of potassium often prevent potassium deficiency from occurring. However, your doctor may prescribe either a potassium supplement or a second diuretic that conserves potassium to prevent this effect, especially if you are also taking digoxin (see Drug Interactions). In any case, your doctor will periodically order a laboratory test that measures the concentration of potassium in the blood. The symptoms of too low a concentration of potassium in the blood include profound muscle weakness, muscle cramps or pain, and irregular heartbeats.

If you experience any of these symptoms, contact your doctor.

Furosemide sometimes causes an increase in the amount of glucose in the blood, which could unmask latent diabetes or require an increase in your insulin or other drug requirement if you already have diabetes. Prevention of excess potassium loss decreases the risk of this problem. Furosemide can also increase the concentration of uric acid in your blood, but it rarely causes gout, the clinical manifestation of too much uric acid in the blood. Your doctor will order periodic laboratory tests to monitor for these and other, rarer possible problems before they cause symptoms.

All diuretics have the potential for causing dehydration when fluid loss is accelerated by hot weather or flulike illness. Whenever you experience fever, vomiting, or diarrhea, whatever the cause, be sure to increase your fluid intake to prevent dehydration. If the symptoms are severe, you should contact your doctor.

Other side effects are too rare to list here. If you experience any unusual symptoms, contact your doctor.

DRUG INTERACTIONS Several drugs can interact with furosemide. Your doctor will take special precautions to ensure that no problems occur if any of these drugs need to be taken with furosemide:

Antidiabetic drugs, such as *insulin* or the *sulfonylureas.* Furosemide can increase the concentration of glucose in the blood. If this occurs, despite the protective effect of correcting for potassium loss, your doctor may increase the dosage of your diabetic medication to compensate for this interaction. If you are taking chlorpropamide (Diabinese) or tolbutamide (Orinase), your doctor will monitor for a second, less frequent possible interaction. These drugs sometimes decrease the concentration of sodium in the blood by a mechanism other than that of furosemide. (Other sulfonylureas do not share this property.) In some older individuals, this combination of drugs can lead to too low a concentration of sodium in the blood (hyponatremia). If you experience weakness, confusion, or muscle cramps, contact your doctor.

Corticosteroids, such as *dexamethasone, hydrocortisone, and prednisone,* cause potassium to be lost from the body, and this side effect is additive with that of furosemide. To prevent problems, your doctor will monitor the concentration of potassium in your blood and may prescribe a potassium supplement or a potassium-conserving diuretic in addition to furosemide.

Clofibrate (Atromid-S), which is used to decrease the concentration of cholesterol and triglycerides in the blood, and furosemide compete with each other for the same binding or storage sites on certain proteins that circulate in the blood. This interaction, which results in increased effects of both drugs, has occurred only in individuals who had abnormally low concentrations of plasma protein (albumin) circulating in their blood. Your doctor will measure your plasma albumin before prescribing this combination. If you experience muscle stiffness or pain or notice a greater diuretic effect than usual while taking this combination of drugs, contact your doctor.

Digoxin (Lanoxin) and furosemide are often prescribed together because they work by different and complementary mechanisms in relieving the symptoms of congestive heart failure. However, an interaction can occur because of furosemide's promotion of potassium loss from the body. If the amount of potassium in the blood becomes too low, then digoxin toxicity may develop. To prevent this problem, your doctor will monitor the concentration of potassium in your blood and may prescribe a potassium supplement or a potassium-conserving diuretic in addition to furosemide.

Indomethacin (Indocin) and perhaps other *nonsteroidal anti-inflammatory drugs,* which are used for the treatment of arthritis, may decrease the effects of furosemide. If such an interaction occurs, your doctor may have to increase the dose of furosemide or prescribe another anti-inflammatory drug.

ALCOHOLIC BEVERAGES Furosemide will make you more sensitive to the blood-pressure-lowering effects of alcohol. Limit your consumption of alcoholic beverages and watch for excessive dizziness from alcohol.

FOOD If furosemide upsets your stomach, a rare problem, take it with food.

Be sure to follow any dietary advice, such as low-salt diet or increasing the amount of potassium-containing foods (such as bananas, orange juice, raisins), you may have been given with your prescription.

HOW DOES AGE AFFECT THE RESPONSE TO THIS DRUG? Because furosemide must be excreted into the urine to exert its effects, and kidney function declines with aging, decreased effects would be expected. Not surprisingly, several studies comparing equal doses of furosemide in younger and older individuals have demonstrated lesser effects in the older subjects.

Nevertheless, the dosage of this drug varies from individual to individual, and, more importantly, advancing age is accompanied by greater sensitivity to dehydration, excessive potassium loss, and excessive sodium loss from potent diuretics like furosemide. Therefore, the older you are, the more carefully your doctor will monitor your response to this drug.

GLIPIZIDE

OTHER NAMES Glipizide (pronounced *GLIP-i-zide)* is the common or generic name of this drug. A frequently used brand name for glipizide is Glucotrol. Glipizide belongs to a group of chemically related drugs called sulfonylureas.

WHAT IS IT SUPPOSED TO DO? Glipizide decreases the concentration of glucose (a form of sugar) in the blood, so it is used in the treatment of certain types of diabetes. Glipizide works by making the body more sensitive to its own insulin. It also increases the production of insulin by the pancreas, but this effect is probably less important over the long run.

Diabetes that occurs in middle and late life is usually best controlled by diet and exercise. If these measures fail to decrease the concentration of glucose in the blood, then either insulin or a sulfonylurea drug such as glipizide may be required in addition. The symptoms of too high a concentration of glucose in the blood (*hyper*glycemia) are excessive thirst, excessive urination, fatigue (which can lead to loss of consciousness and coma), and low resistance to infection. Even if you don't have any symptoms, your doctor will want you to control your blood glucose. Control of blood glucose is essential in preventing or reducing the complications of diabetes, which include damage to vision, loss of feeling in the extremities, kidney damage, heart attack, and stroke.

SIDE EFFECTS   *Hypo*glycemia (too low a concentration of glucose in the blood) can occur from any drug that lowers the blood sugar. Glipizide is no exception, although this problem is not likely to occur unless you stop eating, are severely ill, or follow an extremely irregular diet. The symptoms of hypoglycemia, which include lethargy, nausea, cold sweats, pounding or racing heartbeat, shakiness, headache, confusion, and dizziness, are quickly reversed with a glass of fruit juice or with food. If untreated, hypoglycemia can lead to loss of consciousness and coma. If you think you are experiencing hypoglycemia, have something to eat and contact your doctor.

Other side effects from glipizide are infrequent. Stomach upset occurs in one or two persons per hundred; take it with food if this problem bothers you. Rash occurs in about one person per hundred; contact your doctor if rash occurs.

Other side effects are too rare to list here. Contact your doctor if you experience any unusual symptoms.

DRUG INTERACTIONS   A number of drugs can interact with glipizide or affect your diabetes. These are the most likely to cause problems:

Aspirin. Large doses of aspirin (for example, twelve or more tablets a day) have a mild antidiabetic effect. This effect is too mild to be used as a treatment for diabetes, but it adds to the effect of glipizide. If you are taking large doses of aspirin, you should be aware of this effect. If you start or stop using large doses of aspirin, ask your doctor to determine if it is necessary to alter the dosage of your glipizide. Occasional use of aspirin will not affect your response to glipizide.

Some *beta-blocking drugs,* such as *propranolol (Inderal), pindolol (Visken), nadolol (Corgard), or timolol (Blocadren).* Diabetic patients should not take these drugs unless there is no other alternative. They can block some of the warning signs of hypoglycemia (especially rapid heartbeat or palpitations), delay the recovery from hypoglycemia, cause high-blood-pressure episodes during hypoglycemia, and impair circulation to the extremities in diabetics. Other beta-blocking drugs, such as metoprolol (Lopressor) and atenolol (Tenormin), are less likely to cause these problems, but there is some risk. If a beta-blocker is required, keep in mind that sweating, but not rapid heartbeat, is a sign of hypoglycemia.

Clofibrate (Atromid-S), which is sometimes used to lower the concentrations of triglycerides in the blood, may increase the response to glipizide in some patients. If you start or stop taking clofibrate, ask your doctor to reevaluate your response to glipizide.

Corticosteroids, such as *dexamethasone, hydrocortisone, or prednisone,* can make diabetes more difficult to control. This effect is well known. If you require a corticosteroid, your doctor will check your blood glucose concentration and may increase the dosage of your glipizide.

Diuretics, such as *hydrochlorothiazide (HydroDIURIL and others) or furosemide (Lasix),* can reduce the effects of glipizide. If your diuretic causes your blood glucose concentration to increase, your doctor may increase the dosage of your glipizide.

Guanethidine (Ismelin), which is sometimes used to treat high blood pressure, increases the effects of glipizide. If you start or stop taking guanethidine, ask your doctor to reevaluate your response to glipizide.

Nifedipine (Procardia), which is used in the treatment of angina, may decrease your response to glipizide. If you start or stop taking nifedipine, ask your doctor to reevaluate your response to glipizide.

Phenylbutazone (Butazolidin) and *oxyphenbutazone,* which are sometimes used for brief periods to control gout attacks or severe arthritic pain, can markedly increase the effects of drugs that are chemically related to glipizide. Although glipizide does not interact with phenylbutazone in test-tube experiments, some caution is warranted. Since hypoglycemia could result, your doctor may want to decrease the dosage of your glipizide temporarily. Check with your doctor.

Rifampin (Rifadin, Rimactane, Rifamate), which is used in treating tuberculosis and other infections, may stimulate the metabolism of glipizide. Therefore, it may decrease the effects of glipizide. If you start or stop taking rifampin, ask your doctor to reevaluate your response to glipizide.

Smoking antagonizes the effects of insulin and may impair your response to glipizide as well.

Sulfonamides may increase your response to glipizide. Do not start or stop taking sulfonamides without asking your doctor to reevaluate your response to glipizide.

Thyroid hormones can affect your response to glipizide. If you are starting to take thyroid, or if the dosage of your thyroid hormone is being changed, ask your doctor to reevaluate your response to glipizide.

ALCOHOLIC BEVERAGES A number of potential problems can arise from your use of alcoholic beverages. Some doctors tell their patients to avoid alcohol. Others advise their patients to limit their alcohol use to a glass of wine or two with dinner. The American Diabetes Association allows the inclusion of small amounts of alcoholic beverages in the diet of diabetics. You should avoid sweetened alcoholic beverages. Here is a summary of the potential problems that alcohol can cause:

First, alcohol temporarily lowers the concentration of glucose in the blood. If you drink alcohol on an empty stomach, it can cause hypoglycemia. The risk of hypoglycemia is increased while you are taking glipizide. Therefore, you should avoid large amounts of alcohol and avoid drinking on an empty stomach. If you drink small amounts of alcohol with meals, hypoglycemia is not likely to occur.

Second, regular *heavy* use of alcohol may stimulate the enzymes that metabolize glipizide, thereby causing it to be eliminated from the body more rapidly. As a result, the effects of glipizide may be decreased. Alcohol consumption should be limited to small amounts for this reason and because of the danger of hypoglycemia during acute alcohol intoxication.

FOOD   Glipizide does not replace diet as the primary means for controlling blood glucose. In addition to avoiding simple sugars, you should increase the amount of roughage (such as fruits, vegetables, and whole grains) in your diet. These foods slow the absorption of complex carbohydrates. Furthermore, you should restrict your consumption of saturated fats (butter, animal fat), because they increase the risk of cardiovascular disease, and cardiovascular disease is more common among diabetics. Finally, most diabetics who take glipizide are overweight. Obesity causes resistance to the body's natural insulin and increases the concentration of glucose in the blood. Weight loss, even if you remain a little heavy, will help control your diabetes. Follow the diabetic diet prescribed by your doctor.

A regular diet is important. If you skip meals because of illness or some other reason, you may experience hypoglycemia (see Side Effects). If you cannot eat because of illness, check with your doctor.

I advise patients to take their glipizide at the start of a meal to prevent stomach upset and to help them remember to take it. Food delays the absorption of glipizide tablets somewhat, and there is limited evidence that taking glipizide thirty minutes before meals might give a better response. But this requires confirmation, and taking it on an empty stomach can lead to problems if you forget to eat. Hypoglycemia can occur if you fail to eat within an hour or two after taking it on an empty stomach.

HOW DOES AGE AFFECT THE RESPONSE TO THIS DRUG? Hypoglycemia from drugs like glipizide is more common among older people than it is among younger people. Be sure to take your glipizide as directed, follow a careful but regular diet, and be sure that you and those around you are familiar with the signs and symptoms of hypoglycemia.

Age also affects the way your body responds to high concentrations of glucose in the blood. As the kidneys age, they become less efficient. In younger people, when the concentration of glucose in the blood gets much higher than normal, glucose appears in the urine. The threshold for glucose spilling into the urine increases with age, and older people can have much higher concentrations of glucose in their blood without having any in their urine. This effect varies from individual to individual, of course, but urine tests for glucose may be less reliable as indicators of blood glucose in older people. So don't be misled by negative urine tests for glucose. Your doctor can compare your blood glucose with your urine glucose and give you some idea of how reliable urine tests might be for you.

GLYBURIDE

OTHER NAMES   Glyburide (pronounced *GLYE-byoor-ide)* is the common or generic name of this drug. Frequently used brand names of glyburide are DiaBeta and Micronase. Glyburide belongs to a group of chemically related drugs called sulfonylureas.

WHAT IS IT SUPPOSED TO DO?   Glyburide decreases the concentration of glucose (a form of sugar) in the blood. Therefore, it is used in the treatment of certain types of diabetes. Glyburide works by making the body more sensitive to its own insulin. It also increases the production of insulin by the pancreas, but this effect does not persist with normal continued use.

Diabetes that occurs in middle and late life is usually best controlled by diet and exercise. If these measures fail to decrease the concentration of glucose in the blood, then either insulin or a sulfonylurea drug such as glyburide may be required in addition. The symptoms of too high a concentration of glucose in the blood (*hyper*glycemia) are excessive thirst, excessive urination, fatigue (which can lead to loss of consciousness and coma), and low resistance to infection. Even if you don't have any symptoms, your doctor will want you to control your blood glucose. Control of blood glucose is essential in preventing or reducing the complications of diabetes, which include damage to vision, loss of feeling in the extremities, kidney damage, heart attack, and stroke.

SIDE EFFECTS   *Hypo*glycemia (too low a concentration of glucose in the blood) can occur from any drug that lowers the blood sugar. Glyburide is no exception, although this problem is not likely to occur unless you stop eating, are severely ill, or follow an extremely irregular diet. The symptoms of hypoglycemia, which include lethargy, nausea, cold sweats, pounding or racing heartbeat, shakiness, headache, confusion, and dizziness, are quickly reversed with a glass of fruit juice or with food. If untreated, hypoglycemia can lead to loss of consciousness and coma. If you think you are experiencing hypoglycemia, have something to eat and contact your doctor.

Other side effects from glyburide are infrequent. Stomach upset occurs in one or two persons per hundred; take it with food if this problem bothers you. Rash occurs in about one person per hundred; contact your doctor if rash occurs.

Other side effects are too rare to list here. Contact your doctor if you experience any unusual symptoms.

DRUG INTERACTIONS   A number of drugs can interact with glyburide or affect your diabetes. These are the most likely to cause problems:

Aspirin. Large doses of aspirin (for example, twelve or more tablets a day) have a mild antidiabetic effect. This effect is too mild to be used as a treatment for diabetes, but it adds to the effect of glyburide. If you are taking large doses of aspirin, you should be aware of this effect. If you start or stop using large doses of aspirin, ask your doctor to determine if it is necessary to alter the dosage of your glyburide. Occasional use of aspirin will not affect your response to glyburide.

Some *beta-blocking drugs,* such as *propranolol (Inderal), pindolol (Visken), nadolol (Corgard), or timolol (Blocadren).* Diabetic patients should not take these drugs unless there is no other alternative. They can block some of the warning signs of hypoglycemia (especially rapid heartbeat or palpitations), delay the recovery from hypoglycemia, and impair circulation to the extremities in diabetics. Other beta-blocking drugs, like metoprolol (Lopressor) and atenolol (Tenormin), are less likely to cause these problems, but there is some risk. If a beta-blocker is required, keep in mind that sweating, but not rapid heartbeat, is a sign of hypoglycemia.

Clofibrate (Atromid-S), which is sometimes used to lower the concentration of triglycerides in the blood, may increase the response to glyburide in some patients. If you start or stop taking clofibrate, ask your doctor to reevaluate your response to glyburide.

Corticosteroids, such as *dexamethasone, hydrocortisone, or prednisone,* can make diabetes more difficult to control. This effect is well known. If you require a corticosteroid, your doctor will check your blood glucose concentration and may increase the dosage of your glyburide.

Diuretics, such as *hydrochlorothiazide (HydroDIURIL and others) or furosemide (Lasix),* can reduce the effects of glyburide. If your diuretic causes your blood glucose concentration to increase, your doctor may increase the dosage of your glyburide.

Guanethidine (Ismelin), which is sometimes used to

treat high blood pressure, increases the effects of glyburide. If you start or stop taking guanethidine, ask your doctor to reevaluate your response to glyburide.

Nifedipine (Procardia), which is used in the treatment of angina, may decrease your response to glyburide. If you start or stop taking nifedipine, ask your doctor to reevaluate your response to glyburide.

Phenylbutazone (Butazolidin) and *Oxyphenbutazone,* which are sometimes used for brief periods to control gout attacks or severe arthritic pain, can markedly increase the effects of drugs that are chemically related to glyburide. Although glyburide does not interact with phenylbutazone in test-tube experiments, some caution is warranted. Since hypoglycemia could result, your doctor may want to decrease the dosage of your glyburide temporarily. Check with your doctor.

Rifampin (Rifadin, Rimactane, Rifamate), which is used in treating tuberculosis and other infections, may stimulate the metabolism of glyburide. Therefore, it may decrease the effects of glyburide. If you start or stop taking rifampin, ask your doctor to reevaluate your response to glyburide.

Smoking antagonizes the effects of insulin and may impair your response to glyburide as well.

Sulfonamides, which are used in treating infections, may increase your response to glyburide. If you start or stop taking a sulfonamide, ask your doctor to reevaluate your response to glyburide.

Thyroid hormones can affect your response to glyburide. If you are starting to take thyroid, or if the dosage of your thyroid hormone is being changed, ask your doctor to reevaluate your response to glyburide.

ALCOHOLIC BEVERAGES A number of potential problems can arise from your use of alcoholic beverages. Some doctors tell their patients to avoid alcohol. Others advise their patients to limit their alcohol use to a glass of wine or two with dinner. The American Diabetes Association allows the inclusion of small amounts of alcoholic beverages in the diet of diabetics. You should avoid sweetened alcoholic beverages. Here is a summary of the potential problems that alcohol can cause:

First, alcohol temporarily lowers the concentration of glucose in the blood. If you drink alcohol on an empty stomach, it can cause hypoglycemia. The risk of hypoglycemia is increased while you are taking glyburide. Therefore, you should avoid large amounts of alcohol and avoid drinking on an empty stomach. If you drink small amounts of alcohol with meals, hypoglycemia is not likely to occur.

Second, regular *heavy* use of alcohol may stimulate the enzymes that metabolize glyburide, thereby causing it to be eliminated from the body more rapidly. As a result, the effects of glyburide may be decreased. Alcohol consumption should be limited to small amounts for this reason and because of the danger of hypoglycemia during acute alcohol intoxication.

FOOD Glyburide does not replace diet as the primary means for controlling blood glucose. In addition to avoiding simple sugars, you should increase the amount of roughage (such as fruits, vegetables, and whole grains) in your diet. These foods slow the absorption of complex carbohydrates. Furthermore, you should restrict your consumption of saturated fats (butter, animal fat) because they increase the risk of cardiovascular disease, and cardiovascular disease is more common among diabetics. Finally, most diabetics who take glyburide are overweight. Obesity causes resistance to the body's natural insulin and increases the concentration of glucose in the blood. Weight loss, even if you remain a little heavy, will help control your diabetes. Follow the diabetic diet prescribed by your doctor.

A regular diet is important. If you skip meals because of illness or some other reason, you may experience hypoglycemia (see Side Effects). If you cannot eat because of illness, check with your doctor.

Glyburide is best taken at the start of a meal to prevent stomach upset and to help you remember to take it. Food does not affect the absorption of glyburide tablets. Hypoglycemia can occur if you fail to eat within an hour or two after taking it on an empty stomach.

HOW DOES AGE AFFECT THE RESPONSE TO THIS DRUG? Hypoglycemia from drugs like glyburide is more common among older people than it is among younger people. Be sure to take your glyburide as directed, follow a careful but regular diet, and be sure that you and those around you are familiar with the signs and symptoms of hypoglycemia.

Age also affects the way your body responds to high concentrations of glucose in the blood. As the kidneys age, they become less efficient. In younger people, when the concentration of glucose in the blood gets much higher than normal, glucose appears in the urine. The threshold for glucose spilling into the urine increases with age, and older people can have much higher concentrations of glucose in their blood without having any in their urine. This effect varies from individual to individual, of course, but urine tests for glucose may be less reliable as indicators of blood glucose in older people. So don't be misled by negative urine tests for glucose. Your doctor can compare your blood glucose with your urine glucose and give you some idea of how reliable urine tests might be for you.

HALAZEPAM

OTHER NAMES Halazepam (pronounced *hal-AZ-eh-pam)* is the common or generic name of this drug. A frequently used brand name of halazepam is Paxipam. Halazepam belongs to a large group of similar drugs called benzodiazepines.

WHAT IS IT SUPPOSED TO DO? Halazepam relieves the symptoms of anxiety and tension.

SIDE EFFECTS Drowsiness is the principal side effect from halazepam. You may find yourself unsteady on your feet as well. Evaluate these effects for yourself and regulate your activities accordingly. You should be especially cautious about driving an automobile. If drowsiness or unsteadiness persists, stop taking the drug and contact your doctor.

Infrequently, halazepam causes dizziness, weakness, confusion, impaired memory, or loss of coordination. If you experience any of these effects, which suggest you are extremely sensitive to halazepam, stop taking it and contact your doctor.

If you have been taking halazepam regularly for a long time and in large doses, you may experience mild withdrawal symptoms several days after stopping this drug. Typical symptoms include difficulty in sleeping, unusual irritability, and unusual nervousness. If these occur, contact your doctor.

Other side effects are too rare to list here. Contact your doctor if you experience any unusual symptoms.

DRUG INTERACTIONS Sedation is a common side effect of antidepressant drugs, antihistamines, tranquilizers, narcotic analgesics, and other drugs. Be careful of additive effects between halazepam and any of these drugs.

In addition, several drugs can interact with halazepam by other mechanisms. These are the interactions most likely to cause problems:

Cimetidine (Tagamet), which is used for the treatment of ulcers, slows the metabolism of halazepam and thereby enhances its effects. It may be necessary to decrease the dosage of your halazepam while taking both drugs; ask your doctor.

Disulfiram (Antabuse), which is used in the treatment of alcoholism, slows the metabolism of halazepam and thereby enhances its effects. It may be necessary to decrease the dosage of your halazepam while taking both drugs; ask your doctor.

Isoniazid (INH), which is used in the treatment of tuberculosis, may slow the metabolism of halazepam and thereby enhance its effects. It may be necessary to decrease the dosage of your halazepam while taking both drugs; ask your doctor. Rifampin, another drug used in treating tuberculosis, has the opposite effect (see be-

low). When rifampin and isoniazid are used together
for the treatment of tuberculosis, the effects of rifampin
predominate in the interaction with halazepam.

Levodopa (Dopar, Larodopa, L-dopa) is used in the
treatment of Parkinson's disease, and halazepam may
block its effect. If you are taking both drugs and notice
a worsening of your parkinsonism, stop taking your
halazepam and contact your doctor.

Rifampin (Rifadin, Rimactane), which is used in the
treatment of tuberculosis, increases the metabolism of
halazepam and thereby decreases its effect. If your doctor increases the dosage of your halazepam to compensate for this interaction, remind him or her to readjust
your halazepam dosage when you stop taking rifampin.

ALCOHOLIC BEVERAGES   Halazepam adds to alcohol's depressant effects on the nervous system. If you
are taking halazepam regularly, the combined effects
of alcohol and halazepam can occur even if the last
time you took your halazepam was one or even several
days previous. The active metabolites of halazepam remain in the body for many days. Therefore, you should
limit your alcohol consumption to small amounts while
taking halazepam. Needless to say, the effects of this
combination on driving can be dangerous.

FOOD   Halazepam can be taken with food or on an
empty stomach.

**HOW DOES AGE AFFECT THE RESPONSE TO THIS
DRUG?**   The older you are, the more sensitive you
will be to halazepam. There are several mechanisms
involved:

First, older people are inherently more sensitive to
the effects of halazepam. This may have something to
do with the effects of aging on the brain. There is good
evidence that older people experience much more
sedation than younger people with the same concentration of the drug in their blood.

Second, aging changes the distribution of desmethyldiazepam, the principal active metabolite of halazepam,
within the body. As a result, it takes much longer for

the maximum effect of repeated doses to become apparent. An older person who takes halazepam every day will experience slightly more effect each day for several weeks, and *then* repeated doses will maintain the same level of effect. If the dosage is too high for you, you may not notice it as soon as you might expect.

Third, and for some unknown reason this applies more to men than to women, the metabolism of desmethyldiazepam, the active metabolite of halazepam, becomes slower with advanced age. Therefore, some older people develop higher concentrations of drug in their blood than would be expected, and they are more likely to develop side effects. In these individuals, it may take longer than a month before the full effects of repeated doses become apparent.

In any case, side effects increase with age. Confusion, weakness, fainting, dizziness, impaired memory, and loss of coordination, which are infrequent side effects from halazepam, occur far more often in older people than they do in younger people. All of these side effects are reversible. However, because their onset can be so slow, they are sometimes not associated with the offending drug. Furthermore, just as these side effects are often slow to appear, they are equally slow in disappearing after halazepam is stopped. If you are aware of this possibility, it probably won't become a problem for you.

Your doctor will take your age into consideration in selecting a dose and dosage schedule that are likely to be appropriate for you.

HALOPERIDOL

OTHER NAMES   Haloperidol (pronounced *ha-loe-PER-i-dole)* is the common or generic name of this drug. Its principal brand name is Haldol. It belongs to a large group of drugs called neuroleptics or tranquilizers.

WHAT IS IT SUPPOSED TO DO?   Haloperidol controls the symptoms of severe mental problems. People who are extremely agitated, hearing voices that are not there, or are abnormally aggressive or hostile become calmed by haloperidol. Less frequently, it is used to control muscle tics, including those associated with uncontrollable vocal utterances. The precise means by which it accomplishes these effects is unknown, but it probably works by blocking the effects of dopamine, a naturally occurring chemical transmitter in the central nervous system.

SIDE EFFECTS Haloperidol's ability to block the effects of dopamine is beneficial in the part of the brain that is responsible for thinking and feeling (the cortex), but this same effect can cause problems in other parts of the brain. The most common problems arise from its effects in the part of the brain that controls posture and the involuntary aspects of body movement (this part of the brain is called the extrapyramidal system). These side effects, if they occur, may include trembling fingers or hands, slowed body movement, stiffness of arms and legs, shuffling walk, or masklike facial expression (which may give others the impression of depression). Because these side effects resemble the symptoms of Parkinson's disease, they are often referred to as parkinsonian symptoms. Related side effects, which are less common, include severe restlessness (with an apparent need for constant movement and often with difficulty in sitting down) and muscle spasms, especially of the head, neck, and back. Any of these side effects should be promptly reported to your doctor; they are reversible and can be treated with additional drug therapy.

A related side effect, which is rare but serious, sometimes appears when haloperidol is discontinued or the dosage is reduced after prolonged treatment. It is called tardive dyskinesia, which means late-appearing abnormal body movements. The symptoms include rhythmical involuntary movements of the tongue, mouth, or jaw. Typical of these involuntary movements are lip smacking or puckering, puffing of the cheeks, chewing movements, and sticking out of the tongue. Call your doctor if any of these symptoms occur. Because there is no effective treatment for tardive dyskinesia, haloperidol should be used only when it is necessary and in the smallest effective dosages.

Although haloperidol is less likely to cause dizziness, light-headedness, or fainting than related drugs, these side effects can occur, especially in older individuals. Standing up too quickly is likely to cause problems, so care should be exercised. Severe dizziness or light-headedness is an indication for medical attention.

Likewise, drowsiness is less likely to occur from haloperidol than it is from related drugs, but some individuals are sensitive to this effect.

Haloperidol can also cause dry mouth. Often sugarless candy or gum is helpful for this problem.

A stool softener is helpful in preventing or relieving constipation caused by haloperidol.

Other side effects are too rare to list here. Contact your doctor promptly if any unexpected symptoms occur.

DRUG INTERACTIONS   Other drugs that cause sedation can add to this side effect of haloperidol. Examples include antihistamines, narcotics, barbiturates, and benzodiazepines.

In addition, special caution is warranted when haloperidol is prescribed with any of the following drugs:

Levodopa (Dopar, Larodopa), which is used in the treatment of Parkinson's disease, works by increasing the amount of dopamine in the brain, and haloperidol blocks dopamine receptors. Therefore, haloperidol would be expected to antagonize the effects of levodopa.

Lithium (Eskalith, Lithobid, Lithonate), which is used to treat the manic phase of manic-depressive illness, is often taken with haloperidol without adverse effects. However, occasional patients develop unusual adverse mental and neurologic effects from this combination, so any adverse effect should be promptly brought to your doctor's attention.

Methyldopa (Aldomet), which is used in the treatment of high blood pressure, can cause adverse mental effects when taken with haloperidol. Any adverse mental effect should be promptly brought to your doctor's attention.

ALCOHOLIC BEVERAGES   Alcohol should be consumed sparingly with haloperidol because it can add to any dizziness or sedation that haloperidol might cause.

FOOD   Haloperidol can be taken either with food or on an empty stomach. It should be taken with food if it causes stomach upset, which is infrequent. The liquid form of haloperidol should not be added to coffee or tea, because they can cause haloperidol to separate out of the solution.

HOW DOES AGE AFFECT THE RESPONSE TO THIS DRUG?   Older individuals are more likely to experience dizziness or light-headedness from haloperidol.

It was once thought that older individuals are more sensitive to the parkinsonian effects of haloperidol, but more recent studies suggest that older individuals may be *less* sensitive than younger individuals to these side effects.

HYDRALAZINE

OTHER NAMES   Hydralazine (pronounced *hye-DRAL-a-zeen)* is the common or generic name of this drug. Some frequently used brand names for hydralazine are Alazine and Apresoline. Hydralazine is sometimes prescribed as tablets or capsules that also contain a thiazide diuretic (Apresazide, Apresodex, Apresoline-Esidrix, Aprozide, Hydralazine Plus, Hydralazine-Thiazide), reserpine (Serpasil-Apresoline), or both a thiazide diuretic and reserpine (Cherapas, Rezide, Ser-A-Gen, Ser-Ap-Es, Serathide, Serpazide, Tri-Hydroserpine, and Unipres).

WHAT IS IT SUPPOSED TO DO?   Hydralazine relaxes the smooth muscle (not under voluntary control) in arterioles (small arteries). As a result, the resistance to blood flow is decreased, which in turn lowers blood pressure. Hydralazine is most often used in the treatment of moderate to severe hypertension (high blood pressure).

Hypertension causes no symptoms, but untreated hypertension substantially increases the risk of the subsequent development of congestive heart failure, angina, heart attack, stroke, kidney problems, or visual problems. Antihypertensive drugs such as hydralazine decrease these risks.

SIDE EFFECTS Hydralazine's ability to dilate small blood vessels and decrease the resistance to blood flow sometimes causes the heart to react by beating faster. Therefore, racing heartbeat and palpitations are common side effects (although the likelihood of this problem lessens with older age). Hydralazine is often prescribed with a beta-blocker or reserpine, drugs that usually counteract this side effect and add to hydralazine's therapeutic effect. If you experience chest pain, rapid heartbeat, or palpitations, contact your doctor. Hydralazine should not be used by those with angina (chest pain).

Headache (most common), dizziness or light-headedness, or flushing of the face also sometimes occur because of hydralazine's circulatory effects. These side effects may go away as your body becomes accustomed to the drug, but if any of them are persistent or bothersome, contact your doctor.

Diarrhea, nausea, and loss of appetite may occur with large doses or at the beginning of therapy with hydralazine. Less frequently, hydralazine causes stuffy nose or watery eyes. If any of these are persistent or bothersome, contact your doctor.

Fluid retention (common symptoms are rapid weight gain and swelling of the feet or lower legs) occurs less frequently and is usually prevented by the thiazide diuretic that is often prescribed with hydralazine to add to its therapeutic effect. If you experience fluid retention, contact your doctor.

There is a specific kind of allergic reaction (called hydralazine lupus) that some people develop after taking hydralazine for a period of time, most often after a year or more. The symptoms include joint pain (most common), fever, weakness, and rash. Contact your doctor if you develop signs of this side effect, which is dose related (less frequent at doses less than 200 mg per day) and occurs more often in women than in men. Hydralazine is metabolized by a process called acetylation, and people tend to be either slow or fast acetylators of drugs, which doesn't change much with aging. Slow acetylators are more prone to this side effect than fast acetylators, but there is no convenient test for predicting how fast one acetylates hydralazine, and about 50 percent of black or white Americans are slow acetylators. Asians are often fast acetylators.

Rarely, hydralazine cause numbness, tingling, pain, or weakness in the hands or feet. If you experience these symptoms, which may be due to vitamin B deficiency (hydralazine may antagonize vitamin B), contact your doctor.

Other side effects are too rare to list here. Contact your doctor if you experience any unusual symptoms.

DRUG INTERACTIONS   Hydralazine does not interact adversely with most other drugs. Watch for signs of abnormally low blood pressure (dizziness is a sign) when other antihypertensive drugs are added to your therapy.

ALCOHOLIC BEVERAGES   Headache or dizziness are more likely to occur after drinking alcohol. Be cautious in the amount of alcohol you drink.

FOOD   Both increased and decreased absorption have been observed when hydralazine was taken with food. This discrepancy can be explained by differences in measurement techniques, but it is clear hydralazine should always be taken at the same time in relation to meals to prevent day-to-day variation in its effects. Take hydralazine in the way that is most convenient for you (just before or after meals works well for most people), and be consistent with this schedule.

If your doctor has prescribed a restricted-salt diet, be sure to follow it.

HOW DOES AGE AFFECT THE RESPONSE TO THIS DRUG?   Hydralazine is more likely to cause dizziness in older individuals.

HYDROCHLOROTHIAZIDE

OTHER NAMES   Hydrochlorothiazide (pronounced *high-dro-klor-oh-THIGH-a-zide*) is the common or generic name of this drug. It has many brand names, most of which roll off the tongue a bit more easily—Esidrix, HydroDIURIL, Oretic, and Thiuretic are its most frequently used brand names. Hydrochlorothiazide is sometimes combined with a second drug in the same tablet or capsule. The most frequently used combinations are Aldactazide (with spironolactone), Aldoril (with methyldopa), Apresazide (with hydralazine), Capozide (with captopril), Dyazide (with triamterene), Inderide (with propranolol), Maxzide (with triamterene), Moduretic (with amiloride), Timolide (with timolol), and Vaseretic (with enalapril).

Hydrochlorothiazide is the principal member of a group of closely related drugs that are known as the thiazides. Because the thiazides are so similar to one another and because *hydrochlorothiazide* isn't very easy to say, the terms *thiazides* or *thiazide diuretics* are probably more widely used among health professionals. By whatever name, hydrochlorothiazide is the single most commonly prescribed drug in the United States. About 5 percent of all prescriptions contain hydrochlorothiazide. Sometimes its name is abbreviated as HCTZ.

WHAT IS IT SUPPOSED TO DO?   Hydrochlorothiazide is a diuretic, meaning that it increases the amount of urine that is excreted from the body. Hydrochlorothiazide acts on the kidneys, causing them to eliminate extra water and salt from the body and into the urine.

It is used to treat congestive heart failure, high blood pressure, and other medical problems.

Use in Congestive Heart Failure. Extra salt and water may accumulate in the body for a variety of reasons, but congestive heart failure is a common cause in older persons. In congestive heart failure, which is the result of some types of heart disease, the heart's pumping action weakens and the circulation slows. When the kidneys do not get enough circulation, they become less efficient in removing extra salt and water from the body. As a result, veins become swollen and fluid leaks out of them and into surrounding tissue. Usually, the first symptom of this problem is swelling of the ankles and lower legs. (The medical term for this swelling, which can also be caused by less potentially serious circulatory problems, is edema.) Later, fluid accumulates in the lungs, causing shortness of breath. Hydrochlorothiazide's ability to promote salt and water removal by the kidneys is the basis for its use in congestive heart failure.

Use in Hypertension. The diuretic effects of hydrochlorothiazide are important here because too much salt in the body may be part of the cause of hypertension (high blood pressure). In addition, and perhaps more important in hypertension, hydrochlorothiazide causes small blood vessels to dilate. This dilation of blood vessels eases the resistance to blood flow, and blood pressure is thereby lowered. Whether your hypertension is mild or severe, hydrochlorothiazide may be the first drug your doctor prescribes to control it.

SIDE EFFECTS   Serious side effects from hydrochlorothiazide are rare. The most annoying side effect you will notice when you begin taking this drug is a need to urinate frequently. You should avoid taking hydrochlorothiazide too late in the day. Otherwise, you may find yourself being frequently awakened from sleep by a need to urinate.

Hydrochlorothiazide causes potassium to be removed from the body along with salt and water. In most cases, this causes no problem. Dietary sources of potassium usually prevent potassium deficiency from occurring. However, your doctor may prescribe either a potassium supplement or a second diuretic that conserves potassium to prevent this effect, especially if you are also taking digoxin (see Drug Interactions) and will periodically order a laboratory test that measures the concentration of potassium in the blood. The symptoms of too low a concentration of potassium in the blood include profound muscle weakness, muscle cramps or pain, and irregular heartbeats. If you experience any of these symptoms, contact your doctor.

Hydrochlorothiazide sometimes causes an increase in the amount of glucose in the blood, which could unmask latent diabetes or require an increase in your insulin or other drug requirement if you already have diabetes. Prevention of excess potassium loss decreases the risk of this problem. Hydrochlorothiazide can also increase the amount of uric acid in your blood, but it rarely causes gout, the clinical manifestation of too much uric acid in the blood. Your doctor will order periodic laboratory tests to monitor for these and other, rarer possible problems before they cause symptoms.

All diuretics have the potential for causing dehydration when fluid loss is accelerated by hot weather or flulike illness. Whenever you experience fever, vomiting, or diarrhea, whatever the cause, be sure to increase your fluid intake to prevent dehydration. If the symptoms are severe, you should contact your doctor.

Other side effects are too rare to list here. If you should develop a rash or any other unusual symptom while taking this drug, contact your doctor.

DRUG INTERACTIONS   Several drugs interact with hydrochlorothiazide, and your doctor will take special precautions to ensure that no problems occur if any of these drugs need to be taken with hydrochlorothiazide:

Antidiabetic drugs, such as *insulin* or the *sulfonylureas.* Hydrochlorothiazide can increase the concentration of glucose in the blood. If this occurs, despite the protective effect of correcting for potassium loss, your doctor may increase the dosage of your diabetic medication to compensate for this interaction. If you are taking chlorpropamide (Diabinese) or tolbutamide (Orinase), your doctor will monitor for a second, less frequent, possible interaction. These drugs sometimes decrease the concentration of sodium in the blood by a mechanism separate from that of hydrochlorothiazide. (Other sulfonylureas do not share this property.) In some older individuals, this combination of drugs can lead to too low a concentration of sodium in the blood (hyponatremia). If you experience weakness, confusion, or muscle cramps, contact your doctor.

Corticosteroids, such as dexamethasone, hydrocortisone, or prednisone, cause potassium to be lost from the body, and this side effect is additive with that of hydrochlorothiazide. To prevent problems, your doctor will periodically order a laboratory test that measures the concentration of potassium in the blood and, if necessary, will prescribe either a potassium supplement or a second diuretic that conserves potassium.

Digoxin (Lanoxin). Although hydrochlorothiazide is often prescribed together with digoxin, an interaction can occur because of hydrochlorothiazide's promotion of potassium loss from the body. If the amount of potassium in the blood becomes too low, then digoxin toxicity may develop. To prevent this problem, your doctor will periodically order a laboratory test that measures the concentration of potassium in the blood and, if necessary, will prescribe either a potassium supplement or a second diuretic that conserves potassium.

Bile-acid sequestrants, such as cholestyramine resin (Questran) and colestipol (Colestid), are used to lower the concentration of cholesterol in the blood. They are also used to treat the itching that sometimes occurs with jaundice. These drugs may bind to hydrochlorothiazide in the gastrointestinal tract and thereby prevent its full absorption. If therapy with one of these drugs is necessary, the hydrochlorothiazide dose should be taken two hours before the cholestyramine or colestipol dose to minimize any interaction.

Lithium (Eskalith, Lithane, and others), which is prescribed by psychiatrists for mood problems, is removed from the body by the kidneys. Hydrochlorothiazide significantly slows this removal, and the concentration of lithium in the blood increases, sometimes to toxic levels. When these drugs must be used together, your doctor will probably decrease the dose of your lithium, using a laboratory test for monitoring the concentration of lithium in your blood as a guide.

Nonsteroidal anti-inflammatory drugs (NSAIDs), such as *diflunisal, ibuprofen, indomethacin, fenoprofen, meclofenamate, naproxen, piroxicam, sulindac, tolmetin, or large amounts of aspirin.* These drugs can cause fluid retention and edema in older people who are sensitive to this effect. If you are taking hydrochlorothiazide for fluid retention and edema (such as that caused by congestive heart failure or liver disease) and you experience a worsening of your symptoms while taking one of these NSAIDs, stop taking the NSAID and contact your doctor.

ALCOHOLIC BEVERAGES Alcoholic beverages have a more pronounced effect on some people than on others; if you become dizzy when drinking, hydrochlorothiazide might make things worse. You can carefully evaluate this effect for yourself. Most people do not notice any effect at all.

FOOD Many pharmacists recommend taking hydrochlorothiazide with meals. Food does not impair its absorption, and some people (probably fewer than one in a hundred) experience an upset stomach. Taking it with a meal will help you set up a routine for taking it and thereby prevent you from missing too many doses. Take your morning dose with breakfast and, if you take a second daily dose, take it with a late-afternoon snack or dinner.

Be sure to follow any dietary advice, such as low-salt diet or increasing the amount of potassium-containing foods (such as bananas, orange juice, raisins), you may have been given with your prescription.

HOW DOES AGE AFFECT THE RESPONSE TO THIS DRUG? Older people are more sensitive to the effects of diuretics. The effects of too much diuretic, which are rare in younger people, are more likely to occur with advancing age. The most common problem is dizziness or faintness from abnormally low blood pressure. If you experience such a symptom, contact your doctor. Another problem, which is infrequent, is too low a concentration of sodium in the blood. If you experience weakness, confusion, or muscle cramps, contact your doctor.

Your doctor will take your age into consideration in selecting a dosage that is likely to be appropriate for you.

IBUPROFEN

OTHER NAMES Ibuprofen (pronounced *eye-BYOO-pro-fen)* is the common or generic name of this drug. Ibuprofen was first marketed as a prescription drug in the United States in 1974, under the brand name Motrin. Subsequently, equally effective generic ibuprofen tablets became available. In 1984, a form of ibuprofen became available without prescription, marketed under the brand names Advil and Nuprin. These tablets, and the more recently marketed Medipren, contain the same drug that is in their prescription counterparts, but the dose is smaller. Even at this small dose, ibuprofen is an effective pain reliever. Ibuprofen belongs to a large group of drugs called nonsteroidal anti-inflammatory drugs (NSAIDs).

WHAT IS IT SUPPOSED TO DO? Ibuprofen is very effective in relieving pain. It is also effective in relieving the inflammation, swelling, and stiffness caused by arthritis. A number of studies have shown ibuprofen to be as effective, or nearly as effective, as large doses of aspirin for the treatment of arthritic symptoms. However, ibuprofen is much less likely to cause stomach upset than aspirin, and this quality has led to its widespread acceptance among physicians. Ibuprofen is now one of the most widely used prescription drugs.

Although some relief of arthritic symptoms should be apparent shortly after you take your first dose, maximum relief occurs after one or two weeks of regular use.

SIDE EFFECTS Indigestion, heartburn, nausea, stomach discomfort, excessive gas, diarrhea, and other problems related to the digestive tract are the most common side effects from ibuprofen. These side effects can sometimes be prevented by taking ibuprofen with a full glass of water, perhaps in addition to food or an antacid. If these side effects persist, or if they become severe, stop taking the drug and contact your doctor.

Rarely, ibuprofen causes more severe problems in the digestive tract. These include ulcer with bleeding into the gastrointestinal tract (evidenced by bloody stools or stools that are discolored dark red or black) and small amounts of painless blood loss (which can cause anemia). The risk of these problems is lower than it is with aspirin.

Ibuprofen can also cause mental effects such as drowsiness, headache, or dizziness, although these problems don't occur very often. Because ibuprofen can cause decreased alertness in some individuals, you should evaluate how this drug affects you before you drive an automobile or operate any potentially dangerous machinery. If you should develop any sort of visual difficulty (such as blurred or dim vision) or hearing problem (such as buzzing or ringing in your ears), stop taking ibuprofen and contact your doctor.

Kidney problems caused by ibuprofen and similar drugs are relatively rare, but most of the cases that have been reported in the medical literature involved older individuals. Some of the medical problems that are more prevalent among older people place them at greater risk of this side effect. When the kidneys are stressed by congestive heart failure, dehydration, or any kind of kidney impairment (even modest impairment), the body responds by producing substances called prostaglandins. Prostaglandins increase the flow of blood to the kidneys and increase their efficiency. Ibuprofen and related drugs can block this compensatory response, and kidney failure (usually reversible) can occur as a result. (All nonsteroidal antiinflammatory drugs work by preventing the body from manufacturing prostaglandins, which are also mediators of pain and inflammation.) Considering the widespread use of ibuprofen among older people and the extremely small number of kidney problems that have been reported, the risk appears to be quite small. However, you should return to your doctor for regular medical checkups while taking this drug. Contact your doctor promptly if you experience sudden weight gain, swelling of your feet or ankles, or markedly decreased urine production.

Skin problems, such as rashes or unusual reactions to the sun, are extremely rare side effects from ibuprofen. Contact your doctor if you experience anything unusual.

Ibuprofen is very effective in lowering fever. This effect, combined with its pain-relieving and antiinflammatory actions, could be considered a side effect if the signs of an infection were masked and the infection went undetected (and untreated) too long.

If you have ever developed asthma as an allergic reaction to aspirin, you should not take ibuprofen, because a similar allergic reaction could occur.

Other side effects from ibuprofen are too rare to list here. Contact your doctor if you experience any unusual symptoms.

DRUG INTERACTIONS Several drugs have the potential to interact with ibuprofen:

Aspirin is potentially irritating to the digestive tract, and its irritant effects could become troublesome when added to those of ibuprofen. Check with your doctor before taking this drug combination.

Diuretics, such as *hydrochlorothiazide (HydroDIURIL and other brands) or furosemide (Lasix).* Infrequently, ibuprofen causes fluid retention and edema. If you are taking a diuretic for fluid retention and edema (such as that caused by congestive heart failure or liver disease) and you experience a worsening of your symptoms while taking ibuprofen, contact your doctor.

Warfarin (Coumadin). Ibuprofen can cause some gastrointestinal bleeding, which could be worsened by the anticoagulant effects of warfarin. In addition, ibuprofen decreases the effectiveness of blood platelets in forming blood clots, so the risk of side effects from warfarin is increased somewhat while you are taking ibuprofen.

ALCOHOLIC BEVERAGES Alcohol adds to ibuprofen's irritating effects on the gastrointestinal tract. Avoid taking them at the same time.

FOOD It's a good idea to take your ibuprofen with food to minimize any gastric irritation that might occur.

HOW DOES AGE AFFECT THE RESPONSE TO THIS DRUG? Age does not significantly affect the way in which ibuprofen is absorbed from the gastrointestinal tract or eliminated from the body. However, advancing age does increase the risk of side effects from ibuprofen.

When ibuprofen became available without a prescription, as Advil and Nuprin, there was some concern that kidney problems (see Side Effects) caused by the drug would become more frequent because of unsupervised use in older people. The Food and Drug Administration replied that the risk, at the doses used for self-medication, is too low to warrant any special warning to the consumer. To be safe, do not take ibuprofen without your doctor's approval if you have chronic kidney problems, if you take diuretics, if you have liver disease, or if you have congestive heart failure.

IMIPRAMINE

OTHER NAMES Imipramine (pronounced *im-IP-ra-meen*) is the common or generic name of this drug. Some frequently used brand names for imipramine are Janimine, SK-Pramine, Tipramine, Tofranil, and Tofranil-PM. Imipramine belongs to a group of drugs called tricyclic antidepressants. *(Tricyclic* describes their chemical structure; *antidepressant* refers to their principal pharmacological effect.)

WHAT IS IT SUPPOSED TO DO?   Imipramine relieves mental depression. The precise means by which it works has not been established, but its mechanism of action involves an increase in the concentration of certain naturally occurring substances (serotonin and norepinephrine) within the brain. Elevation of mood and reversal of the various symptoms that can accompany depression (such as sleep problems, decreased energy, or loss of appetite) require a minimum of several weeks of regular use. Your doctor may prescribe less than several weeks' supply of medication initially, so it is important that you return to your pharmacy to have your prescription refilled. Your doctor may want you to continue taking imipramine for several months after your mood returns to normal.

SIDE EFFECTS   Nearly everyone experiences dry mouth while taking imipramine. It doesn't seem to be related to dosage, and it tends to diminish with time. Sugar-free candy or gum is often helpful in alleviating this problem.

Drowsiness is another common side effect. Avoid driving until you are sure that your alertness and coordination are not impaired.

The most common potentially serious side effect involves the temporary decrease in blood pressure that occurs when you stand up quickly. This decrease in blood pressure is exaggerated by imipramine and is likely to make you dizzy, light-headed, or faint if you stand up too quickly. If this side effect is severe (especially if it causes you to fall or causes your heart to pound or race), contact your doctor. Be very careful to stand up slowly.

The dry mouth caused by imipramine is an example of what pharmacologists call an anticholinergic effect. It can be caused by any drug that blocks the receptors for acetylcholine, a substance the body produces to regulate certain functions that are beyond conscious control. When imipramine is taken with other drugs that have anticholinergic side effects, these side effects are more likely to cause problems (see Drug Interactions). A common anticholinergic side effect is constipation. Ask your pharmacist for appropriate treatment; a stool softener is often helpful. Contact your doctor if constipation becomes severe. Another anticholinergic side effect is the sudden onset of confusion or disorientation, sometimes with visual hallucinations. If this occurs, contact your doctor; it is a sign that the dosage is too high for you. Other anticholinergic side effects that require your doctor's attention (and these are infrequent or rare) include blurred vision, difficulty in urinating (more common in older men with prostate difficulties), and eye pain (a possible indication that narrow-angle glaucoma, not the usual type of glaucoma, has been aggravated).

Effects on the heart—excessively fast, slow, or irregular heartbeats—are infrequent. Contact your doctor if any of these occur.

Other side effects include nausea, unpleasant taste, diarrhea (infrequent), and excessive sweating (infrequent). These side effects may diminish or go away as your body adjusts to the effects of this drug. Contact your doctor if they are severe or bothersome. A fine tremor is not an uncommon side effect in older people; tell your doctor if this occurs.

Other side effects are too infrequent to list here. Contact your doctor if you experience any unexpected symptoms.

DRUG INTERACTIONS Imipramine interacts with a number of drugs. Here are the most common sources of potential problems:

Anticholinergic drugs, such as *belladonna (Donnatal) or propantheline (Pro-Banthine),* which are used for peptic-ulcer disease, *benztropine (Cogentin),* which is used in the treatment of Parkinson's disease and to treat the side effects sometimes caused by tranquilizers, and *scopolamine (Transderm Scōp)*, which is used to prevent motion sickness, all work by blocking acetylcholine (see Side Effects). These drugs are more likely to cause anticholinergic side effects when taken with imipramine. In many cases, the anticholinergic side effects of imipramine obviate the need for these other drugs. Check with your doctor before taking them.

Antihistamines, which are included in many nonprescription cold and allergy medicines, have sedative and anticholinergic (see above) side effects. Avoid these products while taking imipramine.

Antihypertensive drugs can interact with imipramine by several mechanisms. First, some of them (beta-blockers, clonidine, methyldopa, and reserpine) can cause depression as a side effect. Second, the action of a few antihypertensive drugs is blocked by imipramine. If you are taking clonidine (Catapres, Combipres), guanethidine (Ismelin), or guanadrel (Hylorel), your doctor will need to prescribe another drug to control your blood pressure. Third, if your antihypertensive drug causes dizziness, imipramine will make this side effect worse. Your doctor may need to decrease the dose of your antihypertensive drug before you start taking imipramine.

Cimetidine (Tagamet), which is used in the treatment of peptic-ulcer disease, slows the metabolism of imipramine and thereby increases its effects. Contact your doctor if you experience an increase in imipramine side effects while taking cimetidine; your doctor may have to lower the dosage of your imipramine temporarily.

Monoamine oxidase inhibitors, such as *isocarboxazid (Marplan), phenelzine (Nardil), or tranylcypromine (Parnate),* which are also used in the treatment of depression, sometimes cause dangerous toxic reactions when taken with imipramine. This combination of drugs should only be used in hospitalized patients who are under careful observation. Normally, one or two weeks are allowed to elapse between the use of imipramine and one of these drugs.

Phenobarbital, which is used to prevent seizures and is also sometimes included as an ingredient in certain medications for its sedative effects, stimulates the metabolism of imipramine and thereby decreases its effects. If you require treatment with phenobarbital, your doctor will take this into consideration in adjusting your imipramine dosage. Otherwise, your doctor may replace your phenobarbital-containing medication with another drug product.

Phenothiazine tranquilizers, such as *perphenazine (Trilafon), thioridazine (Mellaril), or trifluoperazine (Stelazine),* are more likely to cause anticholinergic side effects (see Side Effects) when taken with imipramine. In addition, these drugs may slow the metabolism of imipramine and thereby increase its effects. There are instances when these drugs need to be given with imipramine, but you should be sure that your doctor intends that you take this combination.

ALCOHOLIC BEVERAGES   Alcohol will increase the dizziness or faintness you may feel upon standing up too quickly. It will also add to any drowsiness that imipramine might cause. Therefore, you should avoid alcohol or use it sparingly while taking imipramine.

FOOD   Take your imipramine with meals to help you maintain a regular schedule for taking it and to prevent any nausea it might cause.

HOW DOES AGE AFFECT THE RESPONSE TO THIS DRUG?   There is considerable variation among individuals in the rate at which imipramine is removed from the blood by metabolism in the liver. However, several studies have shown that advancing age is accompanied by a slower metabolism of imipramine, and that older people tend to develop higher concentrations of imipramine in their blood. Therefore, older people usually require smaller doses than younger people.

In addition, older people are more sensitive to side effects from imipramine. Your doctor will try to prescribe a dose that is likely to be effective without causing serious side effects, but you should contact him or her promptly if you experience extreme dizziness or faintness (which could cause you to fall), confusion or disorientation (which is alarming but goes away when the dose is reduced or the drug is stopped), or any other serious side effect. Your doctor may make use of a laboratory test that measures the concentration of imipramine in your blood to evaluate your dosage.

INDOMETHACIN

OTHER NAMES Indomethacin (pronounced *in-doe-METH-a-sin)* is the common or generic name of this drug. A frequently used brand name for indomethacin is Indocin. Indomethacin belongs to a large group of drugs called nonsteroidal anti-inflammatory drugs (NSAIDs).

WHAT IS IT SUPPOSED TO DO? Indomethacin relieves the pain, inflammation, swelling, and stiffness associated with arthritis and related conditions. Although some relief should be apparent shortly after you start taking indomethacin, maximum relief occurs after one or two weeks of regular use.

SIDE EFFECTS Although indomethacin is very effective and is widely used, many people cannot tolerate its side effects.

Headache is the most common side effect. Less frequently, it causes confusion or severe mood changes. If any of these occur, contact your doctor. Dizziness and light-headedness are other frequent mental effects from indomethacin. Because indomethacin can cause decreased mental alertness in some individuals, you should evaluate how this drug affects you before you drive an automobile or operate any dangerous machinery.

Stomach pain, indigestion, loss of appetite, nausea, vomiting, diarrhea, and other problems related to the digestive tract are not uncommon effects from indomethacin. These side effects can sometimes be prevented by taking indomethacin with a full glass of water, perhaps in addition to food or an antacid. If these side effects persist, or if they become severe, stop taking the drug and contact your doctor.

Infrequently, indomethacin causes more serious problems in the digestive tract. These include ulcer with bleeding (evidenced by bloody stools or stools that are discolored dark red or black) and small amounts of painless blood loss (which can cause anemia).

Kidney problems caused by indomethacin and similar drugs are relatively rare, but most of the cases that have been reported in the medical literature involved older individuals. Some of the medical problems that are more prevalent among older people place them at greater risk for this side effect. When the kidneys are stressed by congestive heart failure, dehydration, or any kind of kidney impairment (even modest impairment), the body responds by producing substances called prostaglandins. Prostaglandins increase the flow of blood to the kidneys and increase their efficiency. Indomethacin, which is among the most potent inhibitors of prostaglandin synthesis, can block this compensatory response, and kidney failure (usually reversible) can occur as a result. (All nonsteroidal antiinflammatory drugs work by preventing the body from manufacturing prostaglandins, which are also mediators of pain and inflammation.) Considering the widespread use of indomethacin among older people and the relatively small number of kidney problems that have been reported, the risk is probably small. However, you should return to your doctor for regular medical checkups while taking this drug. Contact your doctor promptly if you experience sudden weight gain, swelling of your feet or ankles, or markedly decreased urine production.

Skin problems, such as rashes or unusual reactions to the sun, are extremely rare side effects from indomethacin. Contact your doctor if you experience anything unusual.

Indomethacin is very effective in lowering fever. This effect, combined with its pain-relieving and anti-inflammatory actions, could become a side effect if the signs of an infection were masked and the infection went undetected (and untreated) too long.

If you have ever developed asthma as an allergic reaction to aspirin, you should not take indomethacin, because a similar allergic reaction could occur.

Other side effects occur infrequently. Contact your doctor if you experience any unusual symptoms.

DRUG INTERACTIONS Several drugs have the potential to interact with indomethacin:

Angiotensin-converting-enzyme (ACE) inhibitors, such as *captopril (Capoten) or enalapril (Vasotec).* Indomethacin can block the antihypertensive effects of these drugs. It is also possible that indomethacin can block the beneficial effects of these drugs on congestive heart failure. Ask your doctor to monitor for loss of captopril or enalapril effect.

Aspirin is potentially irritating to the digestive tract, and its irritant effects could become troublesome when added to those of indomethacin. Don't take this combination of drugs unless it is specifically recommended by your doctor.

Beta-blocking drugs, such as *atenolol (Tenormin), metoprolol* (Lopressor), nadolol (Corgard), pindolol (Visken), propranolol (Inderal), or timolol (Blocadren). Indomethacin can impair the blood-pressure-lowering effects of these drugs and may impair their other effects as well. If you are taking a beta-blocking drug and indomethacin is required, your doctor will need to evaluate whether there is any decrease in the effect of your beta-blocking drug.

Diuretics, such as *hydrochlorothiazide (HydroDIURIL and other brands) or furosemide (Lasix).* Infrequently, indomethacin causes fluid retention and edema. If you are taking a diuretic for fluid retention and edema (such as that caused by congestive heart failure or liver disease) and you experience a worsening of your symptoms while taking indomethacin, stop taking your indomethacin and contact your doctor. It can also block the antihypertensive effects of diuretics. If you are taking a diuretic for high blood pressure, your blood pressure should be checked while you are taking indomethacin, to be sure that it has not impaired your response to the diuretic.

Potassium-sparing diuretics, such as *amiloride (Midamor) or triamterene (Dyrenium),* and indomethacin can cause impaired kidney function when taken together. This combination is best avoided.

Warfarin (Coumadin). Indomethacin can cause some gastrointestinal bleeding, which could be worsened by the anticoagulant effects of warfarin. In addition, indomethacin decreases the effectiveness of blood platelets in forming blood clots, so the risk of gastrointestinal bleeding from warfarin is increased while you are taking indomethacin.

ALCOHOLIC BEVERAGES Alcohol adds to the gastric-irritant effects of indomethacin. Avoid taking them at the same time.

FOOD It's a good idea to take your indomethacin with food to minimize any gastric irritation that might occur.

HOW DOES AGE AFFECT THE RESPONSE TO THIS DRUG? Advancing age increases the risk of side effects from indomethacin.

INSULIN

OTHER NAMES Insulin (pronounced *IN-su-lin),* a hormone secreted by the pancreas, is injected as a drug when the natural supply is inadequate. There are many insulins on the market because it comes from several biological sources and each insulin can be prepared in a variety of ways. The various preparations prolong its action for different periods of time. Although insulin is available without a prescription, insulin regimens are highly individualized and should not be altered without medical supervision.

Insulins obtained from beef and pork sources have been used for many years. More recently, synthetic human insulin, prepared either by modification of pork insulin or by employment of genetically altered bacteria (utilizing recombinant DNA technology), has become commercially available. Various brands of insulin utilize different sources of insulin, and your body may be more or less sensitive to each of these insulins. Therefore, you should not change brands unless your pharmacist can assure you that the source and purity are the same; purity may be a less important issue, since all currently marketed insulins are highly purified. If you change to a brand that utilizes insulin from a different source (after checking with your doctor), your insulin requirements could change as well, and you should monitor for this possibility.

There are several insulin preparations that release insulin into the blood at differing rates. Be careful to buy only the preparation(s) prescribed by your doctor. The various insulin preparations, their approximate onsets and durations of action (which will vary depending on the dose and your responsiveness), and some of their frequently used brand names (with sources in parentheses) are listed below:

Regular insulin. Also called Insulin Injection, this is the only insulin that is clear in appearance. It begins working within thirty to sixty minutes, its peak effects occur in two to four hours, and it lasts for five to seven hours. Some frequently used brand names are Humulin R (human insulin created by recombinant DNA), Novolin R (human insulin created by modification of pork insulin), Regular Iletin I (combined beef-pork origin), Regular Iletin II (beef or pork origin), Regular Insulin (pork origin), and Velosulin (pork origin).

Semilente insulin. Also called Prompt Insulin Zinc Suspension. It begins working in one to two hours, its peak effects occur in four to six hours, and it lasts for twelve to sixteen hours. Some frequently used brand names are Semilente Iletin I (combined beef-pork origin) and Semilente Insulin (beef origin).

NPH insulin. Also called Isophane Insulin Suspension. It begins working in one to two hours, its peak effects occur in six to fourteen hours, and it lasts for more than twenty-four hours. Some frequently used brand names are Humulin N (human insulin created by recombinant DNA), Insulatard NPH (pork origin), Novolin N (human insulin created by modification of pork insulin), NPH Iletin I (combined beef-pork origin), NPH Iletin II (beef or pork origin), and NPH Insulin (beef origin).

Mixed NPH and regular insulin. The brand name of this product is Mixtard (pork origin). It begins working in thirty to sixty minutes, its peak effects occur in four to eight hours, and it lasts for up to twenty-four hours.

Lente insulin. Also called Insulin Zinc Suspension. It begins working in one to three hours, its peak effects occur in six to fourteen hours, and it lasts for more than twenty-four hours. Some frequently used brand names are Humulin L (human insulin created by recombinant DNA), Lente Iletin I (combined beef-pork origin), Lente Iletin II (beef or pork origin), Lente Insulin (beef), and Novolin L (human insulin created by modification of pork insulin).

PZI insulin. Also called Protamine Zinc Insulin Suspension. It begins working in four to six hours, its peak effects occur in fourteen to twenty-four hours, and it lasts for more than thirty-six hours. Some frequently used brand names are Protamine Zinc & Iletin I (combined beef-pork origin) and Protamine Zinc & Iletin II (beef or pork origin).

Ultralente insulin. Also called Extended Insulin Zinc Suspension. It begins working in four to six hours, its peak effects occur in eighteen to twenty-four hours, and it lasts for more than thirty-six hours. Some frequently used brand names are Ultralente Iletin I (beef-pork origin) and Ultralente Insulin (beef origin).

If your doctor tells you to mix two types of insulin in the same syringe in order to more accurately meet your requirements in a single dose, always follow the same sequence of mixing, and follow your doctor's directions carefully.

Although most insulin contains 100 units/ml, there are other strengths, so be careful to buy the correct strength and appropriate syringes.

WHAT IS IT SUPPOSED TO DO?   Insulin is essential to normal carbohydrate, protein, and fat metabolism. When the body is unable to provide enough insulin for its needs, the metabolic syndrome known as diabetes mellitus occurs. The primary symptoms of diabetes can be related to impaired carbohydrate metabolism. In the absence of insulin, glucose (a sugar formed during the digestion of carbohydrates) is poorly utilized by the body, and its concentration increases in the blood. The symptoms of too high a concentration of glucose in the blood (*hyper*glycemia) are loss of appetite, fruitlike breath odor, unusual thirst (less reliable as a symptom in some older people), excessive urination, and drowsiness (which can progress to loss of consciousness and coma). Careful dosage of insulin, along with regulation of diet and exercise, restores normal metabolism and lowers the concentration of glucose in the blood.

In addition to promoting the entry of glucose into muscle cells, where it becomes a source of energy, and promoting the storage of glucose in the liver (as glycogen), insulin is essential to several other aspects of healthy food and energy metabolism. In its absence, there are not only high concentrations of glucose in the blood, but also high concentrations of fatty acids from the abnormally rapid breakdown of fat. Protein is converted into glucose at an abnormally high rate in the absence of insulin. These metabolic problems are corrected or prevented by insulin injections.

Even if you don't have any symptoms, your doctor will want you to control your blood glucose. Control of blood glucose prevents or reduces the long-term complications of diabetes, which include deterioration of vision, kidney disease, loss of feeling in the extremities, damage to blood vessels, heart attack, and stroke.

SIDE EFFECTS   *Hypo*glycemia (too low a concentration of glucose in the blood) is the most important side effect from insulin. Hypoglycemia occurs from too much insulin effect, but the inadvertent administration of too large a dose isn't the only cause. Vigorous exercise shares insulin's ability to promote the transport of glucose into muscle cells, and, of course, exercise uses glucose for energy. An unaccustomed increase in exercise will therefore add to the effect of insulin and can cause hypoglycemia. Failure to eat is another common cause of hypoglycemia. Hypoglycemia can also occur during illness that is accompanied by vomiting or the inability to eat, but you still need insulin when you are sick—contact your doctor for directions. Hypoglycemia can be prevented by regulation of diet, activity, and insulin dosage and by monitoring the blood glucose.

The symptoms of hypoglycemia, which include the rapid onset of weakness, hunger or nausea, cold sweats, pounding or racing heartbeat, shakiness, headache, blurred vision, nervousness, crabbiness, tingling lips or mouth, numb fingers, drowsiness, confusion, light-headedness, or dizziness, are quickly reversed with a small amount of rapidly acting carbohydrate. Individuals vary in the symptoms they experience first (and there are other, less common symptoms), but weakness, shakiness, sweating, and nervousness are the most prevalent early signs of hypoglycemia. Examples of appropriate amounts and sources of carbohydrate for treating a hypoglycemic episode are one-half cup (four ounces) of fruit juice, one-half cup (four ounces) of sugar-containing soft drink, one cup (eight ounces) of milk (an excellent treatment because it contains both carbohydrate and protein), one-half cup (four ounces) of water with two teaspoonfuls of sugar dissolved in it, or five or six Life Savers. If relief does not occur within ten minutes, the carbohydrate should be repeated. After treating yourself with carbohydrate, measure your blood glucose or contact your doctor. Have a snack of toast or crackers or half a sandwich if you are not planning to eat within the next hour. You should always carry hard candy or some form of carbohydrate when you go out. You should also carry an identification card or bracelet with pertinent medical information. If untreated, hypoglycemia can lead to loss of consciousness and coma.

Other side effects are too rare to list here. Contact your doctor if you experience any unusual symptoms.

DRUG INTERACTIONS   A number of drugs can interact with insulin or affect your diabetes. These are the most important:

Aspirin. Large doses of aspirin (for example, a dozen or more tablets a day) have a mild antidiabetic effect. This effect is too mild to be used as a treatment for diabetes, but it adds to the effect of insulin. If you are taking large doses of aspirin, you should be aware of this effect. If you start or stop using large doses of aspirin, your insulin requirement may change. Small amounts of aspirin (fewer than six tablets a day) will not affect your response to insulin.

Some *beta-blocking drugs, such as pindolol (Visken), propranolol (Inderal), nadolol (Corgard), or timolol (Blocadren).* Diabetic patients should not take these drugs unless there is no other alternative. They can block some of the warning signs of hypoglycemia (especially rapid heartbeat or palpitations), delay the recovery from hypoglycemia, cause high-blood-pressure episodes during hypoglycemia, and impair circulation to the extremities in diabetics. Other beta-blocking drugs, such as metoprolol (Lopressor) and atenolol (Tenormin), are less likely to cause problems, but there is some risk, and all beta-blockers prevent racing or pounding heartbeat from occurring during hypoglycemia. If a beta-blocker is required, keep in mind that sweating is a sign of hypoglycemia.

Corticosteroids, such as *dexamethasone, hydrocortisone, or prednisone,* can make diabetes more difficult to control. If you require a corticosteroid, your insulin requirement may increase.

Diuretics, such as *hydrochlorothiazide (HydroDIURIL and others) or furosemide (Lasix),* tend to increase the concentration of glucose in the blood. When you begin taking a diuretic, your insulin requirement may increase.

Guanethidine (Ismelin) and guanadrel (Hylorel), which are sometimes used to treat high blood pressure, increase the effects of insulin. If you start or stop taking guanethidine or guanadrel, your insulin requirement may change.

Nifedipine (Procardia), which is used in the treatment of angina, may decrease your response to insulin. If you start or stop taking nifedipine, your insulin requirement may change.

Smoking antagonizes the effects of insulin somewhat. Heavy smokers require larger doses of insulin. If you stop smoking, your insulin requirement may decrease.

Thyroid hormones can affect your response to insulin. If you are starting to take thyroid, or if the dosage of your thyroid hormone is being changed, your insulin requirement may change.

ALCOHOLIC BEVERAGES Some doctors tell their patients to avoid alcohol. Others advise their patients to limit their alcohol use to a glass of wine or two with dinner.

If your doctor says it is all right for you to drink small amounts of alcohol with meals, you should observe some precautions. First, avoid sweetened alcoholic beverages. Second, you should know that alcohol temporarily lowers the concentration of glucose in the blood. If you drink alcohol on an empty stomach, it can cause hypoglycemia. Therefore, you should avoid large amounts of alcohol and avoid drinking on an empty stomach. If you drink small amounts of alcohol with meals, hypoglycemia is not likely to occur.

FOOD Insulin does not replace diet as the primary means of controlling blood glucose. In addition to avoiding simple sugars, you should increase the amount of roughage (such as fruits, vegetables, and whole grains) in your diet. These foods slow the absorption of complex carbohydrates, thereby preventing large increases in blood glucose after meals. Furthermore, you should restrict your consumption of saturated fats (butter, animal fat), because they increase the risk of cardiovascular disease, which is more common among diabetics. Your doctor will recommend a diet that is balanced in protein, carbohydrate, and unsaturated fats

This diet can be as varied as you like, as illustrated by the standard food-composition tables and exchange lists that you should obtain.

Be careful in measuring your portions, especially with the more concentrated forms of calories—a tablespoon of cooking oil and two slices of bread both contain about 120 calories, but it's easier to underestimate the measurement of the cooking oil. Seasoning with lemon, vinegar, salt, onion, garlic, or spices does not add calories, but seasoning with butter, meat fat, or sugars adds undesirable foods as well as calories to your diet.

A regular diet is important. If you skip meals because of illness or for some other reason, you may experience hypoglycemia (see Side Effects). If you cannot eat because of illness, check with your doctor.

HOW DOES AGE AFFECT THE RESPONSE TO THIS DRUG? Hypoglycemia is a potential problem among all people who use insulin, but older people are more susceptible to hypoglycemia. The confusion that is sometimes caused by hypoglycemia often complicates its recognition, especially among some older people. Be sure to take your insulin as directed, follow a careful but regular diet, and be sure that you and those around you are familiar with the signs and symptoms of hypoglycemia.

Age also affects the way your body responds to high concentrations of glucose in the blood. As the kidneys age, they become less efficient. In younger people, when the concentration of glucose in the blood gets much higher than normal, glucose appears in the urine. The threshold for glucose spilling into the urine increases with age, so older people can have much higher concentrations of glucose in their blood without having any in their urine. This effect varies from individual to individual, of course, but urine tests for glucose may be less reliable as indicators of blood glucose in older people. Don't be mislead by negative urine tests for glucose. Your doctor can compare your blood glucose with your urine glucose and give you some idea of how reliable urine tests are for you. Many diabetics are able to measure their own blood glucose concentrations.

If you have trouble injecting your insulin because of poor vision or arthritis in your fingers, train someone to help you or discuss the problem with your doctor.

ISOSORBIDE DINITRATE

OTHER NAMES   Isosorbide dinitrate (pronounced *eye-soe-SOR-bide dye-NYE-trate)* is the common or generic name of this drug. Some frequently used brand names for isosorbide dinitrate are Dilatrate, Iso-Bid, Isonate, Isordil, Isotrate, Sorbide, and Sorbitrate. It is available in a variety of dosage forms, including chewable tablets, regular tablets (to be swallowed), extended-release tablets and capsules (to be swallowed), sublingual tablets (to be dissolved under the tongue), and buccal tablets (to be dissolved between the cheek and gum or between the lip and gum). Be sure you know how to take your isosorbide dinitrate; each form is designed to release the drug into the blood at a specific rate. Isosorbide dinitrate belongs to a large group of drugs called organic nitrates, which have been used in the treatment of angina for more than a hundred years.

WHAT IS IT SUPPOSED TO DO?   Angina pectoris, the chest pain that may be precipitated by exercise, stress, or meals, is caused by a deficiency of oxygen in the heart muscle. Isosorbide dinitrate relaxes the smooth muscle within the walls of veins and arteries, causing them to dilate (their diameter gets wider). This dilation is beneficial in angina for two reasons. First, blood flow (and therefore oxygen supply) within the heart muscle is increased. Second, circulatory changes throughout the body decrease the heart's workload and therefore its demand for oxygen.

Isosorbide dinitrate relieves angina attacks when it is taken sublingually (dissolved under the tongue). This route of administration can also be used to prevent an angina attack that can be predicted (such as by the need to walk up a flight of stairs). When it is taken buccally (dissolved between the cheek or lip and gum) or chewed and held in the mouth for at least two minutes before swallowing (this requires chewable tablets), the effect is longer lasting. Tablets or capsules that are intended to be swallowed contain a larger amount of the drug; they are taken regularly for the prevention of angina attacks.

If sublingual, buccal, or chewed isosorbide dinitrate does not relieve your angina attack within five minutes, you may take another dose. This procedure can be repeated if necessary, but not for more than three doses. If your chest pain continues after three doses taken within fifteen minutes, contact your doctor or go to a hospital emergency room immediately.

Although the treatment of angina is the most common use of isosorbide dinitrate, it is sometimes used in the treatment of congestive heart failure (because of its ability to decrease the heart's workload).

SIDE EFFECTS Although the circulatory changes brought about by isosorbide dinitrate are beneficial to the heart, they can cause unpleasant effects elsewhere in the body. Headache is the most common side effect. Headache often decreases with continued use. Acetaminophen or aspirin may provide some relief. If your headaches are particularly severe, ask your doctor if the dose can be decreased. You may experience dizziness and weakness, especially when you are standing up. Sit or lie down if you feel dizzy or light-headed (if you don't, you might faint); this will restore circulation to your brain. Exercise, hot weather, standing in one position for a long time, and alcohol can provoke this drug-induced dizziness or light-headedness. Flushing of the face and neck, rapid pulse (unless you are taking a beta-blocker), and nausea can also occur as a result of the circulatory changes brought about by this drug. Contact your doctor if any of these side effects is persistent or severe; the dosage may be too high for you.

After taking isosorbide dinitrate on a regular basis

for a while, you may develop some tolerance to it, and stopping it suddenly could cause a withdrawal reaction. The likelihood of such tolerance is unknown at this time; it may be only a theoretical risk. To be safe, don't stop taking isosorbide dinitrate without first checking with your doctor, who may wish that you slowly decrease the dosage when stopping it.

Blurred vision, dry mouth, and rash are rare side effects. Contact your doctor if you experience these or any other unexpected symptoms.

DRUG INTERACTIONS Any drug that lowers the blood pressure (as a therapeutic effect or side effect) will make you more sensitive to the dizziness or light-headedness that isosorbide dinitrate may cause. Nasal decongestants often contain drugs that can provoke an angina attack; check with your pharmacist before using such drugs.

ALCOHOLIC BEVERAGES Alcohol can add significantly to the dilation of blood vessels caused by isosorbide dinitrate, making dizziness, light-headedness, or fainting much more likely to occur. Be very careful to limit the amount of alcohol you drink.

FOOD Remember that overeating can cause angina attacks. Exercise immediately after meals is another situation you should avoid. Also, obesity places a strain on your heart and increases the likelihood that you will have angina attacks.

HOW DOES AGE AFFECT THE RESPONSE TO THIS DRUG? Advancing age increases the susceptibility to dizziness or light-headedness from isosorbide dinitrate. Therefore, your doctor will begin treatment with small doses. However, there is considerable variation among individuals in the dosages they require.

LORAZEPAM

OTHER NAMES Lorazepam (pronounced *lor-AZ-eh-pam)* is the common or generic name of this drug. A frequently used brand name for lorazepam is Ativan. Lorazepam belongs to a large group of similar drugs called benzodiazepines.

WHAT IS IT SUPPOSED TO DO? Lorazepam relieves the symptoms of anxiety and tension.

SIDE EFFECTS Drowsiness is the principal side effect from lorazepam. You may find yourself unsteady on your feet as well. Evaluate these effects for yourself and regulate your activities accordingly. You should be especially cautious about driving an automobile. If drowsiness or unsteadiness persists, stop taking the drug and contact your doctor.

Infrequently, lorazepam causes dizziness, weakness, confusion, impaired memory, or loss of coordination. If you experience any of these effects, which suggest you are extremely sensitive to lorazepam, stop taking it and contact your doctor.

If you have been taking lorazepam regularly for a long time and in large doses, you may experience mild withdrawal symptoms a day or two after stopping this drug. Typical symptoms include difficulty in sleeping, unusual irritability, and unusual nervousness. If these occur, contact your doctor.

Other side effects are too rare to list here. Contact your doctor if you experience any unusual symptoms.

DRUG INTERACTIONS Sedation is a common side effect of antidepressant drugs, antihistamines, tranquilizers, narcotic analgesics, and other drugs. You may become excessively sedated while taking lorazepam with these drugs.

ALCOHOLIC BEVERAGES Lorazepam adds to alcohol's depressive effects on the nervous system. You should limit your alcohol consumption to small amounts while taking lorazepam. Needless to say, the effects of this combination on driving can be dangerous.

FOOD Lorazepam can be taken either with food or on an empty stomach.

HOW DOES AGE AFFECT THE RESPONSE TO THIS DRUG?   Age does not affect the rate at which lorazepam is removed from the body. However, older people are more sensitive to side effects from lorazepam. Confusion, weakness, dizziness, impaired memory, and loss of coordination, which are infrequent side effects from lorazepam, occur more often in older people.

MECLOFENAMATE

OTHER NAMES   Meclofenamate (pronounced *mehklo-fen-AM-ate)* is the common or generic name of this drug. A frequently used brand name for meclofenamate is Meclomen. Meclofenamate belongs to a large group of drugs called nonsteroidal anti-inflammatory drugs (NSAIDs).

WHAT IS IT SUPPOSED TO DO?   Meclofenamate relieves the pain, inflammation, swelling, and stiffness associated with arthritis. Although some relief should become apparent shortly after you begin taking meclofenamate, maximum relief occurs after one or two weeks of regular use.

SIDE EFFECTS   The most common side effect from meclofenamate is diarrhea. If you experience severe diarrhea, stop taking the drug and call your doctor. Sometimes this side effect goes away if the dose is reduced. Nausea, vomiting, and stomach pain can also be caused by meclofenamate. These side effects can sometimes be prevented by taking meclofenamate with a full glass of water, perhaps with the addition of food or an antacid. If they persist, or if they are severe, stop taking the drug and contact your doctor.

Rarely, meclofenamate causes more severe problems in the digestive tract. These include ulcer with bleeding into the gastrointestinal tract (evidenced by bloody stools or stools that are discolored dark red or black) and small amounts of painless blood loss (which can cause anemia). The risk of these problems is lower than it is with aspirin.

Meclofenamate can also cause mental effects such as dizziness or headache. Because meclofenamate can cause decreased alertness in some individuals, you should evaluate how this drug affects you before you drive an automobile or operate any potentially dangerous machinery. If you should develop any sort of visual difficulty (such as blurred or dim vision) or hearing problem (such as buzzing or ringing in your ears), stop taking the drug and contact your doctor.

Rashes from meclofenamate are not uncommon. On rare occasions, meclofenamate causes other, more severe skin problems or unusual reactions to the sun. Contact your doctor if you experience any sort of rash or skin problem while taking meclofenamate.

Kidney problems caused by meclofenamate and similar drugs are relatively rare, but most of the cases that have been reported in the medical literature involved older individuals. Some of the medical problems that are more prevalent among older people place them at greater risk for this side effect. When the kidneys are stressed by congestive heart failure, dehydration, or any kind of kidney impairment (even modest impairment), the body responds by producing substances called prostaglandins. Prostaglandins increase the flow of blood to the kidneys and also their efficiency. Meclofenamate and related drugs can block this compensatory response, and kidney failure (usually reversible) can occur as a result. (All nonsteroidal anti-inflammatory drugs work by preventing the body from manufacturing prostaglandins, which are also mediators of pain and inflammation.) Considering the widespread use of meclofenamate among older people and the extremely small number of kidney problems that have been reported, the risk is probably small. However, you should return to your doctor for regular medical checkups while taking this drug. Contact your doctor promptly if you should experience sudden weight gain, swelling of your feet or ankles, or markedly decreased urine production.

Meclofenamate is very effective in lowering fever. This effect, combined with its pain-relieving and anti-inflammatory actions, could be considered a side effect if the signs of an infection were masked and the infection went undetected (and untreated) too long.

Other side effects from meclofenamate are too rare to list here. Contact your doctor if you experience any unusual symptoms.

DRUG INTERACTIONS Several drugs have the potential to interact with meclofenamate:

Aspirin is potentially irritating to the digestive tract, and its irritant effects could become troublesome when added to those of meclofenamate. Avoid this combination.

Diuretics, such as *hydrochlorothiazide (HydroDIURIL and other brands) or furosemide (Lasix).* Infrequently, meclofenamate causes fluid retention and edema. If you are taking a diuretic for fluid retention and edema (such as that caused by congestive heart failure or liver disease) and you experience a worsening of your symptoms while taking meclofenamate, stop taking your meclofenamate and contact your doctor.

Warfarin (Coumadin). Meclofenamate can cause some gastrointestinal bleeding, which could be worsened by the anticoagulant effects of warfarin. In addition, meclofenamate decreases the effectiveness of blood platelets in forming blood clots, so the risk of side effects from warfarin is increased somewhat while you are taking meclofenamate.

ALCOHOLIC BEVERAGES Alcohol adds to the gastric-irritant effects of meclofenamate. Avoid taking them at the same time.

FOOD Food slows the absorption of meclofenamate somewhat, but it doesn't impair its absorption. It's a good idea to take your meclofenamate with food to minimize any gastric irritation that might occur.

HOW DOES AGE AFFECT THE RESPONSE TO THIS DRUG? Advancing age increases the risk of side effects from meclofenamate.

METHYLDOPA

OTHER NAMES   Methyldopa (pronounced *meth-ill-DOE-pa)* is the generic or common name for this drug. A frequently used brand name for methyldopa is Aldomet. Methyldopa is sometimes prescribed as tablets that also contain a thiazide diuretic. Examples of such combinations are Aldoril (methyldopa and hydrochlorothiazide) and Aldoclor (methyldopa and chlorothiazide).

WHAT IS IT SUPPOSED TO DO?   Methyldopa works inside the brain (by stimulating alpha$_2$-adrenergic receptors) to lower blood pressure. It is often used in combination with a thiazide diuretic, which lowers the blood pressure by additional mechanisms.

Hypertension (high blood pressure) causes no symptoms by itself, but untreated hypertension substantially increases the risk for the subsequent development of congestive heart failure, angina, heart attack, stroke, kidney problems, or visual problems. Antihypertensive drugs such as methyldopa decrease these risks.

SIDE EFFECTS   The most common side effects are sedation, dizziness (especially when standing up quickly), nasal stuffiness, and dry mouth. Sedation tends to decrease or go away after a week or so of taking methyldopa. Be careful at first. Contact your doctor if troublesome side effects persist.

When methyldopa is taken by itself, without a diuretic, it can cause fluid retention. Symptoms are rapid weight gain and swelling of the feet and ankles. When taken with a diuretic, this side effect is not likely to occur; if it does, contact your doctor.

Since methyldopa works inside the central nervous system, mental side effects do occur in some people, although infrequently. These include sleep disturbances, anxiety, impotence (it is the brain that sends out the signals to the genitals), headache, and depression. Contact your doctor if you develop any of these problems.

A rare side effect from methyldopa is drug-induced fever, which is most common during the first month of treatment. If you develop a fever that has no other apparent cause, contact your doctor. Other rare side effects include liver and blood reactions. Contact your doctor promptly if you notice yellowing of the skin or eyes, pale stools, dark or amber urine, persistent stomach pain and diarrhea, unusual bleeding or bruising, or any other unusual symptoms.

DRUG INTERACTIONS   Except for some drugs that are used only in hospitals, the drugs that are likely to cause problems in combination with methyldopa are relatively few. These are the most important drug interactions:

Haloperidol (Haldol). Slowed thinking and disorientation occurred in several patients who took this tranquilizer with methyldopa. This interaction may not occur in all people, but you should be aware of the possibility.

Lithium (Eskalith, Lithane, Lithonate), which is prescribed by psychiatrists for mood problems, interacts with methyldopa in a potentially dangerous way. For unknown reasons, patients taking both of these drugs have developed lithium toxicity. Normally, the concentration of lithium in the blood is used as a guide to lithium dosage; toxicity does not usually occur unless the concentration of lithium in the blood is elevated. However, in patients who developed lithium toxicity while taking methyldopa, the concentration of lithium in the blood was normal. If it is necessary for you to take lithium, ask your doctor if another drug can be used to control your blood pressure.

ALCOHOLIC BEVERAGES   There is no need to avoid alcoholic beverages, but be careful of the sedation that methyldopa may cause. Alcohol could add to that sedation. Also, dizziness upon standing up too quickly is a side effect of both alcohol and methyldopa, and the effects could be additive.

FOOD It doesn't matter whether you take your methyldopa with food or on an empty stomach. Some people take their methyldopa with a meal to help them to remember to take it.

You should restrict your salt intake while taking methyldopa. Excess salt intake contributes to high blood pressure, and salt retention is a possible side effect of methyldopa.

HOW DOES AGE AFFECT THE RESPONSE TO THIS DRUG? Brief episodes of low blood pressure, such as the dizziness or light-headedness you feel if you stand up too suddenly, occur more frequently as you get older. Methyldopa will make you more prone to this dizziness, so extra caution is warranted. Persistent dizziness or light-headedness is an indication that the dose may be too high; contact your doctor.

The sedation that methyldopa sometimes causes may result in an unacceptable decrease in mental alertness. If it does, discuss this problem with your doctor.

METOPROLOL

OTHER NAMES Metoprolol (pronounced *meh-TOE-proe-lole*) is the common or generic name of this drug. Its most frequently used brand name is Lopressor. Metoprolol is sometimes prescribed as tablets that also contain the diuretic hydrochlorothiazide; the brand name of this drug combination is Lopressor HCT. Metoprolol belongs to a group of drugs known as beta-blockers. Health professionals sometimes refer to metoprolol as a cardioselective beta-blocker or a $beta_1$-blocker, names that are precise pharmacological descriptions of how metoprolol works.

WHAT IS IT SUPPOSED TO DO? Metoprolol lowers blood pressures that are too high, prevents angina attacks, and reduces the risk of recurrence of heart attack. It accomplishes these beneficial effects by acting on the autonomic nervous system, the part of the nervous system that is beyond our conscious control—the part that regulates the heart, blood vessels, and various internal organs. Needless to say, the autonomic nervous system is complex. It has parasympathetic and sympathetic parts that generally work in opposition to one another. The sympathetic part responds to two types of stimulation, alpha and beta.

Metoprolol molecules temporarily bind with highly specialized nervous tissues called beta-receptors, thereby preventing them from recognizing the chemical messengers that normally set them off. (That is why pharmacologists refer to metoprolol as a beta-blocker.) The beta-receptors are one of several means by which the cardiovascular system gets the messages that tell it what to do. An increase in heart rate and an increase in blood pressure are examples of beta responses that are blocked by metoprolol.

There are beta-receptors throughout the body, but they are not all the same. The beta-receptors in the heart and kidneys, which are more sensitive to the effects of metoprolol, are called beta$_1$-receptors. The beta receptors in the lungs and pancreas, which are called beta$_2$-receptors, are less sensitive to the effects of metoprolol. This relative lack of effect on beta$_2$-receptors is particularly desirable in people who have lung problems or diabetes, because beta-blockers that are not as selective in their action as metoprolol can complicate these conditions. Because metoprolol has a greater affinity for beta$_1$-receptors, and therefore greater selectivity for cardiovascular beta-blocking effects, pharmacologists call it a cardioselective beta-blocker.

SIDE EFFECTS   Despite the wide distribution of beta-receptors throughout the body, side effects from metoprolol are infrequent and generally mild. Most people experience no side effects at all.

The most important side effect you should know about is the possibility of withdrawal symptoms if you suddenly stop taking metoprolol after taking it regularly. This side effect can be understood by considering how metoprolol works (see above). While the beta-receptors are blocked by metoprolol, they can become overly sensitive to the chemical messengers that normally set them off. If metoprolol is withdrawn abruptly, these receptors will overrespond. The most common symptom is headache, but there is also the danger of angina attacks, a sudden rise in blood pressure, irregular heartbeats, or even a heart attack, depending on what condition was being treated initially. If your doctor wants you to stop taking metoprolol, he or she will gradually reduce the dose, or may substitute another drug that has similar effects.

Your doctor will carefully check your heart before prescribing metoprolol. When metoprolol is taken by individuals with untreated congestive heart failure, a condition in which the heart is unable to carry out its job of pumping blood through the circulatory system adequately, this heart failure is likely to be worsened. Infrequently, it causes congestive heart failure in individuals with no previous symptoms. Most patients whose congestive heart failure is corrected by other drugs are able to take metoprolol without problem. However, you should contact your doctor at once if you experience swelling of your feet or ankles, sudden weight gain, or difficulty in breathing. Metoprolol's ability to slow the heart and lower the blood pressure is usually beneficial, but occasional individuals experience too much of these effects. An unusually slow pulse rate (less than fifty beats per minute) or dizziness (possibly from abnormally low blood pressure) are other reasons to get in touch with your doctor.

Stomach upset, constipation, or diarrhea occur infrequently from metoprolol. When any of these side effects does occur, it often goes away with continued use of the drug. If it continues to be bothersome, contact your doctor.

Although metoprolol enters the brain, its effects there are usually imperceptible, except for occasional drowsiness. However, it sometimes causes adverse mental effects, including dizziness, fatigue, confusion, nightmares, insomnia, and depression. If you experience any unusual and persistent mental symptoms, contact your doctor.

Other side effects are too rare to mention here. Contact your doctor if you experience anything unusual.

DRUG INTERACTIONS   Several drugs can interact with metoprolol. Your doctor will monitor your therapy with special care if any of these drugs need to be taken with metoprolol:

Antidiabetic drugs, such as *insulin* or the *sulfonylureas.* Metoprolol can block the rapid heartbeat or palpitations that occur as warning signs of hypoglycemia (too low a concentration of glucose in the blood), but sweating and dizziness remain as signs of hypoglycemia. Overdosage of metoprolol can delay the recovery from hypoglycemia.

Breathing medications, such as *isoproterenol (Isuprel) inhalation, terbutaline (Brethine, Bricanyl),* or *theophylline (Elixophyllin, Slo-Phyllin, Theobid, Theo-Dur, and others),* which are used for the treatment of asthma, emphysema, or other lung problems, stimulate $beta_2$-receptors, whereas metoprolol blocks $beta_1$-receptors. Theoretically, there should be no interaction, but large doses of metoprolol will also block $beta_2$-receptors and will therefore block the ability of breathing medications to open up the air passages in the lungs. These drugs can be used together safely, but you should be alert for the possibility of poor response to your respiratory medication. If this occurs, contact your doctor.

Cimetidine (Tagamet), which is used to treat ulcers, reduces the rate at which metoprolol is metabolized by the liver. Thus, cimetidine causes individuals to respond to smaller amounts of metoprolol than would otherwise be expected. If you are taking cimetidine, your physician will either lower your metoprolol dose accordingly or stop the cimetidine in favor of another drug.

Clonidine (Catapres), which is used to control high blood pressure, can cause a rebound hypertensive reaction if it is stopped abruptly. This reaction is worse in patients who are also taking metoprolol. If you are taking both of these drugs and must stop taking clonidine, your doctor may slowly discontinue your metoprolol first. In any case, don't stop taking this drug combination without careful supervision.

Phenobarbital, which is sometimes included in drug combinations for its sedative effects and is also used in the prevention of seizures, increases the rate at which metoprolol is metabolized by the liver. While you are taking phenobarbital, a larger than usual metoprolol dose may be required. If you stop taking phenobarbital, be sure to ask your physician to reevaluate your metoprolol dosage.

ALCOHOLIC BEVERAGES Usually there is no interaction between metoprolol and alcohol. However, you should establish for yourself that metoprolol does not make you drowsy or dizzy before you drink anything with alcohol in it.

FOOD It's a good idea to take metoprolol with meals to help you to develop a regular routine for taking it. In addition, food may improve its absorption. If your doctor has prescribed a restricted-salt or restricted-calorie diet, be sure to follow it.

HOW DOES AGE AFFECT THE RESPONSE TO THIS DRUG? Although metoprolol is eliminated from the body more slowly with advancing age, thereby allowing it to accumulate to higher concentrations in the blood, advancing age also brings changes in the beta-receptors that make them less sensitive to drugs. These two effects tend to offset one another. Therefore, older people usually respond similarly to the doses required by younger people. There is, however, wide variation in the doses required by different individuals, regardless of age.

The risk of side effects, particularly those related to the heart (see Side Effects), increases with advancing age. Be sure to return to your doctor for regular checkups. Most older people, including those who have achieved considerable age, are able to take metoprolol without problems.

NADOLOL

OTHER NAMES   Nadolol (pronounced *na-DOE-lole)* is the common or generic name of this drug. A frequently used brand name for nadolol is Corgard. Nadolol is sometimes prescribed as tablets that also contain the diuretic bendroflumethiazide; the brand name of this drug combination is Corzide. Nadolol belongs to a group of drugs known as beta-blockers.

WHAT IS IT SUPPOSED TO DO?   Nadolol lowers blood pressures that are too high, prevents angina attacks, and corrects several other medical problems. It is most often prescribed for its beneficial effects on high blood pressure and on heart problems.

  Nadolol accomplishes these various remedies by acting on the autonomic nervous system, the part of the nervous system that is beyond our conscious control—the part that regulates the heart, blood vessels, and various internal organs. Needless to say, the autonomic nervous system is complex. It has parasympathetic and sympathetic parts that generally work in opposition to one another. The sympathetic part responds to two types of stimulation, alpha and beta.

  Nadolol molecules temporarily bind with highly specialized nervous tissues called beta-receptors, thereby preventing them from recognizing the chemical messengers that normally set them off. (That is why pharmacologists refer to nadolol as a beta-blocker.) The beta-receptors are one of several means by which the organs get the messages that tell them what to do. An increase in heart rate and an increase in blood pressure are examples of beta responses that are blocked by nadolol. Because it is long-acting, its beneficial effects require only a single daily dose.

SIDE EFFECTS   Despite the wide distribution of beta-receptors throughout the body, side effects from nadolol are infrequent and generally mild. Most people experience no side effects at all.

The most important side effect you should know about is the possibility of withdrawal symptoms if you suddenly stop taking nadolol after taking it regularly. This side effect can be understood by considering how nadolol works (see above). While the beta-receptors are blocked by nadolol, they can become overly sensitive to the chemical messengers that normally set them off. If nadolol is withdrawn abruptly, these receptors will overrespond. The most common symptom is headache, but there is also the danger of angina attacks, a sudden rise in blood pressure, irregular heartbeats, or even a heart attack, depending on what condition was being treated initially. If your doctor wants you to stop taking nadolol, she will gradually reduce the dose, or she may substitute another drug that has similar effects.

Your doctor will carefully check your heart before prescribing nadolol. When nadolol is taken by individuals with untreated congestive heart failure, a condition in which the heart is unable to carry out its job of pumping blood through the circulatory system adequately, this heart failure is likely to be worsened. Infrequently, it causes congestive heart failure in individuals with no previous symptoms. Most patients whose congestive heart failure is corrected by other drugs are able to take nadolol without problem. However, you should contact your doctor at once if you experience swelling of your feet or ankles, sudden weight gain, or difficulty in breathing. Nadolol's ability to slow the heart and lower the blood pressure is usually beneficial, but occasional individuals experience too much of these effects. An unusually slow pulse rate (less than fifty beats per minute) or dizziness (possibly from abnormally low blood pressure) are other reasons to get in touch with your doctor.

Stomach upset, constipation, or diarrhea occur infrequently from nadolol. When any of these side effects does occur, it often goes away with continued use of the drug. If it continues to be bothersome, contact your doctor.

Another infrequent side effect is coldness of the hands or feet that may occur as a result of the circulatory changes that are brought about by nadolol. Be sure to dress warmly in cold weather.

Adverse mental effects from nadolol are infrequent Fatigue or dizziness occur in about one person in fifty. Other adverse mental effects, which are rare, include sleep disturbances, depression, disorientation, memory loss, and emotional changes. If you experience any unusual and persistent mental symptoms, contact your doctor.

There are some diseases that increase the risk of side effects from nadolol. Your doctor will not prescribe nadolol if you have asthma or emphysema, since the effects of nadolol are just the opposite of those that are helpful for lung diseases. In diabetics, nadolol can cause several problems (see Drug Interactions, Antidiabetic Drugs), And, as already stated, uncontrolled congestive heart failure is worsened by nadolol. Because the kidneys are the sole means by which nadolol is eliminated from the body, your doctor will evaluate your kidney function before prescribing nadolol.

Other side effects are too rare to mention here. Contact your doctor if you experience any unusual symptoms.

DRUG INTERACTIONS   Several drugs can interact with nadolol. These are the principal ones:

Antidiabetic drugs, such as *insulin* and the *sulfonylureas.* Diabetic patients should not take nadolol unless there is no other alternative. Nadolol can block some of the warning signs of hypoglycemia (rapid heartbeat or palpitations), delay the recovery from hypoglycemia, cause high-blood-pressure episodes during hypoglycemia, and impair circulation to the extremities. If nadolol is required, keep in mind that sweating, but not rapid heartbeat, is a sign of hypoglycemia. Other beta-blocking drugs, such as metoprolol and atenolol, are less likely to cause these problems, but there is some risk.

Breathing medications, such as *isoproterenol (Isuprel) inhalation, terbutaline (Brethine, Bricanyl),* or *theophylline (Elixophyllin, Slo-Phyllin, Theobid, Theo-Dur, and others),* which are used for the treatment of asthma, emphysema, or other lung problems, don't mix well with nadolol. The ability of these drugs to open up the air passages in the lungs is antagonized by nadolol. Although its effects on normal lungs are minimal, nadolol can be dangerous in those with asthma or other lung problems.

Clonidine (Catapres), which is used to control high blood pressure, can cause a rebound hypertensive reaction if it is stopped abruptly. This reaction is worse in patients who are also taking nadolol. If you are taking both of these drugs and must stop taking clonidine, your doctor may stop your nadolol first. In any case, don't stop taking this drug combination without careful supervision.

Indomethacin (Indocin) can block the antihypertensive and antianginal effects of nadolol. If indomethacine is required, your doctor will need to evaluate whether there is any decrease in nadolol effect.

Prazosin (Minipress), which is used to control high blood pressure, sometimes causes a severe drop in blood pressure when the person taking it stands up too quickly. This side effect is most common when the drug is first started, and there is some evidence that nadolol makes it more likely to occur. If you are taking nadolol and starting to take prazosin, your doctor will start with smaller doses and may advise you to take the prazosin at bedtime.

Sympathomimetics, which are contained in some nonprescription remedies for nasal congestion, can cause hypertensive reactions in susceptible individuals. There is some evidence that the risk of this reaction is greater in patients with high blood pressure who are taking nadolol. Check with your pharmacist before taking any medication for nasal congestion.

ALCOHOLIC BEVERAGES Usually there is no interaction between nadolol and alcohol. However, you should establish for yourself that nadolol does not make you drowsy or dizzy before you drink anything with alcohol in it.

FOOD It's a good idea to take nadolol with meals to help you to develop a regular routine for taking it. Food does not affect its absorption. If your doctor has prescribed a restricted-salt or restricted-calorie diet, be sure to follow it.

HOW DOES AGE AFFECT THE RESPONSE TO THIS DRUG? Aging slows the rate at which nadolol is removed from the body by the kidneys, thereby allowing it to accumulate to higher concentrations in the blood, but advancing age also brings changes in the beta-receptors that make them less sensitive to drugs. These two effects tend to offset one another. Therefore, older people usually respond similarly to the doses required by younger people. There is, however, wide variation in the doses required by different individuals, regardless of age.

The risk of side effects, particularly those related to the heart (see Side Effects), increases with advancing age. Be sure to return to your doctor for regular checkups. Most older people, including those who have achieved considerable age, are able to take nadolol without problems.

NAPROXEN

OTHER NAMES Naproxen (pronounced *na-PROX-en*) is the common or generic name of this drug. Frequently used brand names for naproxen are Anaprox and Naprosyn. Naproxen belongs to a large group of drugs called nonsteroidal anti-inflammatory drugs (NSAIDs).

WHAT IS IT SUPPOSED TO DO? Naproxen relieves the pain, inflammation, swelling, and stiffness associated with arthritis. It also relieves the pain caused by injuries, surgery, or cancer.

Although some relief of arthritic symptoms should be apparent shortly after the first dose, maximum relief occurs after two or three weeks of regular use.

SIDE EFFECTS Indigestion, heartburn, nausea, stomach discomfort, excessive gas, diarrhea, and other problems related to the digestive tract are the most common side effects. These side effects can sometimes be prevented by taking naproxen with a full glass of water, perhaps in addition to food or an antacid. If they persist, or if they are severe, stop taking the drug and contact your doctor.

Rarely, naproxen causes more severe problems in the digestive tract. These include ulcer with bleeding into the gastrointestinal tract (evidenced by bloody stools or stools that are discolored dark red or black) and small amounts of painless blood loss (which can cause anemia). The risk of these problems is lower than it is with aspirin.

Naproxen can also cause mental symptoms such as drowsiness, headache, or dizziness. Because naproxen can cause decreased alertness in some individuals, you should evaluate how this drug affects you before you drive an automobile or operate any potentially dangerous machinery. If you should develop any sort of visual difficulty (such as blurred or dim vision) or hearing problem (such as buzzing or ringing in your ears), stop taking the drug and contact your doctor.

Kidney problems caused by naproxen and similar drugs are relatively rare, but most of the cases that have been reported in the medical literature involved older individuals. Some of the medical problems that are more prevalent among older people place them at greater risk for this side effect. When the kidneys are stressed by congestive heart failure, dehydration, or any kind of kidney impairment (even modest impairment), the body responds by producing substances called prostaglandins. Prostaglandins increase the flow of blood to the kidneys and increase their efficiency. Naproxen and related drugs can block this compensatory response, and kidney failure (usually reversible) can occur as a result. (All nonsteroidal anti-inflammatory drugs work by preventing the body from manufacturing prostaglandins, which are also mediators of pain and inflammation.) Considering the widespread use of naproxen among older people and the extremely small number of kidney problems that have been reported, the risk appears to be quite small. However, you should return to your doctor for regular medical checkups while taking this drug. Contact your doctor promptly if you experience sudden weight gain, swelling of your feet or ankles, or markedly decreased urine production.

Skin problems, such as rashes or unusual reactions to the sun, are extremely rare side effects from naproxen. Contact your doctor if you experience anything unusual.

Naproxen is very effective in lowering fever. This effect, combined with its pain-relieving and anti-inflammatory actions, could be considered a side effect if the signs of an infection were masked and the infection went undetected (and untreated) too long.

If you have ever developed asthma as an allergic reaction to aspirin, you should not take naproxen, because a similar allergic reaction could occur.

Other side effects from naproxen are too rare to list here. Contact your doctor if you experience any unusual symptoms.

DRUG INTERACTIONS   Several drugs have the potential to interact with naproxen:

Aspirin is potentially irritating to the digestive tract, and its irritant effects could become troublesome when added to those of naproxen. Check with your doctor before taking this drug combination.

Diuretics, such as *hydrochlorothiazide (HydroDIURIL and other brands) or furosemide (Lasix).* Infrequently, naproxen causes fluid retention and edema. If you are taking a diuretic for fluid retention and edema (such as that caused by congestive heart failure or liver disease) and you experience a worsening of your symptoms while taking naproxen, stop taking your naproxen and contact your doctor.

Warfarin (Coumadin). Naproxen can cause some gastrointestinal bleeding, which could be worsened by the anticoagulant effects of warfarin. In addition, naproxen decreases the effectiveness of blood platelets in forming blood clots, so the risk of side effects from warfarin is increased somewhat while you are taking naproxen.

ALCOHOLIC BEVERAGES Alcohol adds to the gastric-irritant effects of naproxen. Avoid taking them at the same time.

FOOD Food slows the absorption of naproxen somewhat, but it doesn't impair its absorption. It's a good idea to take your naproxen with food to minimize any gastric irritation that might occur.

HOW DOES AGE AFFECT THE RESPONSE TO THIS DRUG? There is preliminary evidence that advancing age is accompanied by decreased naproxen binding to protein storage sites in the blood, which could cause more intense effects in older individuals. In a study that compared equal doses of naproxen in younger (age twenty-two to thirty-nine) and older (age sixty-six to eighty-one) healthy men, the concentration of drug that was not bound to protein in the blood was twice as high in the older individuals. Since the unbound concentration of a drug is usually closely related to its effects, older individuals may be more sensitive to naproxen. The older individuals also tended to metabolize naproxen less efficiently, but the higher unbound drug concentrations in their blood compensated for this effect by making more drug available for metabolism.

NIFEDIPINE

OTHER NAMES Nifedipine (pronounced *nigh-FED-i-peen)* is the common or generic name of this drug. Its most frequently used brand name is Procardia. Nifedipine belongs to a group of drugs called calcium channel blockers.

WHAT IS IT SUPPOSED TO DO? Nifedipine decreases the occurrence of angina pectoris, the chest pain caused by a deficiency in oxygen supply to the heart muscle. It works by inhibiting the movement of calcium into the cells of the specialized muscle tissue in the walls of certain blood vessels (arterioles), thereby causing a relaxation of this muscle and dilation of the blood vessel. This widening in the diameter of the vessels that carry blood to the heart muscle improves its circulation and supplies it with more oxygen. Nifedipine also causes a widening in the diameter of the blood vessels the heart pumps into (the ones that create a resistance to the heart's pumping action). The heart's workload is thereby decreased—pharmacologists call this a decrease in afterload. This decrease in workload causes the heart to use less oxygen.

Although the current primary use of nifedipine is for angina, its effects on blood vessels are also of value in the treatment of high blood pressure.

Like other calcium channel blockers, nifedipine's effects on calcium are limited to specialized muscle tissues. It has no effect on the concentration of calcium in the blood, and, under normal circumstances, it is unaffected by calcium in the diet or by calcium supplements.

SIDE EFFECTS The circulatory changes brought about by nifedipine, while generally beneficial, can also cause dizziness, light-headedness, flushing or warm tingling sensations, headache, or nausea. If you experience dizziness or light-headedness, be especially careful not to stand up too quickly; allow your body time to adjust to changes in position. Less frequently, nifedipine causes constipation, and rarely it causes nasal congestion, stomach cramps, weakness, or nervousness. These side effects often go away or decrease in severity as your body becomes accustomed to the drug. If any of these is persistent or bothersome, contact your doctor.

The decrease in blood pressure brought about by nifedipine occasionally causes the heart to beat faster. If you experience racing or pounding heartbeat, contact your doctor.

Occasionally, nifedipine's circulatory changes lead to fluid retention. Contact your doctor if you experience swelling of your feet, ankles, or lower legs, or (less likely) if you experience shortness of breath, wheezing, or coughing.

A rare side effect, in certain individuals with severe angina, is a paradoxical worsening of angina, occurring about thirty minutes after a dose is taken. It is thought that this side effect is caused by excessive dilation of blood vessels that don't need dilation (thus stealing blood from areas of the heart whose blood supply is already insufficient) or by a racing or pounding heart that is working hard to supply blood to excessively dilated blood vessels. Contact your doctor if you experience this paradoxical worsening of angina or if you experience racing or pounding heartbeat.

An extremely rare side effect from nifedipine is alteration of the sense of smell or taste. If this occurs, contact your doctor.

Other side effects are too rare to list here. If you experience anything unexpected, contact your doctor.

DRUG INTERACTIONS Several drugs may interact with nifedipine:

Antidiabetic drugs, such as *insulin* and the *sufonylureas.* Nifedipine causes an increase in the concentration of sugar in the blood of some individuals. It may be necessary to increase the dosage of your sulfonylurea or your insulin. Check with your doctor.

Beta-blocking drugs, such as *atenolol (Tenormin), metoprolol (Lopressor), nadolol (Corgard), propranolol (Inderal), pindolol (Visken),* or *timolol (Blocadren).* A beta-blocking drug is often prescribed together with nifedipine because the two drugs work by different mechanisms that complement each other in the treatment of angina or hypertension. For most patients, it's a beneficial combination. However, in some instances this drug combination can cause abnormally low blood pressure (dizziness, fainting). Contact your doctor if you experience these or other unexpected symptoms.

Calcium, if taken in large enough amounts, can bloc the effects of nifedipine. This is true of intravenous infusions of calcium and calcium taken in combination with large doses of vitamin D. It is unlikely that a diet rich in calcium or one that is modestly supplemented with calcium would cause this effect. However, you should be alert for the possibility of loss of nifedipine effect if you are taking calcium supplements.

Cimetidine (Tagamet), which is used in the treatment of peptic ulcers, slows the metabolism of nifedipine and thereby increases its effects. Ranitidine (Zantac) and famotidine (Pepcid), drugs that work like cimetidine, are less likely to interact with nifedipine in this way.

Digoxin (Lanoxin). In some individuals, nifedipine increases the concentration of digoxin in the blood, but this increase is often too small to be significant. Nevertheless, your doctor should check for evidence of too much digoxin effect.

Quinidine (Cardioquin, Quinaglute). Nifedipine decreases the concentration of quinidine in the blood. If you start or stop taking nifedipine, ask your doctor to reevaluate your quinidine therapy.

ALCOHOLIC BEVERAGES   Alcohol adds to the dilation of blood vessels and lowering of blood pressure caused by nifedipine, making you more susceptible to dizziness, light-headedness, or fainting. Limit your consumption of alcohol.

FOOD   Take your nifedipine with meals to help you maintain a regular schedule for taking it.

HOW DOES AGE AFFECT THE RESPONSE TO THIS DRUG?   Advancing age is accompanied by increased sensitivity to the effects of nifedipine. Older people are more susceptible to dizziness caused by nifedipine. Your doctor will prescribe a dose that is likely to be appropriate for you.

NITROGLYCERIN

OTHER NAMES   Nitroglycerin (pronounced *nye-troe-GLI-ser-in*) is the common or generic name of this drug. Nitroglycerin comes in a variety of dosage forms—

sublingual tablets, extended-release tablets, extended-release capsules, ointments, transdermal disks or patches, and an aerosol spray. Each of these dosage forms releases nitroglycerin into the body at a specific rate, and each dosage form has several product names. The most common form of nitroglycerin is the sublingual tablet, a tablet that is dissolved beneath the tongue. Nitrostat and Nitroglycerin Sublingual Tablets are frequently used brand names for this form of nitroglycerin. Some frequently used brand names for extended-release nitroglycerin capsules or tablets are Cardabid, Klavikordal, Niong, Nitro-Bid Plateau Caps, Nitrocap TD, Nitroglyn, Nitrolin, Nitro-long, Nitronet, Nitrong, Nitrospan, Nitrostat SR, and Trates Granucaps. Nitroglycerin ointment is called just that, or by one of its many brand names, including Nitro-Bid, Nitrol, Nitrong, and Nitrostat ointments. Nitroglycerin disks or patches, which are placed on the skin, are known by the following brand names: Nitrodisc, Nitro-Dur, and Transderm-Nitro. An aerosol form of nitroglycerin, to be sprayed onto or under the tongue, is marketed under the brand name Nitrolingual. Nitroglycerin belongs to a large group of drugs called organic nitrates, which have been used in the treatment of angina for more than a hundred years.

WHAT IS IT SUPPOSED TO DO? Angina pectoris, the chest pain that may be precipitated by exercise, stress, or meals, is caused by a deficiency of oxygen in the heart muscle. Nitroglycerin relaxes the smooth muscle within the walls of veins and arteries, causing them to dilate (their diameter gets wider). This dilation is beneficial in angina for two reasons. First, blood flow (and therefore oxygen supply) within the heart muscle is increased. Second, circulatory changes throughout the body decrease the heart's workload and therefore its demand for oxygen.

Nitroglycerin relieves angina attacks when it is taken sublingually (dissolved under the tongue). This route of administration also prevents angina attacks from occurring immediately after the tablet is dissolved under the tongue, and it is a useful way to prevent an angina attack that can be predicted (such as by the need to walk up a flight of stairs).

The other dosage forms of nitroglycerin—extended-release tablets and capsules, ointment, and patches and disks—contain larger amounts of nitroglycerin that are slowly released into the circulation. They are used for the prevention of angina attacks. Long-acting forms are also sometimes used in the treatment of severe congestive heart failure (because of nitroglycerin's ability to decrease the heart's workload).

Sublingual nitroglycerin usually works within one to five minutes. If your angina attack is unrelieved after five minutes, you may take another dose. This procedure can be repeated if necessary, but not for more than three doses. If your chest pain continues after three doses taken within fifteen minutes, contact your doctor or go to a hospital emergency room immediately.

SIDE EFFECTS Although the circulatory changes brought about by nitroglycerin are beneficial to the heart, they can cause unpleasant effects elsewhere in the body. Headache is the most common side effect. Headache often decreases with continued use. Acetaminophen or aspirin may provide some relief. If headache is particularly severe after a sublingual dose of nitroglycerin, ask your doctor if the dose can be decreased. You may experience dizziness and weakness, especially when you are standing up. Sit or lie down if you feel dizzy or light-headed (if you don't, you might faint); this will restore circulation to your brain. Exercise, hot weather, standing in one position for a long time, and alcohol can provoke this drug-induced dizziness or light-headedness. Flushing of the face and neck, rapid pulse (unless you are taking a beta-blocker), and nausea can also occur as a result of the circulatory changes brought about by this drug. Contact your doctor if any of these side effects is persistent or severe; the dosage may be too high for you.

After taking sustained-release nitroglycerin on a regular basis for a while, you may develop some tolerance to it, and stopping it suddenly could cause a withdrawal reaction. The likelihood of such tolerance is unknown at this time; it may be only a theoretical risk. To be safe, don't stop taking sustained-release nitroglycerin without first checking with your doctor, who may wish that you slowly decrease the dosage when stopping it.

Blurred vision, dry mouth, and rash are rare side effects. Contact your doctor if you experience these or any other unexpected symptoms.

DRUG INTERACTIONS Any drug that lowers the blood pressure (as a therapeutic effect or side effect) will make you more sensitive to the dizziness that nitroglycerin can cause. Nasal decongestants often contain drugs that can provoke an angina attack; check with your pharmacist before using such drugs.

ALCOHOLIC BEVERAGES Alcohol can add significantly to the dilation of blood vessels caused by nitroglycerin, making dizziness, light-headedness, or fainting much more likely to occur. Be very careful to limit the amount of alcohol you drink.

FOOD Remember that overeating can lead to angina attacks. Exercise immediately after meals is another situation you should avoid. Also, obesity places a strain on the heart and increases the likelihood that you will have angina attacks.

HOW DOES AGE AFFECT THE RESPONSE TO THIS DRUG? Advancing age increases the susceptibility to dizziness or light-headedness from nitroglycerin. Therefore, your doctor will begin treatment with small doses. However, there is considerable variation among individuals in the dosages they require.

NORTRIPTYLINE

OTHER NAMES Nortriptyline (pronounced *nor-TRIP-ti-leen)* is the common or generic name of this drug. Some frequently used brand names for nortriptyline are

Aventyl and Pamelor. Nortriptyline belongs to a group of drugs called tricyclic antidepressants. (*Tricyclic* describes their chemical structure; *antidepressant* refers to their principal pharmacological effect.)

WHAT IS IT SUPPOSED TO DO? Nortriptyline relieves mental depression. The precise means by which it works has not been established, but its mechanism of action involves an increase in the concentration of certain naturally occurring substances (serotonin and norepinephrine) within the brain. Elevation of mood and reversal of the various symptoms that can accompany depression (such as sleep problems, decreased energy, or loss of appetite) require a minimum of several weeks of regular use. Your doctor may prescribe less than several weeks' supply of medication initially, so it is important that you return to your pharmacy to have your prescription refilled. Your doctor may want you to continue taking nortriptyline for several months after your mood returns to normal.

SIDE EFFECTS Nearly everyone experiences dry mouth while taking nortriptyline. It doesn't seem to be related to dosage, and it tends to diminish with time. Sugar-free candy or gum is often helpful in alleviating this problem.

Nortriptyline sometimes causes drowsiness. Avoid driving until you are sure that your alertness and coordination are not impaired.

The most common potentially serious side effect involves the temporary decrease in blood pressure that occurs when you stand up quickly. This decrease in blood pressure is exaggerated by nortriptyline and is likely to make you dizzy, light-headed, or faint if you stand up too quickly. If this side effect is severe (especially if it causes you to fall or your heart to pound or race), contact your doctor. Be very careful to stand up slowly.

The dry mouth caused by nortriptyline is an example of what pharmacologists call an anticholinergic effect. It can be caused by any drug that blocks the receptors for acetylcholine, a substance the body produces to regulate certain functions that are beyond conscious control. When nortriptyline is taken with other drugs that have anticholinergic side effects, these side effects are more likely to cause problems (see Drug Interactions). A common anticholinergic side effect is constipation. Ask your pharmacist for appropriate treatment; a stool softener is often helpful. Contact your doctor if constipation becomes severe. Another anticholinergic side effect is the sudden onset of confusion or disorientation, sometimes with visual hallucinations. If this occurs, contact your doctor; it is a sign that the dosage is too high for you. Other anticholinergic side effects that require your doctor's attention (and these are infrequent or rare) include blurred vision, difficulty in urinating (more common in older men with prostate difficulties), and eye pain (a possible indication that narrow-angle glaucoma, not the usual type of glaucoma, has been aggravated).

Effects on the heart—excessively fast, slow, or irregular heartbeat—are infrequent. Contact your doctor if any of these occur.

Other side effects include nausea, unpleasant taste, diarrhea (infrequent), and excessive sweating (infrequent). These side effects may diminish or go away as your body adjusts to the effects of this drug. Contact your doctor if they are severe or bothersome. A fine tremor is not an uncommon side effect in older people; tell your doctor if this occurs.

Other side effects are too infrequent to list here. Contact your doctor if you experience any unexpected symptoms.

DRUG INTERACTIONS Nortriptyline interacts with a number of drugs. Here are the most common sources of potential problems:

Anticholinergic drugs, such as *belladonna (Donnatal) or propantheline (Pro-Banthine),* which are used for peptic-ulcer disease, *benztropine (Cogentin),* which is used in the treatment of Parkinson's disease and to treat the side effects sometimes caused by tranquilizers, and *scopolamine (Transderm Scōp),* which is used to prevent motion sickness, all work by blocking acetylcholine (see Side Effects). These drugs are more likely to cause anticholinergic side effects when taken with nortriptyline. In many cases, the anticholinergic side effects of nortriptyline obviate the need for these other drugs. Check with your doctor before taking them.

Antihistamines, which are included in many nonprescription cold and allergy medicines, have sedative and anticholinergic (see above) side effects. Avoid these products while taking nortriptyline.

Antihypertensive drugs can interact with nortriptyline by several mechanisms. First, some of them (beta-blockers, clonidine, methyldopa, and reserpine) can cause depression as a side effect. Second, the action of a few antihypertensive drugs is blocked by nortriptyline. If you are taking clonidine (Catapres, Combipres), guanethidine (Ismelin), or guanadrel (Hylorel), your doctor will need to prescribe another drug to control your blood pressure. Third, if your antihypertensive drug causes dizziness, nortriptyline will make this side effect worse. Your doctor may need to decrease the dose of your antihypertensive drug before you start taking nortriptyline.

Cimetidine (Tagamet), which is used in the treatment of peptic-ulcer disease, slows the metabolism of nortriptyline and thereby increases its effects. Contact your doctor if you experience an increase in nortriptyline side effects while taking cimetidine; your doctor may have to lower the dosage of your nortriptyline temporarily.

Monoamine oxidase inhibitors, such as *isocarboxazid (Marplan), phenelzine (Nardil), or tranylcypromine (Parnate),* which are also used in the treatment of depression, sometimes cause dangerous toxic reactions when taken with nortriptyline. This combination of drugs should only be used in hospitalized patients who are under careful observation. Normally, one or two weeks are allowed to elapse between the use of nortriptyline and one of these drugs.

Phenobarbital, which is used to prevent seizures and is also sometimes included as an ingredient in certain medications for its sedative effects, stimulates the metabolism of nortriptyline and thereby decreases its effects. If you require treatment with phenobarbital, your doctor will take this into consideration in adjusting your nortriptyline dosage. Otherwise, your doctor may replace your phenobarbital-containing medication with another drug product.

Phenothiazine tranquilizers, such as *perphenazine (Trilafon), thioridazine (Mellaril), or trifluoperazine (Stelazine),* are more likely to cause anticholinergic side effects (see Side Effects) when taken with nortriptyline. In addition, these drugs may slow the metabolism of nortriptyline and thereby increase its effects. There are instances when these drugs need to be given with nortriptyline, but you should be sure that your doctor intends that you take this combination.

ALCOHOLIC BEVERAGES Alcohol will increase the dizziness or faintness that you may feel upon standing up too quickly. It will also add to any drowsiness that nortriptyline might cause. Therefore, you should avoid alcohol or use it sparingly while taking nortriptyline.

FOOD Take your nortriptyline with meals to help you maintain a regular schedule for taking it and to prevent any nausea it might cause.

HOW DOES AGE AFFECT THE RESPONSE TO THIS DRUG? There is considerable variation among individuals in the rate at which nortriptyline is removed from the blood by metabolism in the liver. However, two studies have shown that advancing age is accompanied by a slower metabolism of nortriptyline and that older people tend to develop higher concentrations of nortriptyline in their blood. Therefore, older people usually require smaller doses than younger people.

In addition, older people are more sensitive to side effects from nortriptyline. Your doctor will try to prescribe a dose that is likely to be effective without causing serious side effects, but you should contact him or her promptly if you experience extreme dizziness or faintness (which could cause you to fall), confusion or disorientation (which is alarming but goes away when the dose is reduced or the drug is stopped), or any other serious side effect. Your doctor may make use of a laboratory test that measures the concentration of nortriptyline in your blood in order to evaluate your nortriptyline dosage.

OXAZEPAM

OTHER NAMES Oxazepam (pronounced *ox-AZ-eh-pam)* is the common or generic name of this drug. A frequently used brand name for oxazepam is Serax. Oxazepam belongs to a large group of similar drugs called benzodiazepines.

WHAT IS IT SUPPOSED TO DO? Oxazepam relieves the symptoms of anxiety and tension.

SIDE EFFECTS Drowsiness is the principal side effect from oxazepam. You may find yourself unsteady on your feet as well. Evaluate these effects for yourself and regulate your activities accordingly. You should be especially cautious about driving an automobile. If drowsiness or unsteadiness persists, stop taking the drug and contact your doctor.

Infrequently, oxazepam causes dizziness, weakness, confusion, impaired memory, or loss of coordination. If you experience any of these effects, which suggest you are extremely sensitive to oxazepam, stop taking it and contact your doctor.

If you have been taking oxazepam regularly for a long time and in large doses, you may experience mild withdrawal symptoms a day or two after stopping this drug. Typical symptoms include difficulty in sleeping, unusual irritability, and unusual nervousness. If these occur, contact your doctor.

Other side effects are too rare to list here. Contact your doctor if you experience any unusual symptoms.

DRUG INTERACTIONS Sedation is a common side effect of antidepressant drugs, antihistamines, tranquilizers, narcotic analgesics, and other drugs. You may become excessively sedated while taking oxazepam with these drugs.

ALCOHOLIC BEVERAGES Oxazepam adds to alcohol's depressive effects on the nervous system. You should limit your alcohol consumption to small amounts while taking oxazepam. Needless to say, the effects of this combination on driving can be dangerous.

FOOD Oxazepam can be taken either with food or on an empty stomach

HOW DOES AGE AFFECT THE RESPONSE TO THIS DRUG? Age does not affect the rate at which oxazepam is removed from the body. However, older people are more sensitive to side effects from oxazepam. Confusion, weakness, dizziness, impaired memory, and loss of coordination, which are infrequent side effects from oxazepam, occur more often in older people.

PENTAERYTHRITOL TETRANITRATE

OTHER NAMES Pentaerythritol tetranitrate (pronounced *pen-ta-er-ITH-ri-tole tet-ra-NYE-trate)* is the common or generic name of this drug. It is sometimes abbreviated PETN. A frequently used brand name for pentaerythritol tetranitrate is Peritrate. Pentaerythritol tetranitrate belongs to a large group of drugs called organic nitrates, which have been used in the treatment of angina for more than a hundred years.

WHAT IS IT SUPPOSED TO DO? Angina pectoris, the chest pain that may be precipitated by exercise, stress, or meals, is caused by a deficiency of oxygen in the heart muscle. Pentaerythritol tetranitrate relaxes the smooth muscle within the walls of veins and arteries, causing them to dilate (their diameter gets wider). This dilation is beneficial in angina for two reasons. First, blood flow (and therefore oxygen supply) within the heart muscle is increased. Second, circulatory changes throughout the body decrease the heart's workload and therefore its demand for oxygen.

Pentaerythritol tetranitrate is taken to prevent angina attacks. It works too slowly to relieve an angina attack that has already started.

Although the prevention of angina is the most common use of pentaerythritol tetranitrate, it is sometimes used in the treatment of congestive heart failure (because of its ability to decrease the heart's workload).

SIDE EFFECTS Although the circulatory changes brought about by pentaerythritol tetranitrate are beneficial to the heart, they can cause unpleasant effects elsewhere in the body. Headache is the most common side effect. Headache often decreases with continued use. Acetaminophen or aspirin may provide some relief. If your headaches are particularly severe, ask your doctor if the dose can be decreased. You may experience dizziness and weakness, especially when you are standing up. Sit or lie down if you feel dizzy or lightheaded (if you don't, you might faint); this will restore circulation to your brain. Exercise, hot weather, standing in one position for a long time, and alcohol can provoke this drug-induced dizziness or light-headedness. Flushing of the face and neck, rapid pulse (unless you are taking a beta-blocker), and nausea can also occur as a result of the circulatory changes brought about by this drug. Contact your doctor if any of these side effects is persistent or severe; the dosage may be too high for you.

After taking pentaerythritol tetranitrate on a regular basis for a while, you may develop some tolerance to it, and stopping it suddenly could cause a withdrawal reaction. The likelihood of such tolerance is unknown at this time; it may be only a theoretical risk. To be safe, don't stop taking pentaerythritol tetranitrate without first checking with your doctor, who may wish that you slowly decrease the dosage when stopping it.

Blurred vision, dry mouth, and rash are rare side effects. Contact your doctor if you experience these or any other unexpected symptoms.

DRUG INTERACTIONS Any drug that lowers the blood pressure (as a therapeutic effect or side effect) will make you more sensitive to the dizziness or light-headedness that pentaerythritol tetranitrate may cause. Nasal decongestants often contain drugs that can provoke an angina attack; check with your pharmacist before using such drugs.

ALCOHOLIC BEVERAGES Alcohol can add significantly to the dilation of blood vessels caused by pentaerythritol tetranitrate, making dizziness, light-headedness, or fainting much more likely to occur. Be very careful to limit the amount of alcohol you drink.

FOOD Remember that overeating can cause angina attacks. Exercise immediately after meals is another situation you should avoid. Also, obesity places a strain on your heart and increases the likelihood that you will have angina attacks.

HOW DOES AGE AFFECT THE RESPONSE TO THIS DRUG? Advancing age increases the susceptibility to dizziness or light-headedness from pentaerythritol tetranitrate. Therefore, your doctor will begin treatment with small doses. However, there is considerable variation among individuals in the dosages they require.

PENTAZOCINE

OTHER NAMES Pentazocine (pronounced *pen-TAZ-oh-seen*) is the common or generic name of this drug. Its most frequently used brand name is Talwin. In the United States, pentazocine tablets are marketed under the brand name Talwin Nx. (The *Nx* stands for naloxone, a small amount of which is included in each tablet to prevent abuse by intravenous injection; the naloxone is inactive when the tablet is swallowed, but it promotes withdrawal symptoms should the tablet be dissolved and injected by a narcotic addict.) Pentazocine is sometimes prescribed as tablets that contain either aspirin (Talwin Compound) or acetaminophen

(Talacen). Pentazocine is a synthetic drug that is related to the opiates or narcotics.

WHAT IS IT SUPPOSED TO DO? Pentazocine works inside the brain to alter the sensation of pain. When taken as a tablet, it is approximately equal to codeine, but no more effective than two plain aspirin or acetaminophen tablets. When taken in combination with aspirin or acetaminophen, which relieve pain by other mechanisms, the combination is more effective than either drug alone.

SIDE EFFECTS Pentazocine sometimes causes dizziness, light-headedness, drowsiness, nausea, vomiting, constipation, headache, or sweating. If any of these side effects is persistent or severe, contact your doctor. Nausea is sometimes prevented by lying down.

Avoid driving until you are sure that your alertness and coordination are not impaired.

Some people experience strange and unpleasant mental feelings, nightmares, or confusion from pentazocine. If you experience any unusual thoughts or feelings, stop taking the drug and contact your doctor.

Pentazocine can be habit-forming if taken regularly over a long period of time.

Other side effects are too rare to list here. Contact your doctor if you experience any unexpected symptoms.

DRUG INTERACTIONS Pentazocine will intensify any impairment in coordination or decrease in alertness that you might experience from other drugs, such as antidepressants, antihistamines, barbiturates, or benzodiazepine anti-anxiety or sleeping pills. In addition, pentazocine is chemically related to narcotic antagonists, and it can provoke withdrawal symptoms in individuals who have taken narcotics, such as codeine or morphine, regularly over a long period of time.

ALCOHOLIC BEVERAGES Limit your use of alcohol to small amounts. Alcohol can intensify any dizziness or light-headedness that you may experience from pentazocine, and pentazocine will intensify the intoxicating effects of alcohol. Excessive amounts of both drugs can depress breathing.

FOOD   Pentazocine can be taken with food or on an empty stomach. If you are taking a pentazocine preparation that contains aspirin, take it with a full glass of water and with something to eat.

HOW DOES AGE AFFECT THE RESPONSE TO THIS DRUG?   The effect of age on the response to pentazocine has not been carefully studied, but older people are usually more sensitive to the effects of narcotics, which are related to pentazocine.

PHENOBARBITAL

OTHER NAMES   Phenobarbital (pronounced *fee-noe-BAR-bi-tal*) is the common or generic name of this drug. In Great Britain, its generic name is phenobarbitone. Some frequently used brand names for phenobarbital are Barbita, Luminal, and Solfoton, but phenobarbital is most often prescribed by its generic name. Phenobarbital is sometimes included in tablets or capsules with other drugs. Examples of these combinations are belladonna with phenobarbital (Donnatal), phenytoin with phenobarbital (Dilantin with Phenobarbital), and theophylline, ephedrine, and an expectorant with phenobarbital (Bronkolixer, Bronkotabs, Mudrane). Phenobarbital belongs to a large group of drugs called barbiturates.

WHAT IS IT SUPPOSED TO DO?   Phenobarbital is a general or nonspecific depressant of brain tissue. It was once widely used as a sedative for the relief of tension or anxiety, but its use for this purpose has largely been replaced by the benzodiazepines—drugs like diazepam (Valium) or oxazepam (Serax)—which are more specific in their action on the brain. However, phenobarbital's widespread effect on brain tissue makes it an ideal drug for preventing seizures caused by epilepsy or other medical problems that cause an excessive stimulation of brain tissue, and it is often prescribed for this purpose. It also prevents the seizures that can occur from abrupt withdrawal of alcohol, other barbiturates, and benzodiazepines in individuals who are addicted to these drugs.

Its generalized sedative effects are sometimes used to antagonize the excessive mental stimulation caused by drugs like ephedrine or theophylline.

In addition to its depressant effects on the brain, phenobarbital is a powerful stimulant to some enzyme systems in the liver—enzymes that are responsible for metabolizing certain biological waste products. It is therefore sometimes prescribed for jaundice and other conditions that might benefit from accelerated metabolism. This stimulant effect on the liver can also cause many drug interactions, as described below.

SIDE EFFECTS Phenobarbital often causes drowsiness, dizziness, light-headedness, clumsiness, or unsteadiness. Adjust your activities accordingly. These side effects will decrease or go away as your body adjusts to the drugs, but if they are persistent or bothersome, contact your doctor.

Less commonly, phenobarbital causes confusion, depression, weakness, or excitement. If any of these occur, contact your doctor.

As with all sedative drugs, stopping phenobarbital abruptly after prolonged daily use of large amounts can cause unpleasant symptoms. Your doctor will gradually reduce the dosage if it is necessary for you to stop taking it after prolonged regular use. Symptoms of withdrawal include anxiety, muscle twitching, trembling hands, difficulty in sleeping, and, rarely, seizures. Any signs of withdrawal should be treated by a physician.

Other side effects are too rare to list here. Contact your doctor if you experience any unexpected symptoms.

DRUG INTERACTIONS Phenobarbital stimulates certain enzymes in the liver. Drugs that are metabolized by these enzymes are removed from the blood more quickly, and their effects are thereby diminished.

If the dose of such a drug is increased to compensate for this interaction and phenobarbital is then stopped, the interacting drug will have greater (perhaps too much) effect unless its dosage is reduced accordingly. The list of drugs that are affected in this way is large; most of these interactions are described elsewhere in this book. If you are unsure about any drug you are taking with phenobarbital, ask your pharmacist or physician.

Avoid taking any drug that will add to the central-nervous-system depression caused by phenobarbital. Antihistamines, narcotics, or tranquilizers may cause excessive sedation if taken with phenobarbital.

ALCOHOLIC BEVERAGES Avoid alcohol; the combined effects of alcohol and phenobarbital can cause dangerous depression of the central nervous system.

FOOD Phenobarbital can be taken either with food or on an empty stomach.

HOW DOES AGE AFFECT THE RESPONSE TO THIS DRUG? The rate at which phenobarbital is removed from the body slows with advancing age. In addition, changes within the brain make older people more susceptible to side effects from phenobarbital.

PHENYTOIN

OTHER NAMES Phenytoin (pronounced *FEN-i-toyn)* is the common or generic name of this drug. An earlier generic name for phenytoin, occasionally used today, is diphenylhydantoin, sometimes abbreviated DPH. A frequently used brand name for phenytoin is Dilantin. Different brands of phenytoin capsules vary in the way they release phenytoin into the body, so you should be wary about changing brands, and, if you are taking Dilantin, you should not change brands without your doctor's approval. Phenytoin belongs to a group of drugs called hydantoins.

WHAT IS IT SUPPOSED TO DO?   Phenytoin acts on the central nervous system to prevent convulsions or seizures. It is also sometimes prescribed for its effects on the heart, because it prevents certain types of irregular heartbeats.

SIDE EFFECTS   Phenytoin sometimes causes nausea or stomach upset; take it with food or milk to minimize this problem.

You may experience mild drowsiness, so you should be careful in tasks that require alertness, such as driving, until you are familiar with the drug's effects.

Phenytoin can stimulate excessive gum growth (gingival hyperplasia), which is sometimes accompanied by tender or bleeding gums. Although this problem occurs most frequently in children and adolescents, it can occur in adults. It is prevented by regular tooth brushing and flossing. In addition, you should see your dentist regularly. Toothless portions of the gums are not affected.

Infrequently, phenytoin causes excessive body or facial hair growth. Do not be alarmed if you notice a pinkish or brownish coloration of your urine, which occurs infrequently and doesn't indicate any problem.

Beneficial effects from phenytoin occur within a well-defined range of concentrations of the drug in the blood, which can be determined by a simple laboratory test. Side effects that occur when the concentration is too high include uncontrollable side-to-side eye movements (nystagmus), blurred or double vision, clumsiness or unsteadiness (ataxia), severe drowsiness, slurred speech, confusion, mood or mental changes, and severe dizziness. Contact your doctor if any of these occur.

Rarely, long-term treatment with phenytoin causes folic acid deficiency (megaloblastic anemia) or altered vitamin D and calcium metabolism, which results in softening of the bones (osteomalacia). With routine blood tests, your doctor can detect these problems before they cause symptoms. You should not treat yourself with prophylactic vitamin D or folic acid without checking with your doctor.

Other side effects are too rare to list here. Contact your doctor if you experience a rash or any other unexpected side effect.

DRUG INTERACTIONS   Phenytoin interacts with several drugs. These are the interactions that are most likely to cause problems:

Acetazolamide (Diamox), which is used in the treatment of glaucoma, increases the risk for osteomalacia (see Side Effects) from phenytoin. Your doctor should monitor for signs of this side effect.

Chloramphenicol (Chloromycetin), an antibiotic, slows the metabolism of phenytoin and thereby increases its concentration in the blood. Your doctor should monitor for too much phenytoin effect and, if necessary, temporarily decrease your phenytoin dosage, when you need to take both drugs.

Corticosteroids, such as *dexamethasone, hydrocortisone, or prednisone,* are metabolized more rapidly while you are taking phenytoin. Your doctor may need to prescribe larger doses of corticosteroids to compensate for this effect.

Cimetidine (Tagamet), which is used for the treatment of stomach problems, slows the metabolism of phenytoin, causing increased concentrations of phenytoin in the blood. Ask your doctor to reevaluate your phenytoin dosage when you start or stop taking cimetidine.

Disulfiram (Antabuse), which is used in the treatment of alcoholism, slows the metabolism of phenytoin and thereby increases its concentration in the blood. Ask your doctor to reevaluate your phenytoin dosage when you start or stop taking disulfiram.

Folic acid, which is sometimes prescribed for the megaloblastic anemia that phenytoin can cause (see Side Effects), can decrease the concentration of phenytoin in the blood in some patients. Your doctor should monitor for this effect.

Isoniazid (INH), which is used in the treatment of tuberculosis, inhibits the metabolism of phenytoin and thereby increases its concentration in the blood. Ask your doctor to reevaluate your phenytoin dosage when you start or stop taking isoniazid.

Levodopa (Dopar, Larodopa), which is used in the treatment of Parkinson's disease, may lose some of its effectiveness when taken with phenytoin. Your doctor may need to increase your levodopa dosage if both drugs are required.

Phenobarbital, which is used as a sedative and also for the prevention of seizures, interacts with phenytoin in a complex and variable manner. Phenobarbital stimulates the enzymes that metabolize phenytoin, which could cause *reduced* concentrations of phenytoin in the blood. However, both drugs are metabolized by the same liver enzymes, and there is competition between the two drugs for these enzymes. Particularly in those with limited enzyme capacity (impaired liver function) or those taking large doses of phenobarbital, phenytoin can be metabolized more slowly when it is taken with phenobarbital, resulting in *increased* concentrations of phenytoin in the blood. Both interactions can take place at once, and each could cancel the other's effect. Thus, increased or decreased phenytoin effect or no change at all could occur. Finally, to further confuse matters, phenytoin can increase the concentration of phenobarbital in the blood. Whenever you start or stop taking phenobarbital, watch for either too much or too little phenytoin effect. Both drugs have beneficial effects on seizure control. If the phenytoin is being used for its effects on your heart and the phenobarbital is being used only as a sedative, ask your doctor to prescribe a different sedative.

Phenylbutazone (Butazolidin) and the related drug *oxyphenbutazone,* which are used in treating acute arthritis or gout attacks, can slow the metabolism of phenytoin, thereby increasing its concentration in the blood. In addition, these drugs displace phenytoin from its binding sites on the plasma protein that circulates in the blood, which can also increase phenytoin's effects. (The mechanism by which decreased protein binding can increase phenytoin's effects is discussed below, under How Does Age . . .) Watch for signs of too much phenytoin effect.

Quinidine (Cardioquin, Quinaglute), which is used in preventing irregular heartbeats, is metabolized more rapidly when taken with phenytoin. Therefore, larger quinidine doses may be necessary while you are taking both drugs. Ask your doctor to reevaluate your quinidine therapy if you start or stop taking phenytoin.

Rifampin (Rimactane), an antibacterial used in the treatment of tuberculosis and other infections, stimulates the enzymes that metabolize phenytoin, thereby decreasing its concentration in the blood. Your doctor may need to increase your phenytoin dosage temporarily while you are taking both drugs. If you are taking both isoniazid (see interaction above) and rifampin for tuberculosis, drugs that have opposite effects on phenytoin metabolism, the effect of rifampin can be expected to predominate.

Theophylline, which is used in the treatment of respiratory problems, is metabolized more rapidly when taken with phenytoin. Therefore, larger doses of theophylline may be required while you are taking both drugs. Be sure your doctor monitors for this interaction.

Thyroid hormone metabolism is increased by phenytoin. Normally, your body compensates for this effect by producing more thyroid hormones (although hypothyroidism is a rare side effect of phenytoin therapy). If you are taking thyroid tablets, your doctor will order laboratory tests to determine whether it is necessary to increase the dosage of your thyroid hormone medication.

ALCOHOLIC BEVERAGES   Limit your consumption of alcoholic beverages. Alcohol will add to any drowsiness you may feel from the phenytoin. Regular use of large amounts of alcohol will increase the rate at which phenytoin is metabolized, thereby decreasing its effects. In some individuals, excess alcohol consumption can cause seizures.

FOOD   Take your phenytoin with food to decrease any stomach upset it might cause.

HOW DOES AGE AFFECT THE RESPONSE TO THIS DRUG?   Phenytoin metabolism is unusual; it doesn't follow as predictable a course as most other drugs. With most drugs, each increase or decrease in dosage causes a proportional increase or decrease in concentration of drug in the blood. Phenytoin's metabolic enzymes, however, can be saturated, and each increase or decrease in dosage can cause an increase or decrease in concentration of phenytoin in the blood that is much larger than would be expected (although there are several reliable means for predicting the blood concentrations that are likely to occur from phenytoin dosage modifications). As you might expect, the point at which phenytoin metabolism becomes saturated decreases with age. Although there is considerable variation among individuals, there is a steady decline in phenytoin metabolism throughout life, from childhood to old age. On the average, a sixty- to seventy-nine-year-old person can be expected to require about 80 percent of the daily dosage required by a twenty- to thirty-nine-year-old. A blood test that measures the concentration of phenytoin in the blood, which is becoming increasingly available, will help your doctor in tailoring your phenytoin dosage.

A second effect that aging has on phenytoin response is decreased binding to plasma protein. About 95 percent of the phenytoin circulating in the blood is temporarily bound to albumin, a protein in the blood. You can think of albumin as a sort of storage depot for phenytoin. The concentration of albumin tends to decrease with older age (and it decreases significantly in those with liver or kidney diseases). When the concentration of albumin decreases, the bound concentration of phenytoin also decreases, and there is a proportional increase in the unbound concentration of phenytoin. Because it is the unbound phenytoin that is pharmacologically active, this decrease in binding may be associated with greater drug effect (although more drug is also available for metabolism). Older people tend to experience greater mental changes than do younger patients with the same concentration of phenytoin in their blood, an observation that can be attributed, at least in part, to decreased protein binding. Your doctor will consider the concentration of albumin in your blood in assessing your phenytoin dosage.

PINDOLOL

OTHER NAMES   Pindolol (pronounced *PIN-doe-lole*) is the common or generic name of this drug. A frequently used brand name for pindolol is Visken. Pindolol belongs to a group of drugs known as beta-blockers.

WHAT IS IT SUPPOSED TO DO?   Pindolol lowers blood pressures that are too high, prevents certain kinds of angina attacks, prevents certain kinds of irregular heartbeats, and is occasionally used for other medical problems.

Pindolol accomplishes these various remedies by acting on the autonomic nervous system, the part of the nervous system that is beyond our conscious control— the part that regulates the heart, blood vessels, and various internal organs. Needless to say, the autonomic nervous system is complex. It has parasympathetic and sympathetic parts that generally work in opposition to one another. The sympathetic part responds to two types of stimulation, alpha and beta.

Pindolol molecules temporarily bind with highly specialized nervous tissues called beta-receptors, thereby preventing them from recognizing the chemical messengers that normally set them off (That is why pharmacologists refer to pindolol as a beta-blocker.) The beta-receptors are one of several means by which the organs get the messages that tell them what to do. An increase in heart rate and an increase in blood pressure are examples of beta responses that are blocked by pindolol. There are beta-receptors throughout the body, and a variety of medical problems respond well to treatment with pindolol.

There are other beta-blocking drugs, but pindolol has the unique property of mildly stimulating the receptors that it blocks. This mild stimulation might seem contrary to the primary purpose and prevailing effect of the drug—blockade of beta-receptors—but it is beneficial in preventing some of the side effects that beta-blockers sometimes cause.

SIDE EFFECTS Despite the wide distribution of beta-receptors throughout the body, side effects from pindolol are infrequent and generally mild. Most people experience no side effects at all.

The most important side effect you should know about is the possibility of withdrawal symptoms if you suddenly stop taking pindolol after taking it regularly. This side effect can be understood by considering how pindolol works (see above). While the beta-receptors are blocked by pindolol, they can become overly sensitive to the chemical messengers that normally set them off. If pindolol is withdrawn abruptly, these receptors will overrespond. The most common symptom is headache, but there is also the danger of angina attacks, a sudden rise in blood pressure, irregular heartbeats, or even a heart attack, depending on what condition was being treated initially. Pindolol's ability to cause mild stimulation of the beta-receptors makes withdrawal symptoms less likely than they are with other beta-blockers. Nevertheless, if your doctor wants you to stop taking pindolol, he will gradually reduce the dose, or he may substitute another beta-blocker.

Your doctor will carefully check your heart before prescribing pindolol. When Pindolol is taken by individuals with untreated congestive heart failure, a condition in which the heart is unable to adequately carry out its job of pumping blood through the circulatory system, this heart failure is likely to be worsened. Rarely, it causes congestive heart failure in individuals with no previous symptoms. Most patients whose congestive heart failure is corrected by other drugs are able to take pindolol without problem. Because pindolol mildly stimulates the beta-receptors it blocks, it may be less likely than other beta-blockers to cause adverse effects on the heart. However, you should contact your doctor at once if you experience swelling of your feet or ankles, sudden weight gain, or difficulty in breathing while lying down. Pindolol's ability to slow the heart and lower the blood pressure is usually beneficial, but occasional individuals experience too much of these effects. An unusually slow pulse rate (less than fifty beats per minute) or dizziness (possibly from abnormally low blood pressure) are other reasons to get in touch with your doctor.

Stomach upset, constipation, or diarrhea occur infrequently from pindolol, and they often go away with continued use of the drug. If any of these side effects continues to be bothersome, contact your doctor.

Another infrequent side effect is coldness of the hands or feet, which may occur as a result of the circulatory changes that are brought about by pindolol. Be sure to dress warmly in cold weather.

Although pindolol enters the brain, its effects there are usually imperceptible, except for occasional drowsiness. However, it sometimes causes adverse mental effects, including headache, dizziness, fatigue, confusion, nightmares, insomnia, and depression. If you experience unusual and persistent mental symptoms, contact your doctor.

There are some diseases that increase the risk of side effects from pindolol. Your doctor will not prescribe pindolol if you have asthma or emphysema, since the effects of pindolol are just the opposite of those that help control lung diseases. In diabetics, pindolol can cause several problems (see Drug Interactions, Antidiabetic Drugs). As pointed out above, uncontrolled congestive heart failure is worsened by pindolol.

Other side effects are too rare to mention here. Contact your doctor if you experience any unusual symptoms.

DRUG INTERACTIONS Several drugs can interact with pindolol. Your doctor will monitor your therapy with special care if any of these drugs need to be taken with pindolol:

Antidiabetic drugs, such as *insulin* and the *sulfonylureas.* Diabetic patients should not take pindolol unless there is no other alternative. Pindolol can block some of the warning signs of hypoglycemia (rapid heartbeat or palpitations), delay the recovery from hypoglycemia, cause high-blood-pressure episodes during hypoglycemia, and impair circulation to the extremities in diabetics. If pindolol is required, keep in mind that sweating, but not rapid heartbeat, is a sign of hypoglycemia. Certain other beta-blocking drugs, such as metoprolol (Lopressor) and atenolol (Tenormin), are less likely to cause problems, but there is some risk.

Breathing medications, such as *isoproterenol (Isuprel) inhalation, terbutaline (Brethine, Bricanyl), or theophylline (Elixophyllin, Slo-Phyllin, Theobid, Theo-Dur, and others),* which are used for the treatment of asthma, emphysema, or other lung problems, don't mix well with pindolol. The ability of these drugs to open up the air passages in the lungs is antagonized by pindolol. Although its effects on normal lungs are minimal, pindolol can be dangerous in those with asthma or other lung problems.

Clonidine (Catapres), which is used to control high blood pressure, can cause a rebound hypertensive reaction if it is stopped abruptly. This reaction is worse in patients who are also taking pindolol. If you are taking both of these drugs and must stop taking clonidine, your doctor may slowly discontinue your pindolol first. In any case, don't stop taking this drug combination without careful supervision.

Prazosin (Minipress), which is used to control high blood pressure, sometimes causes a severe drop in blood pressure when the person taking it stands up too quickly. This side effect is most common when the drug is first started, and there is some evidence that pindolol makes it more likely to occur. If you are taking pindolol and starting to take prazosin, your doctor will start with smaller doses and may advise you to take the prazosin at bedtime.

Sympathomimetics, which are contained in some nonprescription remedies for nasal congestion, can cause hypertensive reactions in susceptible individuals. There is some evidence that the risk of this reaction is greater in patients with high blood pressure who are taking pindolol. Check with your pharmacist before taking any medication for nasal congestion.

ALCOHOLIC BEVERAGES   Usually there is no inter-action between pindolol and alcohol. However, you should establish for yourself that pindolol does not make you drowsy or dizzy before you drink anything with alcohol in it.

FOOD   It's a good idea to take pindolol with meals to help you to develop a regular routine for taking it. Food does not affect its absorption. If your doctor has pre-scribed a restricted-salt or restricted-calorie diet, be sure to follow it.

HOW DOES AGE AFFECT THE RESPONSE TO THIS DRUG?   Aging slows the rate at which pindolol is removed from the body, thereby allowing it to accu-mulate to higher concentrations in the blood, but ad-vancing age also brings changes in the beta-receptors that make them less sensitive to drugs. These two ef-fects tend to offset each other. Therefore, older people usually respond similarly to the doses required by dif-ferent individuals, regardless of age.

The risk for side effects, particularly those related to the heart (see Side Effects), increases with advancing age. Be sure to return to your doctor for regular check-ups. Most older people, including those who have achieved considerable age, are able to take pindolol without problems.

PIROXICAM

OTHER NAMES   Piroxicam (pronounced *peer-OX-i-kam)* is the common or generic name of this drug. A frequently used brand name for piroxicam is Feldene. Piroxicam belongs to a large group of drugs called non-steroidal anti-inflammatory drugs (NSAIDs).

WHAT IS IT SUPPOSED TO DO?   Piroxicam relieves the pain, inflammation, swelling, and stiffness associated with arthritis. Although some relief should become apparent shortly after you begin taking piroxicam, maximum relief occurs after two or three weeks.

SIDE EFFECTS   Indigestion, heartburn, nausea, stomach discomfort, excessive gas, diarrhea, and other problems related to the digestive tract are the most common side effects from piroxicam. These side effects can sometimes be prevented by taking your piroxicam with a full glass of water, perhaps in addition to food or an antacid. If they persist, or they are severe, stop taking the drug and contact your doctor.

Rarely, piroxicam causes more severe problems in the digestive tract. These include ulcer with bleeding into the gastrointestinal tract (evidenced by bloody stools or stools that are discolored dark red or black) and small amounts of painless blood loss (which can cause anemia). The risk of these problems is lower than it is with aspirin.

Piroxicam can also cause mental effects such as drowsiness, headache, or dizziness. Because piroxicam can cause decreased alertness in some individuals, you should evaluate how this drug affects you before you drive an automobile or operate any potentially dangerous machinery. If you should develop any sort of visual difficulty (such as blurred or dim vision) or hearing problem (such as buzzing or ringing in your ears), stop taking the drug and contact your doctor.

Kidney problems caused by piroxicam and similar drugs are relatively rare, but most of the cases that have been reported in the medical literature involved older individuals. Some of the medical problems that are more prevalent among older people place them at greater risk for this side effect. When the kidneys are stressed by congestive heart failure, dehydration, or any kind of kidney impairment (even modest impairment), the body responds by producing substances called prostaglandins. Prostaglandins increase the flow of blood to the kidneys and increase their efficiency. Piroxicam and related drugs can block this compensatory response, and kidney failure (usually reversible) can occur as a result. (All nonsteroidal anti-inflammatory drugs work by preventing the body from a manufacturing prostaglandins, which are also mediators of pain and inflammation.) Considering the widespread use of piroxicam among older people and the extremely small number of kidney problems that have been reported, the risk appears to be small. However, you should return to your doctor for regular medical checkups while taking this drug. Contact your doctor promptly if you experience sudden weight gain, swelling of your feet or ankles, or markedly decreased urine production.

Skin problems, such as rashes or unusual reactions to the sun, are rare side effects from piroxicam. Contact your doctor if you experience anything unusual.

Piroxicam is very effective in lowering fever. This effect, combined with its pain-relieving and anti-inflammatory actions, could be considered a side effect if the signs of an infection were masked and the infection went undetected (and untreated) too long.

If you have ever developed asthma as an allergic reaction to aspirin, you should not take piroxicam, because a similar allergic reaction could occur.

Other side effects from piroxicam are too rare to list here. Contact your doctor if you experience any unusual symptoms.

DRUG INTERACTIONS Several drugs have the potential to interact with piroxicam:

Aspirin is potentially irritating to the digestive tract,

and its irritant effects could become troublesome when added to those of piroxicam. Check with your doctor before taking this drug combination.

Diuretics, such as *hydrochlorothiazide (HydroDIURIL and other brands) or furosemide (Lasix).* Infrequently, piroxicam causes fluid retention and edema. If you are taking a diuretic for fluid retention and edema (such as that caused by congestive heart failure or kidney disease) and experience a worsening of your symptoms while taking piroxicam, stop taking your piroxicam and contact your doctor.

Warfarin (Coumadin). Piroxicam can cause some gastrointestinal bleeding, which could be worsened by the anticoagulant effects of warfarin. In addition, piroxicam decreases the effectiveness of blood platelets in forming blood clots, so the risk of side effects from warfarin is increased somewhat while you are taking piroxicam.

ALCOHOLIC BEVERAGES Alcohol adds to the gastric-irritant effects of piroxicam. Avoid taking them at the same time.

FOOD Food slows the absorption of piroxicam somewhat. but it doesn't impair its absorption. It's a good idea to take your piroxicam with food to minimize any gastric irritation that might occur.

HOW DOES AGE AFFECT THE RESPONSE TO THIS DRUG? Advancing age increases the risk of side effects from piroxicam. There has been some public controversy over the safety of piroxicam in older individuals; one health lobby urged that it be declared unsafe for persons older than sixty. However, the Food and Drug Administration concluded, after reviewing various studies, that there is no evidence that the increased risk of side effects in older people is any greater than it is with other nonsteroidal anti-inflammatory drugs.

POLYTHIAZIDE

OTHER NAMES Polythiazide (pronounced *pol-i-THYE-a-zide)* is the common or generic name of this drug. Its most frequently used brand name is Renese. Polythiazide is sometimes prescribed as capsules or tablets that contain other drugs. Minizide is the brand name of capsules that contain polythiazide with the antihypertensive drug prazosin. Renese-R is the brand name of tablets that contain polythiazide with the antihypertensive drug reserpine. Polythiazide belongs to a group of closely related drugs called thiazide diuretics.

WHAT IS IT SUPPOSED TO DO? Polythiazide is a diuretic, meaning that it increases the amount of urine that is excreted from the body. Polythiazide acts on the kidneys, causing them to eliminate extra water and salt from the body and into the urine. It is used to treat congestive heart failure, high blood pressure, and other medical problems.

Use in Congestive Heart Failure. Extra salt and water may accumulate in the body for a variety of reasons, but congestive heart failure is a common cause in older persons. In congestive heart failure, which is the result of some types of heart disease, the heart's pumping action weakens and the circulation slows. When the kidneys do not get enough circulation, they become less efficient in removing extra salt and water from the body. As a result, veins become swollen, and fluid leaks out of them and into surrounding tissue. Usually, the first symptom of this problem is swelling of the ankles and lower legs. (The medical term for this swelling, which can also be caused by less potentially serious circulatory problems, is edema.) Later, fluid accumulates in the lungs, causing shortness of breath. Polythiazide's ability to promote salt and water removal by the kidneys is the basis for its use in congestive heart failure.

Use in Hypertension. The diuretic effects of polythiazide are important here because too much salt in the body may be part of the cause of hypertension (high blood pressure). In addition, and perhaps more important in hypertension, polythiazide causes small blood vessels to dilate. This dilation of blood vessels eases the resistance to blood flow, and blood pressure is thereby lowered. Whether your hypertension is mild or severe, polythiazide may be the first drug your doctor prescribes to control it.

SIDE EFFECTS Serious side effects from polythiazide are rare. The most annoying side effect you will notice when you begin taking this drug is a need to urinate frequently. You should avoid taking polythiazide too late in the day. Otherwise, you may find yourself frequently awakened from sleep by a need to urinate.

Polythiazide causes potassium to be removed from the body along with salt and water. In most cases, this causes no problem. Dietary sources of potassium usually prevent potassium deficiency from occurring. However, your doctor may prescribe either a potassium supplement or a second diuretic that conserves potassium to prevent this effect, especially if you are also taking digoxin (see Drug Interactions). In any case, your doctor will periodically order a laboratory test that measures the concentration of potassium in the blood. The symptoms of too low a concentration of potassium in the blood include profound muscle weakness, muscle cramps or pain, and irregular heartbeat. If you experience any of these symptoms, contact your doctor.

Polythiazide sometimes causes an increase in the amount of glucose in the blood, which could unmask latent diabetes or require an increase in your insulin or other drug requirement if you already have diabetes. Prevention of excess potassium loss decreases the risk of this problem. Polythiazide can also increase the amount of uric acid in your blood, but it rarely causes gout, the clinical manifestation of too much uric acid in the blood. Your doctor will order periodic laboratory tests to monitor for these and other, rarer possible problems before they cause symptoms.

All diuretics have the potential for causing dehydration when fluid loss is accelerated by hot weather or flulike illness. Whenever you experience fever, vomiting, or diarrhea, whatever the cause, be sure to increase your fluid intake to prevent dehydration. If the symptoms are severe, you should contact your doctor.

Other side effects are too rare to list here. If you should develop a rash or any other unusual symptom while taking this drug, contact your doctor.

DRUG INTERACTIONS   Several drugs interact with polythiazide, and your doctor will take special precautions to ensure that no problems occur if any of these drugs need to be taken with polythiazide:

Antidiabetic drugs, such as *insulin* or the *sulfonylureas.* Polythiazide can increase the concentration of glucose in the blood. If this occurs, despite the protective effect of correcting for potassium loss, your doctor may increase the dosage of your diabetic medication to compensate for this interaction. If you are taking chlorpropamide (Diabinese) or tolbutamide (Orinase), your doctor will monitor for a second, less frequent possible interaction. These drugs sometimes decrease the concentration of sodium in the blood by a mechanism separate from that of polythiazide. (Other sulfonylureas do not share this property.) In some older individuals, this combination of drugs can lead to too low a concentration of sodium in the blood (hyponatremia). If you experience weakness, confusion, or muscle cramps, contact your doctor.

Corticosteroids, such as *dexamethasone, hydrocortisone, or prednisone,* cause potassium to be lost from the body, and this side effect is additive with that of polythiazide. To prevent problems, your doctor will periodically order a laboratory test that measures the concentration of potassium in the blood and, if necessary, will prescribe either a potassium supplement or a second diuretic that conserves potassium.

Digoxin (Lanoxin). Although polythiazide is often prescribed together with digoxin, an interaction can occur because of polythiazide's promotion of potassium loss from the body. If the amount of potassium in the blood becomes too low, then digoxin toxicity may develop. To prevent this problem, your doctor will periodically order a laboratory test that measures the concentration of potassium in the blood and, if necessary, will prescribe either a potassium supplement or a second diuretic that conserves potassium.

Bile-acid sequestrants, such as *cholestyramine resin (Questran) and colestipol (Colestid),* are used to lower the concentration of cholesterol in the blood. They are also used to treat the itching that sometimes occurs with jaundice. These drugs may bind to polythiazide in the gastrointestinal tract and thereby prevent its full absorption. If therapy with one of these drugs is necessary, the polythiazide dose should be taken two hours before the cholestyramine or colestipol dose to minimize any interaction.

Lithium (Eskalith, Lithane, and others), which is prescribed by psychiatrists for mood problems, is removed from the body by the kidneys. Polythiazide significantly slows this removal, and the concentration of lithium in the blood increases, sometimes to toxic levels. When these drugs must be used together, your doctor will probably decrease the dose of your lithium, using a laboratory test for monitoring the concentration of lithium in your blood as a guide.

Nonsteroidal anti-inflammatory drugs (NSAIDs), such as *diflunisal, ibuprofen, indomethacin, fenoprofen, meclofenamate, naproxen, piroxicam, sulindac, tolmetin, or large amounts of aspirin.* These drugs can cause fluid retention and edema in older people who are sensitive to this effect. If you are taking polythiazide for fluid retention and edema (such as that caused by congestive heart failure or liver disease) and you experience a worsening of your symptoms while taking one of these

NSAIDs, stop taking the NSAID and contact your doctor.

ALCOHOLIC BEVERAGES Alcoholic beverages have a more pronounced effect on some people than on others; if you become dizzy when drinking, polythiazide might make things worse. You can carefully evaluate this effect for yourself. Most people do not notice any effect at all.

FOOD Many pharmacists recommend taking polythiazide with meals. Food does not impair its absorption, and some people (probably fewer than one in a hundred) experience an upset stomach when they take polythiazide on an empty stomach. Taking it with a meal will help you set up a routine for taking it and thereby prevent you from missing too many doses. Take your morning dose with breakfast and, if you take a second daily dose, take it with a late-afternoon snack or dinner.

Be sure to follow any dietary advice, such as low-salt diet or increasing the amount of potassium-containing foods (such as bananas, orange juice, raisins), you may have been given with your prescription.

HOW DOES AGE AFFECT THE RESPONSE TO THIS DRUG? Older people are more sensitive to the effects of diuretics. The effects of too much diuretic, which are rare in younger people, are more likely to occur with advancing age. The most common problem is dizziness or faintness from abnormally low blood pressure. If you experience such a symptom, contact your doctor. Another problem, which is infrequent, is too low a concentration of sodium in the blood. If you experience weakness, confusion, or muscle cramps, contact your doctor.

Your doctor will take your age into consideration in selecting a dosage that is likely to be appropriate for you.

POTASSIUM CHLORIDE

OTHER NAMES Potassium chloride (pronounced *poe-TASS-ee-um KLOR-ide)* is the common or generic name of this drug. There are many commercial potassium chloride products.

Potassium chloride liquid is often prescribed by its generic name, and your medication bottle may even be labeled with the chemical name for potassium chloride, KCl. Some frequently used brand names for potassium chloride liquid are Cena-K, Kaochlor, Kay Ciel Oral Solution 10%, Klor-10%, Klorvess 10%, Potasalan, and Potassine.

Potassium chloride is also sometimes prescribed as extended-release capsules or tablets. Some frequently used brand names for this form of potassium chloride are Kaon-Cl, K-Tab, Klotrix, Micro-K, and Slow-K.

Packets of flavored potassium chloride powder that are dissolved in a glass of water are another commonly prescribed form of this drug. Some frequently used brand names for these powders are K-Lor, K-Lyte/CL, KATO, and Kay Ciel. A similar dosage form is a tablet that is intended to be dissolved in a glass of water to provide a flavored potassium chloride solution. Some frequently used brands of these tablets for solution are K-Lyte, Klor-Con, and Quic-K.

WHAT IS IT SUPPOSED TO DO? Potassium is an essential constituent of body tissues. Some drugs, such as thiazide diuretics, loop diuretics, and corticosteroids, promote potassium loss, and when dietary replacement is inadequate, potassium is prescribed as a drug. Potassium chloride prevents or corrects hypokalemia (too low a concentration of potassium in the blood).

SIDE EFFECTS Potassium chloride powder is irritating to the digestive tract. Therefore, you should take the liquid form in dilute solution (in a full glass of water or juice). Extended-release potassium chloride tablets are specially formulated to release the drug so slowly that irritation does not occur. Rarely, however, gastrointestinal irritation and ulceration do occur from these tablets. Contact your doctor if you experience persistent stomach discomfort or if you notice blackish stools (a sign of bleeding).

The most serious side effect from potassium chloride is hyperkalemia (too high a concentration of potassium in the blood), but this occurs infrequently. To prevent this side effect, which can cause dangerously irregular heartbeats, your doctor will periodically measure the concentration of potassium in your blood. Your doctor will evaluate your kidney function before prescribing potassium chloride and periodically while you are taking it, because impaired kidney function can lead to the accumulation of potassium in the blood.

DRUG INTERACTIONS Several drugs can increase the concentration of potassium in the blood, especially when taken with potassium chloride. These are the most likely to cause problems:

Angiotensin-converting-enzyme (ACE) inhibitors, such as *captopril (Capoten, Capozide)* or *enalapril (Vaseretic, Vasotec)*, which are used in the treatment of congestive heart failure and high blood pressure, cause potassium to be conserved by the body. To minimize the risk of hyperkalemia, potassium chloride should be used with these drugs only when the concentration of potassium in the blood has been demonstrated to be too low. If you are taking this combination, be sure your doctor is monitoring the concentration of potassium in your blood.

Potassium-sparing diuretics, such as *amiloride (Midamor, Moduretic), spironolactone (Aldactone, Aldactazide), or triamterene (Dyazide, Dyrenium, Maxzide)*, cause potassium to be conserved by the body. When these drugs are taken with potassium chloride, a dangerous hyperkalemia can occur.

Salt substitutes and *low-salt milk* contain potassium and can add to the effect of your potassium chloride medication if taken in sufficient amounts. To avoid hyperkalemia, check with your doctor before using these products.

ALCOHOLIC BEVERAGES Avoid taking potassium chloride and alcoholic beverages at the same time on an empty stomach, because both are potentially irritating to the stomach.

FOOD Potassium chloride should be taken with food to prevent any stomach upset it might cause. If you are on a restricted-salt diet, be sure to follow it, and avoid using salt substitutes (see Drug Interactions). Since foods vary in their potassium content, you should not make a radical change in your regular diet without first checking with your doctor.

HOW DOES AGE AFFECT THE RESPONSE TO THIS DRUG? The risk for hyperkalemia (see Side Effects) from potassium chloride increases because of the steady decline in kidney function that occurs with advancing age. As kidney function declines, potassium is eliminated more slowly. (The assessment of kidney function in older individuals is described in the appendix.)

Older age is more often accompanied by medical problems that add to the risk for hyperkalemia. For example, in some instances, diabetics are more prone to develop hyperkalemia than nondiabetics. Likewise, individuals with malignancies are more likely to develop hyperkalemia.

Lastly, older individuals are more likely to experience adverse effects from drug interactions that don't ordinarily cause problems. For example, nonsteroidal anti-inflammatory drugs (such as ibuprofen, fenoprofen, or naproxen) and beta-blocking drugs (such as metoprolol or propranolol) can cause a small increase in the concentration of potassium in the blood. The effect that these drugs have on potassium, which is ordinarily not clinically apparent, may add to the effect of potassium chloride in people with poor kidney function.

Regular checkups should prevent these problems. Despite this list of potentially dire consequences of potassium chloride use with advancing age, this drug is generally safe and beneficial. Potassium chloride is one of the most commonly used drugs among older people and seldom causes serious side effects.

PRAZEPAM

OTHER NAMES Prazepam (pronounced *PRAY-zeh-pam)* is the common or generic name of this drug. A frequently used brand name for prazepam is Centrax. Prazepam belongs to a large group of similar drugs called benzodiazepines.

WHAT IS IT SUPPOSED TO DO? Prazepam relieves the symptoms of anxiety and tension.

SIDE EFFECTS Drowsiness is the principal side effect from prazepam. You may find yourself unsteady on your feet as well. Evaluate these effects for yourself and regulate your activities accordingly. You should be especially cautious about driving an automobile. If drowsiness or unsteadiness persists, stop taking the drug and contact your doctor.

Infrequently, prazepam causes dizziness, weakness, confusion, impaired memory, or loss of coordination. If you experience any of these effects, which suggest you are extremely sensitive to prazepam, stop taking it and contact your doctor.

If you have been taking prazepam regularly for a long time and in large doses, you may experience mild withdrawal symptoms several days after stopping this drug. Typical symptoms include difficulty in sleeping, unusual irritability, and unusual nervousness. If these occur, contact your doctor.

Other side effects are too rare to list here. Contact your doctor if you experience any unusual symptoms.

DRUG INTERACTIONS Sedation is a common side effect of antidepressant drugs, antihistamines, tranquilizers, narcotic analgesics, and other drugs. Be careful of additive effects between prazepam and any of these drugs.

In addition, several drugs can interact with prazepam by other mechanisms. These are the interactions most likely to cause problems:

Cimetidine (Tagamet), which is used for the treatment of ulcers, slows the metabolism of prazepam and thereby enhances its effects. It may be necessary to decrease the dosage of your prazepam while taking both drugs; ask your doctor.

Disulfiram (Antabuse), which is used in the treatment of alcoholism, slows the metabolism of prazepam and thereby enhances its effects. It may be necessary to decrease the dosage of your prazepam while taking both drugs; ask your doctor.

Isoniazid (INH), which is used in the treatment of tuberculosis, may slow the metabolism of prazepam and thereby enhance its effect. It may be necessary to decrease the dosage of your prazepam while taking both drugs; ask your doctor. Rifampin, another drug used in treating tuberculosis, has the opposite effect (see below). When rifampin and isoniazid are used together for the treatment of tuberculosis, the effects of rifampin predominate in the interaction with prazepam.

Levodopa (Dopar, Larodopa, L-dopa) is used in the treatment of Parkinson's disease, and prazepam may block its effect. If you are taking both drugs and notice a worsening of your parkinsonism, stop taking your prazepam and contact your doctor.

Rifampin (Rifadin, Rimactane), which is used in the treatment of tuberculosis, increases the metabolism of prazepam and thereby decreases its effect. If your doctor increases the dosage of your prazepam to compensate for this interaction, remind him or her to readjust your prazepam dosage when you stop taking rifampin.

ALCOHOLIC BEVERAGES   Prazepam adds to alcohol's depressant effects on the nervous system. If you are taking prazepam regularly, the combined effects of alcohol and prazepam can occur even if the last time you took your prazepam was on the previous day, or even several days previously. The active metabolites of prazepam remain in the body for many days. Therefore, you should limit your alcohol consumption to small amounts while taking prazepam. Needless to say, the effects of this combination on driving can be dangerous.

FOOD Prazepam can be taken with food or on an empty stomach.

HOW DOES AGE AFFECT THE RESPONSE TO THIS DRUG? The older you are, the more sensitive you will be to prazepam. There are several mechanisms involved:

First, older people are inherently more sensitive to the effects of prazepam. This may have something to do with the effects of aging on the brain. There is good evidence that older people experience much more sedation than younger people with the same concentration of the drug in their blood.

Second, aging changes the distribution of desmethyldiazepam, the principal active metabolite of prazepam, within the body. As a result, it takes much longer for the maximum effect of repeated doses to become apparent. An older person who takes prazepam every day will experience slightly more effect each day for several weeks, and *then* repeated doses will maintain the same level of effect. If the dosage is too high for you, you may not notice it as soon as you might expect.

Third, and for some unknown reason this applies more to men than to women, the metabolism of desmethyldiazepam, the active metabolite of prazepam, becomes slower with advanced age. Therefore, some older people develop higher concentrations of drug in their blood than would be expected and they are likely to develop side effects. In these individuals, it may take longer than a month before the full effects of repeated doses become apparent.

In any case, side effects increase with age. Confusion, weakness, fainting, dizziness, impaired memory, and loss of coordination, which are infrequent side effects from prazepam, occur far more often in older people than they do in younger people. All of these side effects are reversible. However, because their onset can be so slow, they are sometimes not associated with the offending drug. Furthermore, just as these side effects are often slow to appear, they are equally slow in disappearing after prazepam is stopped. If you are aware of this possibility, it probably won't become a problem for you.

Your doctor will take your age into consideration in selecting a dose and dosage schedule that are likely to be appropriate for you.

PRAZOSIN

OTHER NAMES Prazosin (pronounced *PRA-zoe-sin)* is the common or generic name of this drug. Its most frequently used brand name is Minipress. Sometimes prazosin is prescribed as capsules that also contain the thiazide diuretic polythiazide; the brand name of this combination is Minizide.

WHAT IS IT SUPPOSED TO DO? Prazosin blocks certain receptors (alpha$_1$-sympathetic receptors) in blood vessels. When stimulated by certain substances in the blood (and when they are not blocked by prazosin), these receptors tell the muscle in blood vessels to constrict and make the diameter of blood vessels narrower. Prazosin therefore widens the diameter of blood vessels, decreases the resistance to blood flow, and lowers blood pressure.

Hypertension (high blood pressure) causes no symptoms, but untreated hypertension substantially increases the risk of the subsequent development of congestive heart failure, angina, heart attack, stroke, kidney problems, or visual problems. Antihypertensive drugs such as prazosin decrease these risks.

SIDE EFFECTS The most common side effect from prazosin is light-headedness or dizziness, especially upon standing up quickly. This side effect is particularly severe during the first thirty to ninety minutes after the first dose and could cause you to faint. Therefore, the first dose of prazosin (which should not exceed 1 mg) is best taken at bedtime, which would allow its effects to occur while you are lying down. This "first-dose effect" may recur if for any reason you stop taking prazosin for a few days and then start again.

After the first dose, you will develop some tolerance to this dizziness, but it will still occur if you stand up too quickly from a sitting or lying position. It can also occur after standing in one position for a long period of time, during vigorous exercise, or if the weather is hot. If you begin to feel dizzy, lie down so that you will not faint; then sit for a while before standing. If dizziness is more than a minor problem, or if you experience pounding or racing heartbeat, contact your doctor.

Prazosin can also cause drowsiness. Do not drive until you are sure the drowsiness or dizziness from prazosin will not affect your abilities.

Headache or nausea can also occur. You may become tolerant to these side effects, but if they are persistent or severe, contact your doctor.

Some people experience fluid retention from prazosin. If you notice weight gain, swelling of your feet or lower legs, or shortness of breath, contact your doctor.

Other side effects are too infrequent to list here. Contact your doctor if you experience any unexpected symptoms.

DRUG INTERACTIONS   Several drugs have the potential for interacting adversely with prazosin:

Antihypertensive drugs. The dizziness that prazosin sometimes causes can be worsened by other antihypertensive drugs, especially beta-blockers. This combination is often used to good therapeutic advantage, but caution is warranted, particularly after the first dose of prazosin (see Side Effects). Although diuretics increase prazosin's effectiveness, they, too, can contribute to prazosin-induced dizziness.

Phenylephrine (Neo-Synephrine), which is used as a nasal decongestant and as eye drops, works by stimulating the alpha-sympathetic receptors in blood vessels. Prazosin has the opposite effect; it blocks these receptors. When enough phenylephrine appears in the blood, it can reverse the effects of prazosin. There is some evidence that sensitivity to this interaction increases with advancing age. Check with your pharmacist or physician before using any nasal decongestant.

ALCOHOLIC BEVERAGES Dizziness is more likely to occur after drinking alcohol. Be cautious about the amount of alcohol you drink.

FOOD Prazosin can be taken either with meals or on an empty stomach. If your doctor has prescribed a low-salt diet, be sure to follow it.

HOW DOES AGE AFFECT THE RESPONSE TO THIS DRUG? Prazosin is more likely to cause dizziness in older individuals.

PREDNISONE

OTHER NAMES Prednisone (pronounced *PRED-ni-sone)* is the common or generic name of this drug. It has many brand names, including Deltasone, Meticorten, Orasone, and SK-Prednisone, but it is most often prescribed by its generic name. Prednisone belongs to a large group of similar drugs known as corticosteroids. Some health professionals refer to corticosteroids simply as *steroids;* others use the terms *glucocorticoids* or *adrenal cortex hormones.*

WHAT IS IT SUPPOSED TO DO? Prednisone is a synthetic hormone, similar to hydrocortisone, the natural hormone that is produced by the adrenal glands. It is prescribed for a number of reasons. Sometimes, small doses are prescribed to correct a deficiency of the body's natural hormone. More commonly, it is used to relieve the symptoms of a wide variety of diseases, including arthritis, lupus, liver disease, kidney disease, lung diseases, and bowel diseases. In addition, prednisone is often combined with anticancer drugs in the treatment of various kinds of cancer.

SIDE EFFECTS Side effects from prednisone are usually the result of prolonged use, and they fall into two distinct categories: *withdrawal* and *continued use of large doses.*

After more than a few weeks of use, natural hormone production becomes suppressed. If prednisone is stopped abruptly, or if the dose is lowered too quickly, symptoms of withdrawal may occur. These include fever, muscle and joint pain, weakness, and risk of severe illness. Abrupt cessation after prolonged use can cause adrenal insufficiency, which can be life-threatening. When your doctor wants you to stop taking prednisone, he or she will slowly reduce the dose over a period of time, to allow the body to readjust to its absence.

When prednisone is used continuously for the symptomatic relief of a chronic problem such as arthritis or lung disease, its side effects increase in proportion to the dosage that is taken and the duration of treatment. For this reason, physicians always strive to give the smallest dose that will provide acceptable relief. A dosage that will provide complete relief of symptoms is considered too large, in terms of risk of side effects.

Side effects from prolonged use are quite varied. They include loss of potassium from the body, increase in blood sugar, fluid retention, increased susceptibility to infection, peptic ulcer, muscle weakness, redistribution of body fat, mood and thought disorders, cataracts, and osteoporosis. Follow your doctor's instructions carefully, and return for regular checkups in order to avoid problems. Promptly report any unusual symptoms.

DRUG INTERACTIONS Several drugs can interact with prednisone. These are the most important interactions:

Anticoagulants, such as warfarin (Coumadin). Prednisone can increase the coagulability of the blood, and this could affect the dosage requirements for anticoagulant drugs. In addition, prednisone's ability to occasionally cause ulcers could lead to problems. If a peptic ulcer does occur, the risk of serious bleeding is increased because of the anticoagulant.

Antidiabetic drugs, such as *insulin* or the *sulfonyl-ureas.* Prednisone can cause the blood sugar to increase. Therefore, the dosage of any drug that is used to control the blood sugar may have to be increased to compensate for this effect.

Diuretics, such as *furosemide (Lasix) or hydrochlo-rothiazide (Hydro-DIURIL and other brands),* can cause potassium to be lost from the body. Since prednisone also has this side effect, hypokalemia (too low a concentration of potassium in the blood) is more likely to occur when these drugs are taken at the same time. Your doctor will measure the concentration of potassium in your blood regularly while you are taking this combination. If necessary, he or she will prescribe either supplemental potassium or a second diuretic that conserves potassium.

Estrogens may increase the effect of prednisone. The mechanism is unknown, but estrogens may slow the metabolism of prednisone. Lower dosages of prednisone may be adequate during treatment with estrogens.

Isoniazid (INH), which is used for the treatment of tuberculosis, may slow the metabolism of prednisone (and increase its effects), and prednisone may increase the metabolism of isoniazid (and decrease its effects). When both drugs are taken together, your doctor will have to evaluate whether or not to increase the dosage of your isoniazid and/or decrease the dosage of your prednisone.

Phenobarbital, which is sometimes included in drug combinations for its sedative effects and is also used in the prevention of seizures, increases the metabolism of prednisone and thereby decreases its effects. Your doctor may have to give you larger doses of prednisone while you are taking phenobarbital.

Phenytoin (Dilantin), which is used to prevent seizures and to treat certain kinds of irregular heartbeats, increases the metabolism of prednisone and thereby decreases its effects. Your doctor may have to give you larger doses of prednisone while you are taking phenytoin.

Rifampin (Rifadin, Rimactane), a drug used for the

treatment of tuberculosis, may increase the metabolism of prednisone and thereby decrease its effects. Your doctor may have to give you larger doses of prednisone while you are taking rifampin.

ALCOHOLIC BEVERAGES Prednisone may make you more sensitive to the stomach irritation caused by alcoholic beverages. Wine or beer with meals will probably not cause problems, but you should check with your doctor.

FOOD You may take your prednisone with meals or on an empty stomach. Food does not impair the absorption of prednisone from the gastrointestinal tract.

Be sure to follow any dietary advice, such as low-salt diet or increasing the amount of potassium-containing foods (such as bananas, orange juice, raisins), you may have been given with your prescription.

HOW DOES AGE AFFECT THE RESPONSE TO THIS DRUG? There is no evidence that age will affect your response to prednisone. However, some of the side effects from prednisone can aggravate the medical problems that normally occur in greater frequency with advancing age. For example, prednisone-induced fluid retention may make congestive heart failure or high blood pressure more difficult to control. Prednisone-induced increases in blood sugar may make diabetes more difficult to control. The most common problem in older people, particularly older women, is osteoporosis.

PROCAINAMIDE

OTHER NAMES Procainamide (pronounced *proe-KANE-a-mide)* is the common or generic name of this drug. Some frequently used brand names for procainamide are Procan, Promine, and Pronestyl.

WHAT IS IT SUPPOSED TO DO? Procainamide suppresses certain types of abnormal heart rhythms. The dosage required for its beneficial effects varies considerably among individuals. Your doctor will determine the correct dosage for you on the basis of electrocardiograms (ECGs) and perhaps on the basis of a laboratory test that measures the concentrations of procainamide and its active metabolite in the blood.

SIDE EFFECTS   Procainamide may cause diarrhea, loss of appetite, and dizziness or light-headedness. If any of these side effects is persistent or severe, contact your doctor. Do not drive an automobile until you are sure that dizziness or light-headedness will not affect your driving skill.

If you are taking a long-acting form of procainamide (the designation *SR*, for sustained release, after the drug name indicates the long-acting form), you may notice tablet residue in your stools. This is normal; it's the waxy part of the tablet that slowly releases the drug.

Many people develop a specific kind of allergic reaction to procainamide after a period of time. Your doctor may test for the possible development of this problem with repeated blood tests, although less than half of those with positive blood tests will develop clinical symptoms. Contact your doctor if you experience arthritic symptoms such as joint pain or swelling (the most common symptoms), pain with breathing, fever, unusual tiredness or weakness, or skin rash or itching.

An infrequent or rare form of allergy, which can occur early in therapy and is potentially very serious, affects the normal formation of blood cells. The possible symptoms include sore mouth, gums, or throat; rash; severe respiratory infection, unusual bleeding or bruising; fever, and signs of infection. Contact your doctor promptly if you experience these or other unexpected symptoms.

If you have a history of allergy to procaine (Novocain), tell your doctor; you may be allergic to procainamide as well.

Effects on the brain are rare. Contact your doctor if you experience depression, confusion, hallucinations, or any other unexpected mental symptoms.

Possible signs that the dosage is too high include severe dizziness or fainting, confusion, drowsiness, unusual decrease in urination, nausea and vomiting, and unusually fast or irregular heartbeat. Contact your doctor if you experience any of these.

Other side effects are too rare to list here. Contact your doctor if you experience any unusual symptoms.

DRUG INTERACTIONS Several drugs can interact with procainamide:

Antihypertensives may add to the dizziness or light-headedness caused by procainamide. If you experience this side effect, which may be an indication of abnormally low blood pressure, have your blood pressure checked.

Cholinergic drugs, such as *neostigmine (Prostigmin) or pyridostigmine (Mestinon),* which are used in the treatment of myasthenia gravis. Procainamide can block the action of these drugs and worsen myasthenic symptoms. Report any worsening of your symptoms to your doctor.

Cimetidine (Tagamet), which is used in the treatment of peptic-ulcer disease, decreases the ability of the kidneys to eliminate procainamide and its active metabolite from the body. Older age increases the magnitude of this interaction. Your doctor may need to decrease the dosage of your procainamide while you are taking cimetidine.

ALCOHOLIC BEVERAGES If you experience dizziness or light-headedness from procainamide, alcohol will worsen this side effect. Be careful until you determine how this combination affects you.

FOOD Food does not impair the absorption of procainamide. You can take your procainamide either with meals or on an empty stomach.

HOW DOES AGE AFFECT THE RESPONSE TO THIS DRUG? The rate at which procainamide and its active metabolite are removed from the body by the kidneys decreases with advancing age, so older people usually require smaller doses than younger people. Your doctor will evaluate your kidney function (see appendix) in determining your procainamide dosage.

However, as pointed out above, procainamide dosage varies considerably and must be individually tailored on the basis of response.

Advancing age increases the sensitivity to dizziness or light-headedness from procainamide.

PROGESTINS

OTHER NAMES Progestins (pronounced *proe-JESS-tins)* are drugs that mimic the natural hormone progesterone, a female hormone that, until menopause, is produced during the last part of the menstrual cycle and during pregnancy. The most commonly used progestins in women over the age of fifty (with brand names in parenthesis) are medroxyprogesterone acetate (Amen, Curretab, Provera), norethindrone (Norlutin), and norethindrone acetate (Aygestin, Norlutate). There are several other progestins, but they are most often used in birth control pills. Progestins are also called progestational agents and progestogens, names that have the benefit of more syllables.

WHAT IS IT SUPPOSED TO DO? In women over the age of fifty, progestins are most often taken with estrogens to treat the deficiency in these hormones that occurs after menopause. The benefits of estrogens, which include the prevention of osteoporosis, are discussed in the section on estrogens. It is now clear that when estrogens are taken by themselves after menopause, the risk for endometrial cancer (cancer of the lining of the uterus) is increased. When a progestin is taken with the estrogen, this increase in risk is prevented.

When used for this purpose, the progestin is taken with the estrogen in a dosage pattern that mimics the production cycle of hormones that occurred before menopause. A typical regimen includes an estrogen taken daily for the first twenty-five days of the month and a progestin taken from day sixteen through day twenty-five; no tablets are taken for the remainder of the month. This sort of hormone-taking pattern causes the uterus to respond much as it did before menopause; at the end of the month, after the progestin is stopped, the endometrium is shed and menstrual bleeding occurs. This bleeding is beneficial in preventing endometrial cancer, the major side effect of estrogens taken after menopause. The risk for endometrial cancer in women who take progestins with estrogens in this manner is lower than it is in women who take no hormones at all. In addition, abnormal bleeding is less likely to occur with combined progestin-estrogen treatment than it is with estrogen alone.

Although postmenopausal estrogen use does not increase the risk for breast cancer, the addition of a progestin may actually decrease this risk. Progestins are also used in the treatment of fibrocystic breast disease.

Lastly, the combination of a progestin and an estrogen is more effective in preventing osteoporosis than is an estrogen alone.

Progestins are used for other purposes, including the treatment of certain types of cancer, the evaluation of endometrial function, and a variety of uses in younger women. However, for this discussion, I am assuming that you are taking a progestin with an estrogen for the treatment of postmenopausal hormone deficiency, which is the most common use of progestins.

SIDE EFFECTS The side effect that most women complain about is the continuation of menstruation after menopause. Of course, this withdrawal bleeding, which is usually more scant than the menstruation that occurred before menopause, is also a beneficial effect, as described above.

You may experience edema, bloating, or premenstrual irritability. These symptoms can also be caused by your estrogen, but your progestin may aggravate them. Occasionally, progestins cause lower abdominal cramps or painful menstruation. If any of these effects is bothersome, contact your doctor. Some of these side effects can be treated by adjusting the dose of one of the two hormones.

There is some concern that progestins may negate the beneficial effects that estrogens appear to have in preventing cardiovascular disease, but this question is still unanswered. It does appear, however, that the combination of one form of progestin, medroxyprogesterone acetate (Provera), and an estrogen has an effect on the concentrations of lipoproteins in the blood that would be expected to be favorable in preventing cardiovascular disease.

Other side effects are too rare to list here. If you experience abnormal bleeding or any unexpected symptoms, contact your doctor promptly. Be sure to return to your doctor for regular checkups.

DRUG INTERACTIONS   In the doses and the cyclic pattern used for hormone replacement after menopause, it is unlikely that any of your other drugs will interact with your progestin.

ALCOHOLIC BEVERAGES   Your progestin will not affect your response to alcohol.

FOOD   You can take your progestin either with food or on an empty stomach.

HOW DOES AGE AFFECT THE RESPONSE TO THIS DRUG?   In 97 percent of women who take a progestin with an estrogen in the cyclical fashion described above, menstrual bleeding continues until age sixty. This menstruation continues to age sixty-five in 60 percent of women.

PROPOXYPHENE

OTHER NAMES   Propoxyphene (pronounced *proe-POX-i-feen*) is the common or generic name of this drug. In Great Britain, its generic name is dextropropoxyphene. A frequently used brand name for propoxyphene is Darvon. The napsylate salt of propoxyphene (as opposed to the hydrochloride salt, the form of the drug in Darvon) is marketed under the brand name Darvon-N. Propoxyphene is often prescribed as tablets or capsules that also contain another pain reliever. Some frequently used brand names of these combinations are Darvocet-N (propoxyphene napsylate and acetaminophen), Darvon with A.S.A. (propoxyphene and aspirin), and Darvon Compound (propoxyphene, aspirin, and caffeine).

WHAT IS IT SUPPOSED TO DO? Propoxyphene, like codeine, works inside the central nervous system to alter the sensation of pain, but it is less potent than codeine. A standard dose of propoxyphene, 65 mg (or 100 mg of propoxyphene napsylate), provides less pain relief than 650 mg of aspirin (two standard tablets) or 650 mg of acetaminophen (two standard tablets). However, when taken in combination with aspirin or acetaminophen, which relieve pain by other mechanisms, propoxyphene is an effective pain reliever.

SIDE EFFECTS Infrequently, propoxyphene causes nausea, abdominal pain, constipation, drowsiness, lightheadedness, or dizziness. If any of these side effects is persistent or bothersome, contact your doctor. Avoid driving until you are sure that your alertness and coordination are not impaired.

Propoxyphene can be addicting if taken regularly over a long period of time.

Contact your doctor promptly if you should ever experience signs of propoxyphene overdose, which include difficulty in breathing, weakness, unusual drowsiness or dizziness, confusion, and anxiety.

Other side effects are too rare to list here. Contact your doctor if you experience any unexpected symptoms.

DRUG INTERACTIONS Propoxyphene will intensify any impairment of coordination or decrease in alertness that you might experience from other drugs, such as antidepressants, antihistamines, barbiturates, or benzodiazepine anti-anxiety or sleeping pills. In addition, several drugs interact with propoxyphene in other ways:

Carbamazepine (Tegretol), which is used to treat the

pain of trigeminal neuralgia and also to treat seizure
disorders, is removed from the blood by metabolism in
the liver. Propoxyphene slows the metabolism of carbamazepine and thereby increases its effects. Several
cases of carbamazepine toxicity have occurred in people taking this combination. If acetaminophen or aspirin cannot be used by themselves for your pain and
you need to take propoxyphene, watch for excessive
carbamazepine effect.

Phenobarbital, which is taken to prevent seizures and
sometimes for its sedative effects, is removed from the
blood by metabolism in the liver. Regular use of propoxyphene (for example, three times a day for more
than several days) may slow the metabolism of phenobarbital and thereby increase its effects. If you experience excessive sedation while taking this combination,
contact your doctor.

Smoking. Propoxyphene may be less effective in
heavy smokers.

Tricyclic antidepressants, such as *amitriptyline
(Elavil), doxepin (Sinequan),* or *imipramine (Trofranil),*
are removed from the blood by metabolism in the liver.
Propoxyphene, taken in repeated doses, slows the metabolism of doxepin, resulting in increased doxepin effects. It is not known whether other tricyclic
antidepressants interact in the same way, but you
should watch for increased side effects from your antidepressant while you are taking propoxyphene.

ALCOHOLIC BEVERAGES Limit your use of alcohol
to small amounts. Propoxyphene will intensify the effects of alcohol, which could be especially dangerous if
you need to drive.

Although propoxyphene does not cause dangerous
respiratory depression when taken by itself in prescribed amounts, excessive use in combination with alcohol is dangerous. Propoxyphene overdose in
combination with heavy alcohol use has caused many
deaths.

FOOD Propoxyphene can be taken either with food
or on an empty stomach. If you are taking a propoxy-

phene preparation that contains aspirin, take it with a full glass of water and with food.

HOW DOES AGE AFFECT THE RESPONSE TO THIS DRUG? The effect of age on the response to propoxyphene has not been carefully studied, but older people are usually more sensitive to the effects of narcotics, which are related to propoxyphene.

PROPRANOLOL

OTHER NAMES Propranolol (pronounced *pro-PRAN-oh-lole)* is the common or generic name of this drug. Its most frequently used brand name is Inderal. There are tablets and capsules that contain a combination of propranolol and the diuretic hydrochlorothiazide; the brand name of this combination is Inderide. Propranolol belongs to a group of drugs known as beta-blockers. It was the first beta-blocker to become widely used.

WHAT IS IT SUPPOSED TO DO? Propranolol lowers blood pressures that are too high, prevents angina attacks, reduces the risk of recurrence of heart attack, prevents irregular heartbeats, prevents migraine headaches, relieves the symptoms of hyperthyroidism, and corrects many other medical problems. It is most often prescribed for its beneficial effects on high blood pressure and on heart problems.

Propranolol accomplishes all these remedies by acting on the autonomic nervous system, the part of the nervous system that is beyond our conscious control—the part that regulates the heart, blood vessels, and various internal organs. Needless to say, the autonomic nervous system is complex. It has parasympathetic and sympathetic parts that generally work in opposition to one another. The sympathetic part responds to two types of stimulation, alpha and beta.

Propranolol molecules temporarily bind with highly specialized nervous tissues called beta-receptors, thereby preventing them from recognizing the chemical messengers that normally set them off. (That is why pharmacologists refer to propranolol as a beta-blocker.) The beta-receptors are one of several means by which the organs get the messages that tell them what to do. An increase in heart rate and an increase in blood pressure are examples of beta responses that are blocked by propranolol. There are beta-receptors throughout the body, and a variety of medical problems respond well to treatment with propranolol.

SIDE EFFECTS   Despite the wide distribution of beta-receptors throughout the body, side effects from propranolol are infrequent and generally mild. Most people experience no side effects at all.

The most important side effect that you should know about is the possibility of withdrawal symptoms if you suddenly stop taking propranolol after taking it regularly. This side effect can be understood by considering how propranolol works (see above). While the beta-receptors are blocked by propranolol, they can become overly sensitive to the chemical messengers that normally set them off. If propranolol is withdrawn abruptly, these receptors will overrespond. The most common symptom is headache, but there is also the danger of angina attacks, a sudden rise in blood pressure, irregular heartbeats, or even a heart attack, depending on what condition was being treated initially. If your doctor wants you to stop taking propranolol, he will gradually reduce the dose, or he may substitute another drug that has similar effects.

Your doctor will carefully check your heart before prescribing propranolol. When propranolol is taken by individuals with untreated congestive heart failure, a condition in which the heart is unable to carry out its job of pumping blood through the circulatory system adequately, this heart failure is likely to be worsened. Infrequently, it causes congestive heart failure in individuals with no previous symptoms. Most patients whose congestive heart failure is corrected by other drugs are able to take propranolol without problem. However, you should contact your doctor at once if you experience swelling of your feet or ankles, sudden weight gain, or difficulty in breathing. Propranolol's ability to slow the heart and lower the blood pressure is usually beneficial, but occasional individuals experience too much of these effects. An unusually slow pulse rate (less than 50 beats per minute) or dizziness (possibly from abnormally low blood pressure) are other reasons to get in touch with your doctor.

Stomach upset, constipation, or diarrhea occur infrequently from propranolol. When any of these side effects does occur, it often goes away with continued use of the drug. If it continues to be bothersome, contact your doctor.

Another infrequent side effect is coldness of the hands or feet, which may occur as a result of the circulatory changes that are brought about by propranolol. Be sure to dress warmly in cold weather.

Although propranolol enters the brain, its effects there are usually imperceptible, except for occasional drowsiness. However, it sometimes causes adverse mental effects, including dizziness, fatigue, confusion, nightmares, insomnia, and depression. If you experience any unusual and persistent mental symptoms, contact your doctor.

There are some diseases that increase the risk of side effects from propranolol. Your doctor will not prescribe propranolol if you have asthma or emphysema. The effects of propranolol are just the opposite of those that are desirable for lung disease, which can be worsened by propranolol. In diabetics, propranolol can cause several problems (see Drug Interactions, Antidiabetic Drugs). As pointed out above, uncontrolled congestive heart failure is worsened by propranolol. The symptoms of an overactive thyroid gland can be masked by propranolol, and that could get you into trouble, but there are laboratory tests for checking up on the thyroid.

Other side effects are too rare to mention here. Contact your doctor if you experience any unusual symptoms.

DRUG INTERACTIONS Several drugs can interact with propranolol. Your doctor will monitor your therapy with special care if you need to take any of these drugs with propranolol:

Antacids can impair the absorption of propranolol. Therefore, antacid and propranolol doses should be taken at least an hour apart.

Antidiabetic drugs, such as *insulin* and the *sulfonylureas.* Diabetic patients should not take propranolol unless there is no other alternative. Propranolol can block some of the warning signs of hypoglycemia (especially rapid heartbeat or papitations), delay the recovery from hypoglycemia, cause high-blood-pressure episodes during hypoglycemia, and impair circulation to the extremities in diabetics. If propranolol is required, keep in mind that sweating, but not rapid heartbeat, is a sign of hypoglycemia. Certain other beta-blocking drugs, such as metoprolol (Lopressor) and atenolol (Tenormin), are less likely to cause problems, but there is some risk.

Breathing medications, such as *isoproterenol (Isuprel) inhalation, terbutaline (Brethine, Bricanyl), or theophylline (Elixophyllin, Slo-Phyllin, Theobid, Theo-Dur, and others),* which are used for the treatment of asthma, emphysema, or other lung problems, don't mix well with propranolol. The ability of these drugs to open up the air passages in the lungs is antagonized by propranolol. Although its effects on normal lungs are minimal, propranolol can be dangerous in those with asthma or other lung problems.

Cimetidine (Tagamet), which is used to treat ulcers, slows the rate at which propranolol is metabolized by the liver. Thus, cimetidine causes individuals to respond to smaller amounts of propranolol than would otherwise be expected. If you are taking cimetidine, your doctor will either lower your propranolol dose accordingly or stop the cimetidine in favor of another drug.

Clonidine (Catapres), which is used to control high blood pressure, can cause a rebound hypertensive reaction if it is stopped abruptly. This reaction is worse in patients who are also taking propranolol. If you are

taking both of these drugs and must stop taking clonidine, your doctor may slowly discontinue your propranolol first. In any case, don't stop taking this drug
combination without careful supervision.

Indomethacin (Indocin) can block the antihypertensive and antianginal effects of propranolol. If indomethacin is required, your doctor will need to evaluate
whether there is any decrease in propranolol effect.

Phenobarbital, which is sometimes included in drug
combinations for its sedative effects and is also used in
the prevention of seizures, increases the rate at which
propranolol is metabolized by the liver. While you are
taking phenobarbital, a larger than usual propranolol
dose may be required. If you stop taking phenobarbital,
be sure to ask your doctor to reevaluate your propranolol dosage.

Prazosin (Minipress), which is used to control high
blood pressure, sometimes causes a severe drop in
blood pressure when the person taking it stands up too
quickly. This side effect is most common when the drug
is first started, and there is some evidence that propranolol makes it more likely to occur. If you are taking propranolol and starting to take prazosin, your
doctor will start with smaller doses and may advise you
to take the prazosin at bedtime.

Sympathomimetics, which are contained in some
nonprescription remedies for nasal congestion, can
cause hypertensive reactions in susceptible individuals.
There is some evidence that the risk of this reaction is
greater in patients with high blood pressure who are
taking propranolol. Check with your pharmacist before
taking any medication for nasal congestion.

ALCOHOLIC BEVERAGES Usually there is no interaction between propranolol and alcohol. However, you
should establish for yourself that propranolol does not
make you drowsy or dizzy before you drink anything
with alcohol in it.

FOOD It's a good idea to take propranolol with meals
to help you to develop a regular routine for taking it.
In addition, food improves its absorption. If your doctor

has prescribed a restricted-salt or restricted-calorie diet, be sure to follow it.

HOW DOES AGE AFFECT THE RESPONSE TO THIS DRUG? The risk for side effects, particularly those related to the heart (see Side Effects), increases with advancing age. In a large study of adverse drug reactions to propranolol in hospitalized patients, age over fifty was associated with nearly double the incidence of adverse effects, and most of these were related to the heart.

The best way to avoid side effects from propranolol is to return to your doctor for regular medical checkups. As long as your heart responds well to the effects of propranolol, there is little reason to expect any problems.

In the above-mentioned study, there was no correlation between dose and the incidence of side effects. Subsequent studies have found that although propranolol is eliminated from the body more slowly with advancing age, thereby allowing it to accumulate to higher concentrations in the blood, advancing age also brings changes in the beta-receptors that make them less sensitive to drugs. These two effects tend to offset one another. Therefore, older people usually respond similarly to the doses required by younger people. There is, however, wide variation in the doses required by different individuals, regardless of age.

QUINIDINE

OTHER NAMES Quinidine (pronounced *KWIN-i-deen*) is the common or generic name of this drug. Pharmaceutical companies manufacture tablets and capsules from the various salts of quinidine, such as quinidine sulfate, quinidine gluconate, quinidine polygalacturonate. Each of these quinidine salts dissolves and enters the body at a different rate. They also vary in the amount of quinidine they contain, so they can't be used interchangeably. Furthermore, some pharmaceutical companies manufacture their quinidine product into special tablets that release the drug at an especially slow rate. Therefore, each quinidine product, regardless of brand name, will provide the same general quinidine effect, but each product is unique: Cardioquin, Cin-Quin, Duraquin, Quinaglute Dura-Tabs, Quinidex Extentabs, Quinora, and Quin-Release.

Quinidine is a close chemical relative to quinine, the drug that is used to treat malaria and nighttime leg-muscle cramps. Both quinidine and quinine occur naturally in the bark of the cinchona tree, which is native to certain parts of South America. The medical use of cinchona bark was well established before its chemical constituents were isolated during the eighteenth century. In 1853, quinidine was prepared synthetically by Pasteur, who gave it its present name. In the early use of cinchona for malaria, it was noted that patients who also had certain kinds of irregular heartbeats were cured of their heart problem during treatment. The effects of quinidine on the heart were carefully studied during the first part of this century, and it was then that quinidine became widely used in treating cardiac arrhythmias (the medical term for irregular heartbeats).

WHAT IS IT SUPPOSED TO DO?　The heart normally beats at a rate of sixty to one hundred times a minute in carrying out its job of pumping blood throughout the body. Its normal "lub-dub" sound, and the pumping of blood that it represents, is the result of a complex series of electrical discharges that cause each part of the heart to beat in rhythm with the others. Your doctor can study these electrical discharges on a video screen or on graph paper with the help of a device called the electrocardiogram (ECG). Quinidine is used in the treatment of several types of rhythm disorders. In all cases, the desired effect is suppression of abnormal heartbeats, which impair the heart's effective pumping action. To do this, quinidine must be present in the blood in an effective concentration. Its effects don't last very long, even with time-release tablets, so you will have to take repeated doses if it is to have consistent effect.

SIDE EFFECTS   At first, you will probably notice some discomfort in your digestive tract. Nausea, bitter taste, loss of appetite, cramping, and diarrhea are common problems. These side effects tend to go away with continued use of the drug. Contact your doctor if they are severe.

Signs of too much quinidine effect (called cinchonism), which can occur after only a few doses in people who are extremely sensitive to quinidine, include ringing or buzzing in the ear, loss of hearing, visual changes, flushed skin, fever, headache, and confusion or delirium. Contact your doctor if you experience any of these symptoms.

Infrequently, quinidine causes allergic reactions. Among these are fever, which can be followed by liver injury (usually reversible) if the drug is not discontinued; rash, hives, or itching; and, rarely, a condition called thrombocytopenia, in which normal blood clotting is impaired—the signs are abnormal bruising or bleeding. Contact your doctor if you experience any of these symptoms.

Adverse effects on the cardiovascular system, which include abnormally low blood pressure and irregular heart rhythms, are infrequent. Report any unusual dizziness, light-headedness, fainting, difficulty in breathing, or rapid heartbeat to your doctor.

Other side effects are too rare to list here. Contact your doctor if you experience any unexpected symptoms.

DRUG INTERACTIONS   Several drugs can interact with quinidine. Your doctor will take special precautions to ensure that no problems occur when any of these drugs need to be taken with quinidine:

Acetazolamide (Diamox), which is used in treating glaucoma, has the usually harmless side effect of making the urine alkaline. When the urine is alkaline, the kidneys remove quinidine from the blood less readily, and the concentration of quinidine in the blood increases. If the quinidine dosage is not adjusted, the result could be too much quinidine effect. Ask your doctor to reevaluate your quinidine dosage whenever you start or stop taking acetazolamide.

Antacids can cause the urine to become alkaline if they are taken regularly in sufficient quantities, as in the treatment of an ulcer. When the urine is alkaline, the kidneys remove quinidine from the blood less readily, and the concentration of quinidine in the blood increases. Therefore, you should not take large doses of antacids on a regular basis without consulting your doctor.

Cimetidine (Tagamet), which is used for the treatment of peptic-ulcer disease, slows the metabolism of quinidine by the liver. If both drugs are required, your doctor may find it necessary to decrease the dosage of your quinidine to compensate for this effect. Don't start or stop taking cimetidine without first asking your doctor to reevaluate your quinidine therapy.

Cholinergic drugs, such as *neostigmine (Prostigmin) and edrophonium (Tensilon),* which are used in the treatment of myasthenia gravis, may be antagonized by the anticholinergic effects of quinidine. Similarly, quinidine can add to the anticholinergic side effects of *tranquilizers, tricyclic antidepressants, and other drugs with anticholinergic side effects.*

Digoxin (Lanoxicaps, Lanoxin). The body's response to digoxin, another drug that is used for heart problems, is altered by quinidine. Quinidine increases the concentration of digoxin in the blood by decreasing its removal by the kidneys, as well as by other mechanisms. If you have been taking digoxin regularly, and your doctor is starting to give you quinidine, you will probably be advised to decrease your dose of digoxin. If you have been taking quinidine regularly and your doctor is now starting you on digoxin, your digoxin dosage will be smaller than it would be if you were not taking quinidine. If you have been taking both drugs and stop taking quinidine, then your doctor will need to reevaluate your digoxin dosage.

Nifedipine (Procardia), which is used in the treatment

of angina, decreases the concentration of quinidine in the blood in some individuals. The mechanism is not known. If you start or stop taking nifedipine, ask your doctor to reevaluate your quinidine therapy.

Phenobarbital, which is used for the prevention of seizures, as a sedative, and for other medical problems, stimulates the metabolism of quinidine by the liver, increasing the rate at which it is inactivated. If you are taking phenobarbital, your doctor may have found it necessary to increase your dose of quinidine to compensate for this effect. Ask your doctor to reevaluate your quinidine dosage if you start or stop taking phenobarbital.

Phenytoin (Dilantin), which is used for the prevention of seizures and also for the prevention of certain types of irregular heart rhythms, stimulates the metabolism of quinidine by the liver, increasing the rate at which it is inactivated. When both drugs are required, the dosage of quinidine is often larger than might be expected. Don't start or stop taking phenytoin without first asking your doctor to reevaluate your quinidine therapy.

Rifampin (Rifadin, Rimactane), which is used in the treatment of tuberculosis and other infections, increases the rate at which quinidine is metabolized by the liver, thereby decreasing its effects. Do not start or stop taking rifampin without asking your doctor to reevaluate your quinidine therapy.

Warfarin (Coumadin). In some patients, quinidine adds to the effects of this anticoagulant. The mechanism is not known. Ask your doctor to monitor your anticoagulant therapy whenever you start or stop taking quinidine.

ALCOHOLIC BEVERAGES   With moderation, it's unlikely that any problems will occur. However, it's possible that quinidine could add to the vascular effects of alcohol (flushing, faintness from low blood pressure), so be careful.

FOOD   Unless your doctor has instructed you otherwise, take your quinidine with food to decrease any digestive upset it might cause. It is also helpful to set up your dosage schedule in some relationship to meals, to help you remember to take your quinidine on schedule.

Extremely large amounts of citrus juice (more than a quart of orange juice a day) can cause the urine to become alkaline, and this could lead to quinidine intoxication (see the acetazolamide and antacid drug interactions, above, for the mechanism). Smaller amounts will not cause problems.

HOW DOES AGE AFFECT THE RESPONSE TO THIS DRUG?   Because of slower metabolism by the liver and decreased rate of excretion by the kidneys, advancing age tends to be accompanied by a smaller dosage requirement for quinidine. However, there is considerable variation among individuals. Your doctor will assess your response to quinidine on the basis of your electrocardiogram and perhaps with additional information from a laboratory test that measures the concentration of quinidine in the blood.

RANITIDINE

OTHER NAMES   Ranitidine (pronounced *ra-NIT-te-deen)* is the common or generic name of this drug. Its most frequently used brand name is Zantac. Pharmacologists refer to ranitidine as a histamine H_2-receptor blocker.

WHAT IS IT SUPPOSED TO DO?   Ranitidine decreases the secretion of stomach acid. Therefore, it is used to treat peptic ulcers and related problems.

Ranitidine works by decreasing the effect that histamine has on the stomach. Histamine, a substance the body produces to regulate a number of its functions, reacts with specialized receptors in the stomach to stimulate the flow of gastric juices. Too great a flow of gastric juices (too much stomach acid, too much pepsin), along with too little tissue resistance to their effects, is the cause of peptic-ulcer disease and related problems. Decreasing gastric-juice production is a key component in the medical treatment of these problems. For years, pharmacologists tried to use antihistamines (like the ones you can buy without prescription) to block the effect of histamine on stomach-acid secretion, but without good results. The histamine receptors in the stomach are H_2-receptors, which are different from the histamine receptors in the rest of the body. Antihistamines are histamine H_1-receptor blockers; they block the effect of histamine on allergic reactions, but not on gastric-acid secretion. Ranitidine, on the other hand, blocks the effect of histamine on the histamine H_2-receptors in the stomach. The primary location of histamine H_2-receptors in the body is in the stomach.

SIDE EFFECTS   Headache or dizziness are infrequent side effects, as is constipation. Contact your doctor if any of these side effects is persistent or bothersome.

Ranitidine does not usually cause any perceptible mental effects, but it can cause confusional states (with symptoms of psychosis, anxiety, disorientation, depression, or dementia) as a rare side effect. Tiredness or weakness are other rare side effects. Contact your doctor promptly if you experience any of these rare side effects.

Other side effects are too rare to list here. Contact your doctor if you develop any other unexpected symptoms.

DRUG INTERACTIONS   These are the most important interactions with ranitidine:

Antacids can decrease the absorption of ranitidine, so don't take both at the same time of day. If you take your ranitidine with a meal and then take the antacid an hour or more afterward, this interaction is not likely to cause any problems.

Metoprolol (Lopressor), which is used in the treatment of high blood pressure, is metabolized fairly rapidly by the liver. In some individuals, ranitidine slows metoprolol's metabolism, and thereby enhances its effects. Contact your doctor if you experience metoprolol side effects while taking ranitidine.

Smoking increases the production of stomach acid

and may therefore decrease the beneficial effects of ranitidine.

ALCOHOLIC BEVERAGES You can drink alcoholic beverages while you are taking ranitidine, but you should remember that they can be irritating to the stomach.

FOOD Take your ranitidine with food. Avoid foods that are irritating to your stomach. Special diets are no longer commonly used in the treatment of peptic-ulcer disease.

HOW DOES AGE AFFECT THE RESPONSE TO THIS DRUG? The elimination of ranitidine from the blood, which occurs by metabolism in the liver and excretion by the kidneys, is slower in older people than it is in younger people. In a study that compared the concentrations of ranitidine in the blood among individuals of various ages who were taking the same dosage of ranitidine, people over fifty had significantly higher concentrations. Therefore, older people require smaller doses than younger people. Adverse effects from ranitidine, which are infrequent or rare, have occurred in older people taking doses that might have been better tolerated by younger individuals. Your doctor will take your age and kidney function (see appendix) into consideration in determining a dosage of ranitidine that is likely to be appropriate for you.

RESERPINE

OTHER NAMES Reserpine (pronounced *re-SER-peen*) is the common or generic name of this drug. Reserpine is derived from the root of the plant *Rauwolfia serpentina*, which was used in ancient Hindu medicine. It was introduced into Western medicine in the 1950s. Some frequently used brand names for reserpine are Sandril, Serpalan, Serpasil, Serpate, and SK-Reserpine.

There are many brand-name drug combinations that contain reserpine along with other antihypertensive drugs. Serpasil-Apresoline contains reserpine and hydralazine. Ser-Ap-Es is the most frequently used brand name for tablets that contain reserpine, hydralazine, and hydrochlorothiazide. Serpasil-Esidrix is a combination of reserpine and hydrochlorothiazide. Diutensen-R is a combination of reserpine and the thiazide diuretic methyclothiazide. Diupres contains reserpine and chlorothiazide. Regroton and Demi-Regroton are mixtures of reserpine and chlorthalidone. Hydropres is the most frequently used brand name for tablets that contain hydrochlorothiazide and reserpine. Salutensin and Salutensin-Demi are frequently used brand names for a combination of reserpine and the thiazide diuretic hydroflumethiazide. Hydromox R is a mixture of another thiazide diuretic, quinethazone, and reserpine. And Renese-R contains reserpine and polythiazide.

WHAT IS IT SUPPOSED TO DO?   Reserpine decreases the activity of certain nerves that would otherwise tell blood vessels to make their passageways narrower. The result is an opening up of these blood vessels and a lowering of blood pressure. It is most often used in combination with a thiazide diuretic, which lowers the blood pressure by additional mechanisms.

Hypertension (high blood pressure) causes no symptoms, but untreated hypertension substantially increases the risk of the subsequent development of congestive heart failure, angina, heart attack, stroke, kidney problems, or visual problems. Antihypertensive drugs such as reserpine decrease these risks.

SIDE EFFECTS   The most common side effects from reserpine are stuffy nose, dry mouth, drowsiness, nausea, and diarrhea. These side effects are usually mild and tend to go away as your body adjusts to the drug. If any of them is persistent or bothersome, check with your doctor.

Less frequently, reserpine causes sodium retention. If you notice swelling of your feet or legs, and especially if you experience shortness of breath, contact your doctor.

In some individuals, reserpine can cause severe mental depression, most often after several months of use. This side effect is infrequent or rare in the doses that are currently prescribed, but reserpine is not recommended for individuals with a history of severe mental depression. If you experience mental depression, inability to concentrate, vivid dreams, or nightmares with early-morning insomnia, tell your doctor.

Other infrequent or rare side effects that should be brought to your doctor's attention are chest pain, irregular or slow heartbeat, dizziness, headache, and impotence.

Rarely, reserpine causes peptic ulcer. If you experience stomach pain, black tarry stools (a sign of gastrointestinal bleeding), or bloody vomiting, contact your doctor promptly.

Other side effects are too rare to list here. Contact your doctor if you experience any unexpected symptoms.

DRUG INTERACTIONS Reserpine should not be used with these drugs:

Levodopa (Dopar, Larodopa), which is used in the treatment of Parkinson's disease, works by replacing neurotransmitters within the brain. Reserpine decreases the concentration of several neurotransmitters within the brain and would therefore be expected to antagonize levodopa's effects.

Monoamine oxidase (MAO) inhibitors, which are sometimes used in the treatment of severe depression, can cause excitation and episodes of severe high blood pressure when reserpine is added to therapy with these drugs.

ALCOHOLIC BEVERAGES Reserpine adds to the mental-depressant effect of alcohol. Be careful until you have determined how this drug affects your response to alcohol.

FOOD Reserpine should be taken with food to decrease any stomach upset it might cause. If your doctor has prescribed a salt-restricted diet, be sure to follow it.

HOW DOES AGE AFFECT THE RESPONSE TO THIS DRUG? Dizziness or faintness, which may be a sign of abnormally low blood pressure, are more likely to occur in older people. Check with your doctor if you experience these symptoms.

SPIRONOLACTONE

OTHER NAMES Spironolactone (pronounced *speer-on-oh-LAK-tone)* is the common or generic name of this drug. A frequently used brand name for spironolactone is Aldactone. It is sometimes prescribed as tablets that also contain hydrochlorothiazide, another diuretic but one with different properties. A frequently used brand name for this hydrochlorothiazide-plus-spironolactone combination is Aldactazide. Pharmacologists refer to spironolactone both as a potassium-sparing diuretic and as a aldosterone antagonist.

WHAT IS IT SUPPOSED TO DO? Spironolactone is a diuretic. It acts on the kidneys, causing them to eliminate extra water and salt from the body and into the urine. It is used in treating high blood pressure and in relieving the symptoms of edema, the abnormal swelling in tissues or congestion in the lungs that results from heart failure or other medical problems. Spironolactone works by blocking the action of aldosterone, a hormone whose principal function is to retain sodium and water in the body and promote the excretion of potassium in the urine. By preventing the effects of this hormone, spironolactone promotes sodium and water excretion and causes potassium to be retained by the body.

Because spironolactone is a mild diuretic, it is often taken with another diuretic, such as hydrochlorothiazide or furosemide. When used in combination with these more potent diuretics, spironolactone counteracts their principal side effect—potassium loss.

SIDE EFFECTS At first you will notice a need to urinate frequently. This effect will decrease with continued use. You should avoid taking spironolactone too close to bedtime, or you may find yourself being frequently awakened from sleep by a need to urinate.

Occasionally, spironolactone causes nausea, vomiting, stomach cramps, or diarrhea. If they occur, these side effects may go away with continued use. Contact your doctor if they are persistent. You should contact your doctor whenever you experience continued vomiting or diarrhea, because these can cause dehydration and electrolyte imbalance.

Infrequently, spironolactone causes breast tenderness and enlargement in both men and women. The medical term for this condition is gynecomastia. It is due to the hormonelike effects of the drug and is slowly reversed when the drug is discontinued. If you experience this problem, contact your doctor.

The most serious side effect from spironolactone is hyperkalemia (too high a concentration of potassium in the blood), but this occurs infrequently. To prevent this side effect, which can cause dangerously irregular heartbeats, you should not take any form of potassium supplement while you are taking spironolactone. Your doctor will periodically measure the concentration of potassium in your blood while you are taking spironolactone. Numbness or tingling in the hands, feet, or lips; weakness; or confusion may be signs of hyperkalemia. Contact your doctor if any of these occur.

Other side effects are too rare to list here. Contact your doctor if you experience any unexpected problems.

DRUG INTERACTIONS Several drugs can interact with spironolactone, and some of these interactions have potentially serious consequences:

Angiotensin-converting-enzyme (ACE) inhibitors, such as *captopril (Capoten, Capozide)* or *enalapril (Vaseretic, Vasotec),* which are used in the treatment of congestive heart failure and high blood pressure, cause potassium to be conserved by the body. To minimize the risk of too high a concentration of potassium in the blood (hyperkalemia), spironolactone should be used with these drugs only when the concentration of potassium in the blood has been demonstrated to be too low. If you are taking this combination, be sure your doctor is monitoring the concentration of potassium in your blood.

Digoxin (Lanoxin), which is used in treating congestive heart failure and certain types of irregular heartbeats, interacts with spironolactone in two ways. Spironolactone interferes with certain of the assays used to measure the concentration of digoxin in the blood, causing false reports of elevated digoxin concentration in the blood. In addition, there is some evidence that spironolactone can also decrease the elimination of digoxin from the body, causing true increases in the concentration of digoxin in the blood and therefore increased digoxin effect. Ask your doctor to carefully monitor your digoxin response while you are taking spironolactone.

Potassium supplements (KCl, potassium chloride). Spironolactone causes potassium to be conserved by the body. When supplemental potassium is given with spironolactone, too high a concentration of potassium in the blood (hyperkalemia) can occur.

Other *potassium-sparing diuretics,* such as *amiloride (Midamor, Moduretic)* or *triamterene (Dyazide, Dyrenium, Maxzide),* should not be taken with spironolactone. There is no reason for taking more than one potassium-sparing diuretic at the same time. Such a combination would substantially increase the risk for developing too high a concentration of potassium in the blood (hyperkalemia).

Salt substitutes and *low-salt milk* contain potassium chloride. Therefore, they can interact with spironolactone in the same way as potassium supplements (see above) if used in sufficient amounts. Check with your doctor before using these products.

ALCOHOLIC BEVERAGES Unless you have other medical reasons for restricting their use, you can continue drinking them. There is no interaction.

FOOD Unless your doctor had advised otherwise, take your spironolactone with meals to decrease any gastrointestinal upset it might cause and to help you set up a routine for taking it regularly.

If you are on a restricted-salt diet, be sure to follow it, and avoid using salt substitutes (see Drug Interactions). Since foods vary in their potassium content, you should not make a radical change in your regular diet without first checking with your doctor.

HOW DOES AGE AFFECT THE RESPONSE TO THIS DRUG? The risk of hyperkalemia (see Side Effects) from spironolactone increases because of the steady decline in kidney function that occurs with advancing age. Potassium is eliminated from the body by the kidneys, and it can accumulate to high concentrations in the blood if kidney function is sufficiently reduced. Evidence of this risk was recently illustrated by a study of hospitalized patients with hyperkalemia of various causes, in which age over sixty was associated with a threefold greater incidence of this problem. Two-thirds of the cases of hyperkalemia in this study were caused by drugs. In another study, which pooled data from nearly four thousand hospitalized patients in seven countries, poor kidney function clearly increased the risk of hyperkalemia from spironolactone. Your doctor will evaluate your kidney function (see appendix) before prescribing spironolactone and periodically thereafter.

SULINDAC

OTHER NAMES Sulindac (pronounced *sull-IN-dak)* is the common or generic name of this drug. A frequently used brand name for sulindac is Clinoril. Sulindac belongs to a large group of drugs called nonsteroidal antiinflammatory drugs (NSAIDs).

WHAT IS IT SUPPOSED TO DO? Sulindac relieves the pain, inflammation, swelling, and stiffness associated with arthritis and related conditions. Although some relief should be apparent shortly after you begin taking sulindac, maximum relief occurs after one or two weeks of regular use.

SIDE EFFECTS   Indigestion, heartburn, nausea, stomach discomfort, excessive gas, diarrhea, constipation, and other problems related to the digestive tract are the most common side effects from sulindac. These side effects can sometimes be prevented by taking the drug with a full glass of water, perhaps in addition to food or an antacid. If they persist, or if they are severe, stop taking the drug and contact your doctor.

Rarely, sulindac causes more severe problems in the digestive tract. These include ulcer with bleeding into the gastrointestinal tract (evidenced by bloody stools or stools that are discolored dark red or black) and small amounts of painless blood loss (which can cause anemia). The risk of these problems is lower than it is with aspirin.

Sulindac can also cause mental effects such as drowsiness, headache, or dizziness. Because sulindac can cause decreased alertness in some individuals, you should evaluate how this drug affects you before you drive an automobile or operate any potentially dangerous machinery. If you should develop any sort of visual difficulty (such as blurred or dim vision) or hearing problem (such as buzzing or ringing in your ears), stop taking the drug and contact your doctor.

Kidney problems caused by sulindac and similar drugs are relatively rare, but most of the cases that have been reported in the medical literature involved older individuals. Some of the medical problems that are more prevalent among older people place them at greater risk of this side effect. When the kidneys are stressed by congestive heart failure, dehydration, or any kind of kidney impairment (even modest impairment), the body responds by producing substances called prostaglandins, which increase the flow of blood to the kidneys and increase their efficiency. Sulindac and related drugs can block this compensatory response, and kidney failure (usually reversible) can occur as a result. Of all the nonsteroidal anti-inflammatory drugs, sulindac is the least likely to cause kidney problems. Considering the widespread use of sulindac among older people and the extremely small number of kidney problems that have been reported, the risk is quite small. However, you should return to your doctor for regular medical checkups while taking this drug. Contact your doctor promptly if you experience sudden weight gain, swelling of your feet or ankles, or markedly decreased urine production.

Rashes from sulindac are not uncommon. On rare occasions, sulindac causes other, more severe skin problems or unusual reactions to the sun. Contact your doctor if you experience any sort of rash or skin problem while taking sulindac.

Sulindac is very effective in lowering fever. This effect, combined with its pain-relieving and anti-inflammatory actions, could become a side effect if the signs of an infection were masked and the infection went undetected (and untreated) too long.

If you have ever developed asthma as an allergic reaction to aspirin, you should not take sulindac, because a similar allergic reaction could occur.

Other side effects from sulindac are too rare to list here. Contact your doctor if you experience any unusual symptoms.

DRUG INTERACTIONS Several drugs have the potential to interact with sulindac:

Aspirin is potentially irritating to the digestive tract, and its irritant effects could become troublesome when added to those of sulindac. Furthermore, there is some evidence that there is no additional benefit to be gained by taking aspirin along with sulindac. Therefore, this combination should be avoided.

Diuretics, such as *hydrochlorothiazide (HydroDIURIL and other brands) or furosemide (Lasix).* Infrequently, sulindac causes fluid retention and edema. If you are taking a diuretic for fluid retention and edema (such as that caused by congestive heart failure or liver disease) and you experience a worsening of your symptoms

while taking sulindac, stop taking your sulindac and
contact your doctor.

Warfarin (Coumadin). Sulindac can cause some gastrointestinal bleeding, which could be worsened by the
anticoagulant effects of warfarin. In addition, sulindac
decreases the effectiveness of blood platelets in forming blood clots, so the risk of side effects from warfarin
is increased somewhat while you are taking sulindac.

ALCOHOLIC BEVERAGES   Alcohol adds to the gastric-irritant effects of sulindac. Avoid taking them at the
same time.

FOOD   Food slows the absorption of sulindac somewhat, but it doesn't impair its absorption. It's a good
idea to take your sulindac with food to minimize any
gastric irritation that might occur.

**HOW DOES AGE AFFECT THE RESPONSE TO THIS
DRUG?**   Advancing age increases the risk of side effects from sulindac.

TEMAZEPAM

OTHER NAMES   Temazepam (pronounced *tem-AZ-e-
pam)* is the common or generic name of this drug. A
frequently used brand name for temazepam is Restoril.
Temazepam belongs to a large group of similar drugs
called benzodiazepines.

WHAT IS IT SUPPOSED TO DO?   Temazepam induces and maintains sleep. It is therefore used for the
treatment of insomnia.

There is some controversy over the use of drugs for
insomnia. It is generally agreed that they are useful for
brief episodes of insomnia caused by grief or stress. In
such a situation, the drug helps to provide restful sleep.
However, most physicians feel that sleeping pills should
not be taken every night on a regular basis.

There are several arguments against regular use of
sleeping pills. First, individuals vary in their requirement for sleep, and many people seem to function quite

well with less sleep than they might think they require. Second, most effective sleeping pills cause some residual effect on the following day (see Side Effects). Third, all sleeping pills are potentially habit forming. Fourth, some medical problems can be complicated by their use.

Furthermore, it is quite normal for your sleep pattern to change as you get older. You are likely to awaken more often during the night and to sleep fewer hours.

SIDE EFFECTS   Ideally, a drug for sleep would cause you to fall asleep, and its effects would last all night, disappearing in the morning, when you would wake up refreshed. If the drug is too short-acting, you might wake up after a few hours, after its effects wear off. If the drug is too long-acting, you may find yourself somewhat drowsy the next day. The duration of action of temazepam is neither too short nor too long, but some residual effects may be apparent on the following day, especially if you take too large a dose, or if you take it in the middle of the night. You may find yourself drowsy on the following day.

Infrequently, temazepam causes light-headedness, headache, weakness, dizziness, confusion, blurred vision, or lack of coordination on the following day. If you take temazepam too many nights in a row, these residual daytime effects might become quite prominent.

If you have been taking temazepam regularly for a long time and in large doses, you may experience mild withdrawal symptoms a day or two after stopping this drug. Typical symptoms include difficulty in sleeping, unusual irritability, and unusual nervousness. If these occur, contact your doctor.

Other side effects are too rare to list here. Contact your doctor if you experience any unusual symptoms.

DRUG INTERACTIONS   Sedation is a common side effect of antidepressant drugs, antihistamines, tranquilizers, narcotic analgesics, and other drugs. These drugs will add to any residual daytime sedation you might experience from temazepam.

ALCOHOLIC BEVERAGES Do not take temazepam if you have been drinking during the evening.

FOOD Temazepam can be taken with food or on an empty stomach, but food will delay its effects.

HOW DOES AGE AFFECT THE RESPONSE TO THIS DRUG? Older people are more sensitive to the effects of temazepam and are more likely to experience residual effects on the following day.

In women, aging slows the rate at which temazepam is removed from the body. Therefore, older women are even more likely to experience residual effects. Older women who take temazepam nightly are more likely to accumulate high concentrations of drug in their blood and to develop side effects. In men, aging does not alter the rate at which temazepam is removed from the body.

THEOPHYLLINE

OTHER NAMES Theophylline (pronounced *thee-OFF-i-lin)* is the common or generic name of this drug. Theophylline is often prescribed as one of its salts, aminophylline and oxtriphylline. Some of the more frequently used brand names for theophylline, aminophylline, or oxtriphylline are Accurbron, Aerolate, Aminodur, Aminophyllin, Aquaphyllin, Bronkodyl, Choledyl, Dilor, Elixophyllin, Lufyllin, Slo-bid, Slo-Phyllin, Somophyllin, Sustaire, Theobid, Theo-Dur, Theolair, Theophyl, Theovent, Quibron, Respbid, and Uniphyl. Theophylline belongs to a group of drugs that pharmacologists refer to as methylxanthines, or simply xanthines. One of the better known xanthines is caffeine, which shares many properties with theophylline but is not as effective in treating asthma and other lung problems.

WHAT IS IT SUPPOSED TO DO? Theophylline relaxes the smooth muscles that surround the bronchi, or branches of airways within the lungs. The result of this relaxation is easier breathing when the lungs are afflicted by asthma, emphysema, or chronic bronchitis.

SIDE EFFECTS Like caffeine, theophylline is a mental stimulant. Therefore, nervousness, restlessness, irritability, and insomnia are common side effects. If these effects become unacceptable, or if you experience headache or dizziness, contact your doctor. Overdose can cause seizures.

Theophylline is irritating to the digestive tract. It can cause nausea, stomach pain, loss of appetite, abdominal pain, and diarrhea. Take your theophylline with a full glass of liquid to minimize its irritating effects. Contact your doctor if you are bothered by anything more than mild discomfort.

Unusually rapid or irregular heartbeat, palpitations, confusion, muscle twitching, dizziness, and severe restlessness are signs of overdose. Contact your doctor promptly.

Other side effects are too rare to list here. Contact your doctor if you experience any unusual symptoms.

DRUG INTERACTIONS Several drugs can interact with theophylline. These are the most important interactions:

Beta-blockers and theophylline have opposite effects on the lungs. Propranolol (Inderal), pindolol (Visken), nadolol (Corgard), and timolol (Blocadren) should not be taken by those with lung problems. Atenolol (Tenormin) and metoprolol (Lopressor) are less likely to cause breathing difficulty in those with lung problems, but there is some hazard.

Carbamazepine (Tegretol), which is used for the prevention of some types of seizures and for the relief of neuralgias, stimulates the metabolism of theophylline. When both drugs are taken together, your doctor may need to increase the dose of your theophylline.

Cimetidine (Tagamet), which is used to treat peptic ulcers, slows the metabolism of theophylline. When both drugs are taken together, your doctor may need to decrease the dose of your theophylline.

Erythromycin, an antibiotic, slows the metabolism of

theophylline. It takes several days for this effect to become apparent, but your doctor may need to decrease the dose of your theophylline temporarily while you are being treated with this antibiotic.

Phenytoin (Dilantin), which is used to prevent seizures and to treat certain kinds of irregular heartbeats, slows the metabolism of theophylline. When both drugs are taken together, your doctor may need to decrease the dose of your theophylline.

Smoking. In addition to its adverse effects on the lungs, smoking increases the metabolism of theophylline. Therefore, smokers require larger doses of theophylline than nonsmokers. When smoking is stopped, this effect on theophylline metabolism disappears slowly over a period of months.

ALCOHOLIC BEVERAGES Except for the possibility that alcoholic beverages may add to the stomach upset sometimes caused by theophylline, there is no reason to avoid alcoholic beverages while taking theophylline.

FOOD Theophylline is most reliably absorbed when taken on an empty stomach, thirty minutes to an hour before meals or two hours after meals. Some time-release theophylline products don't work as well when taken with meals. Other theophylline products can be taken with food to minimize stomach upset. Ask your pharmacist or doctor whether you can take your theophylline with food.

There is preliminary evidence that individuals who consume diets that are high in protein and low in carbohydrate may require larger doses of theophylline. Charcoal-broiled foods may impair the absorption of theophylline. Don't make major changes in your diet without checking with your doctor.

Caffeine, which is present in large amounts in coffee, some teas, and cola beverages, shares many side effects with theophylline. It would be prudent to limit your consumption of caffeine or eliminate it from your diet entirely while you are taking theophylline. Otherwise, you will be more likely to experience nervousness, insomnia, or upset stomach from the combined effects of caffeine and theophylline.

HOW DOES AGE AFFECT THE RESPONSE TO THIS DRUG? The decrease in liver function that occurs with advancing age causes theophylline to remain in the body longer in older individuals. Therefore, smaller doses are usually prescribed. Your doctor will determine your theophylline dosage on the basis of your body weight (adjusted to lean body weight if you are obese), taking your age, other drugs, and other medical problems into consideration. Your doctor may periodically order a laboratory test that measures the concentration of theophylline in the blood.

THYROID HORMONES

OTHER NAMES The thyroid gland, located in the front of the neck, produces two hormones that regulate the body's energy metabolism. When the natural hormone production is deficient, thyroid hormones are given as drugs for replacement. Thyroid hormones are prescribed in several forms. Although all these forms accomplish the same purpose, they are not interchangeable; your pharmacist will dispense the form prescribed by your doctor.

Thyroid Hormones from Natural Sources

Thyroid tablets, also called desiccated thyroid and thyroid extract, contain thyroid hormones derived from the thyroid glands of animals that have been slaughtered for food. The standardization for generic thyroid tablets is not as good as it should be, but Armour brand thyroid tablets are a reliable source of this form of the drug.

Thyroglobulin (pronounced *thye-roe-GLOB-yoo-lin)* is a type of animal thyroid extract that is marketed under the brand name of Proloid.

Synthetic Thyroid Hormones

Both of the natural thyroid hormones, thyroxine (commonly called T-4) and triiodothyronine (commonly called T-3), can be manufactured synthetically and used for thyroid hormone replacement. T-3 and T-4 are closely related to each other chemically and have similar effects on the body. A disproportionately large amount of the hormone produced by the thyroid gland is T-4. Most of the T-3 used by the body is created outside of the thyroid gland by conversion of T-4 to T-3 (by removal of one of the four iodine atoms in the T-4 molecule). Because the body can create T-3 from T-4 (and because T-4 is less likely to cause side effects than T-3, whose effects are more intense and of shorter duration than those of T-4), T-4 is the most frequently prescribed synthetic thyroid hormone.

Levothyroxine (pronounced *lee-voe-thye-ROX-een)* is the common or generic name for T-4. It is also called L-thyroxine and T-4 thyroxine. Frequently used brand names for levothyroxine are Levothroid and Synthroid. Generic levothyroxine tablets from several manufacturers have been shown to contain more or less than their labeled amounts and are therefore unreliable. Synthroid brand tablets manufactured since 1982 and Levothroid brand tablets are equivalent to each other and both contain their labeled amount of levothyroxine.

Liothyronine (pronounced *lye-oh-THYE-roe-neen)* is the common or generic name for T-3. It is also called L-triiodothyronine and T-3 thyronine. A frequently used brand name for liothyronine is Cytomel.

Liotrix (pronounced *LYE-oh-trix)* is a combination of levothyroxine (T-4) and liothyronine (T-3) in the same tablet and is marketed under the brand names Euthroid and Thyrolar. These two brands of liotrix are manufactured as tablets that are not equivalent in dosage, so they cannot be used interchangeably.

All forms of thyroid are called thyroid hormones.

WHAT IS IT SUPPOSED TO DO? Thyroid hormone is taken to replace the hormone normally secreted by the thyroid gland. It is prescribed when natural thyroid hormone production and secretion are insufficient. Thyroid hormone is necessary for normal energy metabolism. The signs of thyroid hormone deficiency (hypothyroidism) are nonspecific and include coldness, constipation, confusion, clumsiness, depression, dry skin, fatigue, muscle aches, sleepiness, sluggishness, unusual weight gain, and weakness. Because these signs are nonspecific (they could have other causes), your doctor will rely on laboratory tests to determine your need for thyroid hormone replacement. Your doctor may prescribe thyroid hormone before your deficiency is severe enough to cause symptoms. You will have to continue taking thyroid hormone on a regular basis to maintain its beneficial effects.

SIDE EFFECTS In most instances, thyroid hormone causes no side effects. It has been described as the ideal drug therapy because it is simple replacement of a natural hormone deficiency. However, individuals vary considerably in the doses they require for replacement. Signs of too much thyroid hormone effect (and these, too, are nonspecific) that should be brought to your doctor's attention include chest pain, rapid or irregular heartbeat, shortness of breath, diarrhea, fever, hand tremors, headache, irritability, nervousness, sensitivity to heat, inability to sleep, and weight loss. If any of these is due to too much thyroid hormone, it can be verified with a simple laboratory test, and the dosage can be corrected.

Other effects are too rare to list here. If you experience a rash (possibly from a dye in the tablet) or any other unexpected symptoms, contact your doctor.

DRUG INTERACTIONS Several drugs can interact with thyroid hormones. These are the interactions most likely to cause problems.

Antidiabetic drugs. If you have been taking insulin or a sulfonylurea drug for diabetes and are starting to take thyroid hormone, your doctor may need to increase the dose of your antidiabetic drug. On the other hand, if you have been taking thyroid hormone and are starting to take an antidiabetic drug, your response will not be altered.

Cholestyramine (Questran) is a drug that is used to treat the itching that occurs with some types of jaundice. It is also used to lower the concentration of cholesterol in the blood. Cholestyramine binds with thyroid hormones in the digestive tract and prevents their full absorption. Separate your daily thyroid dose as far from the nearest cholestyramine dose as possible.

Phenytoin, which is used to prevent seizures and certain kinds of irregular heartbeats, increases the rate at which thyroid is metabolized and removed from the body. Normally, your body would compensate for this effect by producing more thyroid hormone. However, if you are taking thyroid hormone for replacement, your dosage requirement may be increased by this interaction. Check with your doctor if you have recently started to take phenytoin.

Warfarin (Coumadin), an anticoagulant, must be given in larger doses to those who are deficient in thyroid hormone (hypothyroidism). If you have been taking warfarin regularly and are now beginning to take thyroid medication, it may be necessary to decrease the dosage of your warfarin; check with your doctor. If you were taking thyroid hormone regularly before starting to take warfarin, you will respond to warfarin in the same way as someone who has normal thyroid function.

ALCOHOLIC BEVERAGES Your thyroid-hormone therapy will not affect your response to alcoholic beverages.

FOOD Food may decrease the absorption of thyroid hormones, so thyroid medication is best taken on an empty stomach, thirty to sixty minutes before a meal.

HOW DOES AGE AFFECT THE RESPONSE TO THIS DRUG? In people with normal thyroid function, aging is associated with a decline in the production of both T-3 and T-4. This results in a tendency toward lower concentrations of T-3 in the blood. The effect of aging on T-4 is more complex. Although T-4 secretion by the thyroid decreases with aging, this hormone is removed from the blood more slowly with advancing age. Therefore, the concentration of T-4 circulating in the blood does not change despite decreased production. When thyroid hormones are being given for replacement, the lower normal values for T-3 and the slower elimination of T-4 must be considered.

People of any age will vary considerably in the dosages they require, but several studies have shown that the dosage requirement for thyroid hormone decreases steadily with age. Your doctor will monitor your thyroid hormone therapy with laboratory tests to ensure that the dosage is appropriate for you.

If you are beginning to take thyroid hormone for the first time, your doctor will start with a small dose that may be gradually increased. There are two reasons for this slow and cautious approach. First, the older you are, the more likely your heart will be sensitive to an increase in thyroid hormone (natural or synthetic). Second, your dosage requirement may be smaller because of your age, and the small starting dose may turn out to be the correct replacement dose.

TIMOLOL

OTHER NAMES Timolol (pronounced *TYE-moe-lole)* is the common or generic name of this drug. Its most frequently used brand name, as tablets, is Blocadren. Its brand name as an ophthalmic solution is Timoptic. Timolol is sometimes prescribed as tablets that also contain the diuretic hydrochlorothiazide; a frequently used brand name for this drug combination is Timolide. Timolol belongs to a group of drugs know as beta-blockers.

WHAT IS IT SUPPOSED TO DO? When taken as tablets, timolol lowers blood pressures that are too high, prevents angina attacks, reduces the risk of recurrence of heart attack, and corrects several other medical

problems. When applied to the eyes, as eye drops, timolol reduces the intraocular pressure, the pressure inside the eye, an effect that is beneficial in people with
glaucoma. The remainder of this discussion is directed
toward timolol tablets, which are used for their effects
on blood pressure and on the heart. Although some
systemic effects, including side effects, can occur from
timolol eye drops, they are usually the result of taking
the drug as tablets.

Timolol accomplishes all these remedies by acting on
the autonomic nervous system, the part of the nervous
system that is beyond our conscious control—the part
that regulates the heart, blood vessels, and various internal organs. Needless to say, the autonomic nervous
system is complex. It has parasympathetic and sympathetic parts that generally work in opposition to one
another. The sympathetic part responds to two types
of stimulation, alpha and beta.

Timolol molecules temporarily bind with highly specialized nervous tissues called beta-receptors, thereby
preventing them from recognizing the chemical messengers that normally set them off. (That is why pharmacologists refer to timolol as a beta-blocker.) The
beta-receptors are one of several means by which the
organs get the messages that tell them what to do. An
increase in heart rate and an increase in blood pressure
are examples of beta responses that are blocked by
timolol.

SIDE EFFECTS   Despite the wide distribution of beta-
receptors throughout the body, side effects from timolol are infrequent and generally mild. Most people
experience no side effects at all.

The most important side effect you should know
about is the possibility of withdrawal symptoms if you
suddenly stop taking timolol after taking it regularly.
This side effect can be understood by considering how
timolol works (see above). While the beta-receptors are
blocked by timolol, they can become overly sensitive
to the chemical messengers that normally set them off.
If timolol is withdrawn abruptly, these receptors will

overrespond. The most common symptom is headache, but there is also the danger of angina attacks, a sudden rise in blood pressure, or even heart attack, depending on what condition was being treated initially. If your doctor wants you to stop taking timolol, he will gradually reduce the dose, or he may substitute another drug that has similar effects.

Your doctor will carefully check your heart before prescribing timolol. When timolol is taken by individuals with untreated congestive heart failure, a condition in which the heart is unable to carry out its job of pumping blood through the circulatory system adequately, this heart failure is likely to be worsened. Infrequently, it causes congestive heart failure in individuals with no previous symptoms. Most patients whose congestive heart failure is corrected by other drugs are able to take timolol without problem. However, you should contact your doctor at once if you experience swelling of your feet or ankles, sudden weight gain, or difficulty in breathing. Timolol's ability to slow the heart and lower the blood pressure is usually beneficial, but occasional individuals experience too much of these effects. An unusually slow pulse rate (less than fifty beats per minute) or dizziness (possibly from abnormally low blood pressure) are other reasons to get in touch with your doctor.

Stomach upset, constipation, or diarrhea occur infrequently from timolol. When any of these side effects does occur, it often goes away with continued use of the drug. If it continues to be bothersome, contact your doctor.

Another infrequent side effect is coldness of the hands or feet, which may occur as a result of the circulatory changes that are brought about by timolol. Be sure to dress warmly in cold weather.

Although timolol enters the brain, its effects there are usually imperceptible, except for occasional drowsiness. However, it sometimes causes adverse mental effects, including dizziness, fatigue, confusion, nightmares, insomnia, and depression. If you experience any unusual and persistent mental symptoms, contact your doctor.

There are some diseases that increase the risk of side effects from timolol. Your doctor will not prescribe timolol if you have asthma or emphysema. The effects of timolol are just the opposite of those that are desirable for lung diseases, which can be worsened by timolol. In diabetics, timolol can cause several problems (see Drug Interactions, Antidiabetic Drugs). As pointed out above, uncontrolled congestive heart failure is worsened by timolol.

Other side effects are too rare to mention here. Contact your doctor if you experience any unusual symptoms.

DRUG INTERACTIONS   Several drugs can interact with timolol. These are the principal ones:

Antidiabetic drugs, such as *insulin* or the *sulfonylureas.* Diabetic patients should not take timolol unless there is no other alternative. Timolol can block some of the warning signs of hypoglycemia (rapid heartbeat or palpitations), delay the recovery from hypoglycemia, cause high-blood-pressure episodes during hypoglycemia, and impair circulation to the extremities. If timolol is required, keep in mind that sweating, but not rapid heartbeat, is a sign of hypoglycemia. Certain other beta-blocking drugs, such as metoprolol (Lopressor) and atenolol (Tenormin), are less likely to cause these problems, but there is some risk.

Breathing medications, such as *isoproterenol (Isuprel) inhalation, terbutaline (Brethine, Bricanyl),* or *theophylline (Elixophyllin, Slo-Phyllin, Theobid, Theo-Dur, and others),* which are used for the treatment of asthma, emphysema, or other lung problems, don't mix well with timolol. The ability of these drugs to open up the air passages in the lungs is antagonized by timolol. Although its effects on normal lungs are minimal, timolol can be dangerous in those with asthma or other lung problems.

Cimetidine (Tagamet), which is used to treat ulcers, reduces the rate at which timolol is metabolized by the liver. Thus, cimetidine causes individuals to respond to smaller amounts of timolol than would otherwise be expected. If you are taking cimetidine, your doctor will either lower your timolol dose accordingly or stop the cimetidine in favor of another drug.

Clonidine (Catapres), which is used to control high blood pressure, can cause a rebound hypertensive reaction if it is stopped abruptly. This reaction is worse in patients who are also taking timolol. If you are taking both of these drugs and must stop taking clonidine, your doctor may slowly discontinue your timolol first. In any case, don't stop taking this drug combination without careful supervision.

Indomethacin (Indocin) can block the antihypertensive and antianginal effects of timolol. If indomethacin is required, your doctor will need to evaluate whether there is any decrease in timolol effect.

Phenobarbital, which is sometimes included in drug combinations for its sedative effects and is also used in the prevention of seizures, increases the rate at which timolol is metabolized by the liver. While you are taking phenobarbital, a larger than usual timolol dose may be required. If you stop taking phenobarbital, be sure to ask your doctor to reevaluate your timolol dosage.

Prazosin (Minipress), which is used for high blood pressure, sometimes causes a severe drop in blood pressure when the person taking it stands up too quickly. This side effect is most common when the drug is first started, and there is some evidence that timolol makes it more likely to occur. If you are taking timolol and starting to take prazosin, your doctor will start with smaller doses and may advise you to take the prazosin at bedtime.

Sympathomimetics, which are contained in some nonprescription remedies for nasal congestion, can cause hypertensive reactions in susceptible individuals. There is some evidence that the risk of this reaction is greater in patients with high blood pressure who are taking timolol. Check with your pharmacist before taking any medication for nasal congestion.

ALCOHOLIC BEVERAGES Usually there is no inter-action between timolol and alcohol. However, you should establish for yourself that timolol does not make you drowsy or dizzy before you drink anything with alcohol in it.

FOOD It's a good idea to take your timolol with meals to help you develop a regular routine for taking it. Food does not affect its absorption. If your doctor has pre-scribed a restricted-salt or restricted-calorie diet, be sure to follow it.

HOW DOES AGE AFFECT THE RESPONSE TO THIS DRUG? Aging slows the rate at which timolol is me-tabolized, thereby allowing it to accumulate to higher concentrations in the blood, but advancing age also brings changes in the beta-receptors that make them less sensitive to drugs. These two effects tend to offset each other. Therefore, older people usually respond similarly to the doses required by younger people. There is, however, wide variation in the doses required by different individuals, regardless of age.

The risk of side effects, particularly those related to the heart (see Side Effects), increases with advancing age. Be sure to return to your doctor for regular check-ups. Most older people, including those who have achieved considerable age, are able to take timolol without problems.

TOLAZAMIDE

OTHER NAMES Tolazamide (pronounced *tole-AZ-a-mide)* is the common or generic name of this drug. A frequently used brand name for tolazamide is Tolinase. Tolazamide belongs to a group of chemically related drugs called sulfonylureas.

WHAT IS IT SUPPOSED TO DO? Tolazamide de-creases the concentration of glucose (a form of sugar) in the blood. Therefore, it is used in the treatment of certain types of diabetes. Tolazamide works by making the body more sensitive to its own insulin. It was originally thought to increase insulin production by the pancreas, but this effect does not persist with normal continued use.

Diabetes that occurs in middle and late life is usually best controlled by diet and exercise. If these measures fail to decrease the concentration of glucose in the blood, then either insulin or a sulfonylurea drug such as tolazamide may be required in addition. The symptoms of too high a concentration of glucose in the blood (*hyper*glycemia) are excessive thirst, excessive urination, fatigue (which can lead to loss of consciousness and coma), and low resistance to infection. Even if you don't have any symptoms, your doctor will want you to control your blood glucose. Control of blood glucose is essential in preventing or reducing the complications of diabetes, which include damage to vision, loss of feeling in the extremities, kidney damage, heart attack, and stroke.

SIDE EFFECTS   *Hypo*glycemia (too low a concentration of glucose in the blood) can occur from any drug that lowers the blood sugar. Tolazamide is no exception, although this problem is not likely to occur unless you stop eating, are severely ill, or follow an extremely irregular diet. The symptoms of hypoglycemia, which include lethargy, nausea, cold sweats, pounding or racing heartbeat, shakiness, headache, confusion, and dizziness, are quickly reversed with a glass of fruit juice or with food. If untreated, hypoglycemia can lead to loss of consciousness and coma. If you think you are experiencing hypoglycemia, have something to eat and contact your doctor.

Other side effects from tolazamide are infrequent. Stomach upset occurs in one or two persons per hundred; take it with food if this problem bothers you. Rash occurs in about one person per hundred; contact your doctor if rash occurs.

Other side effects are too rare to list here. Contact your doctor if you experience any unusual symptoms.

DRUG INTERACTIONS   A number of drugs can interact with tolazamide or affect your diabetes. These are the most likely to cause problems:

Aspirin. Large doses of aspirin (for example, twelve or more tablets a day) have a mild antidiabetic effect. This effect is too mild to be used as a treatment for diabetes, but it adds to the effect of tolazamide. If you are taking large doses of aspirin, you should be aware of this effect. If you start or stop using large doses of aspirin, ask your doctor to determine if it is necessary to alter the dosage of your tolazamide. Occasional use of aspirin will not affect your response to tolazamide.

Some *beta-blocking drugs,* such as *propranolol (Inderal), pindolol (Visken), nadolol (Corgard), or timolol (Blocadren).* Diabetic patients should not take these drugs unless there is no other alternative. They can block some of the warning signs of hypoglycemia (especially rapid heartbeat or palpitations), delay the recovery from hypoglycemia, cause high-blood-pressure episodes during hypoglycemia, and impair circulation to the extremities in diabetics. Other beta-blocking drugs, such as atenolol (Tenormin) or metoprolol (Lopressor), are less likely to cause these problems, but there is some risk. If a beta-blocker is required, keep in mind that sweating, but not rapid heartbeat, is a sign of hypoglycemia.

Clofibrate (Atromid-S), which is sometimes used to lower the concentration of triglycerides in the blood, may increase the response to tolazamide in some patients. If you start or stop taking clofibrate, ask your doctor to reevaluate your response to tolazamide.

Corticosteroids, such as *dexamethasone, hydrocortisone, or prednisone,* can make diabetes more difficult to control. This effect is well known. If you require a corticosteroid, your doctor will check your blood glucose concentration and may increase the dosage of your tolazamide.

Diuretics, such as *hydrochlorothiazide (HydroDIURIL and other brands) or furosemide (Lasix),* can reduce the effects of tolazamide. If your diuretic causes your blood glucose concentration to increase, your doctor may increase the dosage of your tolazamide.

Guanethidine (Ismelin), which is sometimes used to treat high blood pressure, increases the effects of tolazamide. If you start or stop taking guanethidine, ask your doctor to reevaluate your response to tolazamide.

Nifedipine (Procardia), which is used in the treatment of angina, may decrease your response to tolazamide. If you start or stop taking nifedipine, ask your doctor to reevaluate your response to tolazamide.

Phenylbutazone (Butazolidin) and *oxyphenbutazone,* which are sometimes used for brief periods to control gout attacks or severe arthritic pain, can markedly increase the effects of tolazamide. Since hypoglycemia could result, your doctor may want to decrease the dosage of your tolazamide temporarily. Check with your doctor.

Rifampin (Rifadin, Rimactane, Rifamate), which is used in treating tuberculosis and other infections, may stimulate the metabolism of tolazamide. Therefore, it may decrease the effects of tolazamide. If you start or stop taking rifampin, ask your doctor to reevaluate your response to tolazamide.

Smoking antagonizes the effects of insulin and may impair your response to tolazamide as well.

Sulfonamides, which are used in treating infections, may increase your response to tolazamide. If you start or stop taking a sulfonamide, ask your doctor to reevaluate your response to tolazamide.

Thyroid hormones can affect your response to tolazamide. If you are starting to take thyroid, or if the dosage of your thyroid hormone is being changed, ask your doctor to reevaluate your response to tolazamide.

ALCOHOLIC BEVERAGES A number of potential problems can arise from your use of alcoholic beverages. Some doctors tell their patients to avoid alcohol. Others advise their patients to limit their alcohol use to a glass of wine or two with dinner. The American Diabetes Association allows the inclusion of small amounts of alcoholic beverages in the diet of diabetics. You should avoid sweetened alcoholic beverages. Here is a summary of the potential problems that alcohol can cause:

First, alcohol temporarily lowers the concentration of glucose in the blood. If you drink alcohol on an empty stomach, it can cause hypoglycemia. The risk of hypoglycemia is increased while you are taking tolazamide. Therefore, you should avoid large amounts of alcohol and avoid drinking on an empty stomach. If you drink small amounts of alcohol with meals, hypoglycemia is not likely to occur.

Second, some people who take tolazamide develop a flushing reaction when they drink alcohol. This reaction occurs in fewer than 5 percent of those who take tolazamide. It is known as the disulfiram or Antabuse reaction, because disulfiram (Antabuse), which is more reliable in causing this reaction, is given to alcoholics for precisely this reason. The reaction is usually harmless, but may be unpleasant and may be accompanied by headache. If you are bothered by this reaction and your doctor says it is all right for you to drink small amounts of alcohol with meals, you might try taking an aspirin tablet about an hour before a meal that will include a glass of wine.

Third, regular *heavy* use of alcohol may stimulate the enzymes that metabolize tolazamide, thereby causing it to be eliminated from the body more rapidly. As a result, the effects of tolazamide may be decreased. Alcohol consumption should be limited to small amounts for this reason and because of the danger of hypoglycemia during acute alcohol intoxication.

FOOD Tolazamide does not replace diet as the primary means for controlling blood glucose. In addition to avoiding simple sugars, you should increase the amount of roughage (such as fruits, vegetables, and whole grains) in your diet. These foods slow the absorption of complex carbohydrates. Furthermore, you should restrict your consumption of saturated fats (butter, animal fat) because they increase the risk of cardiovascular disease, which is more common among diabetics. Finally, most diabetics who take tolazamide are overweight. Obesity causes resistance to the body's natural insulin and increases the concentration of glucose in the blood. Weight loss, even if you remain a little heavy, will help control your diabetes. Follow the diabetic diet prescribed by your doctor.

A regular diet is important. If you skip meals because of illness or some other reason, you may experience hypoglycemia (see Side Effects). If you cannot eat because of illness, check with your doctor.

Tolazamide is best taken at the start of a meal to prevent stomach upset and to help you remember to take it. Food does not affect the absorption of tolazamide tablets. Hypoglycemia can occur if you fail to eat within an hour or two after taking it on an empty stomach.

HOW DOES AGE AFFECT THE RESPONSE TO THIS DRUG?

Hypoglycemia from drugs like tolazamide is more common among older people than it is among younger people. Be sure to take your tolazamide as directed, follow a careful but regular diet, and be sure that you and those around you are familiar with the signs and symptoms of hypoglycemia.

As the kidneys age, they become less efficient. In younger people, when the concentration of glucose in the blood gets much higher than normal, glucose appears in the urine. The threshold for glucose spilling into the urine increases with age, and older people can have much higher concentrations of glucose in their blood without having any in their urine. This effect varies from individual to individual, of course, but urine tests for glucose may be less reliable as indicators of blood glucose in older people. So don't be misled by negative urine tests for glucose. Your doctor can compare your blood glucose with your urine glucose and give you some idea of how reliable urine tests might be for you.

TOLBUTAMIDE

OTHER NAMES Tolbutamide (pronounced *toll-BYOO-ta-mide)* is the generic or common name of this drug. A frequently used brand name for tolbutamide is Orinase. Tolbutamide belongs to a group of chemically related drugs called sulfonylureas.

WHAT IS IT SUPPOSED TO DO? Tolbutamide decreases the concentration of glucose (a form of sugar) in the blood. Therefore, it is used in the treatment of certain types of diabetes. Tolbutamide works by making the body more sensitive to its own insulin. It was originally thought to increase insulin production by the pancreas, but this effect does not persist with normal continued use.

Diabetes that occurs in middle and late life is usually best controlled by diet and exercise. If these measures fail to decrease the concentration of glucose in the blood, then either insulin or a sulfonylurea drug such as tolbutamide may be required in addition. The symptoms of too high a concentration of glucose in the blood *(hyper*glycemia) are excessive thirst, excessive urination, fatigue (which can lead to loss of consciousness and coma), and low resistance to infection. Even if you don't have any symptoms, your doctor will want you to control your blood glucose. Control of blood glucose is essential in preventing or reducing the complications of diabetes, which include damage to vision, loss of feeling in the extremities, kidney damage, heart attack, and stroke.

SIDE EFFECTS *Hypo*glycemia (too low a concentration of sugar in the blood) can occur from any drug that lowers the blood sugar. Tolbutamide is no exception, although this problem is not likely to occur unless you stop eating, are severely ill, or follow an extremely irregular diet. The symptoms of hypoglycemia, which include lethargy, nausea, cold sweats, pounding or racing heartbeat, shakiness, headache, confusion, and dizziness, are quickly reversed with a glass of fruit juice or with food. If untreated, hypoglycemia can lead to loss of consciousness and coma. If you think you are experiencing hypoglycemia, have something to eat and contact your doctor.

Other side effects from tolbutamide are infrequent. Stomach upset occurs in one or two persons per hundred; take it with food if this problem bothers you. Rash occurs in about one person per hundred; contact your doctor if rash occurs.

Other side effects are too rare to list here. Contact your doctor if you experience any unusual symptoms.

DRUG INTERACTIONS A number of drugs can interact with tolbutamide or affect your diabetes. These are the most likely to cause problems:

Aspirin. Large doses of aspirin (for example, twelve or more tablets a day) have a mild antidiabetic effect. This effect is too mild to be used as a treatment for diabetes, but it adds to the effect of tolbutamide. If you are taking large doses of aspirin, you should be aware of this effect. If you start or stop using large doses of aspirin, ask your doctor to determine if it is necessary to alter the dosage of your tolbutamide. Occasional use of aspirin will not affect your response to tolbutamide.

Some *beta-blocking drugs,* such as *propranolol (Inderal), pindolol (Visken), nadolol (Corgard), or timolol (Blocadren).* Diabetic patients should not take these drugs unless there is no other alternative. They can block some of the warning signs of hypoglycemia (especially rapid heartbeat or palpitations), delay the recovery from hypoglycemia, cause high-blood-pressure episodes during hypoglycemia, and impair circulation to the extremities in diabetics. Other beta-blocking drugs, such as atenolol (Tenormin) or metoprolol (Lopressor), are less likely to cause these problems, but there is some risk. If a beta-blocker is required, keep in mind that sweating, but not rapid heartbeat, is a sign of hypoglycemia.

Clofibrate (Atromid-S), which is sometimes used to lower the concentration of triglycerides in the blood, may increase the response to tolbutamide in some patients. If you start or stop taking clofibrate, ask your doctor to reevaluate your response to tolbutamide.

Corticosteroids, such as *dexamethasone, hydrocortisone, or prednisone,* can make diabetes more difficult to control. This effect is well known. If you require a corticosteroid, your doctor will check your blood glucose concentration and may increase the dosage of your tolbutamide.

Diuretics, such as *hydrochlorothiazide (HydroDIURIL and other brands) or furosemide (Lasix),* can reduce the effects of tolbutamide. If your diuretic causes your blood glucose concentration to increase, your doctor may increase the dosage of your tolbutamide. There is a second possible interaction between tolbutamide and diuretics. Diuretics and tolbutamide both tend to lower the concentration of sodium in the blood, and they do this by separate mechanisms. In some older individuals, this combination of drugs may lead to too low a concentration of sodium in the blood. This is not a common problem, but you should contact your doctor if you experience weakness, confusion, or muscle cramps.

Guanethidine (Ismelin), which is sometimes used to treat high blood pressure, increases the effects of tolbutamide. If you start or stop taking guanethidine, ask your doctor to reevaluate your response to tolbutamide.

Nifedipine (Procardia), which is used in the treatment of angina, may decrease your response to tolbutamide. If you start or stop taking nifedipine, ask your doctor to reevaluate your response to tolbutamide.

Phenylbutazone (Butazolidin) and *oxyphenbutazone,* which are sometimes used for brief periods to control gout attacks or severe arthritic pain, can markedly increase the effects of tolbutamide. Since hypoglycemia could result, your doctor may want to decrease the dosage of your tolbutamide temporarily. Check with your doctor.

Rifampin (Rifadin, Rimactane, Rifamate), which is used in treating tuberculosis and other infections, stimulates the metabolism of tolbutamide. Therefore, it may decrease the effects of tolbutamide. If you start or stop taking rifampin, ask your doctor to reevaluate your response to tolbutamide.

Smoking antagonizes the effects of insulin and may impair your response to tolbutamide as well.

Sulfonamides, which are used in treating infections, may increase your response to tolbutamide. If you start or stop taking a sulfonamide, ask your doctor to reevaluate your response to tolbutamide.

Thyroid hormones can affect your response to tolbutamide. If you are starting to take thyroid, or if the dosage of your thyroid hormone is being changed, ask your doctor to reevaluate your response to tolbutamide.

ALCOHOLIC BEVERAGES A number of potential problems can arise from your use of alcoholic beverages. Some doctors tell their patients to avoid alcohol. Others advise their patients to limit their alcohol use to a glass of wine or two with dinner. The American Diabetes Association allows the inclusion of small amounts of alcoholic beverages in the diet of diabetics. You should avoid sweetened alcoholic beverages. Here is a summary of the potential problems that alcohol can cause:

First, alcohol temporarily lowers the concentration of glucose in the blood. If you drink alcohol on an empty stomach, it can cause hypoglycemia. The risk of hypoglycemia is increased while you are taking tolbutamide. Therefore, you should avoid large amounts of alcohol and avoid drinking on an empty stomach. If you drink small amounts of alcohol with meals, hypoglycemia is not likely to occur.

Second, some people who take tolbutamide develop a flushing reaction when they drink alcohol. This reaction occurs in fewer than 5 percent of those who take tolbutamide. It is known as the disulfiram or Antabuse reaction, because disulfiram (Antabuse), which is more reliable in causing this reaction, is given to alcoholics for precisely this reason. The reaction is usually harmless, but may be unpleasant and may be accompanied by headache. If you are bothered by this reaction and your doctor says it is all right for you to drink small amounts of alcohol with meals, you might try taking an aspirin tablet about an hour before a meal that will include a glass of wine.

Third, regular *heavy* use of alcohol stimulates the enzymes that metabolize tolbutamide, thereby causing it to be eliminated from the body more rapidly. As a result, the effects of tolbutamide are decreased. Alcohol consumption should be limited to small amounts for this reason and because of the danger of hypoglycemia during acute alcohol intoxication.

FOOD   Tolbutamide does not replace diet as the primary means of controlling blood glucose. In addition to avoiding simple sugars, you should increase the amount of roughage (such as fruits, vegetables, and whole grains) in your diet. These foods slow the absorption of complex carbohydrates. Furthermore, you should restrict your consumption of saturated fats (butter, animal fat), because they increase the risk of cardiovascular disease, which is more common among diabetics. Finally, most diabetics who take tolbutamide are overweight. Obesity causes resistance to the body's natural insulin and increases the concentration of glucose in the blood. Weight loss, even if you remain a little heavy, will help control your diabetes. Follow the diabetic diet prescribed by your doctor.

A regular diet is important. If you skip meals because of illness or some other reason, you may experience hypoglycemia (see Side Effects). If you cannot eat because of illness, check with your doctor.

Tolbutamide is best taken at the start of a meal in order to prevent stomach upset and to help you remember to take it. Food does not affect the absorption of tolbutamide tablets. Some scientists have said that there may be a slight advantage to taking tolbutamide thirty minutes before meals, but research in support of this theory has shown the benefits to be extremely marginal when compared with the effects of taking tolbutamide at the start of meals. Hypoglycemia can occur if you fail to eat within an hour or two after taking it on an empty stomach.

HOW DOES AGE AFFECT THE RESPONSE TO THIS DRUG? Hypoglycemia from drugs like tolbutamide is more common among older people than it is among younger people. Be sure to take your tolbutamide as directed, follow a careful but regular diet, and be sure that you and those around you are familiar with the signs and symptoms of hypoglycemia.

Age also affects the way your body responds to high concentrations of glucose in the blood. As the kidneys age, they become less efficient. In younger people, when the concentration of glucose in the blood gets much higher than normal, glucose appears in the urine. The threshold for glucose spilling into the urine increases with age, and older people can have much higher concentrations of glucose in their blood without having any in the urine. This effect varies from individual to individual, of course, but urine tests for glucose may be less reliable as indicators of blood glucose in older people. So don't be misled by negative urine tests for glucose. Your doctor can compare your blood glucose with your urine glucose and give you some idea of how reliable urine tests might be for you.

TOLMETIN

OTHER NAMES Tolmetin (pronounced *TOLL-met-in*) is the common or generic name of this drug. A frequently used brand name for tolmetin is Tolectin. Tolmetin belongs to a large group of drugs called nonsteroidal anti-inflammatory drugs (NSAIDs).

WHAT IS IT SUPPOSED TO DO? Tolmetin relieves the pain, inflammation, swelling, and stiffness associated with arthritis. Although some relief should become apparent shortly after you start taking tolmetin, maximum relief occurs after one or two weeks of regular use.

SIDE EFFECTS Indigestion, heartburn, nausea, stomach discomfort, excessive gas, diarrhea, and other problems related to the digestive tract are the most common side effects from tolmetin. These side effects can sometimes be prevented by taking the drug with a full glass of water, perhaps in addition to food or an antacid. If they persist, or if they are severe, stop taking the drug and contact your doctor.

Rarely, tolmetin causes more severe problems in the digestive tract. These include ulcer with bleeding into the gastrointestinal tract (evidenced by bloody stools or stools that are discolored dark red or black) and small amounts of painless blood loss (which can cause anemia). The risk of these problems is lower than it is with aspirin.

Tolmetin can also cause mental effects such as lightheadedness, dizziness, or drowsiness. Because tolmetin can cause decreased alertness in some individuals, you should evaluate how this drug affects you before you drive an automobile or operate any potentially dangerous machinery. If you should develop any sort of visual difficulty (such as blurred or dim vision) or hearing problem (such as buzzing or ringing in your ears), stop taking the drug and contact your doctor.

Kidney problems caused by tolmetin and similar drugs are relatively rare, but most of the cases that have been reported in the medical literature involved older individuals. Some of the medical problems that are more prevalent among older people place them at greater risk for this side effect. When the kidneys are stressed by congestive heart failure, dehydration, or any kind of kidney impairment (even modest impairment), the body responds by producing substances called prostaglandins, which increase the flow of blood to the kidneys and increase their efficiency. Tolmetin and related drugs can block this compensatory response, and kidney failure (usually reversible) can occur as a result. (All nonsteroidal anti-inflammatory drugs work by preventing the body from manufacturing prostaglandins, which are also mediators of pain and inflammation.) Considering the widespread use of tolmetin among older people and the extremely small number of kidney problems that have been reported, the risk appears to be quite small. However, you should return to your doctor for regular medical checkups while taking this drug. Contact your doctor promptly if you experience sudden weight gain, swelling of your feet or ankles, or markedly decreased urine production.

Skin problems, such as rashes or unusual reactions to the sun, are rare side effects from tolmetin. Contact your doctor if you experience anything unusual.

Tolmetin is very effective in lowering fever. This effect, combined with its pain-relieving and anti-inflammatory actions, could be considered a side effect if the signs of an infection were masked and the infection went undetected (and untreated) too long.

If you have ever developed asthma as an allergic reaction to aspirin, you should not take tolmetin, because a similar allergic reaction could occur.

Other side effects from tolmetin are too rare to list here. Contact your doctor if you experience any unusual symptoms.

DRUG INTERACTIONS Several drugs have the potential to interact with tolmetin:

Aspirin is potentially irritating to the digestive tract, and its irritant effects could become troublesome when added to those of tolmetin. Check with your doctor before taking this drug combination.

Diuretics, such as *hydrochlorothiazide (HydroDIURIL and other brands) or furosemide (Lasix).* Infrequently, tolmetin causes fluid retention and edema. If you are taking a diuretic for fluid retention and edema (such as that caused by congestive heart failure or liver disease) and you experience a worsening of your symptoms while taking tolmetin, stop taking your tolmetin and contact your doctor.

Warfarin (Coumadin). Tolmetin can cause some gastrointestinal bleeding, which could be worsened by the anticoagulant effects of warfarin. In addition, tolmetin decreases the effectiveness of blood platelets in forming blood clots, so the risk of side effects from warfarin is increased somewhat while you are taking tolmetin.

ALCOHOLIC BEVERAGES Alcohol adds to the gastric-irritant effects of tolmetin. Avoid taking them at the same time.

FOOD Food slows the absorption of tolmetin somewhat, but it doesn't impair its absorption. It's a good idea to take your tolmetin with food in order to minimize any gastric irritation that might occur.

HOW DOES AGE AFFECT THE RESPONSE TO THIS DRUG? Advancing age increases the risk of side effects from tolmetin.

TRAZODONE

OTHER NAMES Trazodone (pronounced *TRAZ-oh-done)* is the common or generic name of this drug. Its most frequently used brand name is Desyrel. Trazodone belongs to a group of drugs called antidepressants.

WHAT IS IT SUPPOSED TO DO? Trazodone relieves mental depression. The precise means by which it works has not been established, but its mechanism of action involves an increase in the concentration of certain naturally occurring substances (particularly serotonin) within the brain. Elevation of mood and reversal of the various symptoms that can accompany depression (such as sleep problems, decreased energy, or loss of appetite) require a minimum of several weeks of regular use. Your doctor may prescribe less than several weeks' supply of medication initially, so it is important that you return to your pharmacy to have your prescription refilled. Your doctor may want you to continue taking trazodone for several months after your mood returns to normal.

SIDE EFFECTS The most common side effect from trazodone is drowsiness. Avoid driving until you are sure that your alertness and coordination are not impaired. Drowsiness will decrease as your body becomes accustomed to the drug.

Trazodone may exaggerate the dizziness, lightheadedness, or faintness you feel when you stand up too quickly. Be careful to stand up slowly. If this side effect is severe (especially if it causes you to fall or causes your heart to pound or race), contact your doctor.

Occasionally, trazodone causes dry mouth. Sugarless candy or gum may be helpful in alleviating this side effect. If it is severe, contact your doctor.

Effects on the heart—excessively fast, slow, or irregular heartbeat—are infrequent. Contact your doctor if any of these occur.

Other infrequent side effects include muscle tremor, sudden onset of confusion, or rash. Contact your doctor if any of these occur.

A rare (the estimated incidence is one in seven thousand) but potentially serious side effect in men is inappropriate, sustained, and sometimes painful erection of the penis. If this occurs, stop taking the drug and contact your doctor.

Other side effects are too rare to list here. Contact your doctor if you experience any unexpected symptoms.

DRUG INTERACTIONS Trazodone is a relatively new drug. However, on the basis of isolated reports and experience with related drugs, the following interactions may occur:

Antihypertensive drugs can interact with trazodone by several mechanisms. First, some of them (betablockers, clonidine, methyldopa, and reserpine) can cause depression as a side effect. Second, the action of a few antihypertensive drugs is blocked by trazodone. If you are taking clonidine (Catapres, Combipres), guanethidine (Ismelin), or guanadrel (Hylorel), your doctor will need to prescribe another drug to control your blood pressure. Third, if your antihypertensive drug causes dizziness, trazodone will make this side effect worse. Your doctor may need to decrease the dose of your antihypertensive drug before you start taking trazodone.

Drugs with sedative effects, such as *antihistamines, benzodiazepine antianxiety or sleeping pills, codeine, and tranquilizers*, should be used with caution with trazodone. Excessive sedation may occur.

ALCOHOLIC BEVERAGES   Alcohol will increase the dizziness or faintness you may feel upon standing up too quickly. It will also add to the drowsiness that trazodone often causes. Therefore, you should avoid alcohol or use it sparingly while taking trazodone.

FOOD   Take your trazodone with meals to help you maintain a regular schedule for taking it. Food decreases the likelihood of it causing dizziness or lightheadedness.

HOW DOES AGE AFFECT THE RESPONSE TO THIS DRUG?   When groups of younger (aged twenty-three to thirty) and older (aged sixty-five to seventy-four) individuals were given the same dose of trazodone, the older individuals had higher concentrations of the drug in their blood. Because advancing age is associated with slower elimination of the drug from the blood, and because advancing age increases the sensitivity to side effects from trazodone, your doctor will start your therapy with small doses and gradually increase to doses that are likely to be effective without causing serious side effects.

TRIAMTERENE

OTHER NAMES   Triamterene (pronounced *try-AM-ter-een)* is the common or generic name of this drug. A frequently used brand name for triamterene is Dyrenium. Triamterene is often prescribed as capsules or tablets that also contain hydrochlorothiazide, another diuretic but one with slightly different properties. The brand names of these combination products are Dyazide and Maxzide; although they both contain triamterene and hydrochlorothiazide, they contain differing amounts of their two ingredients and release them into the body in different ways. Dyazide and Maxzide are by no means interchangeable. Pharmacologists refer to triamterene as a potassium-sparing diuretic.

WHAT IS IT SUPPOSED TO DO? Triamterene is a diuretic—it acts on the kidneys, causing them to eliminate extra water and salt from the body and into the urine. It is used in treating high blood pressure and in relieving the symptoms of edema, the abnormal swelling in tissues or congestion in the lungs that results from heart failure or other medical problems. Because triamterene is a mild diuretic, it is usually taken with another diuretic, such as hydrochlorothiazide or furosemide. Unlike those diuretics, however, triamterene conserves potassium in the body rather than promoting its loss. Therefore, when used in combination with these more potent diuretics, triamterene counteracts their principal side effect—potassium loss.

SIDE EFFECTS At first you will notice a need to urinate frequently. This effect will decrease with continued use. You should avoid taking triamterene too close to bedtime. Otherwise, you may find yourself being frequently awakened from sleep by a need to urinate.

Infrequently, triamterene causes nausea, vomiting, stomach cramps, or diarrhea. Mild gastrointestinal discomfort may go away as your body adjusts to triamterene, and it may be prevented by taking the drug with food. However, you should contact your doctor whenever you experience continued vomiting or diarrhea, because these can cause dehydration and electrolyte imbalance.

The most serious side effect from triamterene is hyperkalemia (too high a concentration of potassium in the blood), but this occurs infrequently. To prevent this side effect, which can cause dangerously irregular heartbeats, you should not take any form of potassium supplement while you are taking triamterene. Your doctor will periodically measure the concentration of potassium in your blood while you are taking triamterene. Numbness or tingling in the hands, feet, or lips; weakness; or confusion may be signs of hyperkalemia. Contact your doctor if any of these occur.

Rarely, triamterene causes headache, dizziness, dry mouth, weakness, or skin rashes. These may be signs that you are extremely sensitive to the drug or allergic to it; contact your doctor.

Other side effects are too rare to list here. Contact your doctor if you experience any unexpected problems.

DRUG INTERACTIONS Several drugs can interact with triamterene, and some of these interactions have potentially serious consequences:

Angiotensin-converting-enzyme (ACE) inhibitors, such as *captopril (Capoten, Capozide)* or *enalapril (Vaseretic, Vasotec),* which are used in the treatment of congestive heart failure and high blood pressure, cause potassium to be conserved by the body. To minimize the risk of too high a concentration of potassium in the blood (hyperkalemia), triamterene should be used with these drugs only when the concentration of potassium in the blood has been demonstrated to be too low. If you are taking this combination, be sure your doctor is monitoring the concentration of potassium in your blood.

Indomethacin (Indocin), a nonsteroidal anti-inflammatory drug, can impair kidney function when taken with triamterene. Triamterene causes a slight reduction of blood flow in the kidneys, which the kidneys compensate for by producing prostaglandins. Indomethacin prevents the formation of prostaglandins; it is among the most potent inhibitors of prostaglandin synthesis. Merck Sharpe & Dohme, the principal manufacturer of indomethacin, warns that these two drugs should not be used together.

Other *potassium-sparing diuretics,* such as *amiloride (Midamor, Moduretic)* or *spironolactone (Aldactone, Aldactazide),* should not be taken with triamterene. There is no reason for taking more than one potassium-sparing diuretic. Such a combination would substantially increase the risk for developing too high a concentration of potassium in the blood (hyperkalemia).

Potassium supplements (KCl, potassium chloride). Triamterene causes potassium to be conserved by the body. When supplemental potassium is taken with triamterene, too high a concentration of potassium in the blood (hyperkalemia) can occur.

Salt substitutes and *low-salt milk* contain potassium chloride. Therefore, they can interact with triamterene in the same way as potassium supplements (see above) if used in sufficient amounts. Check with your doctor before using these products.

ALCOHOLIC BEVERAGES Unless you have other medical reasons for restricting their use, you can continue drinking them. There is no interaction.

FOOD Unless your doctor has advised otherwise, take your triamterene with meals to decrease any gastrointestinal upset that it might cause and to help you set up a routine for taking it regularly.

If you are on a restricted-salt diet, be sure to follow it, and avoid using salt substitutes (see Drug Interactions). Since foods vary in their potassium content, you should not make a radical change in your regular diet without first checking with your doctor.

HOW DOES AGE AFFECT THE RESPONSE TO THIS DRUG? The risk of hyperkalemia (see Side Effects) from triamterene increases because of the steady decline in kidney function that occurs with advancing age. Potassium, triamterene, and the active metabolite of triamterene are all eliminated from the body by the kidneys. If kidney function is sufficiently reduced, potassium and the active metabolite of triamterene can accumulate to high concentrations in the blood. Evidence of this risk was recently illustrated by a study of hospitalized patients with hyperkalemia of various causes, in which age over sixty was associated with a threefold greater incidence of this problem. Two-thirds of the cases of hyperkalemia in this study were caused by drugs. Your doctor will evaluate your kidney function (see appendix) before prescribing triamterene and periodically thereafter.

Older age is more often accompanied by medical problems that add to the risk of hyperkalemia. For example, in some instances, diabetics may be more prone to develop hyperkalemia than nondiabetics. Likewise, individuals with malignancies are more likely to develop hyperkalemia.

Lastly, individuals of more advanced age are more likely to experience adverse effects from drug interactions that don't ordinarily cause problems. For example, triamterene and nonsteroidal anti-inflammatory drugs (NSAIDs) such as ibuprofen, fenoprofen, and naproxen, are commonly taken together without problem, despite the fact that these drugs have the potential for interacting with triamterene in a manner similar to indomethacin (see Drug Interactions). This interaction is probably too rare to warrant routine precautionary warnings, but in someone whose kidneys are already stressed by uncorrected congestive heart failure or by dehydration, this interaction could cause kidney failure (usually reversible), depending on the doses of the drugs and the condition of the individual. Furthermore, the potassium-retaining properties of the NSAIDs, which are ordinarily not clinically apparent, may be additive to those of triamterene in people with poor kidney function.

Regular checkups should prevent these problems. Despite this list of potentially dire consequences of triamterene use with advancing age, this drug is generally safe and beneficial. Triamterene is one of the most commonly used drugs among older people, and it seldom causes serious side effects.

TRIAZOLAM

OTHER NAMES Triazolam (pronounced *try-AZ-oh-lam*) is the common or generic name of this drug. A frequently used brand name for triazolam is Halcion.

Triazolam belongs to a large group of similar drugs called benzodiazepines.

WHAT IS IT SUPPOSED TO DO? Triazolam induces and maintains sleep. It is therefore used for the treatment of insomnia.

There is some controversy over the use of drugs for insomnia. It is generally agreed that they are useful for brief episodes of insomnia caused by grief or stress. In such a situation, the drug helps to provide restful sleep. However, most physicians feel that sleeping pills should not be taken every night on a regular basis.

There are several arguments against regular use of sleeping pills. First, individuals vary in their requirement for sleep, and many people seem to function quite well with less sleep than they might think they require. Second, most effective sleeping pills cause some residual effect on the following day, although this rarely occurs with triazolam. Third, all sleeping pills are potentially habit forming. Fourth, some medical problems can be complicated by their use.

Furthermore, it is quite normal for your sleep pattern to change as you get older. You are likely to awaken more often during the night and to sleep fewer hours.

SIDE EFFECTS Ideally, a drug for sleep would cause you to fall asleep, and its effects would last all night, disappearing in the morning, when you would wake up refreshed. If the drug is too long-acting, you may find yourself somewhat drowsy the next day. If the drug is too short-acting, you might wake up after a few hours, after its effects wear off. Triazolam is the shortest-acting drug for insomnia that is available. However, if you take too large a dose, or if you take it in the middle of the night, you may experience residual effects on the following day. Infrequently, triazolam causes light-headedness, headaches, weakness, dizziness, confusion, blurred vision, or lack of coordination on the following day.

If you have been taking triazolam regularly for a long time and in large doses, you may experience mild withdrawal symptoms a day or two after stopping this drug.

Typical symptoms include difficulty in sleeping, unusual irritability, and unusual nervousness. If these occur, contact your doctor.

Other side effects are too rare to list here. Contact your doctor if you experience any unusual symptoms.

DRUG INTERACTIONS Sedation is a common side effect of antidepressant drugs, antihistamines, tranquilizers, narcotic analgesics, and other drugs. These drugs will add to any residual daytime sedation you might experience from triazolam.

In addition, several drugs can interact with triazolam by other mechanisms. These are the interactions most likely to cause problems:

Cimetidine (Tagamet), which is used for the treatment of ulcers, slows the metabolism of triazolam and thereby prolongs its effects. You will be more susceptible to side effects from triazolam (residual effects on the following day) while taking cimetidine.

Disulfiram (Antabuse), which is used in the treatment of alcoholism, slows the metabolism of triazolam and thereby prolongs its effects. You will be more susceptible to side effects from triazolam (residual effects on the following day) while taking disulfiram.

Isoniazid (INH), which is used in the treatment of tuberculosis, may slow the metabolism of triazolam and thereby prolong its effect. You will be more susceptible to side effects from triazolam (residual effects on the following day) while taking isoniazid. Rifampin, another drug which is used for tuberculosis, has the opposite effect (see below). When isoniazid and rifampin are used together for the treatment of tuberculosis, the effects of rifampin are likely to predominate in the interaction with triazolam.

Levodopa (Dopar, Larodopa, L-dopa) is used in the treatment of Parkinson's disease, and triazolam may block its effect. If you are taking both drugs and notice a worsening of your parkinsonism, stop taking your triazolam and contact your doctor.

Rifampin (Rifadin, Rimactane), which is used in the treatment of tuberculosis, increases the metabolism of triazolam and thereby decreases its effect. If your doctor increases the dosage of triazolam to compensate for this interaction, and you stop taking rifampin while continuing to take the same dosage of triazolam, you may experience side effects from triazolam.

ALCOHOLIC BEVERAGES Do not take triazolam if you have been drinking during the evening.

FOOD Triazolam can be taken either with food or on an empty stomach, but food will delay its effects.

HOW DOES AGE AFFECT THE RESPONSE TO THIS DRUG? Age does not affect the rate at which triazolam is removed from the body. However, older people are more sensitive to the effects of triazolam and are therefore more likely to experience residual effects on the following day.

VERAPAMIL

OTHER NAMES Verapamil (pronounced *ver-AP-a-mill)* is the common or generic name of this drug. Some frequently used brand names for verapamil are Calan and Isoptin. Verapamil belongs to a group of drugs called calcium channel blockers.

WHAT IS IT SUPPOSED TO DO? Verapamil decreases the occurrence of angina pectoris, the chest pain caused by poor oxygen supply to the heart muscle. It also prevents certain types of irregular heartbeats and lowers high blood pressure.

Verapamil prevents angina attacks by inhibiting the movement of calcium into the cells of the specialized muscle tissue in the walls of certain blood vessels (arterioles), thereby causing a relaxation of this muscle and dilation of the blood vessel. This widening in the diameter of the blood vessels that carry blood to the heart muscle improves its circulation and supplies it with more oxygen. Verapamil also causes a widening of the diameter of the blood vessels that the heart pumps into (the ones that create a resistance to the heart's pumping action). The heart's workload is thereby decreased (because it is pumping against less resistance—pharmacologists call this a decrease in afterload). This decrease in workload causes the heart to use less oxygen.

Verapamil also has a direct effect on specialized muscle tissue within the heart (the A-V node). There, the inhibition of calcium movement across cell membranes slows the heart and makes it beat more regularly when it is following certain abnormal rhythms.

Although the current primary uses of verapamil are for the prevention of irregular heartbeats and the prevention of angina attacks, its effects on blood vessels are also of value in the treatment of high blood pressure.

Like other calcium channel blockers, verapamil's effects on calcium are limited to specialized muscle tissues. It has no effect on the concentration of calcium in the blood, and, under normal circumstances, it is unaffected by calcium in the diet or by calcium supplements.

SIDE EFFECTS Occasionally, verapamil causes constipation, nausea, dizziness, light-headedness, or headache. If you experience dizziness or light-headedness, be especially careful not to stand up too quickly—allow your body time to adjust to changes in position. Rarely, it causes flushing or warm, tingling sensations; shakiness or weakness; or unusual tiredness. If these side effects persist or if they are severe, contact your doctor.

Verapamil does not usually have a noticeable effect on the heartbeat, but in those with certain types of heart diseases, it can cause too slow a heartbeat (bradycardia). Therefore, you should learn to take your pulse and should contact your doctor if it should become slower than fifty beats per minute. Irregular or unusually fast, pounding heartbeat is another, rarer occurrence that may be related to a specific heart problem; it, too, requires your doctor's attention.

Likewise, you should contact your doctor if you develop shortness of breath or swollen feet or ankles. These side effects are infrequent.

Other side effects are too rare to list here. If you experience anything unexpected, contact your doctor.

DRUG INTERACTIONS Several drugs may interact with verapamil:

Beta-blocking drugs, such as *atenolol (Tenormin), metoprolol (Lopressor), nadolol (Corgard), propranolol (Inderal), pindolol (Visken), or timolol (Blocadren).* A beta-blocking drug is often prescribed together with verapamil because the two drugs work by different mechanisms, which complement each other. For most patients, it's a beneficial combination. However, in some instances this drug combination can cause abnormally low blood pressure (dizziness, fainting), too slow a pulse rate (less than fifty beats per minute), or congestive heart failure (swelling of feet or ankles, difficulty in breathing). Contact your doctor if you experience these or other unexpected symptoms.

Calcium, if taken in large enough amounts, can block the effects of verapamil. This is true of intravenous infusions of calcium and calcium taken in combination with large doses of vitamin D. It is unlikely that a diet rich in calcium or one that is modestly supplemented with calcium would cause this effect. However, you should be alert for the possibility of loss of verapamil effect if you are taking calcium supplements.

Digoxin (Lanoxin). Verapamil increases the concentration of digoxin in the blood. Your doctor should watch for this effect and, if necessary, decrease your digoxin dose. Also, both drugs slow the heart, and their effects can be additive.

ALCOHOLIC BEVERAGES Alcohol adds to the dilation of blood vessels and lowering of blood pressure caused by verapamil, making you more susceptible to dizziness, light-headedness, or fainting. Limit your consumption of alcohol.

FOOD Take your verapamil with meals to help you maintain a regular schedule for taking it.

HOW DOES AGE AFFECT THE RESPONSE TO THIS DRUG?   The rate at which verapamil is removed from the body decreases with advancing age. Therefore, older people may require smaller doses than younger people. Your doctor will prescribe a dose that is likely to be appropriate for you.

WARFARIN

OTHER NAMES   Warfarin (pronounced *WAR-fa-rin*) is the common or generic name of this drug. Some frequently used brand names for warfarin are Coumadin and Panwarfin. Pharmacologists refer to warfarin as an anticoagulant.

WHAT IS IT SUPPOSED TO DO?   Warfarin prevents harmful blood clots from forming on the inside of blood vessels. It does this by modifying some of the clotting factors in the blood so that it takes longer for the blood to clot than normally. (The term *blood thinner* is an overly literal description of what it does.)

Warfarin is prescribed after a clot has already occurred, to prevent more clots from forming. Or it is prescribed in situations where there is a reasonable risk of a blood clot. The principal danger in such clot formation is that the clot will break loose and travel through the circulation to some vital organ, such as the brain, the heart, or the lungs, where its presence could block the circulation to that organ.

SIDE EFFECTS   The main side effects from warfarin are the result of its pharmacological effect—prolongation of the time it takes for your blood to clot. A therapeutic prolongation of clotting time doesn't usually cause adverse effects, but you should watch for signs of too much effect, such as bleeding gums, bloody urine (pink or red urine), rectal bleeding (black stools), or excessive bruising. About 5 percent of the people treated with warfarin experience a minor bleeding problem. Another 2 or 3 percent experience more serious bleeding problems. Your doctor will test your blood regularly to see that the desired effect is being obtained, and this information will be used to modify the dosage, if necessary. If you observe signs of excessive bleeding, contact your doctor at once. It's a good idea to carry a card in your wallet and to wear a special identification bracelet stating that you are taking warfarin should you require emergency medical care.

If you are scheduled to have any sort of surgery, including dental surgery, be sure to notify your doctor or dentist that you are taking warfarin. Its effects can be temporarily antagonized with vitamin K, or you may be instructed to discontinue the warfarin before surgery.

Contact your doctor if you develop any expected symptoms.

DRUG INTERACTIONS Quite a few drugs can interact with warfarin. Don't take any new medication (including nonprescription drugs) without first asking your doctor or pharmacist if an interaction with warfarin might occur. Obviously, it's best to avoid such an interaction, but situations sometimes arise where both drugs are needed. In these cases, your doctor may prescribe the interacting drug and monitor for the interaction in anticipation of a need to increase or decrease your warfarin dosage. If you are already taking a drug that interacts with warfarin, you should not stop taking the drug without your doctor's knowledge. If your warfarin dosage has been adjusted to take an interaction into account and you suddenly stop taking the interacting drug, then your warfarin dosage may become either too great or insufficient, depending on the interaction.

Acetaminophen (Tylenol, Datril), which is a nonprescription pain reliever, can slightly increase the effect of warfarin if taken regularly in adequate amounts. You would probably have to take about six tablets a day for several days for this effect to become apparent. An occasional dose of one or two tablets for pain will not affect your response to warfarin. If you need to take something for pain while you are taking warfarin, acetaminophen is safer then either aspirin or ibuprofen (Advil, Nuprin).

Allopurinol (Zyloprim, Lopurin), which is used to prevent gout attacks and to prevent some of the side effects of certain cancer drugs, slows the metabolism of warfarin. As a result, usual doses of warfarin may have greater effect than anticipated.

Anabolic steroids, such as *methyltestosterone (Metandren)* or *testosterone*, hormones that are used for a variety of medical problems, increase the effect of warfarin considerably. Even the small amount of testosterone that is absorbed from an ointment applied to the skin is sufficient to increase the effect of warfarin.

Aspirin increases the effect of warfarin by several mechanisms. In addition, aspirin causes a small amount of bleeding in the digestive tract with each dose. Normally, this doesn't cause problems, but severe bleeding could occur while you are taking warfarin. You should avoid aspirin while taking warfarin. Aspirin is the active ingredient in many brand-name drugs. Check with a pharmacist before taking any nonprescription medication.

Barbiturates, such as *phenobarbital, pentobarbital (Nembutal), secobarbital (Seconal), and others*, increase the metabolism of warfarin and thereby decrease its effect.

Carbamazepine (Tegretol), which is used for seizure disorders and certain kinds of painful nerve conditions, increases the metabolism of warfarin and thereby decreases its effect.

Chloral hydrate (Noctec), a sleeping capsule, displaces warfarin from its binding sites on the proteins in the blood (where it is stored), thereby increasing warfarin's effects.

Chloramphenicol (Chloromycetin), an antibiotic, may increase the effect of warfarin.

Cholestyramine (Questran), which is used to relieve the itching associated with liver disease and for the treatment of high blood cholesterol, decreases the absorption of warfarin and thereby decreases its effect.

Cimetidine (Tagamet), which is used to treat ulcers,

slows the metabolism of warfarin and thereby increases its effect.

Clofibrate (Atromid-S), which is used to lower the concentration of triglycerides in the blood, increases the effect of warfarin.

Corticosteroids, such as *dexamethasone, hydrocortisone, or prednisone*, may increase the risk of ulcers. Should an ulcer occur, the risk of significant bleeding is increased while taking warfarin. Another effect of corticosteroids is to increase clotting factors, which could decrease warfarin's effect.

Dextrothyroxine (Choloxin), which is used to lower the concentration of cholesterol in the blood, increases the effect of warfarin.

Disulfiram (Antabuse), which is used in the treatment of alcoholism, increases the effect of warfarin. Most physicians avoid this combination of drugs.

Erythromycin, an antibiotic, may slow the metabolism of warfarin and thereby increase its effect.

Ethacrynic acid (Edecrin), a potent diuretic, may displace warfarin from its binding sites on proteins in the blood (where it is stored), thereby increasing warfarin's effect. In addition, gastrointestinal bleeding is a possible side effect of ethacrynic-acid therapy.

Glutethimide (Doriden), a sedative that was more widely used in former years, increases the metabolism of warfarin and thereby decreases its effect.

Griseofulvin (Fulvicin, Grifulvin, Grisactin), an antifungal antibiotic, increases the metabolism of warfarin and thereby decreases its effect.

Influenza vaccination may increase the effect of warfarin. Some researchers have observed this effect, while others were unable to substantiate it.

Metronidazole (Flagyl), which is used in the treatment of trichomonal and other infections, slows the metabolism of warfarin and thereby increases its effect.

Nonsteroidal anti-inflammatory drugs, such as *diflunisal (Dolobid), fenoprofen (Nalfon), ibuprofen (Motrin, Rufen, Advil, Nuprin), indomethacin (Indocin), meclofenamate (Meclomen), naproxen (Anaprox, Naprosyn), piroxicam (Feldene), sulindac (Clinoril), tolmetin (Tolec-*

tin), and others, may increase the effect of warfarin and also may cause some gastric bleeding themselves. If one of these drugs is needed for the treatment of arthritis while you are taking warfarin, it appears that ibuprofen, naproxen, or tolmetin are the least likely to cause problems. Check with your doctor before taking nonprescription ibuprofen.

Phenylbutazone (Butazolidin) and *oxyphenbutazone,* which are sometimes used for acute arthritic pain or for gout attacks, increase the effect of warfarin by several mechanisms. In addition, they may cause gastrointestinal ulceration, which could cause serious bleeding while taking warfarin. Since there are other drugs that can produce similar therapeutic effect with less risk of adverse interaction, this combination should be avoided.

Phenytoin (Dilantin), which is used for the prevention of seizures and for the treatment of irregular heartbeats, may increase or decrease the effect of warfarin, depending on which of several mechanisms predominates. In addition, warfarin may affect your response to phenytoin. Most of the reports of adverse interactions between phenytoin and anticoagulants have been with anticoagulants other than warfarin. If you require both warfarin and phenytoin, your doctor will monitor your response to both of these drugs.

Rifampin (Rifadin, Rimactane), an antibacterial drug, increases the metabolism of warfarin and thereby decreases its effect.

Sulfinpyrazone (Anturane), which is used in the treatment of gout, increases the effect of warfarin by several mechanisms.

Sulfonamides, which are used for their antibacterial effects, increase the effect of warfarin by several mechanisms.

Thyroid hormones, such as *levothyroxine (Levothroid, Synthroid), liotrix (Euthroid, Thyrolar), and others,* may increase the breakdown of clotting factors and thereby increase warfarin's effect. This effect occurs in patients who are hypothyroid (deficient in thyroid hormone) and are already being treated with warfarin before thyroid replacement is begun. If you are taking thyroid regularly, then you will respond to warfarin in the same way as someone who has normal thyroid function.

Vitamin E can increase the effect of warfarin. You should not treat yourself with vitamin E while you are taking warfarin.

Vitamin K antagonizes the effect of warfarin, and this effect is sometimes valuable therapeutically. (Also see Food.)

ALCOHOLIC BEVERAGES Alcoholic beverages do not affect the response to warfarin, provided they are consumed in moderation (no more than two drinks a day). However, heavy drinkers require larger than normal doses of warfarin while they are sober, because these individuals metabolize warfarin more rapidly, thereby decreasing its effect. This decrease in effect in heavy drinkers occurs only while they are sober. Heavy drinking itself has the opposite effect. It increases the effect of warfarin. Because of the complexity of this interaction, you should limit your consumption of alcohol while you are taking warfarin.

FOOD Vitamin K, which occurs in large amounts in leafy green vegetables and beef liver, antagonizes the effect of warfarin. No special diet is required while taking warfarin, but you should avoid radical changes in your diet. Food doesn't appreciably affect the absorption of warfarin, so it doesn't matter whether you take your daily dose with a meal or on an empty stomach. However, to help you remember to take your daily dose, it might be helpful to take it with a meal.

HOW DOES AGE AFFECT THE RESPONSE TO THIS DRUG? Older people generally require smaller amounts of warfarin than younger people, because the rate at which warfarin is removed from the body decreases by about 1 percent per year of age, and perhaps because of greater inherent sensitivity to warfarin with aging. However, there is considerable variation in response among individuals, and warfarin dosage is always individualized. Your warfarin dosage will be determined on the basis of daily blood tests when you start taking the drug and on frequent tests thereafter.

APPENDIX

Predicting the Effect of Aging on Kidney Function

As pointed out in the beginning of this book ("Your Body"), drug effects decline as drug molecules are inactivated by the liver or removed by the kidneys, or some combination of these two processes. Successive doses of drug are taken to replace the drug that is lost by these processes, and a continued drug effect is thereby maintained. If drug removal is substantially slowed, as sometimes happens with aging, then the drug or its active metabolites can accumulate to higher concentrations than expected, and toxic effects can occur. Therefore, with some drugs (not all), your doctor will prescribe smaller doses or less frequent doses to compensate for the normal decline in liver or kidney function that occurs with aging.

Although both the liver and the kidneys become less efficient with advancing age, there is considerable variation among individuals in the degree to which these organs are affected by aging. The routine laboratory tests that evaluate liver function are not of much help in figuring out precisely how fast your liver can metabolize drugs. Furthermore, the liver metabolizes drugs by several processes, depending on the drug it is dealing with, and some of these processes become less efficient with aging, while others do not.

Unlike the liver, the efficiency with which the kidneys remove a number of drugs from the blood can be readily evaluated with routine laboratory tests. That is the subject of this appendix. This material appears here, in an appendix rather than with specific drugs, because this isn't really practical patient information—it's up to your doctor to figure out your drug dosages. Yet, this material is too interesting to leave out entirely.

CREATININE CLEARANCE The efficiency with which the kidneys carry out their task of removing normal waste products, drugs, and drug metabolites from the blood is rated by a laboratory test called the creatinine clearance. Creatinine is a normal metabolic waste product (produced by muscle tissue) that is filtered out of the blood by the kidneys and excreted in the urine. Your body produces creatinine at a constant rate. By collecting all the urine that is produced over a twenty-four-hour period and by measuring the concentration of creatinine in that urine, the volume of that urine, and the concentration of creatinine in the blood, the rate at which creatinine is cleared from the blood can be accurately calculated.

Some drugs (digoxin, allopurinol, cimetidine, aminoglycoside antibiotics, and other drugs) are removed from the blood at a rate that is directly proportional to the rate at which creatinine is removed, and the creatinine clearance provides valuable information in figuring out what dose and dosage schedule are likely to be effective but not toxic.

But there are several practical problems in using this test. It requires extremely accurate urine collection over a twenty-four-hour period. If any urine is lost (for example, by going down the toilet instead of into the collection container), then the calculated results will be in error. Also, it's cumbersome; a lot of urine gets produced in twenty-four hours. Furthermore, the results aren't available until more than a day after the test is started—long after your doctor wants information on which to base your drug dosage. Finally, this test is expensive, and to ensure accuracy in urine collections, it is generally reserved for patients who are in the hospital. Therefore, procedures for *estimating* creatinine clearance have become widely used in recent years.

ESTIMATED CREATININE CLEARANCE The concentration of creatinine in the blood is commonly measured, along with other blood constituents, by routine laboratory tests. An elevated concentration of creatinine in the blood is an indication of kidney impairment. However, a "normal" value for an older person can be misleading, because muscle mass, and therefore creatinine production, decreases steadily with age. When both the production and elimination of creatinine are slowed to the same degree, the concentration of creatinine in the blood will not be elevated, despite poor kidney function. For example, when the concentration of creatinine in the blood was compared among young (age twenty to forty) and old (age sixty to eighty) individuals, there was little difference, but the *creatinine clearance* (the rate of creatinine removal by the kidneys) of the older individuals was half that of the younger individuals.[1] A number of researchers have figured out how the creatinine clearance can be estimated on the basis of the concentration of creatinine in the blood (which is easy to measure), age, sex, and weight.[2] The most commonly used technique is this equation:[3],[4]

$$\frac{\text{creatinine}}{\substack{\text{clearance}\\ \text{in ml/min}}} = \frac{(140 - \text{age in years})\,(\text{weight in kilograms})}{(72)\,(\text{creatinine concentration in blood, mg/100 ml})}$$

(Multiply this result by 0.85 for women, to compensate for smaller muscle mass. For obese individuals, ideal body weight should be used. This technique assumes that the kidney function is not rapidly changing, as it might during a disease process or drug toxicity that affects the kidneys.)

This estimated creatinine clearance can be used in determining the dose and dosage schedule of drugs that are eliminated primarily by the kidneys.[5] For many drugs, there are dosage guidelines based on creatinine clearance in the *Physicians' Desk Reference,* or *PDR.* Once this dosage has been determined, it can be modified on the basis of tests that measure the concentration of drug in the blood, if such tests are available, and on the basis of clinical response.

1. R.D. Lindeman, "The Aging Kidney," *Comprehensive Therapy* 12 (1986): 43–49.
2. R.S. Lott and W.L. Hayton, "Estimation of Creatinine Clearance From Serum Creatinine Concentration—A Review," *Drug Intelligence and Clinical Pharmacy* 12 (1978): 140–50.
3. D.W. Cockcroft and M.H. Gault, "Prediction of Creatinine Clearance from Serum Creatinine," *Nephron* 16 (1976): 31–41.
4. M.M. Reidenberg, "Kidney Function and Drug Action," *The New England Journal of Medicine* 313 (1985): 816–18.
5. W.M. Bennett, G.R. Aronoff, G. Morrison, et al. "Drug Prescribing in Renal Failure: Dosing Guidelines for Adults," *American Journal of Kidney Diseases* 3 (1983): 155–193.

PERSONAL MEDICATION RECORD

If you take more than two drugs on a regular basis, fill out the form on the following pages. Bring it with you every time you visit your doctor or have a prescription filled.

List all of your drugs on the "Current Drug List." Then fill in the "Daily Drug Schedule." For most drugs, it doesn't matter if you get an hour or two off schedule, but a schedule is useful. Drugs that are intended to be taken on an "as needed" basis should be listed under "Occasional-Use Drugs." Examples of occasional-use drugs are sleeping pills or pain pills. Include any non-prescription drugs that you use more than once a week.

Keep all of your drugs in their original containers. That way, everything will remain properly labeled. If you are unable to open any medication bottle, return it to your pharmacist and ask for a more suitable container.

Store all drugs out of the reach of children.

Store drugs in a cool, dry place. The bathroom is usually a poor place for drug storage because of the moisture created by showers. Most drugs deteriorate rapidly in the presence of heat. Never keep your drugs on top of your stove or on a sunny windowsill.

Discard all old drugs you are no longer using.

PERSONAL MEDICATION RECORD

Name: _____ Age: _____ Weight: _____
Medical Problem(s): _____
_____
Drug Allergies: _____

CURRENT DRUG LIST

Drug Name and Strength	Physician	Date Started	Purpose
_____	_____	_____	_____
_____	_____	_____	_____
_____	_____	_____	_____
_____	_____	_____	_____
_____	_____	_____	_____
_____	_____	_____	_____

DAILY DRUG SCHEDULE

Time   Drug(s)
7 AM _____
8 AM _____
9 AM _____
10 AM _____
11 AM _____
Noon _____
1 PM _____
2 PM _____
3 PM _____
4 PM _____
5 PM _____
6 PM _____
7 PM _____
8 PM _____
9 PM _____
10 PM _____
11 PM _____

OCCASIONAL-USE DRUGS:

_____   _____
_____   _____

GLOSSARY

ACE inhibitors   See angiotensin-converting-enzyme inhibitors.

active metabolite   See metabolite.

aldosterone   A hormone secreted by the adrenal glands. Aldosterone acts on the kidneys to retain sodium (and therefore water) in the body and promote the excretion of potassium.

angina pectoris   The sudden and intense chest pain caused by inadequate supply of oxygen to the heart muscle.

angiotensin-converting-enzyme inhibitors   Drugs that inhibit angiotensin-converting enzyme (ACE). Angiotensin-converting-enzyme inhibitors prevent the formation of angiotensin II, a potent elevator of blood pressure, from angiotensin I, an inactive substance. Examples of widely used angiotensin-converting-enzyme inhibitors are captopril and enalapril.

anticholinergic   A drug action that opposes the effects of acetylcholine, a chemical produced by the body to transmit nerve impulses.

anticoagulants   Drugs that prevent abnormal blood clots within the circulation by slowing blood clotting (coagulation). An example of a widely used anticoagulant is warfarin.

antiarrhythmic   A drug action that makes the heart beat more regularly.

arrhythmia   An irregularity in the normal rhythm of the heartbeat.

arthritis   Inflammation of the joints.

autonomic nervous system   The part of the nervous system that regulates involuntary action, as of the intestines, glands, and heart. The autonomic nervous system is divided into two, generally opposing parts—sympathetic and parasympathetic.

benzodiazepines   Drugs that work within the brain to relieve tension or anxiety and, in high enough doses, promote sleep. Examples of widely used benzodiazepines include alprazolam, chlordiazepoxide, clorazepate, diazepam, flurazepam, halazepam, lorazepam, oxazepam, prazepam, and triazolam.

beta-blockers Drugs that block certain receptors within the sympathetic division of the autonomic nervous system. Examples of widely used beta-blockers include atenolol, metoprolol, nadolol, pindolol, propranolol, and timolol.

brand name The name that has been trademarked by the manufacturer.

calcium channel blockers Drugs used in the treatment of cardiovascular problems because of their ability to dilate blood vessels or make the heart beat more regularly. Examples of widely used calcium channel blockers include diltiazem, nifedipine, and verapamil.

clearance Removal of a drug, drug metabolite, or natural substance from the body.

congestive heart failure A condition in which the heart is unable to pump adequately.

corticosteroids Drugs that resemble the natural hormones produced by the adrenal cortex. The most widely used corticosteroid is prednisone.

creatinine A normal metabolic waste produced by muscle tissue. Elevation of the concentration of creatinine in the blood is a signal of poor kidney function.

creatinine clearance The rate at which creatinine is removed from the blood by the kidneys. The creatinine clearance is a precise measurement of the kidneys' efficiency.

dementia Deterioration in intellectual function, often accompanied by emotional disturbance. Dementia can be caused by any of several problems within the brain, but drugs should always be suspected as a cause.

diabetes mellitus Several conditions in which either the production or utilization of insulin is impaired. Characterized by abnormally high concentrations of sugar in the blood, diabetes mellitus is treated by dietary control, often with the addition of insulin or a sulfonylurea drug.

distribution The volume within the body that a dose of drug disperses to. Drugs vary in their affinity for various tissues, such as fat, muscle, or the proteins that circulate in the blood. Individual differences in body makeup and the properties of a drug (along with the dose and the rate at which it is removed from the body) will determine the drug's concentration at its site of action.

diuretics Drugs that increase the amount of urine production, thereby removing excess salt and water from the body. Commonly used diuretics are bendroflumethiazide, bumetanide, chlorothiazide, chlorothalidone, furosemide, hydrochlorothiazide, and polythiazide.

edema An excessive accumulation of fluid in tissues.

endometrium The mucous membrane lining the uterus.

extrapyramidal system The part of the brain that controls posture and the involuntary aspects of body movement.

gastric Pertaining to the stomach.

gastrointestinal Pertaining to the stomach and intestines.

generic name The name that is not trademarked by any manufacturer.

glucose A form of sugar used by the body as its chief source of energy. Although higher concentrations of glucose occur in the blood with aging, marked elevations are associated with diabetes mellitus. The concentration of glucose in the blood is regulated by the hormone insulin.

glucocorticoids See corticosteroids.

H_2-blockers Drugs that decrease the production of stomach acid by blocking the effect of histamine on the stomach. Commonly used H_2-blockers are cimetidine, famotidine, and ranitidine.

half-life The time it takes for the concentration of a drug in the blood to decrease by 50 percent. Drugs vary in their half-lives, and the half-lives of some drugs are increased by the normal changes that occur with aging. Many drugs are taken repeatedly at regular intervals shorter than the half-life of the drug. In this situation, the drug accumulates in the body at first, and then the concentration in the blood remains fairly constant. The time it takes to reach this constant concentration in the blood is approximately equal to four or five half-lives.

hormone A chemical manufactured by an organ and carried in the blood to other parts of the body, where it stimulates some activity. Estrogens, insulin, and thyroid hormones are examples of hormones that are also taken as drugs.

hyperglycemia Too high a concentration of glucose (sugar) in the blood.

hyperkalemia Too high a concentration of potassium in the blood.

hypertension Blood pressure that is repeatedly elevated above a normal range. Left untreated, hypertension increases the risk of heart attack, stroke, and kidney damage.

hypoglycemia   Too low a concentration of glucose (sugar) in the blood.

hyponatremia   Too low a concentration of sodium in the blood.

hypokalemia   Too low a concentration of potassium in the blood.

hypothyroidism   Insufficient production of hormones by the thyroid gland. Treated by thyroid hormones taken as drug therapy.

menopause   The permanent cessation of natural menstruation in women, usually occurring around the age of fifty.

metabolism   1. Conversion of a drug to another form. This changed form may be either active or inactive. 2. The physical and chemical processes involved in maintaining life.

metabolite   A drug that has been changed to another form, usually by the liver. Drug metabolites can be either active, possessing pharmacological properties similar to the parent drug, or inactive.

neurotransmitter   A substance that is released by a nerve to either excite or inhibit another nerve or specialized muscle tissue. Many drugs work by blocking or mimicking the various neurotransmitters produced by the body.

nonsteroidal anti-inflammatory drugs   Drugs that relieve pain and inflammation, probably by preventing the synthesis of prostaglandins. Examples of these drugs include aspirin, diflunisal, fenoprofen, ibuprofen, indomethacin, meclofenamate, naproxen, piroxicam, sulindac, and tolmetin.

NSAIDs   See nonsteroidal anti-inflammatory drugs.

osteoporosis   Loss of enough bone mass with aging to markedly increase the risk of fractures.

platelets   Disk-shaped structures in the blood, smaller than red blood cells, that play a role in blood clotting.

progesterone   A female hormone produced during the last part of the menstrual cycle and during pregnancy.

progestins   Drugs that mimic progesterone. Examples of commonly used progestins are medroxyprogesterone and norethindrone.

prostaglandins   Substances that regulate a variety of physiological functions, including uterine contraction, blood pressure, body temperature, inflammation, and the action of a number of hormones.

receptor A highly specialized tissue that combines with a hormone, neurotransmitter, or drug molecule to cause some sort of response.

salt 1. Sodium chloride or table salt. 2. A form of a drug, such as cimetidine *hydrochloride, sodium* phenobarbital, or ferrous *sulfate.*

steroids See corticosteroids.

sulfonylureas Drugs that increase the utilization of the body's insulin. Examples of commonly used sulfonylureas include acetohexamide, chlorpropamide, glipizide, glyburide, tolazamide, and tolbutamide.

thiazide diuretics Drugs that remove salt from the body and lower blood pressure. Examples of widely used thiazide diuretics are bendroflumethiazide, chlorothiazide, chlorthalidone, hydrochlorothiazide, and polythiazide.

tricyclic antidepressants Drugs that relieve depression. Examples of widely used tricyclic antidepressants include amitriptyline, desipramine, doxepin, imipramine, and nortriptyline.

REFERENCES

American Hospital Formulary Service, *Drug Information 86.* Bethesda, Md.: American Society of Hospital Pharmacists, 1986.

Baum, C.; Kennedy, D.L.; and Forbes, M.B. "Drug Utilization in the Geriatric Age Group." In Moore, S., and Teal, T.W., eds. *Geriatric Drug Use—Clinical and Social Perspectives,* New York: Permagon Press, 1985.

Baum, C.; Kennedy, D.L.; Forbes, M.B.; and Jones, J.K. "Drug Use and Expenditures in 1982." *JAMA, the Journal of the American Medical Association* 253 (1985): 382–86.

Boss, G.R.; and Seegmiller, J.E. "Age-Related Physiological Changes and Their Significance." *The Western Journal of Medicine* 135 (1981): 434–40.

Cohen, J.L. "Pharmacokinetic Changes in Aging." *The American Journal of Medicine* 80, suppl. 5A (1986): 31–8.

Gilman, A.G.; Goodman, L.S.; Rall, T.W.; Murad, F., eds. *Goodman and Gilman's The Pharmacological Basis of Therapeutics,* 7th edition. New York: Macmillan, 1985.

Greenblatt, D.J.; Sellers, E.M.; Shader, R.I. "Drug Disposition in Old Age." *The New England Journal of Medicine* 306 (1982): 1081–88.

Hansten, P.D. *Drug Interactions,* 5th edition. Philadelphia: Lea & Febiger, 1985.

Ouslander, J.G. "Drug Therapy in the Elderly." *Annals of Internal Medicine* 95 (1981): 711–22.

Schmucker, D.L. "Aging and Drug Disposition: An Update." *Pharmacological Reviews* 37 (1985): 133–48.

United States Pharmacopeial Convention. *USP DI, Volume I: Drug Information for the Health Care Provider* and *Volume II: Advice for the Patient,* 6th edition. Rockville, Md.: United States Pharmacopeial Convention, 1986.

ACETAMINOPHEN

Divoll, M.; Abernethy, D.R.; Ameer, B.; and Greenblatt, D.J. "Acetaminophen Kinetics in the Elderly." *Clinical Pharmarcology and Therapeutics* 31 (1982): 151–56.

Divoll, M.; Greenblatt, D.J.; Ameer, B.; and Abernethy, D.R.

"Effect of Food on Acetaminophen Absorption in Young and Elderly Subjects." *The Journal of Clinical Pharmacology* 22 (1982): 571–76.

ANGIOTENSIN-CONVERTING-ENZYME INHIBITORS

Ajayi, A.A.; Hockings, N.; and Reid, J.L. "Age and the Pharmacodynamics of Angiotensin-converting-enzyme Inhibitors Enalapril and Enalaprilat." *British Journal of Clinical Pharmacology* 21 (1986): 349–57.

Anon. "Enalapril for Hypertension." *The Medical Letter on Drugs and Therapeutics* 28 (1986): 53–54.

Anon. "Captopril for Mild to Moderate Hypertension." *The Medical Letter on Drugs and Therapeutics* 27 (1985): 103–104.

Burnakis, T.G.; and Mioduck, H.J. "Combined Therapy With Captopril and Potassium Supplementation—A Potential for Hyperkalemia." *Archives of Internal Medicine* 144 (1984): 2371–72.

Chobanian, A.V. "Antihypertensive Therapy in Evolution." *The New England Journal of Medicine* 314 (1986): 1701–1702.

Cleland, J.G.F.; Dargie, H.J.; McAlpine, H., et al. "Severe Hypotension After First Dose of Enalapril in Heart Failure." *British Medical Journal* 291 (1985): 1309–12.

Cleland, J.G.F.; Dargie, H.J.; East, B.W.; et al. "Total Body and Serum Electrolyte Composition in Heart Failure: The Effects of Captopril." *European Heart Journal* 6 (1985): 681–88.

Creasey, W.A.; Funke, P.T.; McKinstry, D.N.; and Sugerman, A.A. "Pharmacokinetics of Captopril in Elderly Healthy Male Volunteers." *The Journal of Clinical Pharmacology* 26 (1986): 264–68.

Croog, S.H.; Levine, S.; Testa, M.A.; et al. "The Effects of Antihypertensive Therapy on the Quality of Life." *The New England Journal of Medicine* 314 (1986): 1657–64.

Dzau, V.J.; and Hollenberg, N.K. "Renal Response to Captopril in Severe Heart Failure: Role of Furosemide in Natriuresis and Reversal of Hyponatremia." *Annals of Internal Medicine* 100 (1984): 777–82.

Hockings, N.; Ajayi, A.A.; and Reid, J.L. "Age and the Pharmacokinetics of Angiotensin-Converting-Enzyme Inhibitors

Enalapril and Enalaprilat." *British Journal of Clinical Pharmacology* 21 (1986): 341–48.

Jenkins, A.C.; Knill, J.R.; and Dreslinski, G.R. "Captopril in the Treatment of the Elderly Hypertensive Patient." *Archives of Internal Medicine* 145 (1985): 2029–31.

Kelley, J.G.; Doyle, G.; Donohue, J.; et al. "Pharmacokinetics of Enalapril in Normal Subjects and Patients With Renal Impairment." *British Journal of Clinical Pharmacology* 21 (1986): 63–69.

Lowenthal, D.T.; Irvin, J.D.; Merrill, D.; et al. "The Effect of Renal Function on Enalapril Kinetics." *Clinical Pharmacology and Therapeutics* 38 (1985): 661–66.

Muller, H.M.; Overlack, A.; Heck, I.; et al. "The Influence of Food Intake and Pharmacodynamics and Plasma Concentration of Captopril." *Journal of Hypertension* 3, suppl (1985): 135–36.

Ohman, K.P.; Kagedal, B.; Larsson, R.; Karlberg, B.E. "Pharmacokinetics of Captopril and Its Effects on Blood Pressure During Acute and Chronic Administration and in Relation to Food Intake." *Journal of Cardiovascular Pharmacology* 7, suppl 1 (1985): 20–24.

Packer, M.; Medina, N.; and Yushak, M. "Relation Between Serum Sodium Concentration and the Hemodynamic and Clinical Responses to Converting Enzyme Inhibition with Captopril in Severe Heart Failure." *Journal of the American College of Cardiology* 3 (1984): 1035–43.

Schuna, A.A.; Schmidt, G.R. and Petterle, M.E. "Serum Potassium Concentrations After Initiation of Captopril Therapy." *Clinical Pharmacy* 5 (1986): 920–23.

Schwartz, J.B.; Taylor, A.; Abernethy, D.; et al. "Pharmacokinetics and Pharmacodynamics of Enalapril in Patients With Congestive Heart Failure and Patients With Hypertension." *Journal of Cardiovascular Pharmacology* 7 (1985): 767–76.

Swanson, B.N.; Vlasses, P.H.; Ferguson, R.K.; et al. "Influence of Food on the Bioavailability of Enalapril." *Journal of Pharmaceutical Sciences* 73 (1984): 1655–57.

Todd, P.A., and Heel, R. "Enalapril—Review of Its Pharmacodynamic and Pharmacokinetic Properties, and Therapeutic Use in Hypertension and Congestive Heart Failure." *Drugs* 31 (1986): 198–248.

Vlasses, P.H.; Conner, D.P.; Rotmensch, H.H.; et al. "Double-Blind Comparison of Captopril and Enalapril in Mild to

Moderate Hypertension." *Journal of the American College of Cardiology* 7 (1986): 651–60.

Vlasses, P.H.; Larijani, G.E.; Conner, D.P.; Ferguson, R.K. "Enalapril, a Nonsulfhydryl Angiotensin-Converting-Enzyme Inhibitor." *Clinical Pharmacy* 4 (1985): 27–40.

ANTIARRHYTHMICS

Bonde, J.; Pedersen, L.E.; Bodtker, S.; et al. "The Influence of Age and Smoking on the Elimination of Disopyramide." *British Journal of Clinical Pharmacology* 20 (1985): 453–58.

Higbee, M.D.; Wood, J.S.; and Mead, R.A. "Procainamide-Cimetidine Interaction: A Potential Toxic Interaction in the Elderly." *Journal of the American Geriatrics Society* 32 (1984): 162–64.

Nestico, P.F., and Morganroth, J. "Cardiac Arrhythmias in the Elderly: Antiarrhythmic Drug Treatment." *Cardiology Clinics* 4 (1986): 285–303.

Siddoway, L.A., and Woosley, R.L. "Clinical Pharmacokinetics of Disopyramide." *Clinical Pharmacokinetics* 11 (1986): 214–22.

Strathman, I.; Schubert, E.N.; Cohen, A.; Nitzberg, D.M. "Hypoglycemia in Patients Receiving Disopyramide Phosphate." *Drug Intelligence and Clinical Pharmacy* 17 (1983): 635–38.

Totoritis, M.C., and Rubin, R.L. "Drug Induced Lupus." *Postgraduate Medicine* 78 (1985): 149–61.

ANTIDIABETICS

Adir, J.; Miller, A.K.; and Vestal, R.E. "Effects of Total Plasma Concentration and Age on Tolbutamide Plasma Protein Binding." *Clinical Pharmacology and Therapeutics* 31 (1982): 488–93.

Anon. "Glyburide and Glipizide." *The Medical Letter on Drugs and Therapeutics* 26 (1984): 79–80.

Antal, E.J.; Gillespie, W.R.; Phillips, J.P.; and Albert, K.S. "The Effect of Food on the Bioavailability and Pharmacodynamics of Tolbutamide in Diabetic Patients." *European Journal of Clinical Pharmacology* 22 (1982): 459–62.

Edwards, T.H.; Braunstein, G.L.; and Davidson, M.B. "Glyburide-Induced Hypoglycemia in an Elderly Patient: Similarity of First-Generation and Second-Generation Sulfonylurea Agents." *The Mount Sinai Journal of Medicine* 52 (1985): 644–46.

Gerich, J.E. "Sulfonylureas in the Treatment of Diabetes Mellitus—1985." *Mayo Clinic Proceedings* 60 (1985): 439–43.

Klosiewski, M. "Hypoglycemia—What Does the Diabetic Experience?" *The Diabetes Educator* 10 (Fall 1984): 18–21.

Kreisberg, R.A. "The Second Generation Sulfonylureas: Change or Progress?" *Annals of Internal Medicine* 102 (1985): 125–26.

Lipson, L.G. "Diabetes in the Elderly: Diagnosis, Pathogenesis, and Therapy." *The American Journal of Medicine* 80 suppl 5A (1986): 10–21.

Liu, G.C.; Coulston, A.M.; Lardinois, C.K.; et al. "Moderate Weight Loss and Sulfonylurea Treatment of Non-Insulin-Dependent Diabetes Mellitus: Combined Effects." *Archives of Internal Medicine* 145 (1985): 665–69.

Matz, R. "Diabetes Mellitus in the Elderly." *Hospital Practice* 21 (1986): 195–218.

Owens, D.R. "Effects of Oral Sulfonylureas on the Spectrum of Defects in Non-Insulin-Dependent Diabetes Mellitus." *The American Journal of Medicine* 79 (1985, suppl 2B): 27–32.

Prendergast, B.D. "Glyburide and Glipizide, Second-Generation Oral Sulfonylurea Hypoglycemic Agents." *Clinical Pharmacy* 3 (1984): 473–85.

Redmon, J.E. "Treatment of Diabetes in the Elderly." *Comprehensive Therapy* 10 (1984): 24–28.

Sartor, G.; Melander, A.; Schersten, B.; and Wahlin-Boll, E. "Influence of Food and Age on Single-Dose Kinetics and Effects of Tolbutamide and Chlorpropamide." *European Journal of Clinical Pharmacology* 17 (1980): 285–93.

Steiner, G., and Lawrence, P.A., eds. *Educating Diabetic Patients.* New York: Springer, 1981.

ANTIHYPERTENSIVES

Amery, A.; Brixko, P.; Clement, D.; et al. "Mortality and Morbidity Results From the European Working Party on High Blood Pressure in the Elderly Trial." *The Lancet* 1 (June 15, 1985): 1349–54.

Appelgate, W.B.; Carper, E.R.; Kahn, S.E.; et al. "Comparison of the Use of Reserpine Versus Alpha-methyldopa for Second Step Treatment of Hypertension in the Elderly." *Journal of the American Geriatrics Society* 33 (1985): 109–15.

Cameron, H.A., and Ramsay, L.E. "The Lupus Syndrome Induced by Hydralazine: A Common Complication With Low Dose Treatment." *British Medical Journal* 289 (1984): 410–12.

Elliott, H.L.; Sumner, D.J.; Mclean, K.; and Reid, J.L. "Effect of Age on the Responsiveness of Vascular Alpha-Receptors in Man." *Journal of Cardiovascular Pharmacology* 4 (1982): 385–92.

Franklin, S.S. "Geriatric Hypertension." *The Medical Clinics of North America* 67 (1983): 395–415.

Horowitz, R.I., and Feinstein, A.R. "Exclusion Bias and the False Relationship of Reserpine and Breast Cancer." *Archives of Internal Medicine* 145 (1985): 1873–75.

Luxenberg, J., and Feigenbaum, L.Z. "The Use of Reserpine for Elderly Hypertensive Patients." *Journal of the American Geriatrics Society* 31 (1983): 556–59.

O'Malley, K., and O'Brien, E. "Management of Hypertension in the Elderly." *The New England Journal of Medicine* 302 (1980): 1397–1401.

Rubin, P.C.; Peter, J.W.S.; and Reid, J.L. "Prazosin Disposition in Young and Elderly Subjects." *British Journal of Clinical Pharmacology* 12 (1981): 401–404.

Shepherd, A.M.M.; Irvine, N.A.; and Ludden, T.M. "Effect of Food on Hydralazine Levels and Response in Hypertension." *Clinical Pharmacology and Therapeutics* 36 (1984): 14–18.

ASPIRIN

Montgomery, P.R.; Berger, L.G.; Mitenko, P.A.; and Sitar, D.S. "Salicylate Metabolism: Effects of Age and Sex in Adults." *Clinical Pharmacology and Therapeutics* 39 (1986): 571–76.

Needs, C.J., and Brooks, P.M. "Clinical Pharmacokinetics of the Salicylates." *Clinical Pharmacokinetics* 10 (1985): 164–77.

Roberts, M.S.; Rumble, R.H.; Wanwimolruk, S.; et al. "Pharmacokinetics of Aspirin and Salicylate in Elderly Subjects and Patients with Alcoholic Liver Disease." *European Journal of Clinical Pharmacology* 25 (1983): 253–61.

BENZODIAZEPINES

Bonnet, M.H., and Kramer, M. "The Interaction of Age, Performance and Hypnotics in the Sleep of Insomniacs." *Journal of the American Geriatrics Society* 29 (1981): 508–12.

Cook, P.J.; Flanagan, R.; and James, I.M. "Diazepam Tolerance: Effect of Age, Regular Sedation, and Alcohol." *British Medical Journal* 289 (1984): 351–53.

Cook, P.J.; Huggett, A.; Graham-Pole, R.; et al. "Hypnotic Accumulation and Hangover in Elderly Inpatients: A Controlled Double-Blind Study of Temazepam and Nitrazepam." *British Medical Journal* 286 (1983): 100–102.

Dement, W.C.; Miles, L.E.; and Caskadon, M.A. " 'White paper' on Sleep and Aging." *Journal of the American Geriatrics Society* 30 (1982): 25–46.

Divoll, M.; Greenblatt, D.J.; Harmatz, J.S.; and Shader, R.I. "Effect of Age and Gender on Disposition of Temazepam." *Journal of Pharmaceutical Sciences* 170 (1981): 1104–1107.

Greenblatt, D.J.; Shader, R.I.; and Abernethy, D.R. "Current Status of Benzodiazepines." In two parts. *The New England Journal of Medicine* 309 (1983): 354–58 and 410–16.

Klotz, U.; Avant, G.R.; Hoyumpa, A.; et al. "The Effects of Age and Liver Disease on the Disposition of Diazepam in Adult Man." *The Journal of Clinical Investigation* 55 (1975): 347–59.

Meyer, B.R. "Benzodiazepines in the Elderly." *The Medical Clinics of North America* 66 (1982): 1017–35.

Pomara, N.; Stanley, B.; Block, R.; et al. "Adverse Effects of Single Therapeutic Doses of Diazepam on Performance in Normal Geriatric Subjects: Relationship to Plasma Concentrations." *Psychopharmacology* 84 (1984): 42–46.

Reidenberg, M.M., et al. "Relationship Between Diazepam Dose, Plasma Level, Age, and Central Nervous System Depression." *Clinical Pharmacology and Therapeutics* 23 (1978): 371

Smith, R.B.; Divoll, M.; Gillespie, W.R.; Greenblatt, D.J. "Effect of Subject Age and Gender on the Pharmacokinetics of Oral Triazolam and Temazepam." *The Journal of Clinical Psychopharmacology* 3 (1983): 172–76.

Thompson, T.L.; Moran, M.G.; and Nies, A.S. "Psychotropic Drug Use in the Elderly." In two parts. *The New England Journal of Medicine* 308 (1983): 134–38 and 194–99.

BETA-BLOCKERS

Benfield, P.; Clissold, S.P.; and Brogden, R.N. "Metoprolol: An Updated Review of Its Pharmacodynamic and Pharmacokinetic Properties, and Therapeutic Efficacy, in Hypertension, Ischaemic Heart Disease and Related Cardiovascular Disorders." *Drugs* 31 (1986): 376–429.

Frishman, W.H. "Atenolol and Timolol, Two New Systemic Beta-Adrenoceptor Antagonists." *The New England Journal of Medicine* 306 (1982): 1456–62.

Gonasun, L.M., and Langrall, H. "Adverse Reactions to Pindolol Administration." *American Heart Journal* 104 (1982): 482–86.

Greenblatt, D.J., and Koch-Weser, J. "Adverse Reactions to Propranolol in Hospitalized Medical Patients: A Report from the Boston Collaborative Drug Surveillance Program." *American Heart Journal* 86 (1973): 478–84.

Hale, W.E.; Stewart, R.B.; and Marks, R.G. "Central Nervous System Symptoms of Elderly Subjects Using Antihypertensive Drugs." *Journal of the American Geriatrics Society* 32 (1984): 5–10.

Henningsen, N.C., and Mattiasson, I. "Long-Term Clinical Experience With Atenolol—A New Selective Beta$_1$-blocker With Few Side Effects From the Central Nervous System." *Acta Medica Scandinavica* 205 (1979): 61–66.

Hitzenberger, G.; Fitcha, P.; and Beveridge, T.; et al. "Influence of Smoking and Age on Pharmacokinetics of Beta-receptor Blockers." *Gerontology* 28, suppl 1 (1982): 93–100.

Krupp, P., and Franchamps, A. "Pindolol: Experience Gained in Ten Years of Safety Monitoring." *American Heart Journal* 104 (1982): 486–90.

BUSPIRONE

Cohn, J.B.; Bowden, C.L.; Fisher, J.G.; and Rodos, J.J. "Double-Blind Comparison of Buspirone and Clorazepate in Anxious Outpatients." *The American Journal of Medicine* 80 suppl 3B (1986): 10–16.

Dommisse, C.S., and DeVane, L. "Buspirone: A New Type of Anxiolytic." *Drug Intelligence and Clinical Pharmacy* 19 (1985): 624–28.

Edison, A.S., and Temple, D.L. "Buspirone: Review of Its Pharmacology and Current Perspectives on Its Mechanism of Action." *The American Journal of Medicine* 80, suppl 3B (1986): 1–9.

Ereshefsky, L. "Buspirone's Advantages Over Benzodiazepine Anxiolytics." *Clinical Pharmacy* 3 (1984): 654–55.

Gammans, R.E.; Mayol, R.F.; and Labudde, J.A. "Metabolism and Disposition of Buspirone." *The American Journal of Medicine* 80, suppl 3B (1986): 41–51.

Kastenholz, K.V., and Crismon, M.L. "Buspirone, A Novel

Nonbenzodiazepine Anxiolytic." *Clinical Pharmacy* 3 (1984): 600–607.

Napoliello, M.J. "An Interim Multicentre Report on 677 Anxious Geriatric Out-patients Treated With Buspirone." *British Journal of Clinical Practice* 40 (1986): 71–73.

Newton, R.E.; Marunycz, J.D.; Alderice, M.T.; and Napoliello, M.J. "Review of the Side-effect Profile of Buspirone." *The American Journal of Medicine* 80, suppl 3B (1986): 17–21.

Seppala, T.; Aranko, K.; Mattila, M.J.; and Shrotriya, R.C. "Effects of Alcohol on Buspirone and Lorazepam Actions." *Clinical Pharmacology and Therapeutics* 32 (1982): 201–207.

CALCIUM CHANNEL BLOCKERS

Anon. "Diltiazem for Angina Pectoris." *The Medical Letter on Drugs and Therapeutics* 25 (1983): 17–18.

Boden, W.E.; Korr, K.S.; and Bough, E.W. "Nifedipine-Induced Hypotension and Myocardial Ischemia in Refractory Angina Pectoris." *JAMA, The Journal of the American Medical Association* 243 (1985): 1131–35.

Farringer, J.A.; Green, J.A.; O'Rourke, R.A.; et al. "Nifedipine-Induced Alterations in Serum Quinidine Concentrations." *American Heart Journal* 108 (1984): 1570–72.

Gordon, M., and Goldenberg, L.M.C. "Clinical Digoxin Toxicity in the Aged in Association with Co-administered Verapamil: A Report of Two Cases and Review of the Literature." *Journal of the American Geriatrics Society* 34 (1986): 659–62.

Hermann, P., and Morselli, P.L. "Pharmacokinetics of Diltiazem and Other Calcium Entry Blockers." *Acta Pharmacologica et Toxilogica* 57, suppl II (1985): 10–20.

Johnston, D.L.; Lesoway, R.; Humen, D.P.; et al. "Clinical and Hemodynamic Evaluation of Propranolol in Combination with Verapamil, Nifedipine and Diltiazem in Exertional Angina Pectoris: A Placebo-Controlled, Double-Blind, Randomized, Crossover Study." *The American Journal of Cardiology* 55 (1985): 680–87.

Krikler, D.M.; Harris, L.; and Rowland, E. "Calcium Channel Blockers and Beta-Blockers: Advantages and Disadvantages of Combination Therapy in Chronic Stable Angina Pectoris." *American Heart Journal* 104 (1982): 702–708.

McGourty, J.C., and Silas, J.H. "Beta-blockers and Verapamil:

A Cautionary Tale" (letter). *British Medical Journal* 289 (1984): 1624.

Pepine, C.J.; Feldman, R.L.; Hill, J.A.; et al. "Clinical Outcome After Treatment of Rest Angina With Calcium Blockers: Comparative Experience During the Initial Year of Therapy With Diltiazem, Nifedipine, and Verapamil." *American Heart Journal* 106 (1983): 1341–47.

Quigley, M.A.; White, K.L.; McGraw, B.F. "Interpretation and Application of World-wide Safety Data on Diltiazem." *Acta Pharmacologica et Toxilogica* 57, suppl II (1985): 61–73

Terry, R.W. "Nifedipine Therapy in Angina Pectoris: Evaluation of Safety and Side Effects." *American Heart Journal* 104 (1982): 681–89.

Van Lith, R.M., and Appelby, D.H. "Quinidine-Nifedipine Interaction." *Drug Intelligence and Clinical Pharmacy* 19 (1985): 829–31.

DIGOXIN

Clague, H.W.; Twum-Barima, Y.; and Carruthers, S.G. "An Audit of Requests for Therapeutic Drug Monitoring of Digoxin: Problems and Pitfalls." *Therapeutic Drug Monitoring* 5 (1983): 249–54.

Fleg, J.L.; Gottlieb, S.H.; and Lakatta, E.G. "Is Digoxin Really Important in Treatment of Compensated Heart Failure? A Placebo-Controlled Crossover Study in Patients with Sinus Rhythm." *The American Journal of Medicine* 73 (1982): 244–50.

Impivaara, O., and Iisalo, E. "Serum Digoxin Concentrations in a Representative Digoxin-Consuming Adult Population." *European Journal of Clinical Pharmacology* 27 (1985): 627–32.

Moorman, J.R. "Digitalis Toxicity at Duke Hospital, 1973 to 1984." *Southern Medical Journal* 78 (1985): 561–64.

Roffman, D.S. "Special Concerns of Digitalis Use in Elderly Patients." *Geriatrics* 39 (June 1984): 97–98, 103–105.

Stults, B.M. "Digoxin Use in the Elderly." *Journal of the American Geriatrics Society* 30 (1982): 158–64.

DIPYRIDAMOLE

Borhani, N.O. "Prevention of Coronary Heart Disease in Practice: Implications of the Results of Recent Clinical Trials." *JAMA, The Journal of the American Medical Association* 254 (1985): 257–62.

Klimt, C.R.; Knatterud, G.L.; Stamler, J.; and Meier, P. "Persantine-Aspirin Reinfarction Study: Part II: Secondary Coronary Prevention With Persantine and Aspirin." *Journal of the American College of Cardiology* 7 (1986): 251–69.

DIURETICS

Alm, A.; Berggren, L.; Hartvig, P.; and Roosdorp, M. "Monitoring Acetazolamide Treatment." *Acta Ophthalmologica* 60 (1982): 24–34.

Anderson, C.J.; Kaufman, P.L.; and Sturm, R.J. "Toxicity of Combined Therapy With Carbonic Anhydrase Inhibitors and Aspirin." *American Journal of Ophthalmology* 86 (1978): 516–19.

Andreasen, F.; Hansen, U.; Husted, S.E.; et al. "The Influence of Age on Renal and Extrarenal Effects of Frusemide." *British Journal of Clinical Pharmacology* 18 (1984): 65–74.

Andreasen, F.; Hansen, U.; Husted, S.E.; et al. "The Pharmacokinetics of Frusemide Are Influenced by Age." *British Journal of Clinical Pharmacology* 16 (1983): 391–97.

Anon. "Triamterene and the Kidney" (editorial). *The Lancet* 1 (February 22, 1986): 424.

Cowan, R.A.; Hartnell, G.G.; Lowderll, C.P.; et al. "Metabolic Acidosis Induced by Carbonic Anhydrase Inhibitors and Salicylates in Patients With Normal Renal Function." *British Medical Journal* 289 (1984): 347–48.

Favre, L.; Glasson, P.H.; Riondel, A.; Vallotton, M.B. "Interaction of Diuretics and Nonsteroidal Anti-inflammatory Drugs in Man." *Clinical Science* 64 (1983): 407–15.

George, C.F. "Amiloride Handling in Renal Failure." *British Journal of Clinical Pharmacology* 9 (1980): 94–95.

Heller, I.; Halevy, J.; Cohen, S.; and Theodor, E. "Significant Metabolic Acidosis Induced by Acetazolamide." *Archives of Internal Medicine* 145 (1985): 1815–17.

Kerremans, A.L.M.; Tan, Y.; van Baars, H.; et al. "Furosemide Kinetics and Dynamics in Aged Patients." *Clinical Pharmacology and Therapeutics* 34 (1983): 181–89.

Knauf, H.; Mohrke, W.; and Mutschler, E. "Delayed Elimination of Triamterene and Its Active Metabolites in Chronic Renal Failure." *European Journal of Clinical Pharmacology* 24 (1983): 453–56.

Knauf, H.; Reuter, K.; and Mutschler, E. "Limitation on the

Use of Amiloride in Early Renal Failure." *European Journal of Clinical Pharmacology* 28 (1985): 61–66.

Lawson, D.H.; O'Connor, P.C.; and Jick, H. "Drug Attributed Alterations in Potassium Handling in Congestive Cardiac Failure." *European Journal of Clinical Pharmacology* 23 (1982): 21–25.

Lynn, K.L.; Bailey, R.R.; Swainson, C.P.; et al. "Renal Failure With Potassium-Sparing Diuretics." *The New Zealand Medical Journal* 98 (1985): 629–33.

Madias, J.E., et al. "Nonarrhythmogenicity of Diuretic-Induced Hypokalemia. Its Evidence in Patients With Uncomplicated Hypertension." *Archives of Internal Medicine* 144 (1984): 2171–76.

Millson, D.; Borland, C.; Murphy, P.; and Davison, W. "Hyponatremia and Moduretic (Amiloride Plus Hydrochlorothiazide)." *British Medical Journal* 289 (1984): 1308–1309.

Moore, T.D., and Bechtel, T.P. "Hyponatremia Secondary to Tolbutamide and Chlorothiazide." *American Journal of Hospital Pharmacy* 36 (1979): 1107–1110.

Oles, K.S., and Denham, J.W. "Hyponatremia Induced by Thiazide-like Diuretics in the Elderly." *Southern Medical Journal* 77 (1984): 1314–15.

Ponce, S.P.; Jennings, A.E.; Madias, N.E.; and Harrington, J.T. "Drug-Induced Hyperkalemia." *Medicine* 64 (1985): 357–70.

Shemer, J.; Modah, M.; Ezra, D.; and Cabili, S. "Incidence of Hyperkalemia in Hospitalized Patients." *Israel Journal of the Medical Sciences* 19 (1983): 659–61.

Smith, W.E., and Steele, T.H. "Avoiding Diuretic-Related Complications in Older Patients." *Geriatrics* 38 (February 1983): 117–24.

ESTROGENS, PROGESTINS, AND CALCIUM

Anon. "Estrogen Plus a Progestin for Prevention of Postmenopausal Osteoporosis." *The Medical Letter on Drugs and Therapeutics* 27 (1986): 91–92.

Bailar, J.C. "When Research Results Are in Conflict." *The New England Journal of Medicine* 313 (1985): 1080–81.

Barrett-Connor, E. "Postmenopausal Estrogens—Current Prescribing Patterns of San Diego Gynecologists." *The Western Journal of Medicine* 144 (1986): 620–21.

Bush, T.L. "The Adverse Effects of Hormonal Therapy," *Cardiology Clinics* 4 (1986): 145–52.

Bush, T.L., and Barrett-Connor, E. "Noncontraceptive Estrogen Use and Cardiovascular Disease." *Epidemiologic Reviews* 7 (1985): 80–104.

Cali, R.W. "Estrogen Replacement Therapy—Boon or Bane?" *Postgraduate Medicine* 75 (March 1984): 279–86.

Council on Scientific Affairs. "Estrogen Replacement in the Menopause." *JAMA, The Journal of the American Medical Association* 249 (1983): 359–61.

Crona, N.; Silfverstolpe, G.; and Samsioe, G. "The Influence of Hormonal Replacement on Lipid and Lipoprotein Metabolism." *Acta Obstetricia et Gynecologica Scandinavica* 130 suppl (1985): 49–52.

Cummings, S.R., and Black, D. "Should Perimenopausal Women Be Screened for Osteoporosis?" *Annals of Internal Medicine* 104 (1986): 817–23.

Cummings, S.R.; Kelsey, J.L.; Nevitt, M.C.; et al. "Epidemiology of Osteoporosis and Osteoporotic Fractures." *Epidemiologic Reviews* 7 (1985): 178–208.

Cummings, S.R.; Nevitt, M.C.; and Haber, R.J. "Prevention of Osteoporosis and Osteoporotic Fractures." *The Western Journal of Medicine* 143 (1985): 684–87.

DeFazio, J., and Speroff, L. "Estrogen Replacement Therapy: Current Thinking and Practice." *Geriatrics* 40 (November 1985): 32–48.

Ettinger, B.; Genant, H.K.; and Cann, C.E. "Long-Term Estrogen Replacement Therapy Prevents Bone Loss and Fractures." *Annals of Internal Medicine* 102 (1985): 319–24.

Gambrell, R.D. "The Menopause." *Investigative Radiology* 21 (1986): 369–78.

Gambrell, R.D.; Maier, R.C.; and Sanders, B.I. "Decreased Incidence of Breast Cancer in Postmenopausal Estrogen-progestin Users." *Obstetrics and Gynecology* 62 (1983): 435–43.

Gambrell, R.D.; Bagnell, C.A.; and Greenblatt, R.B. "Role of Estrogens and Progesterone in the Etiology and Prevention of Endometrial Cancer: Review." *American Journal of Obstetrics and Gynecology* 146 (1983): 696–707.

Gambrell, R.D. "Clinical Use of Progestins in the Menopausal Patient: Dosage and Duration." *The Journal of Reproductive Medicine* 27 (1982): 531–38.

Gordon, G.S., and Vaughan, C. "Calcium and Osteoporosis." *The Journal of Nutrition* 116 (1986): 319–22.

Gordon, G.S. "Dead Wrong: Estrogens, Osteoporosis, Cancer and Public Policy." *Journal of Medicine* 11 (1980): 203–22.

Greenblatt, R.B.; Gambrell, R.D.; and Stoddard, L.D. "The Role of Progesterone in the Prevention of Endometrial Cancer." *Pathology, Research, and Practice* 174 (1982): 297–318.

Gruber, J.S., and Luciani, C.T. "Physicians Changing Postmenopausal Sex Hormone Prescribing Regimens." *Progress in Clinical and Biological Research* 216 (1986): 325–35.

Gustavson, L.E.; Legler, U.F.; and Benet, L.Z. "Impairment of Prednisolone Disposition in Women Taking Oral Contraceptives or Conjugated Estrogens." *The Journal of Clinical Endocrinology and Metabolism* 62 (1986): 234–37.

Hahn, R.G.; Nachtigall, R.D.; and Davies, T.C. "Compliance Difficulties With Progestin-Supplemented Estrogen Replacement Therapy." *The Journal of Family Practice* 18 (1984): 411–14.

Hammond, C.B., and Maxson, W.S. "Estrogen Replacement Therapy." *Clinical Obstetrics and Gynecology* 29 (1986): 407–30.

Heaney, R.P., and Recker, R.R. "Distribution of Calcium Absorption in Middle-Aged Women." *The American Journal of Clinical Nutrition* 43 (1986): 299–305.

Henstler, L. "Conversation With B. Lawrence Riggs, M.D.: Osteoporosis: First Step Diet Treatment." *Geriatrics* 41 (July 1986): 77–84.

Hulka, B.S. "When Is the Evidence for 'No Association' Sufficient?" *JAMA, The Journal of the American Medical Association* 252 (1984): 81–82.

Jensen, J.; Christiansen, C.; and Rodbro, P. "Cigarette Smoking, Serum Estrogens, and Bone Loss During Hormone-Replacement Therapy Early After Menopause." *The New England Journal of Medicine* 313 (1985): 973–75.

Judd, H.L.; Meldrum, D.R.; Deftos, L.J.; et al. "Estrogen Replacement Therapy: Indications and Complications." *Annals of Internal Medicine* 98 (1983): 195–205.

Kaufman, D.W.; Miller, D.R.; Rosenberg, L.; et al. "Noncontraceptive Estrogen Use and the Risk of Breast Cancer." *JAMA, The Journal of the American Medical Association* 252 (1984): 63–67.

Kennedy, D.L.; Baum, C.; and Forbes, M.B. "Noncontraceptive Estrogens and Progestins: Use Patterns Over Time." *Obstetrics and Gynecology* 65 (1985): 441–46.

Kolata, G. "How Important Is Dietary Calcium in Preventing Osteoporosis?" *Science* 233 (1986): 519–20.

Korenman, S.G. "Menopausal Endocrinology and Management." *Archives of Internal Medicine* 142 (1982): 1131–36.

Ott, S. "Should Women Get Screening Bone Mass Measurements?" *Annals of Internal Medicine* 104 (1986): 874–76.

Persson, I. "The Risk of Endometrial and Breast Cancer After Estrogen Treatment: A Review of Epidemiological Studies." *Acta Obstetricia et Gynecologica Scandinavica* 130 suppl (1985): 59–66.

Pogrund, H.; Bloom, R.A.; and Menczel, J. "Preventing Osteoporosis: Current Practices and Problems." *Geriatrics* 41 (May 1986): 55–71.

Reid, I.R., and Ibbertson, H.K. "Calcium Supplements in the Prevention of Steroid-Induced Osteoporosis." *The American Journal of Clinical Nutrition* 44 (1986): 287–90.

Riggs, B.L., and Melton, L.J. "Involutional Osteoporosis." *The New England Journal of Medicine* 314 (1986): 1676–86.

Rosenberg, S.H.; Fausone, V.; and Clark, R. "The Role of Estrogens as Risk Factor for Stroke in Postmenopausal Women." *The Western Journal of Medicine* 133 (1980): 292–96.

Semmens, J.P.; Tsai, C.C.; Semmens, E.C.; et al. "Effects of Estrogen Therapy on Vaginal Physiology During Menopause." *Obstetrics and Gynecology* 66 (1985): 15–28.

Semmens, J.P., and Wagner, G. "Estrogen Deprivation and Vaginal Function in Postmenopausal Women." *JAMA, The Journal of the American Medical Association* 248 (1982): 445–48.

Shapiro, S.; Kelly, J.P.; Rosenberg, L.; et al. "Risk of Localized and Widespread Endometrial Cancer in Relation to Recent and Discontinued Use of Conjugated Estrogens." *The New England Journal of Medicine* 313 (1985): 969–72.

Specht, E.E. "Hip Fracture, Skeletal Fragility, Osteoporosis and Hormonal Deprivation in Elderly Women." *The Western Journal of Medicine* 133 (1980): 297–303.

Spencer, H., and Kramer, L. "NIH Consensus Conference: Osteoporosis." *The Journal of Nutrition* 116 (1986): 316–19.

Stampfer, M.J.; Willet, W.C.; Colditz, G.A.; et al. "A Prospective Study of Postmenopausal Estrogen Therapy and Coronary Heart Disease." *The New England Journal of Medicine* 313 (1985): 1044–49.

Tikkanen, M.J.; Kuunsi, T.; Nikkila, E.A.; et al. "Postmenopausal Hormone Replacement Therapy: Effects of Progestogens on Serum Lipids, and Lipoproteins: A Review." *Maturitas* 8 (1986): 7–17.

Thomas, D.B. "Noncontraceptive Exogenous Estrogens and Risk of Breast Cancer: A Review." *Breast Cancer Research and Treatment* 2 (1982): 203–11.

Wasnich, R.D.; Ross, P.D.; and Heilbrun, L.K. "Differential Effects of Thiazide and Estrogen Upon Bone Mineral Content and Fracture Prevalence." *Obstetrics and Gynecology* 67 (1986): 457–62.

Weinstein, M.C., and Schiff, I. "Cost-Effectiveness of Hormone Replacement Therapy in the Menopause." *Obstetrical and Gynecological Survey* 38 (1983): 445–55.

Wilson, P.W.F.; Garrison, R.J.; and Castelli, W.P. "Postmenopausal Estrogen Use, Cigarette Smoking, and Cardiovascular Disease in Women Over Fifty: The Framingham Study." *The New England Journal of Medicine* 313 (1985): 1038–43.

H₂-BLOCKERS

Billings, R.F., and Stein, M.B. "Depression Associated With Ranitidine." *The American Journal of Psychiatry* 143 (1986): 915–16.

Drayer, D.E.; Romankiewicz, J.; Lorenzo, B.; and Reidenberg, M.M. "Age and Renal Clearance of Cimetidine." *Clinical Pharmacology and Therapeutics* 31 (1982): 45–50.

Greene, D.S.; Szego, P.L.; Anslow, J.A.; and Hooper, J.W. "The Effect of Age on Ranitidine Pharmacokinetics." *Clinical Pharmacology and Therapeutics* 39 (1986): 300–305.

Jenike, M.A. "Cimetidine in Elderly Patients: Review of Uses and Risks." *Journal of the American Geriatrics Society* 30 (1982): 170–73.

Mangini, R.J. "Clinically Important Cimetidine Interactions." *Clinical Pharmacy* 1 (1982): 433–40.

Porro, G.B. "Famotidine in the Treatment of Gastric and Duodenal Ulceration: Overview of Clinical Experience." *Digestion* 32 (1985, suppl 1): 62–69.

Ritschel, W.A. "Cimetidine Dosage Regimen for Patients With Renal Failure and for Geriatric Patients." *European Journal of Clinical Pharmacology* 23 (1982): 501–504.

Takabatake, T.; Ohta, H.; Maekawa, M.; et al. "Pharmacokinetics of Famotidine, a New H₂-Receptor Antagonist, in Relation to Renal Function." *European Journal of Clinical Pharmacology* 28 (1985): 327–31.

Zimmerman, T.W., and Schenker, S. "A Comparative Evaluation of Cimetidine and Ranitidine." *Rational Drug Therapy* 19 (April 1985): 1–7.

HALOPERIDOL

Moleman, P.; Janzen, G.; von Bargen, B.A.; et al. "Relationship Between Age and Incidence of Parkinsonism in Psychiatric Patients Treated With Haloperidol." *The American Journal of Psychiatry* 14 (1986): 232–34.

Settle, E.C., and Ayd, F.J. "Haloperidol: A Quarter Century of Experience." *The Journal of Clinical Psychiatry* 44 (1983): 440–48.

IRON

O'Neil-Cutting, M.A., and Crosby, W.H. "The Effect of Antacids on the Absorption of Simultaneously Ingested Iron." *JAMA, The Journal of the American Medical Association* 255 (1986): 1468–70.

Lynch, S.R.; Finch, C.A.; Monsen, E.R.; and Cook, J.D. "Iron Status of Elderly Americans." *The American Journal of Clinical Nutrition* 36 (1982): 1032–45.

NONSTEROIDAL ANTI-INFLAMMATORY DRUGS

Albert, K.S.; Gillespie, W.R.; Wagner, J.G.; et al. "Effects of Age on the Clinical Pharmacokinetics of Ibuprofen." *The American Journal of Medicine* 77 (1984): 47–50.

Baum, C.; Kennedy, D.L.; and Forbes, M.B. "Utilization of Nonsteroidal Anti-inflammatory Drugs." *Arthritis and Rheumatism* 28 (1985): 686–92.

Blackshear, J.L.; Davidman, M.; and Stillman, M.T. "Identification of Risk for Renal Insufficiency From Nonsteroidal Anti-inflammatory Drugs." *Archives of Internal Medicine* 143 (1983): 1130–34.

Carmichael, J., and Shankel, S.W. "Effects of Nonsteroidal Anti-inflammatory Drugs on Prostaglandins and Renal Function." *The American Journal of Medicine* 78 (1985): 992–1000.

Clive, D.M., and Stoff, J.S. "Renal Syndromes Associated With Nonsteroidal Anti-inflammatory Drugs." *The New England Journal of Medicine* 310 (1984): 563–72.

Feinfeld, D.A.; Olesnicky, L.; Pirani, C.L.; and Appel, G.B. "Nephrotic Syndrome Associated With Use of the Nonsteroidal Anti-inflammatory Drugs." *Nephron* 37 (1984): 174–79.

Greenblatt, D.J.; Abernethy, D.R.; Matlis, R.; et al. "Absorption and Disposition of Ibuprofen in the Elderly." *Arthritis and Rheumatism* 27 (1984): 1066–69.

Koopmans, P.P.; Thien, T.; and Gribnau, F.W.J. "Influence of Nonsteroidal Anti-inflammatory Drugs on Diuretic Treatment of Mild to Moderate Essential Hypertension." *British Medical Journal* 289 (1984): 1492–94.

Meyer, H.M., and Temple, R. "Labeling of Ibuprofen for Over-the-Counter Use" (letter). *The New England Journal of Medicine* 312 (1985): 377.

Poirier, T.I. "Reversible Renal Failure Associated With Ibuprofen: Case Report and Review of the Literature." *Drug Intelligence and Clinical Pharmacy* 18 (1984): 27–32.

Reeves, W.B.; Foley, R.J.; Weinman, E.J. "Nephrotoxicity From Nonsteroidal Anti-inflammatory Drugs." *Southern Medical Journal* 78 (1985): 318–22.

Richardson, C.J.; Blocka, K.L.N.; Ross, S.G.; and Verbeeck, R.K. "Effects of Age and Sex on Piroxicam Disposition." *Clinical Pharmacology and Therapeutics* 37 (1985): 13–18.

Roberts, R.G.; Gerber, J.G.; Barnes, J.S.; et al. "Sulindac Is Not Renal Sparing in Man." *Clinical Pharmacology and Therapeutics* 38 (1985): 258–65.

Sitar, D.S.; Owen, J.A.; MacDougall, B.; et al. "Effects of Age and Disease on the Pharmacokinetics and Pharmacodynamics of Sulindac." *Clinical Pharmacology and Therapeutics* 38 (1985): 228–34.

Stern, R.S., and Bigby, M. "An Expanded Profile of Cutaneous Reactions to Nonsteroidal Anti-inflammatory Drugs." *JAMA, The Journal of the American Medical Association* 252 (1984): 1433–37.

Svendsen, U.G.; Gerstoft, J.; Hansen, T.M.; and Christensen, P. "The Renal Excretion of Prostaglandins and Changes in Plasma Renin During Treatment With Either Sulindac or Naproxen in Patients With Rheumatoid Arthritis and Thiazide Treated Heart Failure." *The Journal of Rheumatology* 11 (1984): 779–82.

Upton, R.A.; Williams, R.L.; Kelly, J.; and Jones, R.M. "Naproxen Pharmacokinetics in the Elderly." *British Journal of Clinical Pharmacology* 18 (1984): 207–14.

Woolf, A.D.; Rogers, H.J.; Bradbrook, I.D.; and Corless, D. "Pharmacokinetic Observations on Piroxicam in Young Adult, Middle-aged and Elderly Patients." *British Journal of Clinical Pharmacology* 16 (1983): 433–37.

PHENYTOIN

Bauer, L.A., and Bloin, R.A. "Age and Phenytoin Kinetics in Adult Epileptics." *Clinical Pharmacology and Therapeutics* 31 (1982): 301–304.

Ensom, R.J., and Nakagawa, R.S. "Phenytoin Absorption in Adults: Effect of Aging" (letter). *The New England Journal of Medicine* 313 (1985): 697.

Winter, M.E., and Tozer, T.N. "Phenytoin" chapter in Evans, W.E.; Schentag, J.J.; and Jusko, W.J.; eds. *Applied Pharmacokinetics,* Spokane, Wash.: Applied Therapeutics, 1986.

THYROID HORMONES

Dong, B.J.; Young, V.R.; and Rapoport, B. "The Nonequivalence of Levothyroxine Products." *Drug Intelligence and Clinical Pharmacy* 20 (1986): 77–78.

Gambert, S.R., and Tsitouras, P.D. "Effect of Age on Thyroid Hormone Physiology and Function." *Journal of the American Geriatrics Society* 33 (1985): 360–65.

Gambert, S.R. "Atypical Presentation of Thyroid Disease in the Elderly." *Geriatrics* 40 (February 1985): 63–69

Rosenbaum, R.L., and Barzel, U.S. "Levothyroxine Replacement Dose for Primary Hypothyroidism Decreases With Age." *Annals of Internal Medicine* 96 (1982): 53–55

Salwin, C.T.; Herman, T.; Molitch, M.E.; et al. "Aging and the Thyroid: Decreased Requirement for Thyroid Hormone in Older Patients." *The American Journal of Medicine* 75 (1983): 206–209

TRICYCLIC ANTIDEPRESSANTS

Bayer, A.J.; Pathy, M.S.J.; and Ankier, S.I. "Pharmacokinetic and Pharmacodynamic Characteristics of Trazodone in the Elderly." *British Journal of Clinical Pharmacology* 16 (1983): 371–76.

Bock, J.L.; Nelson, J.C.; Gray, S.; and Jatlow, P.I. "Desipramine Hydroxylation: Variability and Effect of Antipsychotic Drugs." *Clinical Pharmacology and Therapeutics* 33 (1983): 322–28.

Coccaro, E.F., and Siever, L.J. "Second-Generation Antidepressants: A Comparative Review." *The Journal of Clinical Pharmacology* 25 (1985): 241–60.

Cutler, N.R., and Narang, P.K. "Implications of Dosing Tricyclic Antidepressants and Benzodiazepines in Geriatrics." *The Psychiatric Clinics of North America* 7 (1984): 845–61.

Davies, R.K.; Tucker, G.J.; Harrow, M.; and Detre, T.P. "Confusional Episodes and Antidepressant Medication." *The American Journal of Psychiatry* 128 (1971): 127–31.

Dawling, S.; Ford, S.; Rangedara, D.C.; and Lewis, R.R. "Amitriptyline Dosage Prediction in Elderly Patients From Plasma Concentration at Twenty-four Hours After a Single 100 mg Dose." *Clinical Pharmacokinetics* 9 (1984): 261–66.

Dawling, S. "Monitoring Tricyclic Antidepressant Therapy." *Clinical Biochemistry* 15 (1982): 56–61.

Dawling, S.; Crome, P.; and Braithwaite, R. "Pharmacokinetics of Single Oral Doses of Nortriptyline in Depressed Elderly Hospital Patients and Young Healthy Volunteers." *Clinical Pharmacokinetics* 5 (1980): 394–401.

Dugas, J.E., and Bishop, D.S. "Nonlinear Desipramine Pharmacokinetics: A Case Study." *Journal of Clinical Psychopharmacology* 5 (1985): 43–45.

Friedel, R.O. "The Relationship of Therapeutic Response to Antidepressant Plasma Levels: An Update." *The Journal of Clinical Psychiatry* 43 (November 1982): 37–43

Halaris, A. "Antidepressant Drug Therapy in the Elderly: Enhancing Safety and Compliance." *The International Journal of Psychiatry in Medicine* 16 (1986): 1–19.

Henry, J.F.; Altamura, C.; Gomeni, R.; et al. "Pharmacokinetics of Amitriptyline in the Elderly." *International Journal of Clinical Pharmacology, Therapy, and Toxicology* 19 (1981): 1–5

Jabbari, B.; Bryan, G.E.; March, E.E.; and Gunderson, C.H. "Incidence of Seizures With Tricyclic and Tetracyclic Antidepressants." *Archives of Neurology* 42 (1985): 480–81.

Livingston, R.L.; Zucker, D.K.; Isenberg, K.; and Wetzel, R.D. "Tricyclic Antidepressants and Delirium." *The Journal of Clinical Psychiatry* 44 (1983): 173–76.

Nelson, J.C.; Jatlow, P.I.; and Mazure, C. "Desipramine Plasma Levels and Response in Elderly Melancholic Patients." *Journal of Clinical Psychopharmacology* 5 (1985): 217–20.

Nelson, J.C., and Jatlow, P.I. "Subjective Complaints During Desipramine Treatment." *Archives of General Psychiatry* 41 (1984): 55–59.

Nelson, J.C.; Jatlow, P.; Quinlan, D.M.; and Bowers, M.B. "Desipramine Plasma Concentration and Antidepressant Response." *Archives of General Psychiatry* 39 (1982): 1419–22.

Nelson, J.C.; Jatlow, P.I.; Bock, J.; et al. "Major Adverse Reactions During Desipramine Treatment." *Archives of General Psychiatry* 39 (1982): 1055–61.

Nelson, J.C., and Jatlow, P.I. "Neuroleptic Effect on Desipramine Steady-State Plasma Concentration." *The American Journal of Psychiatry* 137 (1980): 1232–34.

Nies, A.; Robinson, D.S.; Friedman, M.J.; et al. "Relationship Between Age and Tricyclic Antidepressant Plasma Levels." *The American Journal of Psychiatry* 134 (1977): 790–93.

Preskorn, S.H., and Mac, D.S. "Plasma Levels of Amitriptyline: Effect of Age and Sex." *The Journal of Clinical Psychiatry* 46 (1985): 276–77.

Preskorn, S.H., and Simpson, S. "Tricyclic-Antidepressant-Induced Delirium and Plasma Drug Concentration." *The American Journal of Psychiatry* 139 (1982): 822–23.

Schulz, P.; Turner-Tamiyasu, K.; Smith, G.; et al. "Amitriptyline Disposition in Young and Elderly Normal Men." *Clinical Pharmacology and Therapeutics* 33 (1983): 360–66.

Thayssen, P.; Bjerre, M.; Kragh-Sorenen.; et al. "Cardiovascular Effects of Imipramine and Nortriptyline in Elderly Patients." *Psychopharmacology* 74 (1981): 360–64.

WARFARIN

Mungall, D.R.; Ludden, T.M.; Marshall, J.; et al. "Population Pharmacokinetics of Racemic Warfarin in Adult Patients." *Journal of Pharmacokinetics and Biopharmaceutics* 13 (1985): 213–27.

INDEX

Emitrip, see **amitriptyline**, 33

Empirin, see **aspirin**, 37

Empirin with Codeine, contains
aspirin, 37
codeine, 93

Empracet with Codeine, contains
acetaminophen, 15
codeine, 93

Enalapril, 124

Encaprin, see **aspirin**, 37

Endep, see **amitriptyline**, 33

Enovil, see **amitriptyline**, 33

Entrophen, see **aspirin**, 37

E-Pam, see **diazepam**, 99

Epanutin, see **phenytoin**, 234

Erythrityl Tetranitrate, 127

Esidrex, see **hydrochlorothiazide**, 171

Esidrix, see **hydrochlorothiazide**, 171

Esterfied Estrogens, see **estrogens**, 130

Estinyl, see **estrogens**, 130

Estrace, see **estrogens**, 130

Estraderm, see **estrogens**, 130

Estradiol, see **estrogens**, 130

Estratab, see **estrogens**, 130

Estrogens, 130

Estromed, see **estrogens**, 130

Estrone, see **estrogens**, 130

Estropipate, see **estrogens**, 130

Ethinyl Estradiol, see **estrogens**, 130

Euglucon, see **glyburide**, 157

Euhypnos, see **temazepam**, 293

Euthroid, see **thyroid hormones**, 298

Excedrin, contains
acetaminophen, 15
aspirin, 37

Excedrin P.M., contains
acetaminophen, 15
diphenhydramine, 114

Exdol, see **acetaminophen**, 15

Exdol-8, -15, -30, contains
acetaminophen, 15
codeine, 93

Extended Insulin Zinc, see **insulin**, 187

Famotidine, 137

Feldene, see **piroxicam**, 245

Fenoprofen, 139

Fenopron, see **fenoprofen**, 139

Feosol, see **ferrous sulfate**, 142

Feospan, see **ferrous sulfate**, 142

Fer-In-Sol, see **ferrous sulfate**, 142

Fero-Gradumet, see **ferrous sulfate**, 142

Ferralyn, see **ferrous sulfate**, 142

Ferra-Sul, see **ferrous sulfate**, 142

Ferro-Gradumet, see **ferrous sulfate**, 142

Ferrous Sulfate, 142

Fesofor, see **ferrous sulfate**, 142

Flurazepam, 145

Fortral, see **pentazocine**, 230

Fortunan, see **haloperidol**, 165

Frumil, contains
amiloride, 29
furosemide, 148

Frusemide, see **furosemide**, 148

Frusene, contains
furosemide, 148
triamterene, 323

Frusetic, see **furosemide**, 148

Frusid, see **furosemide**, 148